LEGACY

Also by Thomas Harding

Hanns and Rudolf
Kadian Journal
The House by the Lake
Blood on the Page

LEGACY

One Family,
a Cup of Tea
and the Company that Took on the World

Thomas Harding

WILLIAM HEINEMANN: LONDON

1 3 5 7 9 10 8 6 4 2

William Heinemann
20 Vauxhall Bridge Road
London SW1V 2SA

William Heinemann is part of the Penguin Random House group of companies whose addresses can
be found at global.penguinrandomhouse.com.

Penguin
Random House
UK

First published in Great Britain by William Heinemann in 2019

www.penguin.co.uk

A CIP catalogue record for this book is available from the British Library

ISBN 9781785150883 (Hardback)

ISBN 9781785150890 (Trade Paperback)

Typeset in 12/15.5 pts Bembo Book MT Std
by Integra Software Services Pvt. Ltd, Pondicherry

Printed and bound in Great Britain by Clays Ltd, Elcograf S.p.A.

Penguin Random House is committed to a sustainable future
for our business, our readers and our planet. This book is made from
Forest Stewardship Council® certified paper.

MIX
Paper from
responsible sources
FSC® C018179
FSC
www.fsc.org

For Sam

CONTENTS

CONTENTS

CONTENTS

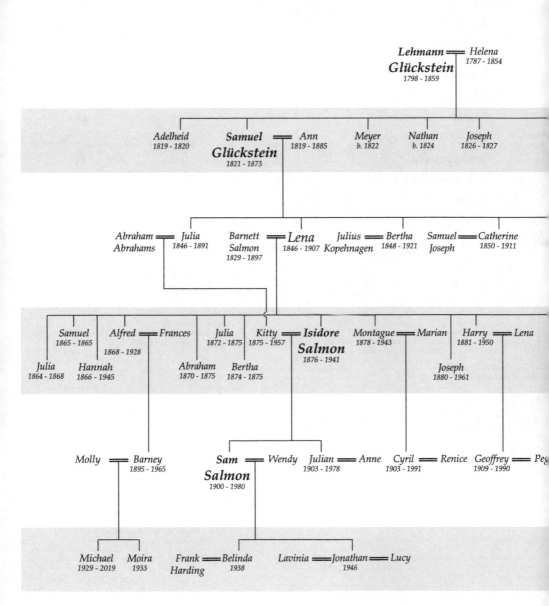

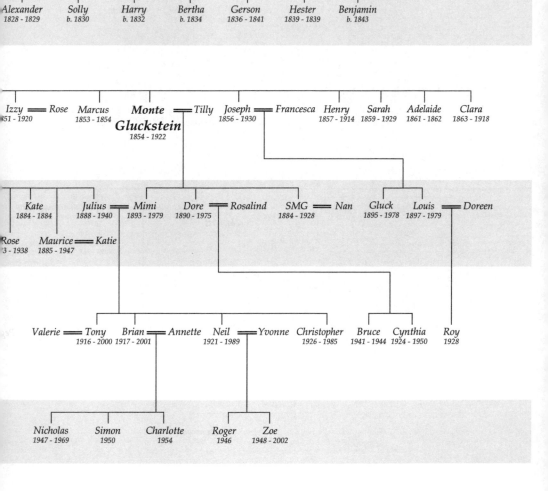

Alexander
1828 - 1829

Solly
b. 1830

Harry
b. 1832

Bertha
b. 1834

Gerson
1836 - 1841

Hester
1839 - 1839

Benjamin
b. 1843

Izzy
1851 - 1920 ══ Rose

Marcus
1853 - 1854

**Monte
Gluckstein**
1854 - 1922 ══ Tilly

Joseph
1856 - 1930 ══ Francesca

Henry
1857 - 1914

Sarah
1859 - 1929

Adelaide
1861 - 1862

Clara
1863 - 1918

Kate
1884 - 1884

Julius
1888 - 1940 ══ Mimi
1893 - 1979

Dore
1890 - 1975 ══ Rosalind

SMG
1884 - 1928 ══ Nan

Gluck
1895 - 1978

Louis
1897 - 1979 ══ Doreen

Rose
3 - 1938

Maurice
1885 - 1947 ══ Katie

Valerie ══ Tony
1916 - 2000

Brian
1917 - 2001 ══ Annette

Neil
1921 - 1989 ══ Yvonne

Christopher
1926 - 1985

Bruce
1941 - 1944

Cynthia
1924 - 1950

Roy
1928

Nicholas
1947 - 1969

Simon
1950

Charlotte
1954

Roger
1946

Zoe
1948 - 2002

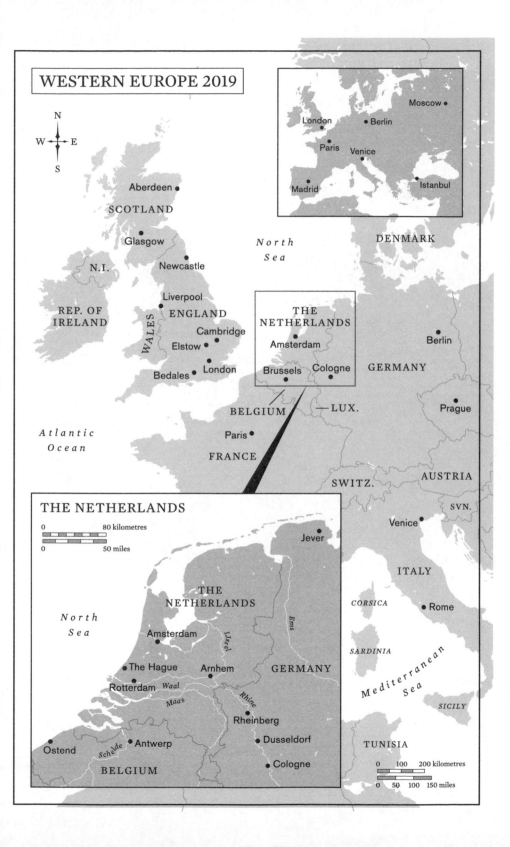

WESTERN EUROPE 2019

N
W · E
S

Aberdeen ●

SCOTLAND

Glasgow ●

N.I.

Newcastle ●

REP. OF
IRELAND

Liverpool ●

ENGLAND

WALES

Cambridge ●

Elstow ●

Bedales ●   London ●

Atlantic
Ocean

BELGIUM — LUX.

Paris ●

FRANCE

London ● ● Berlin

Paris ● Venice ●

Madrid ● Istanbul ●

Moscow ●

North
Sea

DENMARK

THE
NETHERLANDS

Amsterdam ●

Brussels ● Cologne ●

GERMANY

Berlin ●

Prague ●

SWITZ. AUSTRIA

SVN.

Venice ●

ITALY

CORSICA ● Rome

SARDINIA

Mediterranean
Sea

SICILY

THE NETHERLANDS

0   80 kilometres

0   50 miles

North
Sea

Jever ●

THE
NETHERLANDS

Amsterdam ●

Ijssel

Ems

The Hague ● Arnhem ●

Rotterdam ● Waal

Maas

GERMANY

Rhine

Rheinberg ●

Dusseldorf ●

Ostend ● Schelde ● Antwerp

Cologne ●

BELGIUM

0   100   200 kilometres

0   50   100 150 miles

TUNISIA

LONDON

BARNET

HAMPSTEAD
HEATH

BRENT

CAMDEN

• Willesden
Jewish
Cemetery

• Hampstead
Synagogue

St. Johns
Wood
•

REGENTS
PARK

• Maida Vale

Liberal Jewish
Synagogue
(1925-) •

Liberal Jewish
• Synagogue
(1910-1925)

WORMWOOD
SCRUBS

• First S&G Shop
251 Edgware Road

• Bayswater
Synagogue

CITY OF
WESTMINSTER

• Cumberland
Hotel

HYDE PARK

HAMMERSMITH
& FULHAM

HOLLAND
PARK

Blythe Road —

Olympia
•

KENSINGTON
& CHELSEA

• Cadby
Hall

Thames

RICHMOND
UPON
THAMES

BATTERSEA
PARK

WANDSWORTH

0   0.5   1   1.5   2 kilometres

0   0.5   1   1.5 miles

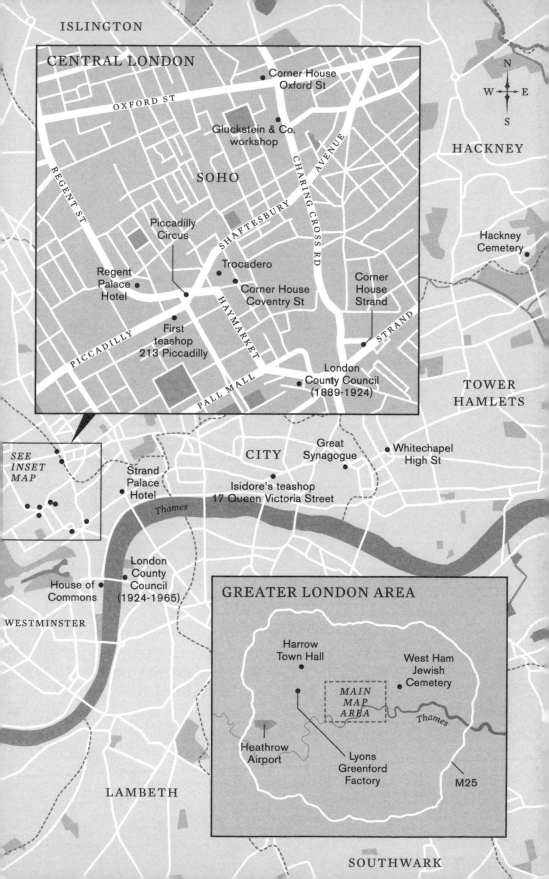

ISLINGTON

CENTRAL LONDON

Corner House
Oxford St

OXFORD ST

Gluckstein & Co.
workshop

SOHO

SHAFTESBURY AVENUE

CHARING CROSS RD

REGENT ST

Piccadilly
Circus

Regent
Palace
Hotel

Trocadero

Corner House
Coventry St

HAYMARKET

PICCADILLY

First
teashop
213 Piccadilly

PALL MALL

Corner
House
Strand

STRAND

London
County Council
(1889-1924)

HACKNEY

Hackney
Cemetery

TOWER
HAMLETS

N
W   E
S

SEE
INSET
MAP

Strand
Palace
Hotel

Thames

CITY

Great
Synagogue

Isidore's teashop
17 Queen Victoria Street

Whitechapel
High St

House of
Commons

London
County
Council
(1924-1965)

WESTMINSTER

GREATER LONDON AREA

Harrow
Town Hall

MAIN
MAP
AREA

West Ham
Jewish
Cemetery

Thames

Heathrow
Airport

Lyons
Greenford
Factory

M25

LAMBETH

SOUTHWARK

'Some day, the history of the Family ought to be written. When it is written, the author must be allowed to write about us as he or she pleases, without being inhibited by the sort of constraint that I for one (and I am sure others also) would want to impose if it were written now. This means that the history will not be written for many years.'

———————————

Geoffrey Salmon, 1974

PROLOGUE

On a clear but cold autumn morning in late September 1906, two very unusual trains were preparing to leave London's Euston station. The concourse was flooded with smoke, the sounds of men barking orders and guards blowing whistles. One train was steadily filling with almost a thousand waiters, cooks, superintendents and kitchen assistants, all smartly dressed and chatting excitedly. The other was being loaded with provisions: 25,000 plates, 64,000 knives, forks and spoons, 12,000 glasses, 4,000 serving dishes, and 1,000 flower ornament centrepieces, not to mention more than 60 tonnes of food and drink. A newspaper described this railway convoy as 'the most curiously laden goods trains that has ever left Euston'.

The trains made their way north, some 850 kilometres up the British east coast to Scotland's granite city, Aberdeen. There the staff and provisions were quickly and skilfully ferried to a giant pavilion erected in the grounds of the University of Aberdeen. The staff marvelled at the structure that had been specially erected, the tall wooden poles festooned with evergreens and roses, illuminated by pearls of gold and pink electric lights; the colourful academic robes that had been brought in from across the United Kingdom and the British Empire. The banquet marked the culmination of a week-long celebration of the university's quadricentennial, which featured honorary degrees being handed to 130 dignitaries, an all-Scottish athletics event and, most importantly, a visit by King Edward VII and Queen Alexandra. Amongst the banquet's guests were the Archbishop of Canterbury, the Prince of Monaco, the Secretary of State for Scotland, and Andrew Carnegie, the American steel magnate and world's richest man.

As the waiters dressed into their sharply creased swallowtails, and the chefs sweated over giant vats and boilers, some of the event's 2,500 guests began to arrive. From a balcony at the far end of the pavilion the 3rd Battalion Gordon Highlanders piped 'God Save the King' and 'Auld Lang Syne'. Then the dinner began.

The food was as opulent as the setting: ten courses in all. To start, *Tortue Claire*, made from ninety turtles that had journeyed up from London, warmed in giant copper cauldrons set up next to the pavilion. Next came an array of mouth-watering dishes: salmon steak and York ham, brazed pigeon and cold quail, beef tongue and asparagus in vinaigrette. Followed by *Mascotte Gateau* filled with praline cream, *Charlotte Russe* – a trifle made of sponge cake, Bavarian cream and strawberries – and fresh fruit. All of this was washed down by 2,900 bottles of sherry, champagne, hock, claret, port and liqueurs; along with the smoking of 3,000 cigars and more than twice that number of cigarettes.

It was an audacious banquet, and the biggest Scotland had ever seen. There was only one firm in the Empire that could have pulled off such an extraordinary feast: J. Lyons & Company. By 1906, Lyons was the undisputed king of British catering, a firm that came to represent the very best of Britishness. It was an enterprise that not only provided food and drink to all the grand events, the annual garden parties at Buckingham Palace and the Wimbledon Lawn Tennis Championships, but also supplied millions of families across the Empire with affordable and high-quality packets of tea, cartons of coffee, loaves of bread and an endless supply of Swiss rolls and other sweet delights. Perhaps most famously, Lyons also revolutionised the nation's eating habits, with a chain of much-loved teashops, from Glasgow in the north to Bournemouth in the south, which were open and accessible to all and were staffed by a small army of loyal 'Nippies'.

In 1906 Lyons was thriving. Yet as the century progressed, the company would occupy a far more important position, creating brands that would become recognisable the world over: Lyons Corner Houses, Lyons Maid ice-cream, Lyons Cakes. They ran a chain of lavish hotels, such as the Cumberland and Regent Palace in London, the Commodore in Paris, the Alpha in Amsterdam and many others. Their factory produced one-seventh of the bombs dropped by the Allies on Germany during the Second World War. They helped to bring women into the workforce in vast numbers, and ensured that their eateries were available to all and excluded none. Lyons would also own a list of mega-brands, such as Tetley Tea, Baskin-Robbins and Dunkin' Donuts, bringing American tastes to the UK and Europe. They even developed the world's first business computer.

Lyons was woven into the fabric of British life: a firm that was a favourite of the royal family and of millions of ordinary Britons. Lyons shaped British taste and in many ways, over a tumultuous century, Britain itself, although few (if any) of Lyons' many millions of customers knew how the company started. And almost no one now remembers the name of the man who began it all – a Hebrew teacher who escaped persecution in Europe, finding opportunity in the slums of east London. A refugee desperate to better himself, in a nation that was not always welcoming to outsiders.

★

I have always been fascinated by my family's past, but for a long time I only really knew about my father's side, the Alexanders. Growing up, I knew that the Alexanders had fled Germany for Britain in the 1930s, forced to start again with nothing. We spent most of our time with my father's family. Theirs was the story I knew best: one of violence and sacrifice, but also one of duty, and perseverance, and love. Of my mother's side – the Salmons and Glucksteins – however, I knew very little, apart from a few odd names.

On a shelf in my parents' living room sat a dark-green book that contained my mother's family tree, going back generations. I used to spend hours leafing through its pages, examining its charts, awed by the sheer number of people mentioned, each carefully labelled with a date of birth, a date of marriage and a date of death. Beneath flowed the names of their children, and their children's children, the branches reaching ever wider. The names were strange to me, sounding funny when I read them aloud: Montague, Barnett and Isidore; Helena, Adelheid and Bertha. And at the very top of the family tree was a single name: Lehmann Meyer Glückstein, born 1787, died 1859. My grandfather's grandfather's grandfather.

When I was nine years old, my mother's father, Sam Salmon, took me out for lunch at the Carvery in Marble Arch. I remember being awed by the plush red-velvet chairs, the perfect white linen that covered the tables and the sparkling chandeliers hanging from the dining room's gold- and silver-painted ceiling. Around us men in pleated chef's hats and starched white jackets pushed carts piled high with more food than I had ever seen: oval platters of roast lamb, chicken and beef and, later, chocolate gateaux, cheesecake, apple strudel and pear flan. 'You can eat as much as you want,' my grandfather told me. He owned the restaurant, after all.

Recently I was walking through central London with my teenage daughter, also called Sam. From Buckingham Palace, we strolled through Green Park and then past the Ritz Hotel and the Royal

Academy to Piccadilly Circus. I pointed to a tall building that housed a designer furniture store, but had once been home to the first Lyons teashop. 'That's where Lyons started,' I told my daughter. 'Lyons?' she asked. I was surprised that we hadn't talked about this before. 'The family company,' I said, 'on your grandmother's side.' I gestured towards some buildings on the other side of Piccadilly Circus. 'I think Lyons owned that entire block as well,' I told her. 'It was, for a while, the biggest hotel in Europe.' She rolled her eyes.

We walked up Shaftesbury Avenue and stopped outside an enormous five-storey pink-stoned building that stretched up the street for 100 metres. Above its main entrance was carved the legend 'Trocadero'. Not so long ago it had been the capital's premier restaurant and retail complex, known for its famous guests, fabulous entertainment and extraordinary food. Now it looked abandoned, its windows covered by plywood, its rooms dark and empty. A tired-looking 'Under construction' sign hung over one of the doors. Lyons had not only owned this building, I explained to Sam, they had built it. 'Who owns it now?' Sam asked. 'I don't know,' I replied. 'The company sold it when they lost everything.' 'What happened?' Sam asked. I wasn't sure. But I realised that I was keen to find out.

Legacy is my family's story. It is the story of Lyons, but also the story of the Salmons and Glucksteins, my grandparents and their ancestors – a family who transformed themselves from penniless immigrants to industrial titans and then to failed entrepreneurs, in five generations. It is a tale of tragedies, triumphs, loves, losses and, above all else, the loyalty that bound the family together.

It is also the story of an astonishing 175 years of British history, during which the nation went from being the global superpower to near bankruptcy. An epoch during which technology moved from horse-drawn carts, salted meat and handwritten ledgers to aeroplanes, frozen food and computers. An epoch in which ordinary people's lives were transformed and their working patterns, social habits and leisure time became unrecognisable, compared to those of their grandparents. An epoch in which women went from being unable to eat in public to winning the right to vote; from being unable to work as waitresses to becoming company executives. An epoch in which immigrants from Ireland, the Caribbean, the Indian subcontinent, Australia and central Europe made a massive contribution to British culture and economy – a contribution that is fundamental to the world we live in today, but all too rarely acknowledged.

To unearth the facts as well as the motivations of my family members, and those around them, I have relied on archival records, interviews, articles, photographs and government reports. One of the benefits of writing about J. Lyons, and the family behind it, is that they were well chronicled by the press. Such coverage has recently been made easily available, thanks to the digitisation of regional and national newspapers. Thankfully, too, the Salmons and the Glucksteins were obsessed with telling their own stories, through private letters and memoirs, biographies, internal memos, reports and testimonies. Fearing the disclosure of confidential information, however, they published none of these histories. Until now. For I have been lucky enough to be trusted with the family's archives.

One of the challenges of writing about a family spanning almost two centuries is that there are hundreds of individuals involved. Clearly it was not possible to describe them all in one book. To offer a pathway through, I focused on a limited number of characters, hoping that through their stories, affiliations and conflicts the larger themes and dramas could be loosened. In this way, I hoped to explain to my daughter what happened to her ancestors: how their business rose to such great heights, how it shaped modern culture and why it collapsed so quickly – from the heights of the Aberdeen banquet to a few scattered memories, in just a few decades. And, ultimately, how the Lyons story echoes that of so many immigrants who arrived on Britain's shores in search of the British Dream.

First, I had to find out about the man at the top of the family tree, Lehmann Glückstein.

PART I

LEHMANN & SAMUEL

'The strength and unity of the Family was at its peak whenever there was danger.'

Mimi Salmon

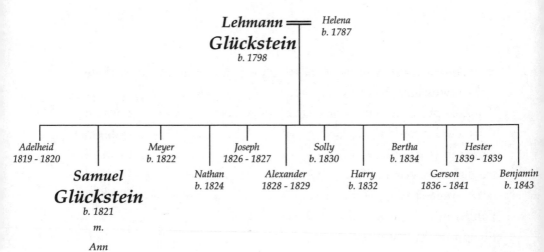

Lehmann Glückstein _b. 1798_ ══ _Helena b. 1787_

| | | | | | | | | |

Adelheid
_1819 - 1820_

Samuel Glückstein
_b. 1821_

_m._

Ann
_b. 1819_

Meyer
_b. 1822_

Nathan
_b. 1824_

Joseph
_1826 - 1827_

Alexander
_1828 - 1829_

Solly
_b. 1830_

Harry
_b. 1832_

Bertha
_b. 1834_

Gerson
_1836 - 1841_

Hester
_1839 - 1839_

Benjamin
_b. 1843_

Chapter 1

1808

Everyone knew that Lehmann was clever. By the age of eight, the tall scrawny boy with almond-shaped eyes could read from the ancient Torah kept in the small synagogue on Wasserpfortstraße in Jever. By thirteen, he could recite Greek, Latin and Aramaic. Now that he was eighteen years old, he could also speak German, French, Flemish and English and was teaching Hebrew to his neighbour's children. His latest interest was poetry, particularly the verse of Alexander Pope. Lehmann's language skills, however, would be of no use this day, as his family had been evicted and he was helping his parents load a cart with their worldly possessions. Through no fault of his own, he was being forced to leave the town of his birth.

With a population of just under 2,500 people, Jever was a small walled community 100 kilometres north-west of Bremen and 20 kilometres south of the North Sea. The town had changed hands three times over the previous twenty years, from Prussia's Prince Frederick Augustus von Anhalt-Zerbst to Russia's Catherine the Great, and then in 1807 to France's Emperor Napoleon. Lehmann, his parents and siblings lived in a tiny two-roomed stone house that backed onto the town wall on Kleine Burgstraße. One of only

3

seventeen Jewish families living in the town, they belonged to an insular but close-knit minority.

Before the arrival of the French, anti-Jewish sentiment had never been far from the surface in Jever. To obtain employment and a place to live, Lehmann's father, Meyer, had to pay a monthly protection fee to Prince Frederick Augustus, and later to Empress Catherine. In return, Meyer was considered to be a *Schutzjude*, or a protected Jew. He was allowed to work as a textile merchant, one of the few permitted occupations for Jews, along with moneylending, slaughtering animals and trade in leather. Forbidden occupations included legal work, politics and trade in sugar, tea and coffee.

The family had hoped that conditions would improve under the French, for Emperor Napoleon had developed a reputation as a man of religious tolerance. At first the news had been positive. A decree announced that the much-hated protection fee was outlawed and then the new French revolutionary code, including the free exercise of worship, was extended to the residents of Jever. Lehmann and his family greeted these announcements with celebration.

Then a new notice had been pinned to the town-hall door. From this point forward, and in an effort at assimilation, family members had to share the same last name. They could no longer simply refer to themselves as being the son of someone, such as 'Meyer son of Asher' or 'Lehmann son of Meyer'. After a long discussion about alternatives, and perhaps hoping for better fortune in the future, the family had chosen the surname 'Glückstein' or 'lucky stone'. It suggested something alchemic, even hopeful – creating gold out of nothing. The application was submitted to the Jever town clerk, a fee was paid and the name was approved.

The change of name and the other decrees, however, could not help the family's financial problems. Following the recent war against Napoleon, the local economy had collapsed. Even more unluckily for Meyer, cheap clothes were now available from France and the

Netherlands. He was bankrupt and was being chased by a long list of creditors. More pressingly, he was behind in his rent to his land-lord. Some of his neighbours, who were also in debt, might have tried appealing to their creditors' generous natures and thereby nego-tiated a payment plan. But these neighbours were not Jewish. A few days earlier, a group of thugs had come to Meyer's door and warned him to be out by the week's end.

Which is why they were leaving. With their belongings now packed, Lehmann, his parents and siblings started on their way. They pulled the cart along the familiar cobbled streets, past the green metal pump where they had taken their water each day, past the red-bricked Catholic church with its tall steeple, past the synagogue on Wasserpfortstraße where Lehmann had performed his *bar mitzvah*, and then up to the three-metre-high wall at the end of Sankt-Annen-Straße. As it was still daylight, the gate was open and, with a greeting to the guard – who knew each of them by name – the small group pushed their way beyond the city wall and headed westwards, in search of a new home.

Over the next few weeks and months, Lehmann travelled widely through the lush flat lands that make up Friesland. Driven by youthful energy and now unencumbered – his parents and younger siblings having settled with relatives – he attempted to find work.

He walked the streets, a clay pipe in his mouth, making enquiries, looking for leads. In Hooksiel, a fishing village on the North Sea, he applied for permission to live and conduct business, but was refused, after the local community argued that Jews 'always sell at the lowest price' (ruining the market for everyone else) and 'mislead their customers' (by selling low-quality goods.) When he did manage to obtain a contract to work as a kosher slaughterman in another town, a complaint was made against him, saying that his meat 'tasted bad' because he smoked during the preparation. Lehmann claimed not to know that smoking was illegal, but this made no difference and he was forced out. Finally, after passing a series of tests, he received a licence from the townspeople of Varel. He would now work as a kosher inspector and Hebrew teacher.

His employment continued until the political context changed once again. In 1813, following Napoleon's defeat in Russia, French troops withdrew from Friesland, including the towns of Varel and Jever, and Prussian troops took their place. This new reality was made permanent on 18 June 1815, with Napoleon's defeat at Waterloo – a week's ride from Jever – by British and Prussian troops. The Napoleonic code was swiftly rescinded. Jews in Friesland were now forbidden from holding public office, serving in the army, teaching in universities or even owning property. Within a year Lehmann saw the first anti-Semitic pamphlets circulating in the market place.

For the next decade he found work as an itinerant teacher, travelling from town to town, hoping that the hostile atmosphere would subside as stability returned to the region. When he was not teaching, Lehmann kept to himself. Shy and lacking in confidence, he struggled to make new friends. As for women, he had little contact with them. They sat apart from the men in synagogue and, without family nearby, Lehmann was not introduced to girls of his age. As for his business contacts, his pupils were all boys and he dealt only with their fathers.

In his spare moments Lehmann wrote *Eduth Aschereth*, or *Witness to Marriage*, a book about Jewish wedding contracts and rituals that was published in 1818. At the time, the ancient myth that Jews used Christian blood in their ceremonies was resurfacing around Europe. One of the most common variations of this so-called 'blood libel' was that Christian blood was applied to the fingers of a Jewish bride to free her from her family. Lehmann's study of wedding rituals proved that this was silliness. Although *Eduth Aschereth* had little impact at the time of its publication, it would be relied upon by future scholars.

It was uncommon for a Jew to be published at this time, particularly given that Lehmann was not formally educated, but it was far from unique. Other published German-Jewish writers included the journalist Ludwig Börne, who edited various liberal newspapers in Frankfurt; and Rahel Levin Varnhagen, who ran an intellectual salon in Berlin and whose superbly written letters would be published after her death. Perhaps most famous of all was Heinrich Heine, who grew up in the Rhineland and wrote enthusiastically about Napoleon's arrival in Düsseldorf. Shortly after Lehmann published his book, Heine wrote 'Edon', a poem about Prussia's prejudices against the Jews: 'A brotherly forbearance has united us for ages. You tolerate my breathing, and I tolerate your rages.'

Each of these authors felt the weight of growing anti-Jewish sentiment in Prussia. Börne, Varnhagen and Heine all chose to assimilate to the dominant culture by converting to Christianity. Lehmann, in contrast, was determined to hang on to his Jewish faith. For him, religion was more important than country.

In the spring of 1819, now aged thirty-two and hoping to secure a long-term position, Lehmann travelled to Rheinberg, a small town on the banks of the River Rhine, 320 kilometres south of Jever and 70 kilometres north of Cologne. There he applied for and was awarded the prestigious position of the community's Hebrew and religious teacher and, as one of the town's most learned scholars, often led the congregation during the Friday-evening and Saturday-morning services.

He moved into a modest room on the second floor of number 55 Rheinstraße, one of the main streets running into Rheinberg. Each morning he was woken by the squawking of chickens and the smell of ducks from the poultry market set up outside his front door. It was only a five-minute walk to the town's small synagogue, across the main square and then down Gelderstraße, and it was here that he gave Hebrew lessons.

With only sixty-five Jewish people living in Rheinberg at the time, word soon spread that an eligible young man had arrived in town. And yet, being timid, Lehmann failed to notice the glances sent his way as he walked down the street. That was until he met Helena Horn, the twenty-two-year-old woman who lived a few doors down from him. It was Helena who picked out the shy, thin, scholarly man from Jever. It was Helena who invited him home for tea; who first kissed him, and then encouraged him to do more.

A few weeks later, and to the dismay of some – in particular Lehmann's mother – Helena announced that she was pregnant. Though pre-marital sex was fairly commonplace within the wider population, it would have been scandalous for a Hebrew teacher to be the father of an illegitimate child, and despite the fact that Lehmann could offer little in the way of financial security, a match was agreed. So it was that, on 21 August 1819, the couple were married at the town hall on the main square. Now five months pregnant, Helena had a bump that was visible for all to see, including the four official witnesses (two merchants, a butcher and a neighbour) as well as the Mayor of Rheinberg, who oversaw the ceremony. Perhaps offended that it was a shotgun wedding, Lehmann's parents did not attend. In contrast, when asked for her view of the nuptials, Helena's mother responded with uncommon enthusiasm, saying that she gave her 'complete consent'. The licence noted that while Lehmann was a teacher, Helena was illiterate and unemployed. The party then retired, as was traditional, to the bride's house on Rheinstraße. As a violinist played, Helena and Lehmann were lifted aloft on chairs and paraded around the courtyard.

While the mood was celebratory, talk soon turned to the anti-Jewish pogroms that had erupted three days earlier in the Bavarian town of Rimpon near Würzburg, 300 kilometres to the south of Rheinberg. That day's local newspaper reported that young men had run through the street armed with hatchets and crowbars, shouting 'Hep! Hep!' – meaning the destruction of Jerusalem – and 'If you don't flee, then you are through!' Vandals had then smashed the windows of four Jewish houses, broken into the Rimpon synagogue and destroyed the sacred scrolls inside. Later that night, Lehmann reassured Helena that the riots would remain in the south; after all, the Jewish community had long been tolerated in the Rhineland, and besides, hadn't they just been married by the mayor himself? Still, as he lay awake, he worried about what would happen.

He didn't have long to find out. The next day, 22 August, a council edict was pinned to the wall of the public reading room in Düsseldorf, less than 50 kilometres from Rheinberg, ordering the expulsion of Jews from the city. Later that night, black arrows were painted on the houses of many Jews, and a notice nailed to the house of Rabbi Löb Aron Scheuer read: 'The domination of Jews over the conduct of trade has already lasted too long. Christians have calmly observed this. Times have changed. If by the 26th of this month, restrictions are not placed on this people, there will be a blood bath.'

Over the next few weeks Lehmann heard of violent pogroms moving ever closer: Bamberg, Heidelberg, Frankfurt. These attacks were the most recent expression of *Judenschuld*, the long-held view that Jews were to be blamed for everything. Such canards were fuelled by fears that Jews had made financial gains during the Napoleonic Wars. Across western and north-western Germany, Jewish homes and shops were looted, Jewish men were beaten with wooden batons and synagogues were set on fire. With few exceptions, priests, the military and local politicians stood by, doing nothing as the beatings continued. Still, despite the violent bloody threats in Düsseldorf, which were as yet unrealised, the left bank of the Rhine where Lehmann and Helena lived remained peaceful.

Then, on 12 October 1819, at the end of the summer festival in the village of Dormagen – 50 kilometres and one day's ride south of Rheinberg – Stoffel Bloemer, the local stonemason, noticed that his seven-year-old daughter Marie Catharina was missing. The child had gone with some others to a nearby village to tend a cow, came back and said to her mother, 'I want to put on my best dress and go out and enjoy myself.' The girl followed the music into the village, passed the church and disappeared. Every house was searched, and people looked down wells and in the River Rhine. Nothing was found.

This story was conveyed by word of mouth from one tradesperson to the next, up the River Rhine: Ürdingen, Duisberg and then on to Rheinberg. The events that followed were recorded by Johann Peter Delhoven, in the *Rheinische Dorfchronik*, the Dormagen village chronicle. According to Delhoven, there were 'thousands of opinions' being discussed as to what happened to the girl:

> The prevailing one is that the Jews captured the child because at times, according to an old legend, they must have Christian blood. And since the disappearance of the child coincides with the end of Sukkot [Feast of Tabernacles], there are all kinds of witnesses who claim to have seen either the Jew Sekel with a sack or the Jew Schimmel lurking around houses at midnight.

Then, on 17 October, a local man, Mathias Heck, found the body of a child lying next to a willow tree in a wood outside Dormagen. It was Marie Catharina. She had been loosely bound twice around the neck, her body impaled to the ground. Her stockings had been pulled down, but not taken off. After examining the body later that evening, a local surgeon announced that the child had been raped. Johann Peter Delhoven noted that on hearing the shocking news, people came to Dormagen from as far as three hours away, to demonstrate their outrage and their support for Marie Catharina's family. This culminated in a rowdy church service. 'On all sides the rumour spread that the child's blood had been sucked and she had bled from 700 wounds,' he wrote. 'I myself saw the child, her arms and legs covered in red spots and I myself knew that the Jews were the perpetrators.'

This was, the chronicler alleged, a *Ritualmordlegende*, or ritual murder myth, based on the ancient fallacy that Jews used Christian blood for their ceremonies. Over the next days, and despite the lack of any evidence to link the crime to a suspect, various Jewish community members were attacked. A teacher and a butcher were assaulted by children and young lads. One trader's windows were smashed, and another had a dead piglet laid at his door. A peddler had his doors smeared with muck and a side of bacon put in front of his house. On 30 October, the Jewish cemetery in Hülchrath, just south of Düsseldorf, was attacked and several gravestones were smashed. The next day a Jewish school was attacked, its windows and blackboard broken. Two adults reported that they were badly abused as they left the school. No one could remember hearing of such violence since the Dark Ages.

As he travelled the region giving Hebrew lessons, Lehmann read the reports of what had become known as the 'Hep Hep riots'. The news, however, was not all bad. In many of the newspapers he read editorials and letters denouncing the anti-Jewish violence. In others, writers suggested that persecuted Jews could come to their countries to find safe haven. The French-language paper *La Renommée*, for instance, published an impassioned column that autumn, saying that the Jews of Germany should 'abandon an ungrateful soil where justice is refused them' and come instead to France, where they can 'enjoy our fine climate, the benefits of law that guarantees the safety of person and property, the freedom of industry, opinions and consciences. Their change will occasion them no regret.' From this and other entreaties, Lehmann understood there were places that would not only accept Jews like himself, but would welcome them. If life became unbearable in Rheinberg, which he still hoped would not be the case, then he and Helena would have to move and find somewhere more tolerant. Perhaps France, perhaps somewhere else.

At noon on 10 December, a month after the riots had finally petered out, Helena gave birth to a daughter named Adelheid. Tragically, the infant died two weeks later. No cause was listed on the death certificate, which was registered at the town hall on 16 January 1820. They tried again and, on Thursday, 4 January 1821, Helena gave birth to a boy, Samuel. Lehmann was not present for the birth – he was teaching in the nearby town of Goch – but he was very much present eight days later for the *brit milah,* or circumcision.

A second boy, Meyer, named after Lehmann's father, followed a year later, and then a third, Nathan, a year after that. Suddenly the Glückstein house seemed small, with three boys all under the age of three, but they were content. Lehmann was busy with his teaching work, while Helena had her hands full with the children. Then, on 13 September 1824, six months after Nathan's birth, word arrived in Rheinberg that further restrictive laws had been passed in Berlin. The Prussian government now decreed not only that the protection fee cancelled under Napoleonic Law was owed once again, but also that the amount that had accumulated over the previous three decades was due immediately. For those not rich enough to pay, the only ways out were bankruptcy, imprisonment or death.

To make matters worse, the new laws also declared that all Jewish religious teachers must apply to the authorities for a licence, providing supporting documents demonstrating that the teacher had all the necessary certificates. Given that he was self-taught, Lehmann quickly realised that he would never be approved. Overnight he lost his position, and another qualified Hebrew tutor was appointed in his place.

Lehmann was now facing huge debts and was unable to support his young family.

Thinking of the entreaties in foreign newspapers, the obvious option was to flee, but how to ensure there would be no retribution for Helena's mother and siblings? After all, according to the new Prussian laws, Lehmann owed the government a vast sum of money. The debt would stay, even if he didn't. Facing ruin, there appeared to be only one solution.

Two weeks later, gravediggers at the Rheinberg cemetery gave a final tamp to the mounded earth and walked away, tools in hand. On the pale-grey headstone were etched the following words:

Glückstein, Lehmann, 1787–1824, from Jever, teacher.

Chapter 2

1824

As the Glücksteins approached from the south, Arnhem rose impressively before them. Five times bigger than Rheinberg, it was the largest town Helena had ever seen. Its church steeples, three in all, seemed taller and more imposing than those back home. Its ancient medieval stone bridge, which spanned the placid river, was wide and without a gatehouse. And unlike Rheinberg, this city's walls had been torn down. This all came as quite a surprise to Helena. For, unlike her husband, she had never travelled more than a few kilometres from her birthplace.

It had been a hard trek. For more than a week they had followed the River Rhine north of Rheinberg, dragging their meagre supplies on a wooden cart into the Netherlands, until they reached the Arnhem town limits. The journey had been made harder by having to look after the three children; harder still, for they were on the run, unsure if they were being chased, unsure if their ruse had been rumbled. For walking alongside Helena was her very-much-alive husband, Lehmann Meyer Glückstein, who had faked his death to allow them to escape without saddling her family with repercussions.

It had been a simple enough scheme to pull off. Record-keeping was unsophisticated at this point, and whilst the law called for all births, marriages and deaths to be registered at the local town hall, many were not. An infant who perished before reaching their first birthday, for instance, was rarely noted. Similarly, those who lived in remote rural areas often changed status without bureaucratic note. So it was that at the same time that his gravestone was being readied in the Rheinberg dirt, Lehmann was leading his family into the heart of the Netherlands in search of safer environs.

Once they had found somewhere to spend the night, he went out in search of employment. Arnhem had a sizeable Jewish community – vital for Lehmann's work – with a synagogue on Nieuwe Walstraat (New Rampart Street), a cemetery, a Jewish school and a society dedicated to study of the Torah. Lehmann soon learned that the wealthier Jews were involved with the country's growing sugar-import trade, as bankers, clerks and wholesalers. There was even a Jewish lawyer living in the town. Less-affluent Jews worked as shop-keepers, salesmen, market labourers and butchers. As such, and with a Jewish population of more than 400 (six times that of Rheinberg), Arnhem was considered one of the most prosperous Jewish communities in the Netherlands. It didn't take long, therefore, for Lehmann to find a few families looking for help with their Hebrew lessons.

As the months rolled by, his reputation for being a good teacher spread, and so his list of clients grew. Yet despite his hard work, there never seemed quite enough income to pay the bills, and the family remained stuck in a constant state of financial jeopardy. The problem was that the people Lehmann worked with did not have much money themselves, and he found it hard to charge when they could ill afford it. When things got particularly tight, Lehmann would hustle around and find extra clients. He would work late into the evening, coming home exhausted, but with a few coins in his pockets.

Helena, meanwhile, was pregnant once again. Her days were filled with the domestic chores of shopping, cooking and washing, while the boys – Samuel, Meyer and Nathan – were all out of cloth nappies and running around the house, causing mayhem. Activity came to a halt every Friday evening for the *Shabbat* and this lasted until sunset the following day. This was a chance to attend synagogue, to better know the Jewish community and to pray.

Lehmann had always been a learned and curious man, someone who thought beyond the here-and-now. It may well have been due to the relative safety of their current situation, or an instinct that things would improve; that there would be a future when people – his children, their descendants – might be interested in his journey; that these times were important, not just for him, but for others. And so one evening, when the family was asleep, he began.

He picked up the small leather-bound book that he had brought with him from Rheinberg. It was 200 years old, a lexicon of ancient Hebrew and Chaldean words written by the Swiss-born Johannes Buxtorf, the so-called 'master of rabbis'. With one hand holding open its back pages, Lehmann picked up a quill with the other, dipped it in black ink and began to write his first entry:

The day of my birth 17 July 1794. Born in Jever (in the Duchy of Oldenburg, near Bremen) Lehmann Meyer Glückstein son of Meyer Lehmann Glückstein and Adele Joseph.

He went on to record his wife's details, their marriage and information about their three sons, including German and Hebrew names, along with dates and place of birth. After his children's names he wrote '*Mazel Tov*', or 'with good fortune'. He also added the portion of the Torah that was read out in synagogue the weeks of their birth. In addition, having studied the secret kabbalah texts, Lehmann noted any numerological significance that he could find. His wedding, for instance, which took place during the Hebrew year of 5579, had the meaning of 'good and sweet', which appeared to please him.

What he did not record, however, was the bad news. In February 1826, his wife gave birth to their fourth son, Joseph, who died a few weeks later. A fifth son, Alexander, was born two years after that, and again he died soon after birth. Neither of these children were chronicled at the back of Lehmann's *Lexicon*. Happily, over the next three years, three more children were born, all of whom survived: Solly, Harry and Bertha. The last was named after Helena's mother; her Hebrew name, Bincha, meant 'dear little bee'.

With six small children to feed, Lehmann set about writing a book, hoping that sales might supplement the income he made from giving Hebrew lessons. Over the summer and winter of 1831 he spent long hours in his study, working and reworking the text. Finally, in early 1832 he delivered the manuscript to the publisher C.A. Theime. It was forty-five pages long, written in Flemish and called *A Simple and Sure Guide to Learn the Gender of French Substantives in Ten Rules*. In his introduction, Lehmann, who now called himself a language teacher, wrote that he hoped his method would make French more comprehensible to Dutch youth – 'a method, which, as far as I know, no other work has used'.

The book was well received, with one critic in the educational magazine *Tijdschrift voor Onderwijzers* recommending it greatly. *A Simple and Sure Guide*, the reviewer wrote, 'can prove helpful to simplify the teaching of French language'. But while it was a critical success, the book made little difference to the family coffers. Fewer copies sold than had been hoped, and the writing had taken much more time than Lehmann had expected, reducing the number of lessons he could provide and worsening the family finances. It was clear to Helena that Arnhem could not fix their pecuniary woes. She had heard that the Jewish merchants working in the port cities were affluent, for international trade was flourishing. They would pay better, she told Lehmann. The solution was to move again, westwards.

In the spring of 1832, the Glücksteins arrived in the city of Rotterdam. It was quite a shock. Unlike Arnhem, the streets teemed with wagons and drays clattering goods to and from the wholesalers and auction houses on the wharves and docks. Hawkers stood in droves, calling out their products. Men in tailored suits and women in beautifully designed dresses were carried past in an assortment of horses and carts: the luxurious four-wheeled barouche, the sedate landau, the speedy phaeton. Government workers attempted to maintain order, shouting instructions and directing traffic. It was organised chaos. For the family from the small town of Rheinberg, Germany, it was all – the noise, the people, the busyness – overwhelming.

They had chosen Rotterdam for two reasons. It was a port city, making it likely to be commercially busy and therefore, hopefully, affluent. Secondly, it was home to more than 2,500 Jews, making it the largest Jewish community in the Netherlands outside Amsterdam. In fact Rotterdam had as many Jews as there were residents of Rheinberg. The Glücksteins made their way to the Jewish quarter, which was centred around the old synagogue in De Boompjes, a neighbourhood abutting the harbour and known for its avenue of lime trees. But when they arrived and had found somewhere to stay, Lehmann and Helena were disappointed to learn that there was no shortage of Hebrew teachers. Worse, there wasn't much need for Lehmann's linguistic skills; the streets and bars were brimming with out-of-work translators and polyglots.

Over the next few days the family discussed various options. They could wait for a job opening. This seemed unwise, given what they had already learned. They could move on to another town, but they were exhausted by travel. Finally, Lehmann could reinvent himself and try something entirely new. But what?

During his visits to taverns and market places across the lowlands, Lehmann had noticed the public's increasing interest in foreign affairs. There was certainly much to discuss. In the two preceding years alone, Belgium and Greece had won their independence. William IV had ascended to the English throne, whilst Charles X of France had abdicated in favour of his grandson Louis Philippe. There was a new pope in Rome. Meanwhile, François Arban had achieved the world's first-ever ascent in a hot-air balloon.

Lehmann had also noted the popularity of streetside entertainments in the larger towns and cities: jugglers and violinists, performing animals and camera obscuras. It was this last that had caught his eye. What if it was possible to combine people's interest in public events with some new way to present them? During the summer of 1832 Lehmann sat at home and experimented. Having purchased a number of small lenses from an optician, he tried out different arrangements. A watercolour picture illuminated by candlelight. Natural light shining through a glass. A hole in a curtain projecting on a wall. The task required great dexterity and patience. He was helped by his eleven-year-old son Samuel, whose small and nimble hands were better suited to manipulating the delicate objects, and who showed such enthusiasm that Lehmann soon viewed him as indispensable to the enterprise's success.

Father and son eventually settled on a device that consisted of a portable wooden viewing box through which coloured painted cards were magnified and illuminated. The illustrations were placed at the back of the box, which was then held up to the light and viewed through a glass lens. Most cards included small cut-out parts through which the light would pass, depicting windows or street lamps, and thus the scene appeared to be illuminated by these light sources. Some cards were also designed to change, so that a scene might appear to alter, for example, from a daytime to a night-time view. They called this device the 'Polyrama Panoptique'.

In one of their first outings, Sam and Lehmann erected a tent next to the harbour wall in Rotterdam. The experiment proved a great success, and before long father and son were taking the attraction around the Netherlands. First they set up on the *Vischbrug*, or 'Fishing Bridge', in the centre of Leiden and invited passers-by to take a view into their magical machine, for a price of course. They moved on to The Hague, Delft and Utrecht. To promote their project, they took out advertisements in the newspapers. In Amsterdam, for instance, they paid for an entry in the *Algemeen Handelsblad* proclaiming that their camera had previously 'found the greatest fame and praise' in cities across the country. For those interested in enjoying the marvel, it continued, the Glücksteins would be exhibiting just across from the French Theatre.

Over the next decade, Lehmann and Samuel criss-crossed the Netherlands and Belgium. In each city or town they found a good location with plenty of traffic, set up the machine, drummed up interest, took in the coins and settled the accounts at the day's end. After a day or two, once they had tapped the local interest, they moved on to the next town. Lehmann was used to the constant travel, but found the endless hawking and peddling tiring. Samuel, by contrast, was a natural salesperson who enjoyed the unpredictability of the road. And so they continued. As the years progressed, they learned the basics of trade: providing quality products that consumers wanted, sold at affordable prices, with patience and – perhaps most important of all – showmanship. The Glücksteins' wondrous contraption was soon talked about in the highest of circles. Indeed, during a stop in The Hague they were even visited by members of the Dutch royal family.

Their most popular picture was that of Napoleon's funeral in 1840. The Polyrama captured the moment after the great man's remains had been controversially returned from his prison on the island of Saint Helena, interred in an oak coffin wrapped in the French tricolour and placed upon an enormous iron-berthed carriage, then paraded with great ceremony and colour before an enormous crowd along the resplendent Champs-Elysées in Paris. To some of the Low-Countries denizens who put their eye to the light box, Napoleon was a fiend, an occupier and dictator. To others, including Lehmann and Samuel, Bonaparte was a liberator, a moderniser and a friend to religious minorities. Either way, he was a larger-than-life character and, most importantly, he was good for business.

It was during this time of commercial experimentation that the family was hit by a double tragedy. Helena gave birth for the ninth time, but the little baby girl, whom they called Hester, died less than a month later. Then, on 11 April 1841, their son Gershom died, at the age of four years and ten months. Lehmann now took out his precious book and, with an uneven hand, scratched out his son's name and information over and over again, until the writing was barely legible.

As the family attempted to come to terms with their loss, another worry loomed large. Holland's economy had weakened significantly over the past few years, with GDP per capita falling from 1.3 per cent in the 1830s to 0.4 per cent in the early 1840s. Salaries were not keeping up with price increases, hitting poorer families such as the Glücksteins particularly hard. Despite their proven charms, Lehmann and Samuel were finding it harder to persuade people to part with their money. As fewer crowds were drawn to the Polyrama Panoptique, they felt more pressure to deliver the funds necessary to make ends meet. And it was then that Samuel, who was now twenty years old, got into trouble.

Late in 1841, in an attempt to turn the family's fortunes around, Samuel sold some items that were of dubious quality. Unhappy with the deal, the purchaser accused him of fraud and went to the police. Samuel told his parents that he was innocent of any wrongdoing and was being made a scapegoat because of his religion. Realising they were unlikely to receive a fair hearing, the Glücksteins hurriedly relocated to Antwerp in Belgium.

In early August 1842, Lehmann wrote to the authorities in Antwerp, asking for a residency permit for Samuel. This was forwarded to the government offices in the capital, Brussels, along with a report from the Antwerp chief of police, which recorded that Samuel 'was convicted for fraud' in the Netherlands, 'but escaped by taking flight'. The following day, 18 August 1842, the Minister of Justice in Brussels replied to the Mayor of Antwerp. 'Concerning S. Glückstein who lives with his father Glückstein master of foreign languages', it began. 'I ask you not to lose sight of him, this foreigner seems to be obliged to leave Holland, after being involved in a swindle.' On 2 November, the Antwerp chief of police wrote to the city's mayor saying that 'Lehmann Glückstein has shown very good character and is arranging his son's affairs', adding that 'it can be painful for parents when they are torn from a child who had made some youthful mistakes, which are anyway easy to rectify'. Two weeks later, the administrator of the Ministry of Justice approved the residency permit for 'Samuel Gluckstein [sic]'.

Despite the official approval, there was now a black mark against Samuel and it was clear that the authorities were keeping an eye on him. Over the winter months, which were memorable for their mild temperatures, lack of rain and the continuing decline in business revenues, the family again had to consider their future. Should Samuel try and clear his name? Should the entire clan relocate? Finally they made a decision. Samuel would journey to London, where it was said the economy was booming and religious tolerance was assured.

Then, on 9 February 1843, shortly before Samuel's departure, Helena gave birth to Benjamin, the traditional Jewish name for the youngest child. The family had grown to nine: Lehmann, Helena, Samuel and his six younger siblings. Samuel would act as the family's vanguard. Once he had established himself, he would send for the others.

Chapter 3

1843

_____

As the *Lord Melville* pushed its way up the River Thames, the twenty-two-year-old Samuel Glückstein stood on deck and marvelled at the relentless industrial activity and the chaotic skyline of wharves, warehouses and tenement buildings that formed the East End of London. It had been almost twenty years since he had left Rheinberg. He had spent most of the intervening time moving from one sleepy Dutch or Belgian city to the next. As for the town of his birth, he could remember little of it. What he could recall was the fear in his father's eyes, and his longing for escape, for safe harbour.

In Samuel's view, his father was wrong. They had never been safe in Germany, or the Netherlands, or Belgium. Not under Napoleon, or the Prussians, or the Dutch king. Why should England be any different? There wasn't some magical city or town that would guarantee their well-being and accept their kind. Such a place didn't exist. At least not yet. What they needed was improved social position – education, contacts, clout. And the only way to obtain all these was through money. This was Samuel's sole ambition, and he was committed to realising it by any means necessary.

He and the other passengers had boarded the schooner eight hours earlier in the Belgium port of Ostend, leaving early to catch the morning tide. Given that it was summertime, the sea had been mercifully calm, the journey uneventful. Now they were in England and his future lay before him: a chance to start afresh and, hopefully, make his family proud.

Once the *Lord Melville* was tied off by the port hands, Samuel disembarked down a narrow wooden stairway and into the frenzied hubbub of London's premier port: stevedores and dockers loading and unloading tea, sugar and timber; seamen, lightermen, ballastmen and coal-heavers preparing for the next voyage; casual workers waiting for the next 'call-on'; prostitutes hoping to turn a mid-afternoon trick; and food-sellers providing lukewarm tea and stale refreshments to those working in the port.

At the customs building Samuel joined the schooner's other passengers, suitcase in hand, as he waited to be processed by a port official. When it was their turn, the master of the *Lord Melville* handed over a one-page 'List of Aliens' that included the names of twenty-nine passengers, of whom thirteen came from Germany, five from Belgium and the rest from France, Norway and Poland. There were no passports to be reviewed, no medical records to be examined and no assets to be enumerated. Having glanced at the form, the official signed his name and added the date of entry: 21 August 1843.

Once clear of customs, Samuel asked one of his fellow passengers where he could find lodgings for the night. There were boarding houses in Whitechapel, he was told; it was a short walk from the Port of London, and they took in newly arrived immigrants such as him. Samuel headed towards the district known as Whitechapel.

A century before, it had been a peaceful, industrious suburb, where breweries, tanneries and slaughterhouses sat cheek-by-jowl with traveller inns and public houses. In the past few decades the neighbourhood had become a melting pot of immigrants from Ireland and

Germany, Poland and the Netherlands. Its maze of narrow streets had been transformed into an overcrowded district, rife with poverty and delinquency. Half the houses had only basic sewage drainage; the rest had none, emptying their waste into cesspools whose foul odour polluted the air and poisoned the water of nearby public pumps. Cholera, smallpox, scarlet fever and whooping cough were endemic. In 1843, the death rate in Whitechapel was 21 per cent higher than in the rest of London.

At this time Whitechapel was fast becoming a Jewish ghetto. Of the capital's 25,000 Jews, the vast majority resided in the East End, making up more than 50 per cent of England's total Jewish population. Living close to each other enabled them to communicate easily (typically in Yiddish), share religious ceremonies, intermarry and do business together. Most of the Jewish families worked as merchants, including those trading in jewels, old clothes, leather, picture frames, toys, antiques and cigars. The majority faced profound economic hardship. By mid-century, 25–30 per cent of Jews in London were receiving poor relief, and half were impoverished or scarcely making a living.

With poverty came crime. Whitechapel was known as a haven for pickpockets and prostitution, prize-fighting and gambling, opium dens and card cheats. This was the domain of colourful characters such as the fence Ikey Solomon (supposedly the basis for Fagin in Dickens' novel *Oliver Twist*); a place where 'people of quality', such as Oscar Wilde's Dorian Gray, visited the 'entertainments', only to return to 'civilised' London when their fun was over. Above all, Whitechapel was infamous for its moneylenders, its men with sharp wits and its thugs – all of whom Samuel was keen to avoid. Finally, as in the rest of Europe, London was also home to virulent anti-Jewish sentiment, so living close to other Jews in Whitechapel provided a form of safety in numbers.

Later that evening Samuel saw a sign announcing a room for rent in a tall, overcrowded boarding house at 9 Freeman Street in

Whitechapel. Although he was fluent in German and Dutch, Samuel spoke little English. Luckily, the building's manager, Conrad Joseph, was also from Holland. Samuel was able to communicate that he had just landed in the capital, would be starting up a new business and needed accommodation until such time as he could afford a larger place. As long as he paid on time, Joseph said, the room was his.

As the centre of the ever-expanding British Empire, London in August 1843 was booming. Over the past eight months the acclaimed engineer Isambard Kingdom Brunel had opened the first tunnel under the River Thames; the Bombay army had won the Battle of Hyderabad, securing the massive Sindh province for the East India Company (at a cost of 2,000 Talpur troops killed); Natal province, almost 100,000 square kilometres of land in the southernmost tip of Africa, was taken from the Boers and proclaimed a British colony; the country was undergoing 'railway mania', with thousands of kilometres of new line being constructed; and the volume of its stock-exchange trade rose ever upwards (driven partly by Britain's monopoly of the telegraph, which transmitted the latest news from around the world via tickertape).

Meanwhile, Britain was simultaneously experiencing a cultural renaissance and mounting self-confidence. Theatres had been liberalised by eliminating the royal patent; and the free press was flourishing – especially compared to the continent (*The Times* described Germany's press that year as existing 'under the thraldom, not only of the censorship, but of absolute and ruinous prohibitions'). At the same time, sympathy for the monarch was at an all-time high, after three assassins over the previous twelve months had tried, and failed, to kill the young Queen Victoria.

The week Samuel set foot in the docks of east London happened to coincide with the launch of *The Economist*, a newspaper set up to promote economic liberalism. 'We seriously believe that free trade, free intercourse, will do more than any other visible agent,' proclaimed its prospectus the previous month, 'to extend civilisation and morality throughout the world – yes, to extinguish slavery itself.' In the newspaper's first edition, published on 2 September 1843, the editorial board noted that 'commercial matters have assumed a more cheerful aspect in every quarter' and that 'the demand for almost every description of foreign and colonial produce has been on a decidedly improved scale'. The home markets for wool, iron, money and corn, they reported in their already-dry but exact tone, were all up.

A different perspective was offered by Friedrich Engels, who at the time was working in his father's textile factory some 320 kilometres to the north, in Manchester. Eight months before Samuel's arrival in London, Engels wrote an article for the *Rheinische Zeitung* describing England as 'feudal' and 'up to its neck in the Middle Ages'. For while industry had made the country rich, it had also created a 'class of unpropertied, absolutely poor people, a class which lives from hand-to-mouth, which multiples rapidly, and which afterwards cannot be abolished, because it can never acquire stable possession of property'. Engels was recounting the situation of many of Samuel's new East End neighbours. Combining the viewpoints of *The Economist* and Engels, it appears that for a young immigrant, 1840s Britain could either be a land of opportunity and promise or a place of never-ending toil and conflict. The outcome would probably be down to hard work, personality and not a little luck.

On his entry documents, Samuel had stated that he was a 'merchant'. He had reported the same to the Antwerp authorities the previous year. What he hadn't disclosed was his interest in tobacco. Like his father, Samuel had long enjoyed smoking. During his various travels around Holland he had become acquainted with many cigar-makers and visited their small workshops. Observant and curious, he had picked up the basics of the manufacturing process.

He now launched himself into his new career. First, he purchased a small quantity of dried leaf direct from the warehouses in the West India Docks. Back in his little room in Whitechapel, he attempted to make the cigars. It was frustrating work, harder than it looked, requiring great dexterity and timing. Pack the tobacco too tight and the flame went out. Pack it too loose and the burn was uneven. Roll it too quickly and the cigar looked ugly or, worse, fell apart. Use the wrong leaf and the cigar would 'char' and a emit foul-smelling odour. The aim was a cigar that looked attractive, tasted good and burned with a clear, steady light, leaving a fine white or pearl-coloured ash. Samuel rolled cigar after cigar after cigar. It was tedious, painstaking and exhausting work.

He kept practising, working long into the night, learning by trial and error, until one day he collapsed and crawled into bed. He had picked up an infection and developed a high fever. Without any family to look after him, he lay alone in his small room, unable to feed himself. At the year's end the medical officer for Whitechapel would report that 2,083 residents had died from fever.

He was fortunate, therefore, that Ann Joseph, the building manager's twenty-four-year-old daughter, was walking past his door and heard Samuel's calls for help. She brought him water and, when he felt better, clear soup. Sitting in a chair next to his bed, she asked about his family, and told him about hers. She had arrived with her parents and brother from Holland thirteen years earlier. Like Samuel, they were Jewish and kept kosher at home. Her father had been found guilty of stealing lottery tickets in Amsterdam – of course he was innocent, she said – and had been sentenced to eighteen months in prison. He had appealed, but just before the hearing they had fled to England.

Lying on his bed, looking at this kind, patient woman, Samuel wondered if he was not the only one to have been falsely accused. Under Ann's careful attention, he soon recovered fully and redoubled his business efforts. After finally filling a box with reasonable-looking cigars, he went out onto the street and tried to sell them. Deploying the techniques he had learned when promoting the Polyrama at the harbourside in Rotterdam and at the Fishing Bridge in Leiden, he was able to sell one cigar and then another. Soon he was selling enough to pay the rent, and then to afford three meals a day. Then enough for a bunch of roses for Ann, and a new suit.

On Sunday, 25 May 1845, two years after Samuel set foot in England, he walked with Ann to the local town hall in Whitechapel. The wedding would be a small affair, as Samuel's parents and siblings were yet to arrive from Holland. On the marriage certificate the registrar added their names and dates of birth, and wrote that Samuel's father was a minister and Ann's was a shoemaker. Samuel then signed his name, and Ann added a mark in the shape of an egg. Like his mother, when she had wed back in Rheinberg, Samuel's bride was illiterate.

Samuel and Ann set about making a home for themselves. They moved into a two-room flat in a rundown building at number 34 Whitechapel High Street, a busy main road just a couple of streets away from Ann's parents. Shortly afterwards, Ann announced that she was pregnant. Samuel was delighted. With a child on the way, he and Ann worked hard to increase the cigar business. With two of them now buying, rolling and selling, profits soon rose. As they moved into winter, Ann's belly swelled, but she kept working. By the year's end she grew tired more quickly, finding it hard to keep up with her husband's long hours. Compared to other pregnant women, her stomach seemed larger, but she was healthy, and for this she was grateful.

On 15 February 1846, almost exactly nine months after the wedding, Ann went into labour. She was at home, and at half-past five in the afternoon she gave birth to a girl. They called her Lena, after Samuel's mother. A few minutes later, and to their great surprise, a second girl was born – a twin, whom they named Julia. These were the family's first British-born grandchildren. When Samuel and Ann registered the birth certificates at the town hall, they omitted the umlaut from the girls' last name; they would now be known by the anglicised form of 'Gluckstein'. Samuel sent word to his parents in Antwerp: they had two grandchildren and the business was looking good – it was time to come to England.

Almost exactly a year later, Samuel's parents and four youngest siblings arrived at the Port of London – his two eldest brothers, Nathan and Meyer, remained in Belgium. After clearing customs, the newcomers walked to Whitechapel and soon were at Samuel and Ann's home. Now, across the crowded kitchen table, a rich mixture of Dutch, German, Yiddish and cockney English was exchanged. Within a few days, however, it became clear there was just not enough room for all of them.

After a quick search, Samuel helped his father find a flat at 14 Castle Place, just a few minutes' walk from 34 Whitechapel High Street. Samuel paid for the first month's rent with the savings they had built up over the last few months. It was a diverse area: half of their neighbours were born in England, while the others were from central and Western Europe. They included a fishmonger, five cap-makers, four tailors, two butchers, a needlewoman, a cane-maker, a sack-maker, a furrier and a customs-house officer. A quarter of the women and half the children aged seven to fourteen were registered as being in paid employment. Many of the residents spoke Yiddish, which was useful, as Samuel's parents and siblings could not speak more than a few words of English.

Once they were settled, three of Samuel's siblings came to work for him: his younger brothers Solly (fourteen) and Harry (twelve), and his sister Bertha (twelve). Samuel's mother Helena remained at home looking after little Benjamin. His sixty-year-old father, Lehmann, was now too old to toil in a workshop, so he also remained at home, improving his English and studying Hebrew texts.

The task of manufacturing cigars could now be divided. Each morning the siblings walked over to Samuel and Ann's flat, which doubled up as a workshop. After a brief tutorial, and having practised and mastered the craft, they were soon able to take over the time-consuming tasks of wrapping and rolling. The greater number of employees resulted in a dramatic rise in production levels and an increase in sales. This in turn liberated greater profits, which allowed for a sharp increase in the purchase of raw materials.

Samuel spent much of his time at the London auction house, sampling, negotiating and purchasing tobacco leaf – in particular tobacco leaf that had just arrived from Virginia.

Chapter 4

1847

The origin of Virginia tobacco can be traced back to 240 years earlier. In the final weeks of 1606, a group of 200 settlers set sail from Plymouth in south-west England, heading for the New World. Consisting of three ships under the command of Captain Christopher Newport, the flotilla arrived five months later on the coast of what became known as Virginia. There, in the middle of May 1607, they erected a small number of dwellings along the banks of the Powhatan River. The new beginning was not an easy one. Within three years, after being ravaged by disease and starvation, only sixty of the original settlers had survived. The community was abandoned until June 1610, when a relief fleet arrived and Jamestown became Britain's first permanent settlement in the Americas.

Four years later, one of the settlers named John Rolfe, who had married Pocahontas, the daughter of a local chief, planted some tobacco seeds that he had picked up in Bermuda. Three years after that, fifty Africans were delivered to Jamestown from a Portuguese slaving ship that had been captured in the West Indies and were set to work in the tobacco fields. The crop was successful and soon Rolfe was sending the harvest back to England. Wishing to support the nascent colony's fragile economy, but disliking the foul-smelling weed, King James I had outlawed tobacco cultivation in England and then, to garner income for the royal coffers, declared all imports to be under royal warrant and taxable. This monopoly continued into the mid-nineteenth century, so that unlike its European neighbours – France, Germany and Austria, which grew much of their own tobacco – England sold tobacco in the London auction houses that was sourced almost entirely from Virginia. It also meant that, for the next few centuries, the vast majority of tobacco products sold in London – including those of Samuel Glückstein – could be traced to plantations worked by slaves.

By the time of Samuel's arrival in London in 1843, the issue of slavery had been highly controversial for many decades. The first concerted British effort to abolish slavery was launched by a Quaker anti-slavery committee in the 1780s. Yet it was not until 1807 that the slave trade was prohibited within the British Empire, and not until 1833 that the House of Commons outlawed the ownership of slaves in Britain. There was, however, no prohibition on importing goods made by slaves over-seas. It would be another thirty years before slavery was abolished in the USA, following the American Civil War of 1861–5.

Like other bulk buyers, Samuel Glückstein was well aware that the tobacco he purchased was produced on the back of slave labour. During the great abolition debates of the 1830s and 1840s, most of the main newspapers ran stories on how tobacco was produced in the USA, along with details of the terrible conditions in which the slaves worked. Indeed, the most prudent and eagle-eyed traders, such as Samuel, prided themselves on knowing the names of the best plantation owners and their agents, as well as the optimal time of year to purchase the harvest. In particular they knew the details of the Virginia tobacco crop-cycle.

Work began in early winter, with the male slaves felling any trees that grew on the land with a pollaxe, while the female slaves grubbed the undergrowth with a mattock and, together with their children, burned the brushwood and roots to clear the ground. In the New Year the slaves hoed the large clumps of earth into finer dirt and, if necessary, added Peruvian guano, then tilled once again. With the start of the rains in early spring, and if the land was considered ready by the overseer, the slaves – who were organised into gangs – then walked up and down the rows, scattering fine tobacco seeds from the baskets they carried on their arms. Next came months of weeding, transplanting, worming, 'hilling up' (mounding earth around the stalk, to protect the roots), topping (pinching the top of the stalk, to prevent flowering) and suckering (removing new shoots). Then, when the sun was at its fiercest and the leaves had thickened and developed yellow spots, came the harvest.

Early in the morning before the arrival of the dew, or late in the evening before the frost had set, the slaves walked up and down the rows, carefully cutting the now-ripened but brittle plants, which were dangled over a 1.5-metre-long wooden pole. Once loaded with seven to nine plants, the poles were carried into the tobacco house and suspended from the roof for drying. Over the next few weeks, small coal fires were maintained within the shed to smoke the tobacco. The purpose of the curing process was to reduce the bitter-tasting chlorophyll and to darken the leaves to a pleasing colour.

When cured, the leaves were stripped of their stalk, then separated by quality, before being prised into enormous 'hogshead' barrels, each containing more than 500 kilograms of product. These were conveyed by horse and cart to Jamestown, Virginia, where they were loaded onto ships and transported to England. It was a never-ending process of brutal, back-breaking and soul-numbing work. Worse, the laws of Virginia afforded the slaves almost no protection from abuse. When mistakes were made, or the effort was considered inadequate, slaves endured terrible assaults including whipping, branding, being half-hanged, raped and locked into a tobacco house filled with smoke. By the middle of the century the black population of Virginia amounted to half a million, of which fewer than 11 per cent were free. The vast majority worked on the cotton and tobacco plantations.

Through their efforts, more than 20,000 tonnes of slave-produced tobacco were shipped annually from Virginia to England.

In taking economic advantage of overseas slaves, the Glucksteins were very much of their time. The Tate sugar family, for instance, continued to rely on cane products imported from the slave plantations of the Caribbean. Importers of Cuban cigars, such as Hunters & Frankau and Robert Lewis, must have known that their much-prized Havanas were cultivated by slave labour. Indeed, the Glucksteins were so unperturbed (or perhaps unmindful) of this issue that as the 1840s moved into the 1850s, and their cigar manufacture increased, they accelerated their purchase of Virginia leaf.

Slave hut on a Virginia tobacco plantation

By 1853 the cigar-making business had outgrown Samuel's home in Whitechapel and had moved into a workshop at 35 Crown Street, off Charing Cross Road in Soho. Meanwhile the clan continued to expand. In addition to their seven-year-old twins Lena and Julia – who were inseparable – Samuel and Ann now had four other children: Bertha, Catherine, Izzy and Monte. Samuel's sister, Bertha, had married local boy Lawrence Abrahams, who had also joined the business. Despite the increasing number of mouths to feed, the family was starting to display the beginnings of wealth. Samuel was now able to pay for a thirty-year-old servant from Ireland, named Helena Dennit, to help his ageing parents. In return for her services, she received a small wage along with free room and board at Lehmann and Helena's home on Castle Place.

The constant drumbeat of positive news did not last, though. In the autumn of 1854, Samuel's fifty-six-year-old mother Helena developed an infected boil known as a carbuncle. Such things were common in the dirt and grime of the East End, where it was a struggle to maintain hygiene. Despite repeated lancing and cleaning, the boil developed into a painful pus-filled abscess under the skin. Over the next few days the infection quickly spread to Helena's kidneys and other organs. Although she was in excruciating agony, there was little to be done. Finally, on 6 October, with Lehmann at her side, she died at home.

Her death did not come as a surprise. Helena had given birth twelve times, had lost four children, had lived in more than ten cities across four countries and her health had been deteriorating for some time. Since her arrival in London, her well-being had only worsened, for unlike her husband, she did not pick up languages easily and found navigating Whitechapel's tumult exhausting. Helena had served as the bedrock to the family. In addition to playing the home-maker – in which she had looked after the children, made meals and done the cleaning – she had guided Lehmann in moments of crisis, as well as moments of opportunity. Now her labours were over.

After making sure that his dear wife's eyes were shut, and having uttered a short prayer, Lehmann covered her with a sheet. He then sent for his eldest son, remaining at his wife's bedside himself, for according to Jewish tradition, a corpse should never be left unattended. When Samuel arrived, father and son spent a few moments sharing condolences, before moving on to logistics. As a man steeped in Jewish practice as well as being a Hebrew scholar, Lehmann well knew that the deceased should be buried quickly, typically within twenty-four hours of death, though not during a holiday period. As this was the day before the autumn celebration of *Sukkot*, Helena must therefore be interred before sunset. That gave them less than nine hours.

Samuel immediately sent two of his younger brothers off into the neighbourhood: one to inform family and friends who might want to attend the burial, and the other to notify the rabbi. Meanwhile Lawrence Abrahams, Samuel's brother-in-law, was sent to register the death at the town hall on Cannon Street. The problem was that Lawrence was illiterate (he added a cross instead of a signature). As a result, the name given for the woman born Helena Horn in Rheinberg, and known by her family as Helena Glückstein, was recorded by the British authorities as 'Leander Gluckstein'.

An hour later, two men arrived at castle Place from the volunteer burial society. They carefully moved the body into a simple wooden coffin and transported it by horse and cart to the cemetery in Hackney. There, inside a red-brick mortuary hall, they were greeted by three women, who watched as the body was gently laid on a table. The men were then ushered out of the room, for it was time for *taharah* – the ritual washing of the body.

First, the women lit candles near Helena's head and then, having uttered a short prayer – 'And I will sprinkle pure water upon you, and you shall be cleansed of all your filth and idols' – they set about removing her clothes. As they worked, they treated the body with great care and respect for, in addition to their love for Helena, they had been taught that the soul lingers for a short while after death. Methodically and in silence they walked around the body, never reaching across, uncovering and washing only a small section at a time. Finally, once the purification was complete, they wrapped Helena in a simple white shroud, without shoes or headscarf, and then sat down next to the corpse. Outside the hall, the men stood guard, wooden staffs in hand, to ensure that nobody stole the body, for this was a time when a corpse could be sold to a doctor in return for sufficient money to feed a family for a month.

Back in Whitechapel, now dressed in their best dark suits and hats, Lehmann and four of his sons – Samuel, Solly, Harry and Benjamin – along with Lawrence Abrahams, walked out of the flat and onto the street. They were joined by neighbours and friends, who greeted them in Yiddish with the customary sayings 'I wish you a long life' and 'You should have no more distress'.

Once it was clear that nobody else was coming, Lehmann said it was time to go and led the crowd up the busy High Street. It was a fifty-minute walk, past the orderlies and porters beavering about outside the London Hospital; through the mayhem of the Bethnal Green markets; along The Drive – a windy road that circumnavigated Victoria Park; and finally onto Grove Street in Hackney. Here they turned right, into the cemetery, an unkempt and gloomy spot, half-filled with disorderly sandstone headstones and chest-tombs overgrown with ivy.

Inside the mortuary hall they were met by rabbi H.L. Harris, who was standing next to Helena's coffin, her feet pointed towards her grave. When everyone had assembled, the rabbi began reciting a prayer and then a psalm, during which Samuel and his siblings ripped the left side of their shirts, in a ritual sign of the grief they dearly felt. After a short eulogy, the body was lifted onto a bier and wheeled outside, followed by Lehmann and the rest of the mourners. As was the custom, they stopped three times on the way to the grave, to check that Helena was not alive.

Finally the procession stopped at the freshly dug hole, just a few steps from the mortuary hall, near the front of the cemetery. The coffin was slowly lowered into the ground, at which point the rabbi intoned the traditional words 'May she rest in peace'. Lehmann stepped forward, gathered a small amount of earth from a mound next to the grave and dropped it into the hole. This first clod made a dull thudding noise as it hit the lid of the coffin.

An hour later, Lehmann and the rest of the family were back at home to commence *Shivah*, the seven-day period of mourning during which the men would cease work; beards remained unshaven, mirrors were covered with cloth, and relatives and friends gathered to comfort the family and pay their respects. That night, after their guests had left, Lehmann made an entry in his leather-bound book, which he had brought all the way from Rheinberg:

'For these things I weep, mine eye, mine eye runneth down with water' for the death of my dear wife Helena

For Lehmann's sixty-fifth birthday, Samuel organised a photographic portrait, sometimes called a daguerreotype, after the French inventor, Louis Daguerre; or a talbotype, after the Welshman, Henry Fox Talbot, who also claimed the patent. Photography was just becoming popular and affordable in London and, as a purchaser of lenses for his Polyrama, Samuel was well aware of the exciting developments in the field of optics and chemical processing. He was a keen early adopter.

So it was that Lehmann found himself sitting in an armchair staring at a shiny lens attached to a wooden box, his *Lexicon* book held open in his hands. Clean-shaven and with his tired almond-shaped eyes looking directly at the camera, he was dressed in a black cloak – like that worn by a reverend or university scholar – a black rimless hat and wide bow-tie. A gold chain hung from his stiff white shirt, whose buttonholes were dressed in shiny studs. This was how Lehmann wanted to be remembered, his gift to the future: a carefully constructed legacy printed on thick yellowing card.

Lehmann Glückstein

Yet despite his efforts to project immortality, the patriarch was by now frail and weary. He moved in with his daughter Bertha, who lived above the cigar workshop at 35 Crown Street in Soho. There he stayed, listening to the constant hum of work downstairs, rarely venturing outside, being visited by his children and grandchildren.

In the early summer of 1859, just after the birth of his ninth grandchild, Sarah, Lehmann caught a nasty cold. This quickly worsened, the infection moving into his lungs. Two weeks later, on 13 June, he stopped breathing. The cause of death was recorded as bronchitis.

This time Lehmann was buried for real – in his eternal home at the Hackney Cemetery next to his beloved wife. Once the mourners had come and gone, the diggers set about filling the grave. Nine months later, after the earth had settled, a round-topped headstone was added to the site. On it was etched in Hebrew the following words:

> Here is buried
> an upright man who walked in blameless ways
> it is the honoured man called Lehmann,
> son of Meyer Glückstein of blessed memory,
> departed on 13 June and buried
> with a good name on 15 June
> in the year [1859]. May his soul be bound
> up in the bond of everlasting life.

Two days after the burial, Lehmann's death notice was placed in the top-left corner of the *Jewish Chronicle and Hebrew Observer*, below a short text announcing the arrival of a baby daughter to the 'wife of Mr Israel Abrahams', and above a 'Help wanted' ad from the Jewish Hawkers' Licence Aid Society, who were looking for a 'responsible collector'. This was the first announcement that the family had ever paid to be published in a newspaper.

With the passing of Helena and Lehmann, Samuel was now head of the Gluckstein family. His responsibility was to protect and provide for the growing clan – sisters and brothers, uncles and aunts, cousins and in-laws – who numbered more than forty people, lived within a couple of streets of each other and were all faced with the same urgent task: building a new life in their adopted country.

Chapter 5

1860

Samuel Glückstein   Ann Glückstein

Despite their business success, the family had not earned enough to leave the chaos of east London. One solution to the noise and pollution of Whitechapel was to seek comfort and respite in organised religion. So it was that at the end of each week Samuel, Ann and the children walked to the Great Synagogue for the Friday-evening service.

Their route took them through Aldgate, through a hubbub of cries being hurled at them: 'flowers' and 'Old Clo', 'mackerel' and 'oranges', 'greens' and 'fire-screen ornaments'. Often the calls came in pairs or, as one irritated journalist from *The Times* described it, 'scarcely has one cry faded on the ear than another takes its place in the occupation and distraction of your restless soul'. The same hack suggested that the Whitechapel residents chose to 'submit to be dinned, stupefied, enfeebled and vulgarized by the tyrant street crier' and that 'if they choose to bear it they deserve the consequences'. Of course the Glucksteins, like so many other recently arrived refugees and economic migrants, had no choice – at least until they could leave the slums.

The family's refuge in Jewish rituals was not a blind continuation of the 'old ways'. As they settled into their new British life, and especially in the months and years following the death of Lehmann, the Glucksteins adopted a more relaxed approach to their religion. They continued to take part in Jewish holidays, fasted on Yom Kippur and sat in *Shivah*, yet soon changes emerged. The older women increasingly showed their hair in public, while the younger generation were wont to wear low-cut dresses, their ribboned manes exposing their bare necks. Similarly, the men rarely wore prayer shawls under their shirts. And while shellfish and pork were avoided, little attempt was made to separate crockery that had touched meat or milk, a kosher practice required in the more observant households. In short, the Glucksteins were mimicking the norms and fashions of the period's higher classes, and they were slowly assimilating.

As with many recently arrived Jewish immigrants, Samuel and Ann considered education to be vital for social advancement and assimilation. So it was that in March 1862, Monte (aged seven) and his elder brother Izzy (aged eleven) started at the Whitechapel Foundation Commercial School – the first children in the family to attend school. The Foundation was a progressive institute that had been recently opened by the Rector of Whitechapel. The fee was £3 a year, and subjects included German, Latin and science.

The boys' formal education, however, did not last long. In 1865, when Monte was just eleven years old, they were withdrawn from school to start work at the cigar-making workshop and learn the tools of the family trade. On their first day, Samuel showed the boys how to make a cigar. To start with, the workers unloaded the dried tobacco from the wooden crates freshly arrived from Virginia. Next, the leaf was checked for weight on a set of brass scales, before being distributed amongst the containers standing at the end of ten wooden benches. A worker then selected two to six palm-sized leaves, bound them in a thick sturdy leaf called a 'binder' and rolled the 'bunch' along the wooden bench. They were then placed for an hour in a wooden mould to produce a smooth, symmetrical shape, before being wrapped one last time with an evenly coloured high-quality leaf and capped with a small piece of pectin. Finally the cigars were cut to size and placed carefully inside a handsomely packaged box, with the family name cheerily embossed on the cover.

By this time the brothers had developed clear personalities. While Izzy was a worrier, pessimistic and prone to ill temper, Monte was optimistic, energetic and blessed with conversational flair. They were competitive, argumentative and feisty, but at a moment's notice would drop their dispute and walk away arm-in-arm. They adored their mother and feared their father, especially his temper. As the youngest members of the team, it would be Monte and Izzy's job to deliver the boxes to clients around London. To get them started, Samuel – who had by now established hundreds of personal relationships – introduced them to the customers.

Monte and Izzy were not the only children to work in the cigar factory. Long before the boys' arrival in Crown Street, their four eldest sisters had mastered the art of rolling and wrapping. Of these, the eldest sister Lena stood out. Though small of stature, she was strong in spirit and energy. And she was intelligent. She not only helped to make the cigars, but also managed the office, for Lena had a good head for numbers and organisation. She ensured that sufficient supplies were always available, tracked customer orders and the payment of bills and invoices. Supported by his siblings and children, Samuel's business had truly become a family affair.

The Glucksteins were not alone in their tobacco-rolling enterprise. By the mid-nineteenth century, improved leaf-drying techniques and a rapidly increased demand for cigars and cigarillos had stimulated a boom amongst cigar manufacturers. There were now hundreds of small cigar-makers in London – men such as Philip Morris, the son of a German immigrant who in 1847 had launched a tobacco business on Bond Street, just a few hundred metres from the Glucksteins' workshop. While genuine Cuban cigars were considered superior, so-called 'British cigars' were less expensive and of better quality than the fake Havanas imported from Belgium.

Driven by Samuel's ambition and iron fist, the company soon employed seventy full-time workers, including nine young women. Samuel's brother Solly was no longer working for the firm – possibly the result of a falling-out – but his other brother Harry was still involved, as was Lawrence Abrahams, his brother-in-law. Indeed the business had done so well that Samuel, Harry and Lawrence had codified their arrangement by forming a partnership. A sign now hung outside their Soho workshop with the hand-painted legend 'Gluckstein & Co.'

Part of the growth was due to the company's employment of hard-working apprentices. It was common practice at this time to employ young unskilled immigrants who, in return for receiving on-the-job training, provided their labour for free. This agreement was annotated in a legally binding contract between the employer and the apprentice's parents or guardian. The arrangement usually lasted for three years and typically satisfied all parties. But not always.

On at least five occasions, according to reports in the newspapers, Samuel had sued apprentices for 'absconding from the service of his master'. One such truant was Henry Broewer, a twenty-year-old boy who had left the company nine months before the end of his contract. When the judge asked Broewer if he would return to service and he said he would not, he was sentenced to prison for a month's hard labour.

On at least one occasion Samuel took the law into his own hands. In the last week of 1858 he was handed a love-letter written by one of his apprentices, fifteen-year-old Joseph De Leon, to one of his employees, eighteen-year-old Miss Savage. 'Dear Miss. Savage,' the boy had written, 'I feel happy in the evening when I walk by your side. Now do say that you love me and keep my company and you make my life happy. I conclude with my present love to you. Yours forever. Joseph D. Leon.' Fraternising with a colleague was strictly forbidden by Gluckstein & Co., and Samuel was not pleased.

The next day, when he saw De Leon in the workshop, Samuel told him it was inappropriate to have a romantic relationship with a fellow worker. Apparently unintimidated, the boy said that he loved Miss Savage and that they had slept together. Shocked by the boy's audacity and lack of mores, Samuel called him a 'scamp'. This angered De Leon, who then called his boss a 'scamp', whereupon Samuel slapped him in the face with the back of his hand, cutting the boy's lip. De Leon later said this 'hurt very much'.

The following week Samuel was charged with assault in Thames Police Court. When the judge asked the boy, 'You are an apprentice, are you not?' De Leon agreed. The judge then declared, 'Then you must not fall in love!', to which the boy responded (to much laughter in the courtroom), 'Me couldn't help it.' At this point De Leon's lawyer said that he would drop the case, if Samuel released his client from his apprenticeship, but the judge was not having this. He asked the boy if he had read his apprentice contract, to which the response was in the negative, whereupon the judge read out the relevant section: 'You must not contract into marriage during your apprenticeship. Falling in love with a girl of eighteen might lead to matrimony' – more laughter in the court. 'You must not fall in love with any girl.' When the judge declared that he was dismissing the case, the boy again asked to be released from his contract. 'You shall not,' said the judge. 'Go back to the factory and attend your work.'

If the lesson learned by Samuel from such employment cases was that, with a firm hand, he would always triumph in court, he was wrong. There are some disputes, he would later learn, from which nobody comes out feeling like a winner.

At the age of forty, Samuel decided it was time to become a British citizen. After twenty years of living in London, he felt some kinship with his adopted country and its customs. It was also a defensive strategy because, given his numerous entanglements with the law, being naturalised would gain him additional property rights and even sympathy from the judge. Samuel now asked his lawyer how he could best make the application.

Prior to the Aliens Act of 1844, the only way for an immigrant to obtain British citizenship was through an individualised Act of Parliament – an option open only to the very few (on average there were eight such cases per year). It had been possible to gain some rights through 'denization', but these could not be passed down to children. The 1844 law changed this, for the first time allowing applicants to apply for citizenship, which, if approved, gave full rights, including the right to vote and to own real-estate property. The only prohibition was that a naturalised citizen could not become a Member of Parliament.

So it was that on 3 August 1861, Samuel stood in the Mansion House before William Cubitt – a former fishmonger and now Lord Mayor of London – and swore the following: 'I will be faithful and bear true Allegiance to Her Majesty Queen Victoria, and will defend Her to the utmost of my Power.' He went on to affirm that, based on the Act of Settlement of 1701, he would support the succession of the Crown, which was 'limited to the Princess Sophia Electress of Hanover, and the Heirs of her Body, being Protestants'. It is unclear whether Samuel understood this complicated aspect of British history, but nevertheless he swore the oath.

In addition, Samuel then filled out a 'memorial' in which he stated his name – retaining the umlaut in 'Glückstein' – and confirmed that he intended to reside permanently in the United Kingdom and that he was a 'faithful and loyal subject'. Supporting the 'memorialist' were four friends, including his brother-in-law and business partner, Lawrence Abrahams. Samuel's application was soon processed and approved. It meant that, as per the 1844 act, Ann automatically became a British citizen, along with Samuel's children. The Glucksteins had taken another big step towards assimilation.

Now that he was a declared loyal subject to Her Majesty the Queen, Samuel decided it was time to take his business to the next level. Until now the enterprise had been limited by the resources within the family. What they needed, Samuel told his children, was to widen the pool of talent and investment, which would lead to accelerated growth. His proposal was to have his seventeen-year-old daughter Lena marry Barnett Salmon, a thirty-four-year-old cigar salesman with whom Samuel had worked in the past. It was a business decision.

What Samuel did not mention was that he was worried about his relationship with his brother Harry and his brother-in-law Lawrence. The three of them increasingly differed when it came to strategy, and to dealing with the staff or customers. In recent months they had argued, and there had even been threats of violence. In case things worsened, Samuel felt that Barnett offered a safe alternative.

Born on 24 May 1829 in the Christchurch district of east London, Barnett Salmon had had a difficult start. His mother Jane died in childbirth, while his father Aaron suffered from severe mental illness. When Barnett was just eight months old, his father left him on the doorstep of the Chevra Jewish orphanage in east London and entered an asylum. Two years later, Aaron was discharged and was living in a workhouse, but given his record – 'lunatic' and 'incurable' – he was unable to care for his son. From a young age Barnett had worked the street, first as a peddler, then as a barrow boy, later as a door-to-door salesman, and had demonstrated a natural talent for enterprise. A tall, serious-looking man with a bushy beard, a penchant for bow-ties and the nervous habit of tapping his fingers against his knee, Barnett was considered a good and reliable businessman.

Lena Salmon   Barnett Salmon

When Samuel suggested the match, Lena accepted. She knew her role in the hierarchy, which was to support her family, and particularly her father and brothers. She was not, however, a passive character in this story. 'She was a remarkable woman with a very fine brain and a strong character,' her grandson Geoffrey Salmon later recalled. 'Nothing was done without first consulting her and throughout her life she exercised great influence in all family affairs.'

The wedding took place at the Great Synagogue on 24 June 1863 and was well attended, following a notice that had been placed in the *Jewish Chronicle*. To their great honour, the ceremony was overseen by the Chief Rabbi, Nathan Adler, who supervised the signing of the *ketubah*, or wedding contract. It is likely that a wedding party was held later that day in the synagogue.

In April the following year, the now eighteen-year-old Lena Salmon gave birth to a daughter, the first of the next generation to be born in England. Sam and Ann's delight at having a grandchild was mitigated only by their sadness that Lehmann and Helena had not lived long enough to enjoy the occasion. In honour of Lena's twin and favourite sister, they called the baby Julia. A year later came Samuel, named after Lena's father. To their great distress, however, the baby died at nine weeks old from diarrhoea – a common cause of infant death at this time. Next came Hannah, born in 1866, and then Alfred, in 1868.

On 4 December 1868, just two months after Alfred's birth, their eldest child, Julia, developed a bad cough. Over the next twenty-four hours her face and neck became covered with tiny red bumps. The rash then spread to the girl's back and legs, and her cough grew more violent. Lena spent the day cleaning the house, disinfecting everything she could lay her hands on. That night the other children were moved to the parents' bedroom. Over the next three days Julia's symptoms worsened. She refused to eat, complaining of a sore stomach, and her body was seized alternatively by chills and a high fever. On 12 December, just eight days after showing the first symptoms, she stopped breathing. She was four years old. After examining the body, the doctor said that the cause of death was 'scarlatina', or scarlet fever. Lena and Barnett had lost two children in four years.

Infant mortality peaked in England during the mid- to late nineteenth century, following rapid urbanisation. Diseases that had been around for years were exacerbated by the numbers of people living in close proximity. According to a report prepared by the Medical Officer of Health, 42 per cent of the total deaths in Whitechapel in 1868 were children under the age of five. Most of those died of smallpox, scarlet fever, diarrhoea and measles. The officer also noted that Whitechapel had a higher infant mortality than the rest of London. In Lena and Barnett's district, one in nine children under five years of age would die, compared to one in fourteen for the whole of London. The figures for small infants were even worse: one in four children died in Whitechapel before reaching their first birthday.

While a parent was more likely to lose a child in the squalid slums of Whitechapel than in the more affluent residences of Kensington, infant mortality affected all levels of society. And the impact everywhere was just as keen. After losing his ten-year-old daughter to tuberculosis, Charles Darwin wrote, 'We have lost the joy of the household, and the solace of our old age. She must have known how we loved her. Oh, that she could now know how deeply, how tenderly we do still and shall ever love her dear joyous face. Blessings on her!'

As 1869 drew to a close, Lena and Barnett hoped that Hannah and Alfred would survive into adulthood, and prayed they would soon be able to give birth to more children. Lena's father Samuel, meanwhile, was struggling with health problems of his own.

Chapter 6

1870

For months now, Samuel had felt lethargic and in pain. He struggled to get out of bed in the morning and was beset by severe headaches and a dry mouth. There were times when he felt confused, disorientated. His wife Ann encouraged him to see a doctor, but Samuel preferred to keep his troubles to himself. Finally even he realised that he needed help.

At the physician's surgery he was asked for a urine sample. When it was tested, the doctor said there was excessive sugar in his urine: Samuel had diabetes. The problem was that nobody knew how to treat this debilitating disease. Insulin was as yet undiscovered, and theories varied as to the proximate cause. He was prescribed the standard treatment: a low-calorie, high-protein, low-carbohydrate diet and, as necessary, agents such as digitalis and opium to suppress his appetite.

On the morning of 25 March 1870, Samuel Glückstein arose feeling worse than usual. A stickler for keeping to the rules and fulfilling his duty, this was the wrong day to stay at home. Yet he knew he wouldn't be able to make it more than a few metres outside the door. He called his second-eldest son, Monte, to his bed. In a quick whispered exchanged, Samuel said that he needed Monte to represent him in Chancery Court that very morning. He was too ill to attend. There was no need to explain the case, for Monte knew all about it. The issues between his father and his two uncles, Harry and Lawrence, had become so intolerable, so intractable, that only a judge could resolve them.

Monte put on his coat and hurried off towards central London. By now fifteen years old, he was a short, slender boy with a long face and short-cropped brown hair parted to one side. It was clear, to anyone who paid attention, that he was Samuel's heir apparent. An hour after leaving home, he arrived in Parliament Square and entered Westminster Hall, whose enormous chamber was covered by a hammer-beamed roof. This was the home of the Chancery Court. Unlike other courts of law, which dealt with criminal matters as well as civil cases that required the payment of damages, the Chancery Court was a 'court of equity', where an injured party could sue for an injunction or file a claim.

Monte proceeded towards the front of the hall, where he sat down on a wooden bench behind his father's lawyer, T. Archibald Roberts. To his right sat his two uncles and their lawyer. At precisely 10 a.m., when the clerk called the court to order Sir Richard Malins, the bewigged Vice-Chancellor of England's High Court, entered the chamber.

The court was now in session.

The case was as simple as it was distressing. Monte's two uncles – the plaintiffs – were accusing his father of a litany of crimes. They said Samuel had 'seriously damaged the character and credit of the firm' by preventing goods being delivered to key customers. Next, and more egregiously, they argued that he had forcibly broken into the company's tin safe and removed a number of bearer bonds. Worst of all, they accused him of being 'very violent and overbearing' and said that he had threatened them with 'personal violence'.

Standing up to respond, T. Archibald Roberts said that his client, Samuel Glückstein, had indeed interfered with the delivery of goods, because his partners were trying to cheat the customers. Specifically, they had instructed the staff to reduce the amount of tobacco leaf in the cigars. To not interfere, declared the lawyer, 'would have been against the welfare of the business'. As to the accusation of theft, his client admitted breaking into the safe box, but there was an innocent explanation: he did not have the key, and needed to see a copy of the workshop's lease that was stored inside. Once Samuel had reviewed the papers he returned the lease to the box and, when he heard from his brother that the bearer bonds were missing, he had, of course, immediately reported the matter to both the insurance company and the police. When prompted by the court, the lawyer provided copies of a police affidavit to confirm the story's truth.

Finally, T. Archibald Roberts said that there had been only one instance when his client had acted aggressively towards the plaintiffs. This was three months previously, when Lawrence 'had attempted to take indecent liberties' with Samuel's daughter, Catherine. Hearing of this, Samuel had confronted Lawrence at the office, calling him a 'scoundrel'. Later, at a public house, Lawrence accused Samuel of being drunk, to which Samuel responded that if he said that again, he would 'knock him down'.

This story about his sister was news to Monte. He was both enraged that this had happened — Catherine was three years older than him, and unmarried at the time — and deeply embarrassed that the incident had been disclosed in court, where anyone might hear it.

T. Archibald Roberts concluded by reading his client's somewhat stilted words (for after all, English was not Samuel's mother tongue) that he did not believe the plaintiffs had proper grounds for instituting the proceedings, and he believed 'it was a most improper attempt on their part to drive him into dissolution so that they may oust me from the business and get it for themselves'.

What the lawyer did not say was that Samuel was the victim of a scam. Harry and Lawrence had fallen into debt to one of Whitechapel's many moneylenders. They were trying to force Samuel to pay for the missing securities, which in all likelihood they still had in their possession, to pay off the usurers. This was known to Monte, and the boy's hatred of loan sharks and money-lenders was never forgotten. Neither did Samuel tell the court, via his lawyer, that he suspected this entire tawdry affair, with all its accusations and counter-accusations, had started only after his wife Ann had gossiped with Lawrence's wife, Bertha. Ann had told Bertha that Samuel was fed up with his partners and planned to set up his own firm.

With the testimony now ended, Vice-Chancellor Malins stated his decision. He ordered the partnership to be dissolved, its effects sold at auction and the assets divided between the partners. Returning home later that day, Monte reported the lawsuit's outcome to his father. Samuel appeared satisfied: he would no longer have to work with his brother and brother-in-law, and he would receive back most of his capital. Monte, by contrast, was devastated. He had watched the proceedings 'in horror', appalled that the sordid details had been publicly aired. Most of all, he was disappointed in his father: that he had allowed his anger and resentment to get the better of him, and that he had set his own needs above those of the family and the business.

Starting at noon on 29 June, the judge-ordered auction was hosted by Bromley, Kelday and Seward at 43 Leman Street, Whitechapel. It consisted of several tonnes of British and foreign cigars, with brand names such as El Cervantes, Queen Havanas and Henry Clay. In addition, tobacco was on sale, made up in bales, crates and serons, as well as various tools of the trade, including scales, office furniture and an iron safe. Once the auctioneer's fee had been paid, £300 was distributed to Harry and Lawrence, the remaining £1,700 being disbursed to Samuel. Several weeks later Samuel used this money – equivalent to £170,000 today – to relaunch the business.

It was immediately clear, however, that Samuel was not up to the task of setting up a new enterprise. Following the court case, his health deteriorated and he rarely left his bed. The rebuilding effort fell instead to Monte, his brother Izzy, his sister Lena and her husband Barnett. They managed to keep the lease for the workshop on Crown Street – Lawrence and Harry set up shop in east London – and persuaded most of the staff to stick with them. The old Gluckstein & Co. sign was taken down and a new one put in its place. It now bore the legend 'Salmon & Gluckstein'.

Samuel never recovered. On 23 January 1873, three years after the trial's end, and aged just fifty-two, Samuel died at the family's home in Whitechapel, after what the papers described as 'a long and protracted illness'. The death certificate was more specific, the primary cause of mortality being diabetes complicated by *Phthisis pulmonalis*, also known as consumption.

Since the Hackney Cemetery where Lehmann and Helena were interred was full, Samuel was buried in West Ham. A few months later, a new cemetery was opened in Willesden, north London, where the rest of the family would be buried. This meant that Samuel Glückstein – loyal son, first-generation immigrant, founder of the family business, fierce and scrappy entrepreneur – would spend the rest of eternity buried two metres under the east London dirt, rarely visited.

On 23 February, thirty days after the burial, and a day after the official mourning period was over, Monte, his uncle Barnett, his mother Ann and his brothers and sisters gathered to hear the reading of Samuel's lengthy will and codicil. This rite of passage, part legal formality, part financial turning point, took place at the office of the family solicitor, John Green, on Canon Street, a few doors down from the Lord Mayor's residence at Mansion House.

'This is the last will and testament,' began the lawyer, 'of Samuel Glückstein of 34 Whitechapel Road in the county of Middlesex cigar manufacturer.' After a few minutes of tedious legal niceties and caveats, the lawyer moved on to a more interesting paragraph. The will, he said, provided that Samuel's 'dear wife' was to be given the sum of £300, as were Montague and the deceased's unmarried but adult daughters, Bertha and Catherine. His younger daughters, Sarah and Clara, who were thirteen and ten years old respectively, were each awarded the princely sum of £1,200, to be held in trust until maturity. And his two sons-in-law, one of whom was Barnett Salmon, would each receive £200. After gifts to the grandchildren and other relatives, the total bequests amounted to £4,500. Given that Samuel had rescued only £1,700 of his capital from the dissolved business with Harry and Lawrence – much of which had been eaten up in the new business launch – the tally was impressive.

As for the cigar business, and to the great relief of those assembled, Samuel wanted it to be 'continued by Barnett Salmon, surviving partner of the deceased and by Ann Gluckstein widow of the deceased'. In practice, all those present knew that the company would be driven by Monte who, at the age of eighteen, already had the energy, guile and tenacity to grow the business in what was fast becoming a highly competitive and quickly evolving market.

As he sat listening to the testament being recited methodically by the lawyer, Monte probably thought of his grandparents' flight from German persecution, their nomadic life in the Netherlands, the death of their four children, their struggle to adapt to life in London, and then his father's awful falling-out with his uncles, which had led to the ugly break-up of the cigar business. He was already telling his family that his father had died of a broken heart.

1870

He swore that he would never again allow the family be torn apart by matters of business. The solution, he concluded, was threefold: a tightening of the family bond, the accumulation of wealth, and assimilation. For this, Monte had a very novel plan.

PART II

MONTE

———————

'If you share, you sleep well, if you take, you ponder it into the night.'

Monte Gluckstein

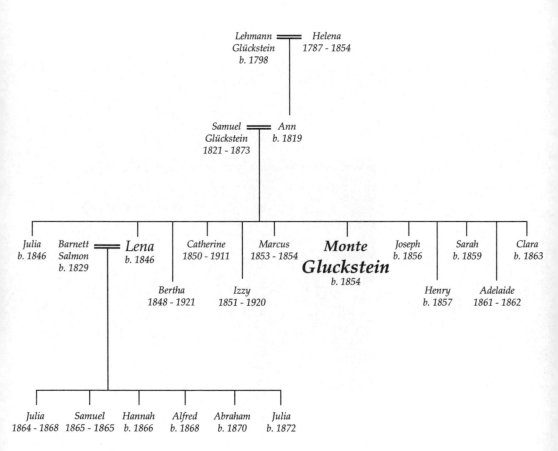

Lehmann
Glückstein
b. 1798
══════
Helena
1787 - 1854

Samuel
Glückstein
1821 - 1873
═══
Ann
b. 1819

Julia
b. 1846

Barnett
Salmon
b. 1829
═══
Lena
b. 1846

Catherine
1850 - 1911

Marcus
1853 - 1854

**Monte
Gluckstein**
b. 1854

Joseph
b. 1856

Sarah
b. 1859

Clara
b. 1863

Bertha
1848 - 1921

Izzy
1851 - 1920

Henry
b. 1857

Adelaide
1861 - 1862

Julia
1864 - 1868

Samuel
1865 - 1865

Hannah
b. 1866

Alfred
b. 1868

Abraham
b. 1870

Julia
b. 1872

Chapter 7

1873

Monte Gluckstein

Now that *Shivah* was over and the will had been read, Monte called a family meeting. In attendance were his three brothers – Izzy, Joseph and Henry – along with his six brothers-in-law, including Barnett Salmon.

Although no minutes were kept, the events of this meeting were told and retold, handed down from generation to generation. They became part of the family's founding mythology. It appears that, standing in front of his close male relatives in the family's Whitechapel flat, Monte made a striking proposal: from this point forward, each of them would pool their incomes. At the end of each year they would distribute a dividend, with every man being paid the same amount. As he spoke, he described this scheme as a 'community of family interests' – or, more simply, as 'the Fund'.

At first Monte was met with silence, even shock. Nobody had ever heard of such an arrangement. Then the first question was asked: surely he wasn't suggesting that a man who had built up his skills and experience would receive the same as a young lad who had just started? Yes, Monte replied, that was exactly what he was proposing. More than this, he added, if someone was injured or grew sick, they would continue to receive a similar income to the others. And what about assets, someone else asked, half-joking, would they be shared as well? Again Monte said yes. When sufficient money had been made, assets would be purchased for all the Fund's members. If one person received a horse and cart, then everyone received a horse and cart.

With these general points answered, the group appeared more comfortable with the proposal and moved on to discussing how the Fund might work in detail. Any male descendant of the original founders would be inducted at the age of twenty-three. Unlike a partnership, where any partner could commit the group to action, decisions would be made collectively in the Fund. If two or more members of the Fund objected, a proposal would be rejected.

As for women, the plan was less egalitarian. Many in the room, if not all, believed that Samuel's legal troubles had been exacerbated by his wife Ann speaking to his sister, Bertha. Despite the important role played thus far by the family's wives, mothers and daughters – particularly as cigar-rollers – it was agreed that the female family members would not be told what went on inside the Fund, and that business must never be discussed in front of women. Furthermore, women would not be admitted, nor could they attend meetings. Widows would be financially taken care of, and upon marriage, daughters would receive a fixed dowry – whose money would be administered by a brother, father or male cousin. Above all else, from this point forward, 'Don't tell the women' was the motto the men would use.

The exception, of course, was Lena. Before the meeting with his brothers and brother-in-laws, Monte had run the idea of the Fund by his sister. Lena had liked the prospect of sharing income and assets, so that everyone, including herself, would reap the rewards of their hard work. So often in England it was the firstborn son who inherited the wealth. The Fund would provide for a more equitable sharing. It had also been Lena who had suggested that wives be looked after following their husband's death. As for women being unable to attend meetings, Lena was unworried. She knew that Monte would always come to her for advice, and she had no interest in spending hours with her male relatives squabbling over details, when she knew that the big decisions had already been made by Monte and herself.

After a few more questions, Monte asked for a vote. Three of his brothers-in-law and one of his brothers, Henry, said they did not support the proposal. Either they had their own businesses they wished to pursue, which they didn't want to contribute to the common pot, or their wives had money, which they did not want to share. To Monte's delight, however, his brothers Izzy and Joseph raised their hands, as did three of his brothers-in-law, including Barnett Salmon. Together with his own vote, that made six. The Fund was now established. The task now was to develop the business.

While Samuel had been alive, there had been little to differentiate Salmon & Gluckstein from the numerous other cigar manufactures in the East End. A single premise served as living quarters, workshop and retail outlet. Sales were made in the street, by Barnett and Monte, or delivered direct to the homes of regular customers. As such, the firm's prosperity was limited by the hard work of the family and its small group of employees spending long hours filling, binding, rolling and wrapping thousands of cigars by hand, and by the salesperson's energy and nous.

Monte's plan was to launch a series of stand-alone tobacconist shops. First they would have to find someone willing to rent them a space, which was easier said than done. Selling hand-rolled cigars generated little profit. Any money they made went into purchasing the next sack of tobacco, paying the rent for the workshop and covering everyone's salaries, meagre though they were. No bank would underwrite them as they had no collateral, besides the cigar boxes waiting to be sold. Between them, though, they had managed to save a little over the months and years. At the next meeting of the Fund they pooled their savings. It was just about enough to cover the first month's rent and the deposit.

After a week of looking, Lena found premises that might work. It was on the busy Edgware Road, just a few hundred metres north of Marble Arch. It was in poor condition, full of old furniture, with paint peeling off the walls but, with a large window overlooking the street and heavy foot traffic, it had potential. She negotiated a long-term lease for a good price and a contract was signed. The family had their first shop.

The plan was not, however, without risk. It would take time to renovate the retail space – perhaps a month – during which no money could be made, and the repairs themselves would be expensive, further depleting their reserves. Opening a shop also meant filling it with stock; stock that had to be purchased which would not provide a return as quickly as it might on the street. Monte and Lena knew that if they didn't make a profit soon, they would be in big trouble.

This would be Lena and Barnett's shop, it had been agreed, and they would be the managers. Together with her husband and her children, she spent the week cleaning and readying the store for business, adding shelves to the walls, a counter near the door and a storeroom for extra stock. Outside the entrance they hung the sign 'Salmon & Gluckstein'.

As planned, they sold cigars made in the family workshop. They opened early and stayed open till late. They were only closed during *Shabbat,* starting at sundown on Friday until sundown on Saturday. The location proved as busy as they had hoped, catching people on the way to work and then again on the way home. People liked Lena's affability and charm. They liked Barnett's knowledge about tobacco leaf and the quality of the cigars. Above all, they liked the affordable prices. When they were close to running out of stock, Lena sent one of the children to the workshop to replenish supplies.

As their customer base grew, requests were made for cigars above and beyond those made by Salmon & Gluckstein. The most common demand was for Havanas from Cuba: *Trabucos*, which were short and thick; *Regalia Imperial*, which were 7 inches (18 cm) long and of the finest leaf; and *Damos*, which were small and for the ladies. Each of these had different qualities, as Lena and Barnett were happy to explain: from *Superfine* at the top end, to *Flor* in the mid-range and *Buenos* at the bottom. The cigars also varied by strength: strong, medium and mild.

Did they sell lucifers? was the next most-common demand. This was a good question. Since their invention at the start of the nineteenth century, phosphorus-tipped matches had been associated with danger. Some exploded when struck or stepped on. Others burned inconsistently, making them hard to use. They also gave off a noxious sulphurous odour. It was not until the early 1860s that a new gener-

Salmon & Gluckstein shop in London

ation of matches had become commercially available in England, separating the combustible elements between the match-head and the striking surface. Lena now stocked an array of these so-called 'safety matches', with names like Fizzes, Euperions, Vesuvians, Vestas, Bells and Blacks, Napoleons and Bismarks. She also ordered in a selection of other cigar-related items: cigar cutters and cigar holders, cigar boxes and ashtrays.

As the shop built a reputation for selling diverse products, customers arrived asking for 'shag' or loose fine-cut tobacco that could be smoked in a pipe. This was an entirely new field for the family, but after a conversation with Monte, Lena agreed to add it to the growing inventory. Now, when cigar tobacco was purchased at the auction house, an order was also put in (small at first, but soon growing) for shag. This, too, had its own plethora of characteristics that had to be memorised and then communicated to the customers: sweet tobacco from Virginia, fire-cured dark tobacco from Kentucky, a highly aromatic leaf from the Ottoman Empire.

It was not long before a selection of pipes could be seen in Lena and Barnett's shop window. Some were carved from a single piece of wood, others finished with mouthpieces made of ivory, ebony or amber. A few dearer items were carved from red stone. The more pipes that were purchased, the more Lena increased her range of products. Soon she was sourcing pipes from around the world: red clay pipes from France, porcelain pipes from Germany, ivory pipes from China. There were straight pipes and bent pipes, short pipes and long pipes. Some were whimsical – in the form of a steam engine with smoke bellowing out of the bowl – while others commemorated historical events, such as Queen Victoria's coronation.

That was not all. Other accoutrements included tobacco boxes of silver, brass and horn, and an assortment of pipe stoppers made from mother-of-pearl, ivory, bone and wood; branded mirrors, handkerchiefs and playing cards; collectibles and antiques; books on tobacco history, customs and techniques. In short, what had started as a one-off family boutique selling its own brand had morphed into a dynamic retail outlet, selling each and every product that was available on the market.

The family was taking advantage of the increasing demand for tobacco products by the general population. This democratisation of tobacco proved to be a disappointment to some. In his book *Tobacco: Its History*, E.R. Billings quoted one British commentator who said that 'in truth, the art of tobacco use is nowhere more ignored, nowhere more contemptuously neglected than in these "favored isles". For one man who smokes with a reason, for a purpose, or by system, you shall find a thousand who smoke without either.' Widespread smoking of cigars and pipes – at the opera, on the street, in pubs, in the home – also prompted pushback from non-users. To them, Billings had this to say: 'The tobacco hater (invariably an illogical creature who hates that which he knows not) will hold up hands in amazement, and sniff with the nose in contempt, to whom reply would be superfluous.'

Salmon & Gluckstein cigar workshop late 19th century

Customers flocked to the Salmon & Gluckstein store and the family worked tirelessly to meet demand. Everyone was involved, including the children, toiling long into the night, all determined to enhance the company. Although he was helped by family, particularly Lena, the person driving the extraordinary company growth was Monte. Though generally patient and tolerant, he was proving to be a forceful and exacting character. He possessed the ability to persuade others, and he took pains to encourage those around him. Two of his sayings were fast becoming family legends. The first had been uttered upon hearing of a relative's misconduct. 'I don't blame you,' he had said, 'I blame those who taught you.' The other was said to a colleague whom he considered unintelligent: 'I can give you the information but I am afraid that I cannot give you the understanding.'

Above all, Monte was ambitious, a quality that was supported by the buoyant economic situation of the time. Since the late 1860s Britain had enjoyed a period of strong economic growth, averaging 3 per cent per year. Politicians and commentators at the time said this stemmed from a combination of international peace, free trade and good harvests. With real wages rising across all classes, there was more money in people's pockets to spend on tobacco products. And this was good for the family business.

The Salmons and Glucksteins, however, were not without their troubles, particularly concerning the sister to whom Monte was closest, Lena.

Chapter 8

1875

By Christmas 1875 and following Samuel's death, Lena had moved in to her parent's small flat at 34 Whitechapel Road. The plan was that while Lena and Barnett worked, her mother Ann would help with the children.

There were now three girls, Hannah, Bertha and another Julia (they had decided to name a second daughter after Lena's twin sister) and two boys, Alfred and Abraham. The family also had the support of three domestic workers: a nursemaid, a 'general servant' and a thirteen-year-old 'errand boy'. The home would soon become even more crowded, for Lena was pregnant once again, the baby being due the following February. With the court case and the shock of Samuel's death behind them, the family was enjoying a time of relative calm. Then London was hit by a new wave of scarlet fever.

The much-feared scourge had been relatively dormant since 1869, but to everyone's horror, the epidemic had returned. More than 200 people were dying each week across London, and most of the victims were young children. Opinion was divided on the best response to the disease. An article published in *The Times* acknowledged that 'the origin and nature of the scarlet fever poison are unknown' and suggested that the best methods to contain the 'evil' included quarantining the patient, drenching the furniture and clothes with disinfectants, and ensuring that the skin was 'imprisoned' with oil, before being cleansed in a bath.

An alternative remedy was published in the *Jewish Chronicle*, suggesting bed rest, ventilation and, quite remarkably for a Jewish paper, 'rubbing the body with bacon several times a day'. The truth was that with the invention of antibiotics still a half-century away, nobody had an effective treatment for the disease. This left Lena, Barnett and the rest of the population in a constant state of fear.

On 14 November 1875, Lena and Barnett were woken during the night by a terrible coughing from the room where their children slept. Lena went to see what was wrong. Pulling back the covers, she saw that Abraham's face and neck were covered with tiny red bumps. Now anxious, she told her oldest son Alfred to fetch the doctor. A few hours later the physician arrived and examined the boy. Once he'd finished, he replaced his tools in his bag and stepped out of the bedroom to where the parents were waiting. He confirmed their worst fears: malignant scarlet fever. Lena and Barnett were distraught.

As had happened with their first child seven years earlier, the fever soon worsened. Overnight Abraham's cough deteriorated, developing into double pneumonia, and he began to make a terrible rasping noise each time he tried to breathe. Shockingly, just thirty-six hours after the doctor's diagnosis, Abraham died. He was only four years old.

They were still reeling from the shock when another child said she was not feeling well. This time it was their three-year-old daughter, Julia. Horrifyingly, the red spots appeared, her lungs became congested, she was beset by a deep, rattling cough and they saw blood in her urine. Then, just as Julia's condition worsened, a rash appeared on their twenty-month-old infant, Bertha. Lena now had two desperately ill children. Two weeks later, on 8 December, baby Bertha stopped breathing. A few hours later that same day, and after two hours of horrific convulsions, Julia also died. Within three weeks Lena and Barnett had lost three children. Following the deaths of baby Samuel and the first Julia, that made five in all. This was an unimaginable, crushing blow.

Monte and Lena's other siblings surrounded the bereaved parents with love. They cooked meals, cleaned the home and kept them company. Keen to distract themselves with matters that made sense, Barnett and Lena tried to immerse themselves in the shop on Edgware Road. The small world of business provided the only sanity they could find: weighing out the tobacco leaf; counting the boxes of cigars. In addition to work at the shop, the now seven-months-pregnant Lena also had to look after their two surviving children, Hannah and Alfred. And when she had no more energy, they went to live with one of the aunts. It was a terrible, dark time, without end or hope.

Lena and Barnett were now desperate to leave Whitechapel and discussed finding a home in west London. But it wasn't that simple. According to the agreement made between the cousins, members of the Fund could only move into a more expensive home when everyone was offered the same opportunity. And for now, at least, the Fund could not afford to move everyone out of east London. As a compromise, it was agreed that Lena, Barnett and their surviving children could live temporarily in the apartment above the tobacconist shop at 251 Edgware Road. It was small and dilapidated, but it was away from east London, so they made it work.

New Year came and went, and so did January. Then on 10 February 1876, Lena gave birth to a son. They called him Isidore, meaning 'strong gift' – which was their hope. Over the next few months they watched him grow warily, desperately hoping that he would stay fit. The thought of losing another child was unbearable. They were lucky, for by now the scarlet-fever epidemic had begun to recede and, by the summer's end, Isidore looked as if he would live to be a strong and healthy boy.

Izzy Gluckstein

By the end of 1876 the shop on Edgware Road was making such a profit that the family agreed to open another in Knightsbridge, to be run by Monte's brother Izzy. And then, the following year, a third on the King's Road in Chelsea, managed by Monte himself. Each of the shops had their own personalities, but they were united by the brand of Salmon & Gluckstein. Around London, the family's products were becoming known for their consistency of product and fairness of price. With three shops now open, it was time to take the next big step: advertising.

Up to this point the company's branding was limited to the signs hanging outside the shop entrances, plus the name printed on the cigar boxes and other products. At a meeting with the other members of the Fund, Monte now proposed that they spend money on a publicity campaign. Some of his brothers and brothers-in-law were sceptical. Was this not wasted money? they asked. Was it not wiser to invest in raw materials or more staff? And, perhaps more importantly, were they not asking for trouble if they grew too quickly? After all, their father was a Jewish immigrant and they were the first generation to be born in the country. They didn't want anyone to think them uppity, climbing the social ladder too fast.

Monte encouraged them to think bigger. If they could develop a reputation for quality and affordability, there was no limit to how large the company could grow. A few weeks later the first advertising display was taken out in a newspaper. The idea was to promote their loyalty scheme, whereby if a customer purchased a number of products – a cigar, a pipe, or tobacco pouch – they were given the next for free. In the end it was a simple but effective message: 'Smoke More, Pay Less'.

At this point in the 1870s the smoking of tobacco was not widely believed to be bad for your health. Indeed, almost everyone in the Salmon and Gluckstein families smoked, both men and women. What *was* widely known was that smoking sometimes led to coughing. This was why Monte now printed up flyers proclaiming that the S&G Plantagenet Pipe was 'healthy', when used correctly. In large capital letters the flyer stated: 'Salmon & Gluckstein's advice to those about to smoke: 'DONT' and then underneath: 'unless you have read this bill'. It then proceeded to explain that 'you won't have to go to the physician, surgeon, chemist or hospital if you smoke on the wonderful healthy Plantagenet pipe'.

Such innovative campaigns were hugely successful. By the mid-1870s, Salmon & Gluckstein had become one of London's most recognised brands.

Advert for Salmon & Gluckstein

Chapter 9

1877

On 22 November 1877, Monte was startled to read in the liberal newspaper *Truth* that Prime Minister Disraeli was being criticised for Britain's recent acquisition of the Suez Canal. It was, said the newspaper, 'a tacit conspiracy […] on the part of a considerable number of Anglo-Hebrews'. This blatant and very public anti-Semitism was deeply disturbing, a reminder of the dark periods that the family had experienced in Germany and the Netherlands.

It had been a proud moment for Monte and the whole Jewish community when, three years previously, Benjamin Disraeli had won the general election against William Ewart Gladstone and had been appointed prime minister. For although he was a converted Christian, it was well known that Disraeli had grown up in a London Jewish family. At a speech at the Crystal Palace during the election, Disraeli had marked out the inclusivity of his ambitions: 'When I say "conservative" I mean it in its purest and loftiest sense,' he had said. 'I mean the people of England, and especially the working class of England, are proud of belonging to a great country, and wish to maintain its greatness – that they are proud of belonging to an imperial country.' In return, Gladstone had attacked Disraeli, claiming that 'he was holding British foreign policy hostage to his Jewish sympathies, and that he was more interested in relieving the anguish of Jews [...] than in any British interests.'

Within months of taking office, prime minister Disraeli had been offered the opportunity to purchase a 44 per cent share in the Suez Canal for £4 million. The Suez Canal had opened five years earlier, and the purchase of a controlling stake in the waterway was significant to Britain, for it provided a far shorter and safer route to the Far East. Compared to the alternative journey around the southern tip of South Africa, it would now take ships half the time to travel to India: from Portsmouth, past Gibraltar and into the Mediterranean, through the Suez Canal and then to Bombay. Rather than borrowing the money from the Bank of England, Disraeli's government borrowed the funds from the banker Lionel Nathan de Rothschild. It was this loan that had triggered the vitriolic conspiracy theory.

Monte was a fan of Disraeli for one other important reason: the prime minister was a leading proponent of free trade. Ever since the arguments over whether tariffs should be imposed on imported food and grains thirty years earlier, known as the Corn Laws, there had roiled a fierce debate in Britain between those who wished to protect domestic producers and businesses, by imposing restrictions on imports, and those who believed that less regulation and open markets led to lower prices that benefited everyone. In June 1876, for instance, *The Economist* dedicated its front three pages to celebrating the hundredth anniversary of Adam Smith's classic, *The Wealth of Nations*. Smith's writings, *The Economist* declared, 'have caused more money to be made, and prevented more money from being wasted, than those of any other author', adding that Smith's political economy has 'by far the most affected the intercourse of nations'.

To Monte, the purchase of the Suez Canal was good news. Since the early 1870s tobacco cultivated in India and East Africa had been sold at the London Tobacco Auction. Such imports not only increased the range of products that could be sold to customers – providing a choice of taste, aroma and colour – but also reduced prices, by disrupting the monopoly held by the North American plantations. Now, by shortening the route, the Suez Canal reduced the costs of transportation from the new tobacco plantations, driving prices down still further.

With increased profits, the family was able to rapidly expand their business. They managed this by always using their own capital, never borrowing from banks or private investors. Over the next few years they rolled out a succession of shops across London: 181 High Street, Camden; 343 Mare Street, Hackney; next to Aldgate railway station; 263 Pentonville Road, King's Cross; Station Buildings, Highbury; 65 Seven Sisters Road, Holloway. On and on they went, so that by 1881 they had built up a network of fifteen Salmon & Gluckstein shops.

With the success of the chain of tobacconist shops, the Fund could finally afford to purchase homes for its six founding members. Now aged twenty-six, Monte moved into a small but comfortable home at 19 Fulham Place in Maida Hill. Lena and Barnett acquired a similar-sized house on Sutherland Avenue, just a short walk down the road from their shop and around the corner from Monte. Meanwhile homes were also purchased nearby for Monte's brothers Izzy and Joseph, and for sisters Catherine and Bertha, along with their spouses and children.

In many ways the Fund was a form of communism, which worked because its members put the family before personal advantage. That is not to say that each member made an equivalent contribution, for Monte was the primary entrepreneurial engine behind this original family enterprise. 'In intellect and vision, he stood head and shoulders above the other members of his generation of the family,' Monte's nephew, Geoffrey Salmon, later recalled. 'The ideas that built the family fortune in the early days were mostly M.G.'s and he had the necessary drive and toughness of fibre to put his ideas into practice.'

While Monte, Izzy, Barnett, Lena and Joseph all now enjoyed homes in central London, the same could not be said for those members of the family who did not belong to the Fund. These other, less fortunate relatives remained in Whitechapel, including Monte's mother, Ann.

By the age of seven, Lena's son Isidore was not only talking and reading, but was also able to add and multiply numbers in his head. This was helpful because each week he helped his mother Lena with the weekly stocktaking at the shop on Edgware Road.

He was also aware of the massive, unspoken hole in the family. Isidore knew that he had arrived after something terrible had happened – being the first child to be born after the loss of Abraham, Bertha and Julia. Their names were never mentioned. They were absent from the album of family photographs kept in the living room. Nobody spoke of them, when telling stories or memories. Nor did people speak of his two older siblings, the first Julia and baby Samuel. Yet they were present – all of them. In the way Isidore heard his mother cry at night. In the absence of his father, always busy with work.

In the seven years since Isidore's birth, Lena had borne four more children: Montague, Harry, Joseph and Rose. He now had six siblings, and Lena was pregnant once again. The age gap between Isidore and his elder brother Alfred was eight years, an eternity in a culture where children were typically born every year. When Alfred started working in the cigar-making workshop downstairs, Isidore was barely able to walk. When Alfred performed his *bar mitzvah*, Isidore was still mastering the skill of tying his laces. He wondered if he would ever catch up.

It was around now that young Isidore started attending Archbishop Tenison's School in the city centre. Each day he set off by himself, as his elder siblings were either already working in the family workshop or too young to attend classes. From his house it was a half an hour's walk, down Oxford Street, through Mayfair, across Piccadilly Circus and Leicester Square and into St Martin-in-the-Fields church on the corner of Trafalgar Square. Once inside the school, down in the cold stone-walled crypt, he learned English literature, numeracy, British history and French. Isidore was particularly good at mathematics, his teachers confirmed. He enjoyed his lessons and, though disappointed when they ended each week, he looked forward to the family getting together on Friday evenings for *Shabbat*.

On one of these *Shabbat* evenings in late 1883 the family met at uncle Monte's house. Isidore's elderly grandmother Ann was there, as were his parents, Lena and Barnett, and his six siblings. His mother's large stomach bulged through her dress. After the women had blessed the candles, and uncle Monte had said the prayers over the wine and bread, they sat down for dinner.

It was now that Monte made an announcement. To their delight, he told them he was engaged to a young schoolteacher called Tilly. She had luxuriant auburn hair, he said, and when he popped the question she had been wearing a long pink dress, which he found … well, captivating. The wedding would be in February the following year. What Monte did not say was that, as ever, he had relied on his sister Lena for advice. It was she who had encouraged him to marry Tilly. It would be good for the business, she had told him, because Tilly's father, Sam Franks, owned a number of successful tobacco shops in London.

Tilly Gluckstein

Two months after the wedding, Lena gave birth to a girl whom they called Kate. The child struggled from the start, suffering from acute diarrhoea and began to lose weight. Alarmed, Lena asked the doctor for help, but his advice was simply to encourage the infant to eat. To the mother's distress, the baby became lethargic and slept much of the day. Finally, on 30 June 1884, Kate died. The cause of death was given as malnutrition. This was the sixth time that Barnett and Lena had lost a child.

Isidore watched as his parents struggled to cope. For days Lena locked herself in her room. Isidore wanted to console her, to do something, but what? Unable to reach out to his mother, he sought the company of his relatives. As Monte and Tilly were busy with their own baby (that October, Tilly had given birth to a boy named Samuel Montague Gluckstein, or 'S.M.G.' for short), Isidore went over to his aunt Julia and uncle Abraham's house. There he spent time with their children who were close to his age, especially the four girls: Kitty, Hannah, Frances and Sarah. Though he was fond of them all, his preference was for Kitty. A year his senior, petite, with a strong will and a deep sense of right and wrong, it was Kitty whose attention and admiration Isidore most sought. Often he would sleep over at her house, when his parents were occupied with some social function. During the winter he accompanied his aunt Julia and the girls on visits to a shop, restaurant or the theatre. In summer they ran around the grass in Hyde Park, which was only a five-minute walk from their house, or took a boat ride on the Serpentine.

Sometimes, late at night, Isidore and Kitty shared secrets. Isidore spoke about his sorrowing parents and the children who had died. He said he sometimes heard his mother cry at night. Kitty talked about her father, Abraham, who drank whisky, even in the morning. She said he could be violent.

That winter the family's attention turned to Lena and Monte's mother, Ann. Like most of the rest of the family she had remained in Whitechapel, where she had lived with her husband Samuel for more than forty years. Born in Holland, Ann had adjusted to the neighbourhood where many spoke Yiddish and several her mother tongue. After years of smoking, she had developed chronic emphysema, made worse by the damp and smog-filled streets of London.

In January 1885 she caught pneumonia and was racked by bouts of coughing. She grew weaker, rarely leaving her bed, finding it increasingly hard to breathe. Her daughter Lena visited her often, crossing London, despite her own grief. On one of these trips she brought Isidore, Alfred and the other children to say goodbye to their grandmother.

Finally, on 3 March, after a week of high fever, Ann died at her home in Whitechapel. She was sixty-six years old. On her death certificate the registrar wrote that she had died of acute bronchitis. After a brief service she was buried, as she had requested, next to her husband in West Ham Jewish cemetery, east London.

In February 1887, on his eleventh birthday and after just four years of formal education, Isidore finished his classes for the last time, said goodbye to his teachers and the next day, just like his uncles before him, began rolling cigars in the family's Soho cigar-making workshop. Any additional training would be provided by the business.

It was now that he was taken aside by his uncle Monte and told the old stories: how his great-grandfather Lehmann Glückstein had escaped from Germany, moved from town to town in the Netherlands and Belgium and finally found a safe haven in Britain. And how Isidore's grandfather, Samuel, had worked hard with his brother and brother-in-law, only to see their business ruined by an argument that tore the family apart.

Seeing that Isidore did not really understand what he was saying, Monte recounted Aesop's Fable 'The Bundle of Sticks'. In this story, he told Isidore, the father invites his sons to break a single twig. When they break the twigs easily, he suggests that they try again, but this time with a number of twigs that have been tied together. They are unable to break them. 'Thus my sons,' says the father in the story, 'as long as you remain united, you are a match for all your enemies; but differ and separate, and you are undone.'

Our family, Monte told his nephew, is like that bundle of sticks. By working together, we are sturdier. The family motto, he said, was *L'Union fait la force* – 'Unity makes strength'.

Chapter 10

1887

_____

'The tobacco business was successful,' Monte would later write, 'but successful though it was, we were a large family growing faster than the business itself. It was obvious, therefore, that sooner or later someone would have to break out a new line.' And so Monte looked to do just that.

Over the previous few years, as he had travelled around the country selling tobacco products at exhibitions and fairs, Monte had noticed that the food on offer tasted bad and was expensive. Even more noteworthy was the lack of beverages provided for women. Social mores dictated that they didn't drink beer, wine or spirits in public, yet they were seldom provided with a non-alcoholic alternative. Here he saw an opportunity.

Ever since the 'Great Exhibition' of manufactured products had been held in 1851 at the Crystal Palace in London, expositions, exhibitions and demonstrations had proved popular, stimulating entrepreneurs and impresarios to host similar, if smaller, enterprises around Britain. And this gave Monte an idea. At the next family meeting in London, he proposed that they launch a side-business. They would use the skills learned in the tobacco trade – management, marketing, human resources and manufacturing – and apply them to a new area: catering.

There was another reason why Monte was attracted to selling tea and cakes to the public. Like most of the rest of the family, he was a teetotaller. Deciding not to drink alcohol was a sign of control in his opinion; it also demonstrated respect for those he spent time with. In his abstention Monte was not alone, for at this time there was a growing temperance movement in the country, being driven, mostly, by women who were fed up with their husbands squandering their earnings on drink.

Barnett Salmon was sceptical about Monte's proposition. Though deeply respectful of his brother-in-law's talents, he believed that the tobacco trade was a safer bet. More and more people were smoking cigar and pipe tobacco, while the newest product – the cigarette – was proving, if anything, even more popular. Why ruin a good thing? Wouldn't diversifying mean draining their limited resources, especially at a time when Monte had been driving them all so hard to expand the business? By 1887 the number of S&G stores had grown to sixty. They now had tobacconist shops outside London, in Manchester, Leeds and Bristol. They had a fleet of horses and carts to pick up and deliver their products. Requests for the opening of new shops and the development of new products were coming in all the time. Surely this was more than enough to satiate their combined energies. Perhaps worst of all, Barnett continued, wouldn't the catering business – associated with lower-class tradesmen and grocers – have the potential to tarnish the family's hard-earned name? A name that had been paid for eighty years earlier, in Jever, and which had been protected ever since. He had a point.

After a long discussion, the men agreed to a compromise: Monte was free to try out his idea as long as it did not interfere with the family's core tobacco business. He therefore could not use either the Salmon or Gluckstein name for his new enterprise, nor could he employ his brothers or brothers-in-law. If he wanted a business associate, he had to look outside of the family. It was hardly a full-throated endorsement.

So, who should be his partner? One man immediately came to mind. Monte had met him through Rose Cohen, Izzy's fiancée. Not quite an impresario, more of a street-seller, he had the gift of the gab, a showman, someone who could whip up excitement about a new gadget or the latest product. He was an extremely likeable fellow, someone you would want to have dinner with, though apparently not good with numbers. He knew little of commerce, but spoke well, and though far from good-looking, he had a great personality, and was considered a real raconteur and humourist. As to the man's name – 'Joseph Lyons' – well, Monte thought, it could work quite well for the business. It was simple and memorable and, perhaps most importantly, didn't sound German or Jewish like Salmon or Gluckstein. Monte was sure the man would not only be glad of the additional income, but would also enjoy the attention. It should be straightforward to persuade him, a commercial transaction.

But first he had to find him.

Joseph Nathaniel Lyons was born on 29 December 1847 into a Jewish family in Newington, just south of the River Thames. His father, Nathaniel Lyons, was a picture dealer. His mother, Hannah, was a home-maker. Joe (as he liked to be called) was educated at the Borough Jewish School near his home and then tried his luck as an artist, but his skills – as he protested to anyone who would listen – went unappreciated. Soon he was travelling the country, touting watches, cheap jewellery and other novelties at exhibitions and fairs.

Joe was just closing his stall in Liverpool – where he had been selling a contraption that combined a microscope, binocular and

Joe Lyons

compass, available for one shilling – when Monte walked up and shared his proposition. Joe confessed that he was on his uppers at this time, and was looking for a new opportunity. After a brief discussion, they reached an agreement, which was memorialised on a single piece of paper: Joe Lyons would afford his name to the business and would act as the front man, whilst the Salmons and Glucksteins would provide the money and management skills. Crucially, the family would retain all the decision-making powers.

Over the first few months of 1887, Monte and Joe set about preparing for their first foray into public catering. They identified an exhibition that was taking place later that spring in Newcastle, contacted the organisers and then tendered and, thankfully, won the beverage and food contract. The commitment having been made, the pressure was on to construct a pavilion, commission the supplies and, most importantly, develop a presentation that would be both attractive and affordable. It was all very different from the S&G shops in London. For one thing, they would be selling tea and cakes, not pipes and cigars. For another, they would be out in the open, working from a temporary structure, making use of a supply chain and staff they had never worked with before. Strangest of all, the contract was for one year only, ending as soon as the exhibition closed. Yet Monte soon realised that many of the elements were the same: they needed to identify their customers, offer a range of desirable products and provide these at the lowest-possible price.

So it was that on 11 May 1887, Monte and Joe stood at the entrance to the 'Mining, Engineering and Industrial Exhibition' in Newcastle, awaiting the arrival of the Duke of Cambridge. Despite it being a blustery, cold and wet spring day, a large crowd had gathered, as this was the first event in the calendar to celebrate the fiftieth anniversary of Queen Victoria's accession. There was much excitement about the exhibition's four main attractions: a complete working model of a coal mine; George Stevenson's first locomotive; a reproduction of the old stone bridge that had spanned the River Tyne for five centuries; and artwork from the Royal Collection. There was less enthusiasm about the local amateur troupe that had been lined up to perform, or about the rusty cannons that had been dragged from the nearby military camp.

Finally, after much muttering and stamping of soggy feet, the royal entourage arrived – a long procession of carts pulled by fine horses, which was greeted by cheers and the waving of flags. Whereupon the Duke – who was cousin to the Queen, head of the Armed Forces and famous for his womanising, as well as for his extravagant grey mutton-chops – was invited to say a few words. As the rain poured down, he thanked the assembled masses for their 'cordial welcome' and wished the exhibition every success. His tone then became more bellicose. He declared his hope that the innovations displayed at the exhibition would deliver 'an England as great and powerful a country in the future as it is now', but that the nation must be cautious, for the most dangerous position any great country could be in was to be unprepared for war. This speech was greeted with loud applause. This was their signal. Monte and Joe ran off to open up the refreshments area.

When visitors first entered, the first thing they noticed were the Chinese decorations: red lanterns, orange streamers and dragon-emblazoned chairs. Looking upstairs, they could see that a second space was Indian-themed, with mandala prints, statues of Ganesh and wooden elephants. At 30 metres long and 12 metres wide, and able to seat more than 1,200 people at one time, the Lyons two-storey pavilion was the second-largest spectacular at the exhibition. According to the fair's programme, the *Jubilee Chronicle*, the pavilion was 'both a matter of enjoyment and surprise. No one could have expected the structures which are to do as refreshment room and sale places would have been nearly so elaborately furnished as they are.'

Back in London the following day, however, Monte's family read the newspaper accounts of the opening of the Newcastle exhibition with growing concern. Despite the family's considerable investment of time and money – and notwithstanding the central place it would later play in the family's mythology or, for that matter, in Britain's cultural history – no mention was made of the exhibition's one truly revolutionary feature, the refreshments pavilion (though much was made of the facsimile River Tyne bridge).

They needn't have worried. Despite the lack of press attention, Monte's newly erected and exquisitely decorated pavilion was overwhelmed by customers. Parched and hungry, they stood in long, polite lines waiting to be served. Monte had cunningly priced his tea and cakes at threepence, rather than the more typical eightpence, generating an immediate buzz. He had also hired a large Hungarian orchestra, which played popular tunes throughout the day and evening; and just in case that was not enough to garner attention, he had also built a shooting gallery in a tent next door, which also proved highly popular. Over the course of the year more than two million people would visit the exhibition, and many of them enjoyed the affordable cups of tea and tasty morsels offered by what was now known as 'J. Lyons.'

Monte would later say that his objective at the Newcastle exhibition had been that 'instead of being an island surrounded by an ocean, I wanted to be the whole show. My belief was that the prices we were charging and the new service we were giving would attract the people of Newcastle.' The shooting gallery, he continued, was 'later destined to become common enough, but in those days it was more than a seven day wonder. It was indeed,' he concluded, 'a marvel.'

At a meeting of the Fund following the success in Newcastle, Monte proposed that he focus his energies on the new catering business. This was accepted without dissent. Securing additional catering concessions for major events would not, however, be cheap. Since the well-publicised success of Schweppes, which had won the highly lucrative franchise at Crystal Palace in 1851, competition had frequently been stiff. The refreshment licence for the Manchester exhibition in 1887, for instance, was sold for £42,690 (equivalent to £4.8 million in today's money). In addition, it was not uncommon for bribes to be offered to those making the decisions. Yet at this time public catering had a reputation for appalling service and quality. In an article published in the *Temperance Caterer*, for example, the writer described the situation as a 'vexed one', in which the licences were typically sold to victualling firms (focused on the sale of alcohol) and the customer was faced with a Hobson's choice between abstention or paying for over-priced and inferior drinks. None of this put Monte off. Conditioned by the hurly-burly world of tobacco retailing, and able to provide high-quality but affordable fare, he became increasingly known as the right man for the job. Over the next four years he won and then successfully delivered catering contracts in Glasgow, London and Paris.

Monte later recalled the secret of his success:

> Any man moving about the country, if he cares, can pick up useful information upon the needs of the public out of the unsatisfied requirements of his own and the people about him, and he can then try to plan a way to meet them. And those of the eighties, I may tell you, fairly shouted for fresh enterprise. It was my experience at exhibitions that first brought home to me the dreary and standstill catering methods of the time.

He had added public catering as second string to the family's corporate bow. The tobacco business was going from strength to strength, and now the catering side was showing real promise. He was living in a beautiful home in west London, as were his sister and brother-in-law – who now had nine surviving children, Lena having given birth to two more boys, Maurice and Julius (the last again named after her twin sister, Julia).

Yet there were still many in the wider Salmon and Gluckstein clan who were yet to escape the violence and poverty of the East End. Monte and Lena's sisters Julia and Sarah still lived off Whitechapel High Street, as did their brother Henry, along with their various spouses and children. In all more than thirty cousins, nephews and nieces were still based in the district.

Monte was deeply shocked, therefore, and not a little afraid when he read in the newspaper that, a few steps from where his sisters lived, a woman had been brutally murdered. And another. And then another. It appeared that Whitechapel had become the hunting ground of a vicious serial killer.

Chapter 11

1888

The first murder took place on Easter Monday, 3 April 1888. Around 6 p.m., forty-five-year-old prostitute Emma Elizabeth Smith left her home on George Road to start the evening trade. During the early morning she was robbed and brutally assaulted. She died the following week. The second attack took place on 7 August at George Yard, also in Whitechapel, when Martha Tabram, a thirty-nine-year-old prostitute, was stabbed thirty-nine times with a knife. Then three weeks later, on 31 August, Mary Ann Nichols, another prostitute, was found in Buck's Row (now Durward Street), with her throat sliced open and her stomach partly ripped wide. Over the next few months at least eight other women were murdered in the Whitechapel area. Many of the local residents believed these victims were linked to the same killer.

The details of these horrendous crimes were extensively reported by the press, providing a boon to both morning and evening sales. With only a small pool of verifiable facts to report – the police refused to divulge many of the investigation's findings – and facing stiff competition, the editors increasingly relied on gruesome rumours and Gothic hyperbole. The *News of the World*'s description of the 7

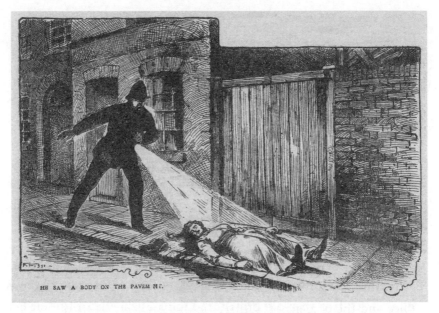

HE SAW A BODY ON THE PAVEMENT.

Mary Ann Nichols, murder victim

October murder of Ann Chapman, for instance, could only have contributed to the growing alarm of Monte and the rest of the family:

> The miscreant had ripped up the sufferer, dragged out a portion of the intestines, and thrown them about her neck. No wild beast could have done such a thing as that. It was all done in a scarcely appreciable portion of time. The marvel is not that there are human brutes in existence, but that no sounds are heard whilst the crime is occurring. The coolness, cunning and hardihood of the criminal are astonishing, but more so is the silence of the deed.

By now the perpetrator had been ascribed various names: 'Whitechapel Murderer', 'Leather Apron' and then, after an anonymous letter from the purported killer was discharged to the police, 'Jack the Ripper'.

The news stories were, of course, terrifying for the inhabitants of Whitechapel, and indeed the rest of London. For the Salmons and Glucksteins, the danger felt immediate, for the killer had murdered his victims within metres of where many of the family lived. And whilst they reassured themselves that they had nothing to fear, there was anxiety that the killer could change his *modus operandi* and that one of the family's women could be targeted.

The police stepped up their investigation. Plain-clothed constables stopped people in the street and asked them about their business. Bloodhounds were brought into the area to try and pick up the killer's scent. A witness gave a detailed description of the killer, which led to the arrest of a number of individuals: a doctor from Birmingham, a Swedish traveller, a Polish cigar-maker. But, when questioned, each of the suspects provided a good alibi and, to the frustration of the police and the citizens of Whitechapel, they were released.

Then, following a well-publicised tip, the police suspected the killer to be a kosher slaughterman who worked on 'Butcher's Row', another name for a section of Aldgate High Street. As it happened, Monte's first cousin, Samuel Abrahams, worked at number 64 Aldgate High Street − as a butcher. Bringing the issue still closer, the investigators borrowed the family's Salmon & Gluckstein tobacconist store next to the Three Nuns Hotel as a stakeout opposite 'Butcher's Row' to monitor a possible suspect.

More generally, and deeply unsettling, were the suspicions, the looks, the whispers. Following centuries of distrust and fear-mongering, many in London blamed the murders on members of the Jewish community, who comprised more than half of Whitechapel's population. The spectre of an anti-Jewish reprisal was heightened with the discovery of graffiti chalked onto a wall the same day as two women were murdered: 'The Juwes are the men that will not be blamed for nothing.' The writing was found on Goulston Street, one street to the west of Castle Place, where Monte's sister Sarah lived; and one street to the east of Middlesex Street, where Monte's other sister Julia lived. There was something scarily familiar about all this. The elder members of the family had not forgotten Lehmann's stories about the Prussians blaming the Jews for violent crimes, and the pogroms that followed. Could such a thing happen in England?

The MP for Whitechapel, Samuel Montagu, certainly thought so. On 13 October 1888, he wrote a letter to the *Pall Mall Gazette* recalling the 'red spectre of bygone ages' when Jews had been falsely blamed for epidemics and murders, inciting acts of violence. 'If the hand-writing on the wall was done by the monster himself,' he wrote, 'can there be any doubt of his intention to throw the pursuers on a wrong track, while showing hostility to the Jews in the vicinity?'

Anti-Semitic sketch (top), graffiti found near one of the victims (below)

The Jewish community was right to be worried. Four days after the MP's letter was published in the *Gazette*, Chief Inspector Donald Swanson, who was in overall charge of the police's Whitechapel murders investigation, wrote a letter to the Home Office describing a recent witness statement. In the margin of the letter Swanson wrote that it was his belief 'that the murderer was a Jew'.

In the midst of this, Monte Gluckstein convened an urgent family meeting. What were the options? Setting up a vigilante group perhaps, but how would the police or the local population respond? An emergency evacuation? But where would they go? Those who lived in west London didn't have room to accommodate everyone. After a long discussion, it was agreed that for now the best option was to send a strongly worded letter to the Home Secretary. It would be signed on behalf of Salmon & Gluckstein, along with family members who lived in Whitechapel, plus more than a hundred other local merchants.

'We the undersigned traders of Whitechapel,' the letter began, 'respectfully submit for your consideration the position in which we are placed in consequence of the recent murders in our District and its vicinity.' For some years, they continued, acts of violence and robbery had been committed 'almost with impunity', owing to the 'insufficiency' of the number of police officers:

> The recent murders and the failure of the authorities in discovering the criminal or criminals have had a most disastrous effect upon the Trade and our district. The universal feeling prevalent in our midst is that the Government no longer ensures the security of Life and Property in East London and that in consequence respectable people fear to go out shopping thus depriving us of our means of livelihood. We confidently appeal to your sense of Justice that the Police in this district may be largely increased in order to remove the feeling of insecurity which is destroying Trade of Whitechapel.

The letter was handed over to Samuel Montagu, MP, who on 28 October passed it along to the Home Secretary. A month later, the parliamentarian stood up in the House of Commons and told the assembled politicians that many of his constituents 'did not care to go now into the streets after dark' and that trade had been terribly depressed, 'owing to the scare which the recent murders had caused'. He added that although he had presented the petition to the Home Secretary some weeks ago, 'signed by the most respectable tradesmen of his constituency', he had received no reply. 'East London very rarely appealed for outside help,' he continued, 'but when it was a case of life and death, and also of the success of the trade of the district', he trusted that the appeal made by his constituents would not be made in vain. If it would help, he added, a reward of £100 had been collected, which the government could use to find the killer.

But it was not to be. The Home Secretary refused to allow the police to accept the reward money; they never responded to the petition, or assigned additional police to Whitechapel. Worst of all, as the winter of 1888 rolled into 1889, five more women were murdered in and around the district, including Alice McKenzie, a prostitute who was found on the pavement of Castle Alley with her throat cut, just round the corner from Monte's sister's Sarah.

Meanwhile, little progress was made in the investigation. The police had their eye on Aaron Kosminski, a Jewish-Polish immigrant who was currently being held in a mental asylum, but they had failed to produce any evidence connecting him to the crimes. No one, therefore, had been charged with the murders. As far as the family was concerned – indeed, as far as London was concerned – the killer remained on the loose. Worse, many people, if not most, continued to blame the Jewish community.

Already unhappy with the rampant poverty, crime and disease of east London, the family felt that accusing Jews of the murders was the final straw. It was time for the rest of the family to leave Whitechapel. To do this, the business would have to grow significantly and quickly.

Chapter 12

1889

Olympia exhibition hall

One morning before breakfast Monte sent word that Alfred and
Isidore should meet him in west London. The brothers – twenty-
one and fourteen respectively – said goodbye to their mother Lena
and, after a short wait on Edgware Road, caught a horse-drawn

omnibus. The half-hour ride took them round Marble Arch, west-wards along the edge of Hyde Park, through Lancaster Gate and Holland Park to West Kensington. At Hammersmith Road they alighted and met Monte, who was waiting for them outside Olympia exhibition hall.

After greeting his nephews, Monte took them inside for a tour. As they walked round, he explained that the business needed to expand rapidly. And what was bigger than this? Monte said, leading them into the Grand Hall. It was enormous; its rounded glass ceiling rose 35 metres into the air, its length 75 metres from one end to the other. Opened just three years earlier, the hall was designed for the very largest exhibitions, being able to host more than 20,000 visitors at a time. And J. Lyons, Monte added, would be providing the catering for the forthcoming attraction to be held in Olympia.

When Isidore asked what this first attraction would be, Monte pointed at a poster on the wall:

Barnum & Bailey presents
The world's largest, grandest, best amusement institution.
The Greatest Show on Earth.

Unlike the Newcastle exhibition where Monte had managed a single pavilion, customers visiting Barnum & Bailey would expect a multitude of cafes, restaurants, snack bars and other eateries. As such, the catering contract for 'The Greatest Show on Earth' had been heavily contested and it had taken weeks of negotiation for Monte to secure the deal. The breaks in the performance were key. As part of the contract, Monte had won the assurance that there would be an interval of 'at least twenty minutes in the course of each of the two daily performances, morning and evening, and that during the interval the band shall not play more than a two-minute overture'. His hope was that such intervals would allow J. Lyons sufficient time to cater to the excited masses and, hopefully, make a sizeable profit in the process.

Leaving the Grand Hall, Monte walked his nephews downstairs to the basement. This was where the food would be made, he said. It would also serve as their offices and headquarters: the engine room of the new business. Isidore and Alfred looked around. It was a large, low-ceilinged, windowless, cavernous space and its brick walls needed a coat of paint. The lack of facilities was alarming. There were no storerooms or prep stations, no ovens or sinks. The place was gloomy and damp. It required great imagination to see this as a commercial kitchen, let alone as the centre of a catering empire, but Monte was enthusiastic about this new venture. It would bring them good fortune.

It would also be a big gamble. For more than a decade Britain's economy had been in a slump. Good jobs were scarce, crime was rising and people struggled to find the money for essentials. The workhouses and poorhouses of Whitechapel were so full they were turning people away. Many were calling this economic contraction the 'Great Depression'. A sour mood hung over the capital. Happily – for the family at least – the population's financial worries seemed if anything to stimulate tobacco sales. It was far from clear, however, how the economic woes would impact ticket sales, let alone the purchase of tea and cake. Monte, though, was bullish. Barnum & Bailey had assured him that tickets would be set at a price so low that even the poorest members of the public would be able to attend. After all, in times of trouble, what better solace than to distract oneself with swinging acrobats, jumping lions and women riding horses bareback?

Over the next few weeks Alfred, Isidore and other members of the family worked tirelessly to prepare for the opening of 'The Greatest Show on Earth'. Once the kitchens were up and running, Isidore's task was to buy food from the early-morning markets in Covent Garden and then, in a fleet of horses and carts, bring it back to the kitchens at Olympia. His days started at 4 a.m., and he seldom finished before 9 or 10 p.m. Most nights he slept on a camp bed in the basement of Olympia.

Eventually, on 11 November 1889, the doors opened and the crowds poured in. They were here to see the extravaganza produced by two of America's most colourful impresarios: Phineas Barnum and James Bailey. Until this point their 'Greatest Show on Earth' had only been available to those living on the other side of the Atlantic. Visitors now swarmed around one of the three circus rings (each measuring 10 metres in diameter) or in front of one of the two stages that had been installed under the expansive Olympia roof. Performances were presented in all five spaces simultaneously. There was a dancing troupe of African tribesmen; a mob of whirling Dervishes; a bearded woman; a legless acrobat; lions and elephants and wild ponies. And, declared the red-jacketed ringmaster who prowled the floor before each show, 'an individual who shows himself possessed of extraordinary powers of chest expansions'. According to the review in *The Times* the following day, 'it is impossible for even the most lynx-eyed onlooker to follow all these performances at once' and 'it is precisely in the immensity, the complexity, the kaleidoscopic variety, the incomprehensibility of the show that Mr Barnum's genius is displayed'.

Watching such energetic and overwhelming entertainment was thirsty work, and soon the men, women and children were milling around Olympia in search of refreshments. They were not disappointed. Around the exhibition hall, Monte, Isidore and Alfred had built a battery of cafés and eating places. From under banners announcing the J. Lyons brand, visitors purchased a selection of freshly made foods and hot beverages. Everything was prepared onsite, in the basement at Olympia. The bread was made overnight, as were the cakes and meat pies; and, as at Newcastle, Monte made sure to set the prices at reasonable levels. This way they avoided accusations of swindling, establishing the reputation that Lyons were purveyors not only of fine foods, but of honest business.

The efforts of Monte and his family did not go unnoticed. An article in the January 1890 edition of the *Caterer* described the Lyons operation as 'bold' and 'winning praise from an appreciative public'. The magazine added that each order was carefully tracked by a numerical tagging system and that, to reward their waiters' hard work, each received 5 per cent of the takings. According to this reporter, the system was 'novel', 'efficient' and 'generous'.

By the year's end, the small team from J. Lyons had served drinks and meals to more than three million visitors. The venture had been a wild success.

The Lyons team at Olympia: Monte (back row second from left), Isidore (centre), Alfred (left of Isidore), Izzy (right of Isidore)

At the start of 1891, Barnum & Bailey decided to end the London run. Recently the ticket sales had seen a downward trend, and it appeared that they were running out of people who had not yet seen 'The Greatest Show on Earth'. It was time to move on.

Monte had been watching Barnum & Bailey carefully over the past year: how they attracted their audiences through mass advertising;

how they hired an army of carpenters and painters to build their sets; how they also managed the less-glamorous aspects of the exhibition, such as the cleaning crews; how they recruited, managed and paid their staff. Granted, it was complicated, but surely with the right management team it was not impossible to replicate. If Lyons could serve tea and cakes to millions of people, why could they not entertain the same number? Above all, Monte had been monitoring the box office. The amount of money that had been taken in was simply staggering. He wanted in.

After the final performance of 'The Greatest Show on Earth', Monte approached the owners of Olympia and was told that a year's lease was available. He now convened a meeting of the Fund to discuss his proposal. His idea was simply too big, and would require too much risk, not to have the approval of his five brothers and brothers-in-law, who sat around him, along with his two nephews Isidore and Alfred. Monte made his pitch. Although overseas travel remained beyond the reach of the vast majority of people, there was a huge appetite for information about the cultures and societies that lay beyond Britain's shores. This hunger was fuelled partly by the increasing numbers of educated people, partly by the growth in the newspaper trade and partly by the ever-expanding reach of the Empire. If the public could not travel the world, Monte suggested, they would bring the world to the public. The first show, he proposed, would recreate one of the world's most romantic cities. They would call it 'Venice in London'.

The cost would be enormous. Not only would they have to build a life-size replica inside Olympia, including buildings and canals, but Monte was also proposing to bring hundreds of men from Venice to steer the gondolas. On top of this would be the colossal cost of marketing and staffing the event. What if they were unable to attract the same numbers who had come to 'The Greatest Show on Earth'? Who would cover the shortfall? In this, Monte was lucky, for the other family business, Salmon & Gluckstein, had continued its phenomenal growth. Over the past few years it had amassed significant reserves, more than enough to underwrite 'Venice in London'.

The only doubter was Barnett Salmon, who was now in his early sixties, frail and increasingly averse to risk. Monte, however, had spoken at length with Lena and knew that she supported the venture. He hoped, therefore, that if Barnett refused to vote for him, he would at least abstain. When the time came for a show of hands, Monte was relieved: all were in favour. Lyons was now in the business of providing public spectacles.

A truly world-class event needed a truly world-class artistic director. The answer, Monte believed, was a forty-five-year-old Hungarian named Imre Kiralfy, who was famous for the scale, colour and ambition of his spectacles, both in Europe and the USA. Having secured Kiralfy's support, Monte travelled to Venice, where he procured more than fifty gondolas at £40 each and the services of a squad of gondoliers. While in the city, he took photographs of some of its most picturesque streets, which would later be used to recreate Venice in London.

Over the summer and into the autumn of 1891, a large team of carpenters, electricians, engineers, artists and scene-painters set up shop in Olympia, carefully reproducing the waterways, cobbled streets and façades, using wood, plaster, tile and glass. They had little time. To take full advantage of the holiday season, Monte had set the opening day for Boxing Day.

But just as the exhibition was coming together, the family suffered another terrible loss. On 17 August 1891, after a twelve-month painful struggle, Lena's twin sister Julia died at the age of forty-five from abdominal cancer. Her husband Abraham had nine surviving children, two of whom had already left home, leaving seven to take care of.

Despite her own worries and responsibilities, Lena immediately took charge. Judging that her brother-in-law would be unable to manage – his drinking had only grown worse – she brought her four young nieces to live at her house. The remaining three boys would stay with the widower. One of the nieces would remember Lena as 'an example of mercy and goodness beyond belief', and said that the house where they all lived 'was full to overflowing, but it was home in the true sense of the word'. Another would add that 'we were never without a mother'.

Fifteen-year-old Isidore was not displeased by the new arrivals, for his interest in Kitty remained acute. They had of course known each other for as long as either could remember, but living in the same house was different. Waiting for his sister to bathe was one thing; waiting for his first cousin quite another. Both being in the midst of puberty, Isidore and Kitty saw each other often and yet, in the midst of so many family members coming in and out, not at all. They also knew that when it came to matrimony, they would of course be consulted, but in the end the decision would be made by their elders. What was good for the business – and primarily for the Fund – would trump any personal preferences. Still, Isidore thought, it was not objectionable to see each other across the breakfast table and hope.

On 25 December 1891, the day before the big opening of the exhibition, the family gathered at Lena and Barnett's house on Edgware Road to celebrate *Chanukah*, the Jewish festival of lights. There had been some debate as to whether it was inappropriate to celebrate the holiday, given the recent bereavement. Those who argued that it was best to stick together, even in hard times, had persevered. Kitty and her three sisters stood around the table, along with Isidore and his eight siblings. Kitty's father Abraham was also there, though in his dishevelled state she barely recognised him. And then just before sunset Barnett stepped forward, said a brief prayer and lit the first candle on the *menorah*. After the candles were aflame and the traditional melody had been sung, everyone retired early, in preparation for the next day's events.

The following morning, and to great fanfare, 'Venice in London' was opened. Fortunately, for Monte and the rest of the family, the day was clear and dry. As one hack pointed out, it would have been hard to conjure up the magic of Venice if London had been hit by one of its perennial pea-souper fogs.

At its heart, the exhibition was a replica of Italy's famed city, divided into two parts, ancient and modern Venice. Modern Venice comprised some of the city's most prized structures – the Doge's Palace, the Ponte di Rialto and the Piazza San Marco – along with a maze of cobbled alleys and stairways, balconies and picturesque shops. The ancient Venice section hosted a theatrical production featuring masked men and women dressed in medieval costumes, as if readying for a masquerade ball. Best of all, to the delight of the growing throng, were the canals.

Running through the centre of the hall was a labyrinth of waterways on which a visitor could relax in a gondola as they shot under one of the many bridges, steered by stripy-shirted Venetians who sang in a romantic baritone. Given the constricted space in which they navigated, the boatmen were cheered on with cries of '*Va bene! Va bene!*'

To Monte's disappointment, however, the theatrical production was hampered by a fault in the pulley system that was meant to change the scenery. Despite this, the crowd was dazzled by the show's scale and sophistication, in which scores of costumed dancers spun and leapt from one floating gondola to the next. The following day Monte was pleased to read in *The Times* that the ballet had been described as 'probably the most imposing spectacle of its kind ever witnessed in London', and that 'the whole entertainment of Venice in London contains, in fact, the elements of success'.

Yet again Monte had been proven right. Over the next year the exhibition was a huge hit, wowing London and attracting 4.9 million visitors.

Within the span of three years, Lyons had gone from running a provincial tea pavilion to delivering a major attraction in the British capital.

After the success of 'Venice', and as 1891 turned to 1892, the obvious question was: what next? Joe Lyons would later tell journalists that the answer to this question was offered by no less a personage than the Prince of Wales who, during dinner one night at Olympia, remarked, 'Why don't your people produce Constantinople when Venice fails to attract!' More likely, Monte had extensively researched the possibilities and, after much consultation, had landed on the Queen of Cities, Constantinople.

Located on the banks of the Bosphorus, on the cusp between Europe and Asia, Constantinople was the capital of the powerful Ottoman Empire. For nine centuries it had been one of the world's richest metropolises. It was now at the centre of a European-wide fight for dominance and was much in the news. In the past two years the city had hosted a major conference between France and Britain on the future of the Suez Canal, as well as a state visit by Wilhelm II, during which the Kaiser had ratified a non-aggression treaty with the Sultan. For a member of the British public, however, Constantinople was not within easy reach. One tour operator was running occasional trips from London to Constantinople via Paris, Venice and Budapest, but even though the journey was made luxurious by the Orient Express, the tour was both arduous and expensive.

With the help of more than 1,000 workmen, the 'Venice in London' exhibition was taken down and the new display was gradually erected in its place. Stonemasons and carpenters, art students and experts in antiquities were all working together to create a three-dimensional facsimile of the ancient Far East. As work continued on the construction, Monte and his team set about hiring more than 2,500 additional employees, who had to be housed, outfitted and trained. To ensure authenticity, a horde of actors would have to be recruited directly from Constantinople. With help from the Foreign Office, Monte engaged in extensive negotiations with the Turkish authorities to allow its citizens to travel to London. After weeks of talks, a deal was agreed in which Lyons guaranteed the employees' return, and Sultan Abdul Hamid II issued an *irade*, or special decree, granting his permission.

In early 1893, while preparations for the 'Constantinople' exhibition were in full swing, the company that owned the Olympia venue went into bankruptcy. Monte did not need to be asked twice. Together with some business associates (including Joe Lyons), he created a holding company and purchased Olympia from bankruptcy. Monte's stake was bankrolled by the Fund, whose coffers were full, following 'Venice in London'. As soon as the financing was in place, Olympia's halls, canteens and other facilities were all purchased by the holding company. In addition to food sales, the family could now potentially profit from property rents, ticket sales, and merchandising.

Over the autumn of 1893, with the exhibition due to open just after Christmas, Lyons invested more than £60,000 in advertising (equivalent to £6.6 million today). The names of Lyons, Olympia and Constantinople were widely strewn across London's billboards, newspapers and horse-drawn omnibuses. One advertising hoarding on the Holloway Road in north London stretched 150 metres long and 4 metres high. Everything seemed set for a smooth grand opening on 26 December, until two things happened.

The first took place on 1 November, when the Turkish Ambassador attended the burlesque *Don Juan* at London's Gaiety Theatre. Unfortunately for all concerned, the performance included a scene in which Sultan Abdul Hamid II was represented as a lecherous old man, chasing and fondling his female slaves. According to a report in *The New York Times*, 'this aroused the Ambassador's ire', and he then withdrew from the theatre in 'high dudgeon' and was driven off urgently in his horse and carriage. Back in the embassy, the Ambassador shot off a caustic note to the Lord Chamberlain, demanding that the play be stopped unless the character of the Sultan was removed. The following day the Lord Chamberlain attended the performance to ensure compliance, which was forthcoming. This, however, was not the end of the matter. Word had seeped back to the Sultan, possibly through the Turkish Secret Police, and he was apparently 'furious' and promptly withdrew his support for the 'Constantinople' exhibition, including the *irade*. As a result, Monte and his team had to smuggle the 100 or so remaining actors out of Turkey. It was another challenge to be conquered by the burgeoning firm.

The second surprise was a happier one. On 7 December, a few weeks earlier than expected, Tilly gave birth to a daughter. They called her Emma Constance, the middle name being a reminder of the exhibition that Monte was in the midst of organising. Within a short period, however, everyone was calling her Mimi. Monte and Tilly now had three children: S.M.G., who was nine years old; a second son, Dore, who was three; and the newborn baby.

On a cold and windy Boxing Day, less than three weeks after Mimi's birth, 'Constantinople' was opened to the public. From the start the halls were packed, the wonders spreading like wildfire through the assembled masses: a bazaar in which Turkish women sold embroidery, lace, jewellery and cigarettes; houses wrapped in trelliswork and mosques dressed in tiled mosaic; Turks in high turbans, Arabian acrobats, Tartars on horseback and camels. Also a harem, described by a hyperventilating journalist from *The Times* as 'a luxurious boudoir with genuine Turkish women, richly habited, and reclining'. Across everything shimmered a mesh of electric light, which gave 'a singularly picturesque effect'.

As with the 'Venice in London' exhibition, the 'most delightful element' was the waterway. Twice each day visitors could board and then traverse the Bosphorus on one of the large curved-keeled caiques, each manned by sailors from Constantinople, ending at the Basilica

Cistern, a cavernous hall comprising more than 1,000 pillars. Once again the spectacle met with widespread praise. 'Entertainment has never been provided by private enterprise to the public on so grand a scale,' raved *The Times*. 'As successful as Venice was, it has been far surpassed by the present effort.'

Over the New Year of 1893 the family discussed the state of the business. Under Izzy's management, Salmon & Gluckstein was doing well. They were opening around fifteen branches each year, with close to 200 in total. Meanwhile Monte, Alfred and Isidore had seen success with 'Venice' and now 'Constantinople'. Already ideas were circulating about possible future exhibitions – the 'Orient' perhaps, or 'South America'. Monte, however, was not satisfied.

The problem was that there was increasing competition in the exhibition market. To remain dominant, Lyons had to slash prices, therefore reducing potential profits. While a name could certainly be made for the firm, the risks were high, the margins low and the energy and time required considerable. Worst of all, one-off exhibitions were sporadic in nature, which put enormous strain on the firm's resources and management.

Monte made a new proposal: If they wished to remain in catering, they needed to develop scale. The solution, he argued, would be to make use of the skills and contacts learned in the exhibitions, by selling hot drinks and baked goods through a more permanent venue. Or, more precisely, a large number of venues.

Chapter 13

1894

By the mid-1890s the British economy was showing strong signs of improvement. For the first time in fifteen years, incomes were rising while unemployment rates were falling. Confidence was at last returning to the streets of London. The cause of the Great Depression (starting in the mid-1870s) and the subsequent recovery (in the mid-1890s) was much debated at the time. Free traders attributed the economy's fall and rise to the imposition and then removal of tariffs by European nations anxious about the impact of globalisation. Union bosses blamed rapid technological advancement, such as the spread of railways and the arrival of cheap steel, which put large numbers of people out of work. Company owners blamed the unions, for pushing wages up to the detriment of enterprise. For the general population, what mattered most was the improvement in their circumstances. Now, with money in their pocket, the public looked for places to spend it, including places to dine. There were, however, very few places at this time where one could enjoyably eat out.

For London's well-to-do, there were private clubs, with names like the 'Beefsteak', the 'Kit-Kat', the 'Reform', 'White's' and the

'Carlton', where a limited range of meals was offered at cost, but such clubs had a reputation for expensive fees, intoxication and exclusivity. Also available were taverns, inns and public houses. These tended to be for the drinking middle classes – tradesmen, clerks, lawyers and the like – where the food served was of variable standard and the atmosphere at times boisterous, if not lewd.

For the working classes and the poor, there were the food industry's other outlets: the chophouses, ham-and-beef shops, coffee-houses and dining rooms. These were squalid, crowded rooms, where cheap, poor-tasting food was available, to be consumed swiftly before departing thankfully. In an article published by the *Daily Mail*, the journalist and poet George Robert Sims remembered these 'slap bangs' as 'mostly dingy places with high-back boxes and a slip-shod waiter or an untidy hand-girl to attend to your wants'. Others commented on the lack of hygiene, the high prices and the dim gas light.

Increased demand, limited supply – this, Monte argued, was the opportunity. Few, if any, of the existing establishments assured quality at a reasonable price. None were part of a chain where the food was supplied centrally, managed by a professional team who knew how to run a national outfit, with standardised prices. The vast majority focused on the sale of alcohol, alienating those who didn't wish to drink or be around rowdy drinkers. And none of the establishments were safe for women, with only a few even permitting them as customers. More than half the population was therefore unable to eat outside their homes, and the other half did so without enjoyment and at a great injury to their pocket books. The answer, Monte believed, was a network of shops selling tea and cake.

Before any investment could be made, however – especially one that would consume such a considerable amount of capital – Monte had to consult his family. By this point the Fund had grown to include the next generation. Alfred Salmon, now twenty-six years old, had joined as the seventh member, while eighteen-year-old Isidore was able to attend, but not yet vote. Monte's two sons were too young to participate. Women were still excluded.

Alfred Salmon

It was from the Fund, and not the business, that each of the members received their annual income. And it was the Fund that owned their houses, paid for their furniture and provided their means of transport (upon entry to the Fund, each member was given the same quality of horse, carriage and driver). Given what was at stake, and the collective implications at hand, Monte was therefore nervous when he stood up before his brothers, cousins and nephews and made his proposal to open a national chain of teashops. After sober questions about the timing of the roll-out, capital requirements, staffing and transportation, and a sombre discussion about optimal scale, desired locations, potential reputational damage and the value of prudence and quality, a decision was made. Monte's proposal was unanimously approved.

So it was that in the spring of 1894 Monte identified a vacant shop lease at 213 Piccadilly, just a few metres from Piccadilly Circus in central London, and fewer than 500 metres from the family's cigar-making workshop on Crown Street in Soho. As it was close also to London's entertainment district, Monte hoped that people would stop off on the way to the theatre.

Lena, as always, handled the contract. She tracked down the owner, charmed and cajoled him, and when the negotiations dragged on, she told the landlord they would walk away unless they were given a better deal. Eventually terms were agreed. At £35,000, the price was substantial, but the location was superb and Lena convinced Monte that the investment would soon be recouped.

Monte's daughter Mimi later recalled Lena as being 'a very clever woman in business as well as in many other ways'. Lena was also famously thrifty, always wearing the same hat. One day a family member mentioned this to her, and she promised to purchase another. The milliner, however, took one look at the hat and then turned it round. She had been wearing it back to front, he told her. Seeing that the hat now looked different, Lena decided there was no need to buy another.

Over the summer, Monte and Lena oversaw the property's renovations. Inspired by the opulent interior decoration of Louis XVI and Marie Antoinette, the walls were draped with colourful silks, the tables were of white marble and the chairs of red velvet. Outside, the shop's exterior was mainly glass – to entice the customers with trays of delicious-looking cakes and pastries. Lena then paid a contractor £15 to paint the exterior woodwork gloss white, upon which was attached a series of large letters made of real gold, reading 'J. Lyons'. Monte was willing to pay the exorbitant cost, believing that it would make replication by others unlikely. The next task was to recruit the employees.

At this time in the mid-1890s the vast majority of waiting staff working in London's hotels and restaurants were male. By making the workplace respectable, Monte and Lena believed they could attract young female employees and, by offering flexible shifts, they might also be able to recruit married women. They were pleased therefore when, in the wake of advertisements in the local newspapers, they were inundated with applications. Interviews were carried out, references checked.

Applicants were expected not only to be friendly and to display good deportment, but to possess a number of key skills. They had to demonstrate the ability to carry trays through a crowded room without spilling the contents, and to make out receipts, which required simple maths. They had to be able to memorise the menu and lay the table according to a precise plan. If successful, the women were then dressed in an elegant brown maid's outfit (whose price would be deducted from their first week's wages) and trained in the skills of customer service.

There was one further innovation. Keen to attract female customers, Monte and Lena had already agreed that alcohol would not be served in their new teashop. This, they hoped, would attract those who were loath to meet at public houses and bars. Now they went one step further, by setting aside a space in the teashop for women only. This, they hoped, would allow women to enjoy eating, drinking and conversing without fear of interruption or hassle.

And so, with a few last-minute straightenings of chairs and adjustments to place settings, they were ready for business.

On 20 September 1894, the first Lyons teashop was officially opened. The initial menu was simple but attractive, comprising fewer than a dozen items. Sweets and pastries were the main offering, including Seed Cake flavoured with caraway, crumbly Dundee cake, along with its moister cousin the Genoa, which boasted cherries in addition to the former's sultanas, currants and almonds. Scones and

Lyons' first teashop, 213 Picadilly

shortbread were also available, as was Scotch gingerbread. These delights were all selected from a display cabinet at the front of the shop. Tea and coffee were brewed in large silver urns and supplied to the tables by smiling waitresses, dressed in matching brown dresses and white hats.

From the start, the teashop on Piccadilly was a success. The customers loved the high-quality, freshly brewed tea, the delicious cakes, the exquisite china and the cheerful service. Best of all were the prices, for this level of quality food was only available at the very finest restaurants and for at least double the cost. It was a hit particularly with married women, who appreciated the women-only spaces; and with theatre-goers, as hoped.

Soon the menu expanded. The range of desserts now included more sophisticated items, such as Swiss rolls, apple tarts, meringues and cream, as well as strawberry and vanilla ices. The most ambitious sampling was the Tennis Cake, a dried-fruit confection that was covered by marzipan and a thin layer of fondant, then decorated with green icing, tennis rackets and a net. In addition to the sweets, customers could now order poached or boiled eggs, pork pies, ham sandwiches, pressed tongue, steak-and-kidney pudding, foie gras and sardines on toast (two slices). The drinks menu was also enlarged. As well as tea and coffee, it boasted iced Bovril and soda, hot cocoa, egg and milk, iced lemonade and potash waters – this last being aerated water containing potassium bicarbonate, which was believed to be good for the health.

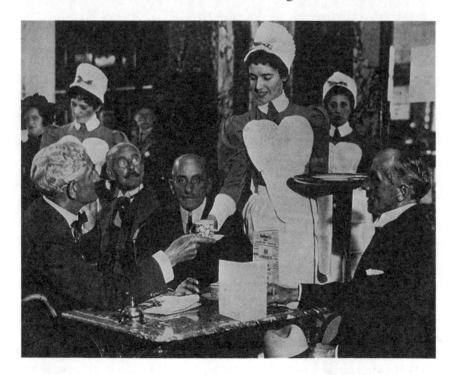

Original waitress Lyons teashop

With the teashop on Piccadilly up and running, Isidore's elder brother, Alfred, was appointed manager. Alfred was perfect for the job. He chatted with the customers, remembering their names and their favourite dishes. He was an excellent supervisor, training new staff and stepping in only when necessary. The place had a family air. It was clean, friendly and efficiently run. Soon customers were returning again and again, becoming regulars.

Meanwhile Monte and Lena identified, and then acquired a lease for, a second shop on Queen Victoria Street near St Paul's Cathedral. This was given to Isidore, who had recently completed an apprenticeship at the Bristol Hotel. He was helped for the first few weeks by his mother Lena, but soon he was on his own, managing staff, greeting customers, tallying the books at the end of each day. It was a big responsibility for the eighteen-year-old, but he was up to the task.

By now Alfred and Isidore had developed very different personalities. The former was a short, outgoing man, who spoke his mind, yet exuded warmth and charm. What he lacked in size, he made up for in personality. He was congenial and was able and willing to talk to anyone, whether it was a supplier, a member of staff, a customer or a man or woman on the street. Though he dressed shabbily, his suit often being crumpled and stained from all the time he spent in the kitchens and warehouses, he was full of energy and quick wit. He also had a distinctive walk, with his hands behind his back and his head down in thought. He was a man of action, who disliked seeing anyone walking around with both hands in their pockets.

Isidore, by contrast, was tall, slender and mostly quiet. What he lacked in charm and warmth, he more than made up for in effort. Always the first to the store in the morning and the last to leave, he worked seven days a week, often sleeping in the staffroom at the back of the stop, as he had in the old days at Olympia. And whilst the two brothers were close, a friendly rivalry existed between them. They vied to see who could tally the highest receipts at the week's end; who could attract the largest number of customers; who could garner the most lavish praise from the celebrity guests who frequently stopped by; and, perhaps most importantly, who could elicit the kindest words from uncle Monte.

Under Monte's direction, Isidore and Alfred's shops were as identical as possible. The same items could be ordered for the same price off the same menu, served by waitresses dressed in the same uniform, whether it was on Queen Victoria Street or Piccadilly. This was highly unusual for the time. More typically, if two or more eateries were owned by the same person, each would have its own distinct personality. Not so for the Lyons teashops, for Monte's aim was to standardise retailing, allowing not only consistency of service – which would be appreciated by the public – but also centralisation of production.

When they opened in 1894, the teashops ordered their baked goods and bread from a local baker. Pies were purchased from a nearby butcher, and tea was procured from a wholesaler in east London. As the chain of teashops expanded, Monte's plan was for Lyons to supply all of these items. To achieve this, he now purchased the lease for an old piano workshop in Hammersmith, known as Cadby Hall. Over the next six months he oversaw the building of a network of workshops, kitchens, stores, warehouse, offices and, perhaps most importantly, a state-of-the art bakery. Food would be prepared here at Cadby Hall, where quality could be assured and efficiencies maximised, and then delivered by horse and cart to the teashops.

Meanwhile the expansion of the teashops – or 'depots', as they were being called by the family – continued. As each was opened, its management was allotted to one of the family's promising young men. One cousin ran Regent Street, a second was in charge of Chancery Lane, a third Ludgate Circus, a fourth the one on Bishopsgate Street, a fifth had the outlet on Budge Row. Within a year, ten teashops were trading, all in central London. By the end of 1894 the Lyons teashop was fast becoming a phenomenon, known for its quality of product, affordability and excellent service.

Monte now proposed that J. Lyons shares be made available for the first time to non-family investors. To do this, they would float the company on the London Stock Exchange. The logic was simple. First, to continue the rapid growth of the teashops (which was their intention) they needed an injection of significant funds. Second, the constant acquiring of new leases was threatening to exhaust the Fund's capital, so they needed to look outside the family for new investment. And third, given the ever-expanding needs of the family – carriages to acquire and maintain, houses to purchase, education fees to cover, medical bills to pay – realising some of the company's equity was not a bad idea.

The problem with going public was that the family did not wish to lose control of their company. The solution was elegant: in order to retain control, the family created two types of shares. 'A Shares' were issued to the new investors, which held the same value as those owned by the family, but had no voting rights, whilst the family now owned 'B Shares', giving the Salmons and Glucksteins 100 per cent of the voting rights. Despite the almost certain lack of accountability and transparency that would follow, the flotation of Lyons was over-subscribed. Investors were apparently less fearful of corporate power dynamics than they were of missing out on the opportunity to be part of one of Britain's fastest-growing brands.

So it was that at twelve o'clock sharp on 20 May 1895, J. Lyons & Company Limited commenced its first annual general meeting at the twin-turreted Cannon Street Hotel in central London. As the public face of the company, Joe Lyons took the position of chair, whilst Monte sat next to him, as managing director. Present also was Lena Salmon, and her two sons Alfred and Isidore, along with the other family members who worked for Lyons.

In this first shareholder address, in front of fewer than twenty investors, Joe revealed that there were now eighteen teashops and declared, 'Your directors have the pleasure to inform you that the shops now opened are doing exceedingly well.' Negotiations were proceeding, he added, for the acquisition of 'several other premises', along with the expansion of the outdoor catering division. Finally, and with an eye to the future, Joe said that the company had recently purchased additional land immediately adjoining Cadby Hall, with regard to the business's 'inevitable growth'. All of this was met with cheers and loud applause.

But, as was almost inevitable, with growth came growing pains.

Early on the morning of Tuesday, 22 October 1895, five months after Lyons' ebullient shareholder meeting, Isidore Salmon arrived at the Queen Victoria Street teashop. The sky was black and it was raining hard. From under his umbrella, Isidore could see that the shop entrance was blocked by a line of women shouting slogans and holding placards. Recognising various faces, he realised that these were his staff. After some brief enquiries, he found out what had happened.

Seven waitresses were refusing to work, upset that their commission (which made up the majority of their earnings, the rest being tips) was being cut in half, from 5 to 2.5 per cent. Isidore spoke calmly to the strikers and, after some discussion, suggested that if they resumed their posts he would transmit their concerns to his uncle Monte. He was, however, unable to convince them, so Isidore unlocked the doors and walked inside. He would manage as best he could when his remaining staff arrived. Meanwhile the strikers marched over to his brother's teashop on Piccadilly, in an attempt to attract more waitresses to their protest.

Strikes had become a feature of British politics since the first general strike in 1842. Occurring initially among the industrial workforce – coalminers, textile workers, shipbuilders – work stoppages had spread into the blossoming service sector. They were, however, almost entirely a male phenomenon. This was partly because women had, until recently, been excluded from the trade-union movement, and partly because of prevailing sexist attitudes. In a speech to the Trade Union Congress in 1875, for example, the TUC's parliamentary secretary, Henry Broadhurst, encouraged the assembly to 'bring about a condition where [our] wives and daughters would be in their proper sphere at home, instead of being dragged into competition for live-lihood against the great and strong men of the world'.

That is not to say that Isidore had never heard of an all-female strike. In July 1888, more than 1,400 workers had famously walked out of the Bryant & May matchbox factory in Bow in east London, protesting at low pay and unsafe conditions. As Bryant & May was one of the largest match manufacturers, whose products were stocked in all the S&G stores, this so-called 'Match-girls' strike' was followed closely by the family – the strike concluded when Bryant & May had effectively given in to all the workers' demands. The establishment, however, was quick to patronise the Bryant & May strikers. *The Times*, for instance, stated that the workers had been 'egged on by irrespon-sible advisers', who were 'pests of the modern industrial world'.

The day after walking out of the Lyons teashops, the striking waitresses met their supporters at St Andrew's restaurant on Bride Street. The location was cleverly chosen, because it was only a short walk from Fleet Street, home to most of the national newspapers. In consequence, the gathering was well attended by journalists. One of the women stood up and said that, after paying for stoppages, clothes washing and what she called her 'costume', she sometimes had no wages left at the end of the week. 'I have reached home at 11.15 p.m.,' said another, 'and after a day's work I have found myself positively out of pocket.' A third added, 'There was no living without the 5 per cent, the whole 5 per cent, and nothing but the 5 per cent.' This last comment met with loud applause.

One of the strike leaders then said they had attempted to meet the Lyons management, but their deputation had been refused. A resolution was adopted which read: 'That this gathering of waitresses and customers of Messrs Lyons and Co. expresses its surprise at the uncivil reception extended by the firm to the deputation, condemns their tyrannical treatment and asks the outside public to leave Messrs Lyons severely alone.' Following a request to the gathered press that they start a public fund, it was agreed that the striking waitresses should meet the Salmon brothers, state the facts of the case and see if the family would receive them back on the old terms of 5 per cent. The meeting was then adjourned.

To the dismay of Isidore and the other family members, the strike was widely and positively reported in the national and regional newspapers. The story caught the public's imagination sufficiently that it entered the world of comment and opinion. The editor of *The Sun* evening paper characterised the protest as 'The Lyons v The Lambs'. Meanwhile a columnist for the *Dundee Advertiser,* wrote that Lyons' 'system is wrong from top to bottom,' adding that 'it is neither fair to the public nor to the waitresses, but I fear the latter will not be able to fight against a strong company which will soon be able to supply their places.'

None of this coverage pleased Isidore's uncles and cousins. It had been less than a year since the launch of the teashops, and the board was relying on continued positive press coverage to attract customers to their growing number of stores. Although they had a sizeable budget for paid-for advertising – so-called 'above the line' marketing – they depended equally on unpaid articles, features and columns, all of which sprang from the goodwill of the newspapers and their writers. Being cast as unfeeling bullies who exploited women, not to mention as unscrupulous capitalists who lacked a sense of fair play, would not help their cause.

1894

A week after the first walk-out, and with the strike growing, Monte, Joe Lyons and the other board members gathered for an emergency meeting. Also in attendance were Isidore and Alfred Salmon. Isidore explained that the dispute had been the result of an unfortunate misunderstanding. The lower commission rate of 2.5 per cent was only meant for new staff, whose wages would be increased to 5 per cent upon satisfactory progress. Sadly, a manageress at his Queen Victoria Street shop had failed to convey this, and the staff had assumed that everyone's commission would be cut in half, prompting the walk-out. Whether it was a failure in communication or a bad policy, the board realised that the current system was now tarnished. 'After mature deliberations and in deference to the strongly expressed public opinion,' read the minutes later, 'the Board has determined upon the abolition of the present system of payment of waitresses.'

Isidore now visited all the teashops personally to explain the new arrangements. Henceforth, he said, waitresses would be paid a fixed salary, and signs with the words 'No gratuities allowed' were to be posted on the teashop walls. All strikers would be welcomed back to their old jobs. If customers insisted on paying a tip, it would be put in a box placed in each teashop, any monies generated being applied to a Provident Fund, to be distributed to employees in times of sickness.

When compared to the previous money they had received (with commissions and tips combined), the income of many of the women was now actually lower, but stability of income appeased the staff. The strikers accepted the new terms. This result pleased Monte enormously. His workforce felt more secure, while the company had burnished its reputation as being both prudent and fair.

Upon this strong foundation, and with one foot on the first rung of the catering industry, Monte decided they could perhaps step higher up the ladder.

Chapter 14

1896

As the century's end approached, a sense of change hung in the air – of the old making way for the new. For the old, the Queen had outlived any other British monarch and was rarely seen in public; whilst for the new, her preening son, the Prince of Wales, was often spotted out-and-about, for instance at the Derby, where his horse Persimmon won in 1896, to uproarious applause. For the old, the great poet Alfred, Lord Tennyson had died just four years earlier, and Thomas Hardy, irritated at the negative response to his new novel *Jude the Obscure*, had put down his pen; whilst for the new, Joseph Conrad's first novel, *Almayer's Folly*, was at the printers, Flora Annie Steel had just published *On the Face of the Waters*, and H.G. Wells was onto his next book, following the success of *The Time Machine*. Similarly the staid tunes of mid-Victorian operetta made way for the zanier, saucier tunes of the music hall, including 'Ta-ra-ra Boom-de-ay' and 'Twiggy-voo'. The exception was the once-in-a-generation sportsman W. G. Grace, who just seemed to keep going. Following his 'Indian Summer', in which he scored his hundredth century, in 1896 he became the first-ever sole recipient of the *Wisden* Cricketer of the Year award.

It was in this climate that the *Penny Illustrated Paper* ran an article suggesting that Monte and his family members might have ambitions beyond their teashops. 'Lyons are proving to be dark horses,' stated the article. 'It is evident that the Piccadilly teashop is not going to be a solus venture. Plans are afoot for something very much grander.'

They were right. Two years earlier, in 1894, Monte had quietly purchased a substantial property at auction on behalf of J. Lyons. Located on the corner of Shaftesbury Avenue and Great Windmill Street, only a few metres from Piccadilly Circus, the building was then near-derelict. In former times it had been a music hall, known variously as the Argyll Rooms, the Trocadero Palace of Varieties and the Royal Trocadero Hall. It was notorious for its salacious shows, and for women who sold themselves by the half-hour. Monte's plan was to demolish the existing structure to make space for a state-of-the-art restaurant and bar complex: a 2,000-square-metre building of the highest quality, which would attract London's elite, its richest and most famous. The building would be known simply as the Trocadero. This was quite an ambitious plan for the son of a German-Jewish immigrant raised in the sordid streets of Whitechapel.

To gather the required capital, the family issued a prospectus extolling the company's past successes and promising likely returns on investment. Advertisements were taken out in the newspapers, encouraging people to invest in the new venture. Some commentators complained that the financial picture given by the company was opaque and failed to provide the necessary detail to enable investors to make an educated decision. Others raised their eyebrows when the new shares that were issued were assigned with non-voting rights, assuring that the family retained absolute control of the board and the company's operations. This did not seem to stop anyone. Given the family's success with the teashops, most newspapers encouraged their readers to subscribe to the new venture. The share issue was over-subscribed.

Work on the site soon ran into difficulties, with the project being beset by delays and rampant over-spending. To control the problem, Monte hired a new architect and surveyor, but was shocked when they reported that the final bill was over budget by £100,000 (equivalent to £10.8 million today). In consequence, at its next meeting the Lyons board announced that it would be unable to distribute dividends to its shareholders. Reflecting this cashflow crisis, no new teashops would be opened for the next three years. Members of the Fund had to tighten their belts, even having to return the horses and carriages they had recently been issued. Some of the national newspapers picked up on the company's financial difficulties, speculating that their initial enthusiasm for J. Lyons might have been misplaced.

In a last-ditch attempt to raise the necessary capital, Monte called an emergency meeting of family members and major investors. Gathered at the centre of the Trocadero's building site, he provided an update on their precarious financial position. When the shareholders expressed their shock, it took all of Monte's charm and powers of oratory to soothe them, explaining the Trocadero's potential and how, once complete, it would bolster the company's reputation. In his attempt to raise additional outside capital, however, he failed.

None of the shareholders were willing to take the risk. In the end, it was the Fund that provided the necessary loan to the company. Later, Monte would grumble that 'the only subscription from outside [the family] amounted to a paltry hundred pounds'. It was a terrifying gamble, which, if it failed, would seriously deplete, if not bankrupt, the Fund – a failure that would be hard to forgive and would probably threaten family unity.

By the late 1880s, steel was increasingly replacing wrought iron in the construction of large buildings. Stronger, more flexible and increasingly cheap to produce, steel enabled architects to design multi-storey structures that soared into the air. In the USA, buildings were being erected whose steel frames supported the entire weight of the walls and floors. Wonders such as the Rand McNally Building in Chicago (completed in 1889) and the Tower Building in New York (also 1889) were early examples. In the UK the use of steel soon followed. The National Liberal Club (1887) was one of the first to make significant use of steel, as would be the Hotel Russell (1900) and the Waring & Gillow shop on Oxford Street, London (1904). Britain's first fully steel-framed building would be the Savoy Hotel extension (1904).

It was within this quickly changing material environment that the Trocadero had been designed and built by the Chicago structural engineer Charles van Childs. It would be the country's first substantially steel-framed restaurant complex. The enormous steel girders were produced in the Middlesbrough mills of Dorman Long, transported by train to London and then by horse and cart through the streets of London to Piccadilly Circus. There, with men hanging off scaffolding and others operating a Scotch derrick – a lifting device comprising a tall mast, a boom, some pulleys and a series of guy-ropes – beams were carefully lifted into place. It was slow, painstaking and dangerous work.

Whilst the construction continued apace, Monte and his relatives worked on the opening gala. It was vital that it was blessed with the stardust of wealth and celebrity. Monte knew that the Trocadero was far too large and expensive an enterprise to be sustained by Lyons' existing customers. A launch event featuring a handful of music-hall regulars and a few titans of the Jewish community would not generate the necessary excitement. What they needed was to bless the Trocadero with royalty and nobility, millionaires and stars of the stage.

As the summer of 1896 drew to a close, Monte, Alfred, Isidore and the rest of the family worked tirelessly to persuade and cajole the good and the great of London to attend the launch party. Messages were carefully sent, gift packages that included fine wines and rare fruits were delivered, intimate lunches at fancy restaurants were arranged and enjoyed, egos were massaged. The message was clear: this was an opening you didn't want to miss. Everyone who was anyone would be there. The family just had to make sure that they were.

Finally, on 1 October 1896, the big day arrived. Twenty-year-old Isidore Salmon spent the afternoon getting ready. After a long soak in the bath, he put on a freshly starched ivory shirt punctured by pearl-coloured buttons, a white bow-tie, black trousers, tails and high-glossed shoes – all of which had been laid out for him by one of the servants. He was excited, not just about the opening of the Trocadero, but also about the ride into town, for not only would he be travelling with his mother, father and siblings, but he would also be escorting his nineteen-year-old cousin, Kitty.

The match had now been approved by his parents, Lena and Barnett, along with Kitty's widowed father, Abraham, but this would be the first time they would be seen in public together as a couple. With the carriage outside the house, Isidore waited in the hall for Kitty. At last the diminutive young woman appeared at the top of the stairs. She was wearing a sparkling ankle-length dress with leg-of-mutton sleeves, and her hair was tied up in a bun topped by a delicate fascinator. Isidore was dazzled. He took Kitty's hand and escorted her outside.

The night was warm and clear, and as they trotted down Regent Street in their smartly appointed hansom cab – past Liberty's, which was known for its fashion and design, then Hamleys, one of the largest and oldest toy shops in the world, and then, to Isidore's great pride, the Lyons teashop – their travel was announced by the gentle silver tinkling of the horses' tackle and the steady 'Ger on, ger on' of the driver. As they approached Piccadilly Circus, they heard the noise from the crowd before they saw it. Thousands had gathered to witness the Trocadero's opening night, see the celebrities, watch the fireworks and be able to tell their friends, 'I was there.'

The Trocadero, 1890s

Others were also arriving. There was the mustachioed diamond-magnate Solly Joel, along with Arthur Collins, the dashing hero of the Anglo-Zulu War. The composer Lionel Monckton, and the poet Sir Edwin Arnold (whose beard resembled a bird's nest). Sir Joseph Renals, who had just stepped down as Lord Mayor of London, and the white-haired Sir Hiram Maxim, inventor of the eponymous machine gun. The popular cartoonist Phil May, and the begowned Katie Christian of the D'Oyly Carte opera company, who would sing the national anthem later that evening. In addition there was an array of baronets, earls, lords, knights and politicians. Each of these names would later be listed in the papers' society pages, along with many others. It is worth noting that none of those mentioned were Jewish.

Having pulled up to the front entrance, Isidore and Kitty were helped down by gold-braided doormen, and then entered the brightly illuminated Italian-style hall, with its columns of Devon marble, walls framed by an elegant frieze depicting the legend of King Arthur and ceiling hung with sparkling chandeliers. As they stepped forward, they were handed a programme, written by one of London's leading playwrights, Clement Scott. 'The Trocadero Restaurant is the newest, the latest, the most luxurious of London's most modern developments in refinement, order and good taste,' gushed the wordsmith. 'The Trocadero has raised its head proudly, and is the ornament of a district whose approach in 1860 would be a positive peril to any woman and to most unguarded men.'

Inside, as the dignitaries glided up the wide marble staircase, they were ushered along by the Band of the Scots Guard, who played popular show tunes. To the Grill Room, its walls decorated in terracotta, its tables covered in starched white linen. Through the Empire Room, an enormous ballroom that could host a banquet for more than 500. Around the numerous dining rooms, which could be hired for private events. Then to the Salon, furnished in the Louis XV style, and finally the Lodge Room, set aside for Masonic meetings. The kitchens, which were not available for touring, were at the top of the building, each efficiently serviced by a series of swift-moving lifts. The entire building was illuminated with electric lights. After they had walked around, the good and the great – who now numbered more than 400 – sat down to a fifteen-course dinner, followed by a lengthy speech of thanks given by Joe Lyons, and more music.

Trocadero foyer

The following day *St James's Gazette* wrote that 'there is very little to remind one that the place had hitherto been a popular musical hall' and that it was furnished with an 'artistic taste of a high order'. Not all the reviews were good. According to the *Pall Mall Gazette*, which apparently had a nose for social climbers, 'The company was large if not distinguished. The speeches were brief, if not bad. The exception was perpetrated by an ex-Lord Mayor, whose name was pronounced in three different ways during the evening. The dinner would doubtless have been good had the service not been atrocious.'

While disappointed by the spotty press notices – there wasn't even a mention in *The Times* or the *Evening Standard* – Monte shrugged it off. He was sure that as soon as people tasted their exquisitely prepared food, ordered from their exclusive and far-ranging wine list and enjoyed their top-quality service, they would be converts. Isidore was similarly unfazed. He had returned home late, after a fabulous night with Kitty. It had been glorious: presenting her to the guests of honour, their first dance and then, at the night's end, a kiss. The only problem was that he had to get up at 4 a.m. to man the kitchens.

Amidst all the positive news, the New Year ushered in some sadness for the family. In the last week of January, Barnett Salmon was gripped by an acute pain in his abdomen. On being visited by his doctor, he was told he had bladder stones. He was taken to hospital where, after the patient was given a dose of laudanum, a surgeon inserted a lithotripter (a long, thin pincer-like metal device) up his urethra and into the bladder and crushed the stones, or calculi, so that they could flow out.

While the procedure went well, the recovery did not. Barnett soon caught an infection, which his body was unable to fight. Late in the evening of Thursday 11 February 1897, surrounded by his wife Lena, sons Isidore and Alfred and other children, Barnett passed away at his home at the age of sixty-seven.

The family turned their attention to his funeral arrangements. Since the graveyard in West Ham, where Lena and Monte's parents were interred, was now full, Barnett would be buried in the new Jewish cemetery in Willesden, north London. The question was when to hold the ceremony. They expected a large turnout, so the family agreed it would be a mistake to rush things. Better to wait until after *Shabbat* was over. So it was that the funeral was held on Sunday, 14 February. It was well attended, with a cortège comprising more than fifty carriages passing through the cemetery's wrought-iron gates. After prayers were spoken in the chapel, Barnett was carried to the family plot. As the first to be buried here, there was plenty of space around him.

Five days later, on 19 February, Isidore read the obituary that ran in the *Jewish Chronicle*. He was pleased. 'Barnett Salmon's career is worthy of note,' it began, 'as an example of what energy and indomitable perseverance can achieve.' It then continued:

> He fought his way from the very lowest rung of the ladder of life and leaves behind him as a record of his labours and abilities what is perhaps one of the largest manufacturing companies in the world; facts of which his family may well be proud. More rapid accumulations of wealth are fairly frequent and sufficiently commented upon, but surely these are less noteworthy than the success which attends the ceaseless efforts of the man who has had to devote his whole life to the task. Mr Salmon's success was undoubtedly due to his shrewd common sense combined with a keen application to business and a knowledge of the world in general far above the average.

Isidore's mother, Lena, was overwhelmed, though deeply gratified by the number of telegrams and letters of condolences she received. She read each one, then carefully stored them away for later viewing.

The will, which was read out five months later, was relatively simple. The assets were valued at £46,491, a ludicrously small amount, given Barnett's significant holding in J. Lyons and S&G. The reason, of course, was that his assets – most importantly Barnett and Lena's house on Sunderland Avenue – were in fact held by the Fund, thus avoiding any problematic inheritance tax that would have been due, following the passage of the Finance Act three years earlier.

Lena was awarded the plates and cutlery, pictures, furniture, horses and carriages – nominally valued at £1,000 – and, per the original agreement between Monte and the other members of the Fund, a trust was set up, valued at £10,000, to be managed by her sons, from which the widow would be paid a regular and sizeable income. The Fund, it appeared, worked well not only during a member's lifetime, but also afterwards.

Now that construction was complete and the operation was running smoothly, the members of the Fund chose the Trocadero as their regular meeting place. Each Wednesday the cousins met for lunch in Room 14, a long high-ceilinged room whose walls were hung with mirrors. After the plates has been cleared, the port served and the cigars lit, the pressing matters of the day were presented and debated.

Following Barnett's death, the Fund now included five of the original partners along with Alfred and Isidore Salmon, making seven in all. While the next generation of men – those aged between eighteen and twenty-three – were excluded from the meal, they were expected to join the after-lunch discussions. These were loud, chaotic and often argumentative occasions, in which conversations were frequently interrupted and little regard was made for age or position. While matters of policy were discussed, these meetings were mostly an opportunity for the members of the Fund to get together and enjoy each other's company.

Although Monte was at this time the undisputed leader of the family, his role should not be exaggerated. 'The Members of the [Fund] were men of very forceful characters,' his nephew Geoffrey Salmon later recalled. 'They were very conscious of the fact they were all equal and they were not to be over-ridden by any members of their generation. Anyone who was present at the glorious rows that took place on a Wednesday would have been left in no doubt about that.' They often disagreed and didn't think well of each other. Yet – and this was key – 'First and foremost was their cohesion. To them it was part of the natural order of things that they should stick together: they didn't reason about it or philosophise about it, it was just a fact of life.'

By the afternoon's end, the business of the meeting was wrapped up. As waiters entered the room to remove the glasses and filled ashtrays, the men said their goodbyes, climbed into their waiting carriages and headed home to their wives and children.

1896

While Monte was responsible for the continued development of the teashops, along with the outside catering business, Alfred and Isidore Salmon were now promoted and were put in charge of the Trocadero.

Their responsibilities were split. Alfred's morning started with a meeting with the front-of-house staff: the maître d', the waiters and waitresses, the porters and the managers. Once the day's schedule had been discussed, including any special events that might be taking place, and the employees were sent on their way, Alfred reviewed the previous day's finances and then dealt with personnel matters. He also met the entertainments manager, ensuring that the night's show was ready and resolving any last-minute problems.

Meanwhile, Isidore's day began with a meeting with the kitchen staff. It was a large group, including the head chef, sous chef, pastry chef, fish cook, saucier and assorted others. There was also a team of kitchen porters, assistants and dishwashers. They reviewed any issues from the night before, along with the day's menu. The food had already been purchased from the markets earlier that morning. If items were missing, this was the moment to alter the menu. As with Alfred, much of the rest of Isidore's day was taken up with matters of personnel and bookkeeping.

It was a good division of labour, playing to the brothers' strengths. Having trained in the kitchens of Olympia and in the teashops, they had both learned the skills of effective management. Within a short time Alfred and Isidore gained the staff's respect for their work ethic, fairness and common sense. The food was of the highest quality, the staff were courteous and well mannered, the evening shows started on time and were highly entertaining. The Trocadero was a well-run machine.

There was one legacy of the Trocadero's music-hall days that Alfred and Isidore found hard to shrug off. Along with their most-welcome refined and elegant fee-paying guests, there were others, typically female, who were looking to pick up customers. In response, Alfred wrote a note to the staff, stating that if they spotted a 'strange lady or ladies in couples (that is the ladies who you know are not regular customers)', they should be placed at tables around the edge of the restaurant, so that 'in case of misbehaviour we can screen the table off'.

The edict to isolate prostitutes seemed to pay off. By December of 1897, the Trocadero was turning a profit, its success mirroring and surpassing that of other recently opened restaurants in central London, such as the Criterion and the Café Monico. Word soon spread that the Trocadero was the destination for foodies, connoisseurs of fine wine and aficionados of the latest music. In an article on the Trocadero published in *The Nation*, for example, a writer named Arnold Better wrote, 'This is a fearful and romantic place. Those artists who do not tingle to the romance of it are dead and have forgotten to be buried.'

George Orwell went further, observing in his essay 'Such, Such Were the Joys' that the Trocadero was a symbol of its time: 'It was the age when crazy millionaires in curly top hats and lavender waistcoats gave champagne parties in rococo houseboats on the Thames [...] the age when people talked about chocs and cigs and ripping and topping and heavenly, when they went for divvy weekends at Brighton and had scrumptious teas at the Troc.'

While the Trocadero was going from strength to strength, a curious thing was happening in Hammersmith.

Back in 1890, when the Lyons catering business had started in Olympia, a handful of bakers' ovens had been installed in the basement to fulfil the onsite needs of the 'Venice in London' and 'Constantinople' exhibitions. Later, when the company had moved into Cadby Hall, an array of ovens had been constructed to provide baked goods to the growing number of tea shops, and later to the restaurants of the Trocadero.

One day, when they had produced too much bread, one of the bakery managers offered the extras to people walking past the entrance to Cadby Hall. The following day these passers-by returned, hoping to purchase more loaves. Word got round, and soon a queue was forming each morning in front of Cadby Hall to purchase freshly baked bread.

Realising that they had an opportunity literally knocking at their door, the family invested in six new ovens, at an average cost of £150. The bakery expanded and quickly became known as the Vienna Bakery, after the highly glazed Viennese-style rolls that were made there. The products proved so popular with the locals that baked goods were wheeled around the neighbourhood in handcarts. On the sides of them were daubed the words 'Lyons Delivers Daily Bread', which promoted sales even further. As word spread, more orders came in, from cafés and restaurants in west and central London. Soon even the Vienna Bakery proved insufficient, and more ovens were built.

The quality of the bread and the efficiency of its delivery now came to the attention of Edward, Prince of Wales. Soon Lyons could brag that it was the official baker to the royal family. For Monte and the rest of the family, this was a moment of great pride. With the royal seal of approval, the demand for Lyons bread grew exponentially. Two 'Titanic' ovens were installed in Q Block of Cadby Hall, which together were capable of producing 10,000 loaves an hour, which were sold via a network of wholesalers around the country.

With the family business now comprising a highly profitable chain of tobacco retail outlets, a national network of teashops, a state-of-the art restaurant complex, a world-class baked-goods factory, as well as an exhibition catering business, the Salmons and Glucksteins had become one of Britain's up-and-coming families. This was no small feat for a German-Jewish family who had stepped off the boat just a half-century before. To mark their arrival on the next rung of the social ladder, they decided it was time for a high-profile event: a society wedding.

On the morning of 19 December 1899, Isidore stood at the front of the Orthodox Bayswater Synagogue in west London, waiting for his bride to arrive. Standing next to him under the *chuppah*, or canopy – decorated with pink and white roses – were his mother Lena and his brother Alfred. Isidore thought of his father, Barnett, and wished again that he was with them.

Behind the group sat more than 600 friends and family, the men wearing morning suits and silky black toppers; the women attired in cheerful dresses accented by a range of millinery choices, from the wide-rimmed Gainsborough to the trumpet and the more modest mushroom. Along the sides of the wooden benches and on the walls hung green palms and chrysanthemums in white and pale yellow, casting a sweet perfume through the hall.

At ten minutes to one, Kitty entered on her father's arm, accompanied by seven bridesmaids, and was led up to the canopy and the nervous groom. The bride's dress was made of rich white satin duchesse, the bodice embroidered with seed pearls, while the yoke, sleeves and underskirt were of chiffon and real Brussels lace. She wore a cluster of orange blossoms in her hair, fastened with diamonds, from which hung a tulle veil, and carried a bouquet of lilies-of-the-valley. To Isidore, Kitty looked absolutely beautiful. No thought was given to the fact that she was his first cousin.

Consanguinity was not unusual in the late nineteenth century, particularly amongst Jewish European immigrants. Of Lena and Barnett's nine surviving children, seven would marry their first cousins. By marrying a close relative, the logic went, assets remained securely within the family. Whilst there was growing concern that inbreeding might have a negative impact on the genetics of future generations, the practice of cousin marriage was legitimised by high-profile couples such as Queen Victoria and Prince Albert, along with Charles and Emma Darwin.

After the vows were spoken and the Chief Rabbi, Dr Adler, had shared his blessings, Isidore smashed a glass with his foot – a symbol of what cannot be undone. The wedding party was then driven to the Trocadero for a sumptuous luncheon in the Empire Room. Almost the entire building was utilised in the celebration and was packed with more than 1,000 additional guests. In the American Bar the waiters wore Stars and Stripes uniforms, while a buffet was offered in the Louis XV Salon. Later, a concert was performed in the Blue Salon and Oak Room.

To the family's delight, the wedding was covered favourably by the major newspapers. One columnist described Isidore as 'highly esteemed for his energy and rare executive ability'. Another enthusiastic reporter wrote that Isidore possessed 'a natural genius' for organisation, and that 'this young Napoleon of caterers will go far'. All spoke favourably about the Trocadero and its staff, thereby promoting the flagship restaurant complex.

It was a moment of celebration and arrival for the family – a ritual that marked an increased sense of belonging. The brothers and sisters, aunts and uncles, cousins and in-laws of the now-sizeable Salmon and Gluckstein families, who had all worked so hard and for so long to fit in, were infused with a greater sense of confidence that things would be all right. Perhaps, finally, they could relax.

Isidore and Kitty

Except for Monte. Because the managing director of Lyons and head of the family knew there was trouble brewing, and that he, the golden boy, lay at the centre of the storm.

Chapter 15

1900

It had all started a decade earlier during the heady days of 'Venice in London' and 'Constantinople', when Monte had purchased the Olympia exhibition complex from bankruptcy.

As part of the acquisition, Monte and the directors of a syndicate had raised funds from shareholders, declaring that the purchase price would be £140,000 and that they would then sell it on almost simultaneously to a third party for £180,000. This was totally legal and provoked no complaint. What was now being alleged by the shareholders was that the original purchase price had actually been £120,000, and that the directors had therefore pocketed £20,000 more than they had disclosed. Having rumbled through the lower courts, the case, which had become known as 'Gluckstein v. Barnes', had now reached the House of Lords, where it was before three of the country's most eminent judges: the Lord Chancellor, Lord Robertson and Lord Macnaghten. To Monte, it felt like his father's far-too-public legal troubles all over again.

On 5 April 1900, four months after hearing evidence from the plaintiff's and defendant's lawyers, the judges issued their verdict. Responding to the evidence, Lord Robertson said that the syndicate's directors had indeed 'misrepresented' their intentions. The Lord Chancellor added that the defendants had committed a 'very gross fraud' and had 'hoodwinked' the shareholders by means of 'nefarious plans'.

In his summary, Lord Macnaghten focused specifically on Monte Gluckstein, saying that he had 'Secretly and therefore dishonestly ... put into his pockets the difference between the real and pretend price and had deliberately misled the shareholders'. Not only must the missing funds be repaid, he stated, but the interest as well. He then went one step further. When discussing the defendant's ability to collect a contribution from the others who had benefited from the scheme, Macnaghten suggested that might be possible, if Monte appealed 'to that sense of honour which was popularly supposed to exist amongst robbers of the humble type'.

This was a real blow. Monte had always prided himself on his reputation for integrity and honest dealing, something made more acute by the phantoms of the past – his great-grandfather's bankruptcy in Jever, his grandfather's flight from Rheinberg, his father's accusation of being a swindler in Antwerp and later a thief and bully in the High Court in London. There was a theme running through each of these, of duplicity and dishonour, of being slippery; a theme not dissimilar from the old medieval tropes of the Jewish moneylender, of Shylock, of Fagan. Of the Jew who takes economic advantage of others, and who in his or her thirst for profit loses touch with what is right and proper, what is decent; who goes too far, and aspires with undeserved hubris to live above their station.

And it was all very public. The day after the judgment, *The Times*, the *Daily Mail* and other national papers took barely hidden joy in poking fun at the businessman with the German-sounding name. The *Pall Mall Gazette* stated, 'It is impossible to describe in less decisive language the tactics adopted by Montague Gluckstein', whilst the *London Daily News* ran a four-line headline:

THE STORY OF 'OLYMPIA'
SECRET PROFITS
MR GLUCKSTEIN'S APPEAL DISMISSED
SCATHING COMMENTS BY LAW LORDS

Perhaps worst of all was the coverage in *The Economist*, the periodical whose arrival in London and later growth had mirrored that of the Salmons and Glucksteins; it had always looked favourably on the family business, printing verbatim the company's annual shareholder meeting (each time taking up three to four pages), and was read not only by Monte, but all of his business associates. After laying out the facts of the decision, the *Economist* concluded with the following simple but damning words: 'Mr Montague Gluckstein was guilty of misfeasance and breach of trust.'

Deeply embarrassed, Monte submitted letters to various newspaper editors, which were published a few days later. This epistle argued that, per legal advice, he had not been obligated to disclose their profits, and whilst he and the other directors might 'technically' owe the money, he had 'acted with perfect *bona fides*' and therefore blame could not be 'attributable' to him. Unsurprisingly, this somewhat self-serving and defensive damage-control exercise failed to improve matters. In business meetings, at the club, even in synagogue, he felt the disapproving looks, heard the judgemental comments.

It is not clear which stung the most: the public humiliation, so similar to what he had felt as a teenage boy, when his father and uncles had fought in court. The harsh humiliating words of the judges. Or the sheer unfairness of it all. After all, as far he was concerned, he had done nothing wrong. But whichever it was, Monte knew that he had become a liability for the company, and therefore for the family.

At the next meeting of the Fund, Monte stood before his male relatives and announced that from this point forward, he would be withdrawing from public life. He would continue running the family businesses from behind the scenes, but he would no longer represent the family at social or business events. In terms of being the face of the company, it was now up to the younger generation, like Alfred and Isidore, to take things forward. Monte was only forty-six years old.

PART III

MONTE & ISIDORE

'God save the King, Uncle Monte and J. Lyons and Co.'

Lena Salmon

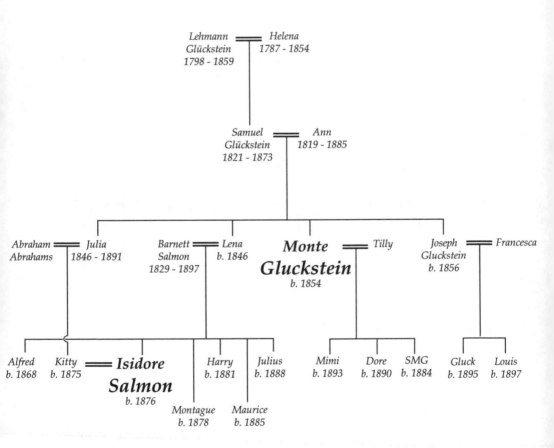

Lehmann
Glückstein
1798 - 1859 ═══ Helena
1787 - 1854

Samuel
Glückstein
1821 - 1873 ═══ Ann
1819 - 1885

Abraham
Abrahams ═══ Julia
1846 - 1891

Barnett
Salmon
1829 - 1897 ═══ Lena
b. 1846

**Monte
Gluckstein**
b. 1854 ═══ Tilly

Joseph
Gluckstein
b. 1856 ═══ Francesca

Alfred
b. 1868

Kitty
b. 1875 ═══ **Isidore
Salmon**
b. 1876

Harry
b. 1881

Julius
b. 1888

Montague
b. 1878

Maurice
b. 1885

Mimi
b. 1893

Dore
b. 1890

SMG
b. 1884

Gluck
b. 1895

Louis
b. 1897

Chapter 16

1901

_____

As is so often the case, just as Monte was becoming obsessed with personal problems – working on legal strategies with his lawyers, writing heartfelt letters to the press, reassuring his customers and shareholders – he was jolted by events far greater than his own. For the British Empire, which he and his family not only benefited from but also wholeheartedly believed in, was hit by two major shocks.

The first took place in South Africa. According to the newspapers, the Boers – descendants of Dutch settlers – had refused to accept British rule. Starting in the autumn of 1899 and continuing for the next two years, the Boers and British had engaged in a series of skirmishes, sieges and then battles in which the imperial forces were harassed, overwhelmed and, even after large reinforcements had been dispatched, embarrassed.

For loyal servants such as the Salmons and the Glucksteins, as well as the staff of Lyons, the reports in the London newspapers were both depressing and frustrating. They wanted to do something, even if it was only a gesture. So in an effort to show their patriotism, Lyons baked thousands of Christmas puddings, loaded them onto carts draped with Union Jacks, took some pictures for the press and then shipped the packages to the troops fighting in Cape Town. Eventually, under the command of Lord Kitchener and Lord Roberts, the British soldiers overwhelmed the rebels, but not without a terrible toll. More than 22,000 British soldiers died in the campaign (mostly of disease) and 6,000 Boer soldiers; more than a quarter-billion pounds was spent; 30,000 Boer houses were razed to the ground; and more than 26,000 Boers died in British concentration camps (many of them children).

The second shock took place closer to home. Queen Victoria, the nation's longest-serving monarch and Empress of India, died on 22 January 1901. Her death triggered a period of mass mourning and soul-searching. The newspapers were filled with stories of all that had been achieved during her long reign. The British Empire was now the largest empire in history, encompassing hundreds of millions of people, speaking scores of languages, across five continents. Many people – especially outside the Empire – asked themselves how a country as small as Great Britain came to control one-quarter of the planet. Others, given the rise of nations such as the USA, Germany and Austria, asked how long it would be possible to continue to exert such an influence.

Many considered the new king, Edward VII, to be a sybarite and a playboy, ill-suited to build on his mother's achievements. Others viewed him as a modern-thinking man, well travelled and, in terms of politics and social matters, liberal. He was without doubt prone to questioning the status quo and tradition, and had surrounded himself with men who some considered unsuitable companions for a monarch, including loud-mouthed parvenus, colourful actors, well-known philanderers, inveterate gamblers and members of the Jewish aristocracy.

The banker Nathaniel Mayer Rothschild, for instance, had met the Prince when they had studied at Cambridge together and had remained a friend. Also close were the bankers Arthur Sassoon and Sir Ernest Cassel – the latter being so friendly with the monarch that he earned the moniker 'Windsor Cassel' – plus the physician Sir Felix Semon and the lawyer Sir George Lewis. As a prince, Edward had stayed overnight with some of these associates, even observing their Friday-evening *Shabbat* rituals. The coronation was planned for the summer of the following year, and many in the Jewish community, including senior members of the Salmon and Gluckstein family, hoped that the new king would usher in a more inclusive atmosphere. They were not disappointed.

At the next Lyons annual general meeting, held once again at the Trocadero, Joe Lyons announced that, to his great pleasure, the company had been appointed, under royal warrant, as 'refreshment contractors' and 'bakers' to the King. In addition, Joe said that the company had shown 'remarkable growth' in the previous year and that the value of its property holdings was close to £1 million. No mention was made of the Olympia scandal.

After a brief question-and-answer session with the shareholders, the chairman announced the election of the directors, amongst them for the first time Isidore Salmon. 'I am very proud of the honour you have done me,' Isidore proclaimed to the shareholders. 'My best efforts will be continued in the interests of the company, I hope they may prove as profitable to the enterprise as I shall endeavour to make them.' With that, the meeting was called to a close.

Still smarting from the allegations made against him in the newspapers, and perhaps looking for a distraction, Monte now threw himself into his business affairs, turning his attention to the family's other major enterprise – tobacco.

In recent years Salmon & Gluckstein profits had risen in line with the phenomenal growth of cigarettes. Brought back to England after the Crimean War in the 1850s, cigarettes were now cheaper to make, easier to smoke and increasingly popular with both men and women. By 1901, more than thirteen million cigarettes were being purchased each year, up from two million just a decade before.

Taking advantage of this boom, Salmon & Gluckstein developed a stable of labels, including Sunshine, Sweethearts, Puck, Saucy Cut, Lifeboat, Snake Charmer and Dandy Firth. These products were manufactured at the family's new bonded factory on Lever Street in Clerkenwell. Between 1896 and 1901 more than a hundred S&G shops were opened around the country. During this same period profits for the company almost trebled, from £23,461 to £61,818.

S&G cigarette card, 1890s, front and reverse

S&G were facing increased competition. By the turn of the century there were more than 6,000 retailers selling tobacco products in Great Britain. Many of them were small family operations, comprising one or two shops. There were other chains, however, not as big as S&G, but nonetheless eager for growth. These groups mounted aggressive cost-cutting campaigns, threatening S&G's market dominance. To take on is rivals, Monte now sat down with his brother Izzy at their cigarette factory in east London and agreed upon an emergency action plan.

Their first move was to invest in machines that could manufacture more quickly and with less wastage, producing as many as half a million cigarettes per week. Then they told shopkeepers that if they didn't sell S&G brands exclusively, they would withdraw their products. Next they radically discounted prices to attract consumers. Finally they rolled out a national marketing campaign, spending more than £10,000 per year on advertising. Part of this consisted of five horse-drawn omnibuses daubed in silver paint proclaiming the virtues of S&G's various products that offered free rides through London. This was, according to *Cigar and Tobacco World*, 'one of the biggest things in the way of street advertisement yet attempted', adding that it was 'so big and so effective that it is a wonder that no one has ever thought of it before'.

Smaller tobacco retailers were enraged by Monte and Izzy's aggressive tactics. Some attempted to match S&G's radical cost-cutting, but when their losses built up they found themselves unable to keep pace. Others refused to stock S&G products and urged their suppliers to respond strongly to the hardball tactics. Still others complained to the press, saying that S&G were bullying them out of business. One of these papers, the *Financial Times*, reported that 'Salmon & Gluckstein threaten to scoop the whole retail trade of the metropolis.' In response, Monte and Izzy told journalists that the small shops were trying to stop free trade, to the detriment of the consumer, and cut their prices even further. This tussle between the British tobacco companies was heralded in *The Daily Telegraph* and other papers as the 'Tobacco Wars'.

Then one of their competitors noticed something strange. Examining an S&G pack one day, he spotted that although the wrapping claimed it had been 'hand-rolled', each of the cigarettes inside were clearly identical – the same length, the same width, the same weight. Obviously they were made by machine. This eagle-eyed competitor filed a suit claiming that S&G were lying about their products. Quick to defuse a potentially explosive situation, Monte apologised and explained that old labels had been used simply as a matter of expediency. His employees had not wanted to waste the 500,000 labels already printed. He promised to rectify the practice. The judge seemed to accept this *mea culpa* as genuine and dismissed the case.

At the next meeting of the Fund, Monte's brothers and brothers-in-law expressed their concerns. S&G could not afford to cut the price of cigarettes for ever, they said. Worse, the company was being singled out by the media, and they worried again about the family's reputation. On this last point, Monte argued that the opposite was true. The press attention had been good for the company. It had proved that S&G was acting in the interests of the consumer. After all, who wouldn't want to purchase their cigarettes at a cheaper price? As for the price-cutting, however, he agreed. For the sake of profits, it would have to end, sooner rather than later. He promised he would fix things. Over the next few days Monte negotiated a truce with the competitors: S&G now guaranteed that they would cease cutting prices outside London, and in return the retailers would stop complaining to journalists. This was a great deal for the family, because most of their profits were generated in the capital city.

Salmon & Gluckstein had now grown to more than 160 shops, making it by far the biggest retail chain in the country. This allowed them to claim on advertisements, playing cards and cigarette boxes that they were the 'largest retail tobacconists in the world'.

In the middle of December 1901, Monte and the other members of the Fund were gathered at the Trocadero in Room 14 for their weekly meeting. Lunch having been served and eaten, they were sitting in their leather wing-backed chairs, with cigars and pipes in their mouths, whiskies on the table, discussing various matters, when Monte said that he had a proposal. He believed it was time to sell S&G.

'Why now?' asked one of his surprised relatives. After all, hadn't they just invested a huge amount of time and money to win the Tobacco Wars? Monte laid out his reasons. In his view, they were at the top of the market. Production was streamlined, their staff were well trained and happy. Their brands were household names and well loved. The problem, he continued, was that their competition was unlikely to lessen any time soon, which meant that – at least for the foreseeable future – they would be obliged to keep prices low, with little prospect of a decent profit. Instead, he believed, they should focus their efforts on the more profitable catering business, J. Lyons, where the margins were higher and the competition weaker. Most importantly, he told his relatives, he had had an offer: from James Buchanan Duke.

James Buchanan Duke was the most powerful tobacco businessman in the world. He owned American Tobacco, which supplied 40 per cent of the cigarettes in the USA. Three years earlier he had made his first move into the European market by purchasing Ogden Ltd in Liverpool, producers of the popular pipe tobacco St Bruno and St Julien. Duke's purchase of Ogden's had triggered a swift response from Britain's largest tobacco manufacturers. To strengthen their position, thirteen of the country's largest firms had merged, including H. D. & H. O. Wills, John

Player & Sons and Lambert & Butler. This new concern had been registered on 10 December 1901, just days before the meeting at the Trocadero. It was called the Imperial Tobacco Company.

S&G faced a dilemma, Monte now told his brothers, cousins and nephews. If they remained independent, they would be 'hurled into the midst of a triangular fight, the end of which would be hidden in obscurity'. The company was simply not big enough to take the heat. They had to make a choice: either go with the American or join their British competitors at Imperial.

Many of his relatives urged Monte to approach Imperial. It was a matter, they said, of honour. After all, it was a British company. Others said they should stick it out and try and remain independent, as the business had been good to them for so long. Still others said that whatever they did, they should act quickly. But Monte was not to be rushed. Realising that the competition might actually be turned to their advantage, he asked the Fund for permission to dangle the bait a bit longer. Once he had obtained their full support, Monte returned to Duke and asked for his best and final offer. With a chance to purchase Britain's largest tobacco retailer, the American industrialist jumped at the opportunity and made a generous proposal. Having secured the deal, Monte then contacted Imperial Tobacco, who considerably improved upon the American's offer.

At the next meeting of the Fund, and with the two offers in his pocket, Monte recommended that they sell to the highest bidder: the British. Thanking him for his efforts and seeing little alternative, the men heartily approved the sale. On 2 January 1902, Monte, Izzy, Alfied and the other members of the family sold their controlling stake in Salmon & Gluckstein Limited to Imperial Tobacco. The family's interest was sold for £400,000. In today's money, that would be equivalent to £41 million. Later, Imperial Tobacco would report that it had paid 'considerably more than the business was worth'.

The family was now wealthy. Any remaining relatives still living in Whitechapel moved out. Those who were members of the Fund migrated en masse into far larger houses in West Hampstead, Kensington and Hammersmith, often in the same neighbourhood. Monte and his wife Tilly installed themselves in a large red-brick house at 14 West Kensington Gardens, in the same street as Joe Lyons and Alfred Salmon, who inhabited numbers 26 and 11 respectively. Isidore and Kitty moved into an enormous house nearby at 30 Holland Villas Road, also in Kensington. Living close together, members of the family continued their practice of socialising with each other, almost to the exclusion of other people.

One morning soon after the sale of S&G, at exactly eleven in the morning, to ensure no jealousy or complaint of favouritism, the doorbell of each member of the Fund rang out. When family members opened the door, they saw standing in front of their house three new horses, a new landau, a new brougham and a new victoria. Each of the carriages was painted smartly in green and black. Next to them awaited a coachman wearing a black silk top hat with a green cockade, a black coat and a green-edged cape, along with a young groom who was similarly attired.

Improvements were also made to personal wardrobes. Monte now ordered his shirts from a particular manufacturer in Karstadt, Germany, and he developed an eye for antique furniture, offering family members suggestions on which pieces might make for a sound investment. Equally, Tilly, Kitty and the other women took to purchasing the finest clothes from the most expensive boutiques.

Monte's daughter Mimi later described it as follows: 'The S and G dames used to receive the most courteous attention in all the West End shops and especially at Jay's, an elegant shop with a dress and tailoring department equal to the best in Paris.' Her mother, Tilly, was always welcomed without making an appointment, and even had her own special fitting room. 'As a very little girl I noticed there was a shade of envy when "the girls" as Father termed all the females bought hats for the family weddings.' Mimi added, 'Tilly came off best. She used to send her worn ones (never more than 2 seasons' wear) back to the Milliner Augrave in the Queen's Road (as it was then called) for the staff to enjoy.'

Though he was close to his two sons, Monte's relationship with his seven-year-old daughter Mimi was special. He would frequently take her to Cadby Hall, the Lyons headquarters in Hammersmith, which had by this point become a sprawling four-hectare complex of factory buildings, warehouses and offices. To the east was the narrow Blythe Road, on the other side of which stood Olympia, the glass-domed exhibition hall. As she visited the offices of her uncles and cousins, Mimi would be welcomed with a warm greeting and would leave with a coin – sometimes small, sometimes large. On her return home, she shared it with her brothers and other little cousins. 'This was done without hesitation by us youngsters,' Mimi remembered. 'It was due to our upbringing. The Fund training started in the nursery.'

At heart, Monte was a Victorian man, criticising extravagance and scolding those who indulged in it, whilst privately enjoying a few luxuries for himself. Nevertheless, according to his daughter, Monte never forgot his working-class roots. Still speaking with a cockney accent, he always remembered the names of the family's parlour maids when they opened the front doors, and further endeared himself by tipping generously, sometimes as much as a golden sovereign given secretly.

As with his sons, Monte educated his daughter about the history of the family, the court case that had broken his father, and the Fund. 'All of us always must give of our very best to [the Fund],' he told her. 'The Family comes first. Unity at all costs. Write this down and read it from time to time.' Yet what he didn't say, but Mimi already realised, was that the Fund was a world she would never know. She would never be able to work for the family business. She might be advised of any major discussions and even be consulted, but when it came to decisions, she would be excluded. That was how it was, as far as Monte was concerned, and how it would always be.

Mimi and Dore

Chapter 17

1905

Five years into the new century and Isidore Salmon was enjoying the gifts of settled family life. He and Kitty had been happily married for six years. They had, to their great delight, two boys: Sam, who was five years old, and Julian, who was three. And they lived in a magnificent house.

Number 30 Holland Villas Road was a large three-storey brown-bricked building with white-painted bay windows, set back from the quiet street, with four bedrooms, a large attic with separate rooms for the live-in nanny and cook, a dining room big enough to sit fourteen guests comfortably, an office for Isidore and a large tree-shaded garden in the back, where the boys learned to walk and later to play football. Nearby was Hyde Park, where nanny took the boys to feed the ducks or run round Kensington Gardens. As Cadby Hall was less than a kilometre away, Isidore was able to walk there in ten minutes. The house was, simply, a wonderful place to live.

It had been shortly after Julian's birth that Kitty had noticed that Sam was having difficulty with his vision. Despite his intelligence, he appeared unable to read and grew frustrated when she encouraged him to learn. A few times he even threw a book across the room.

Not a little worried, she took him to a specialist, who said that Sam was profoundly short-sighted. To help him, Kitty found books with large print, read to Sam daily, and had an optician craft a special pair of spectacles for him. Before long, little Sam was reading for himself, well before other partially-sighted children of the same age. His disability would not prove an obstacle, she told him, provided he didn't let it become so.

While Kitty busied herself with their two young sons, Isidore began thinking beyond the family. As a boy, he had seen the sorrow on his parents' faces when they recalled the deaths of their six children. He had seen the ravages caused by poverty and illness in Whitechapel. Since the age of eleven he had worked full-time, travelling around London selling cigars, working at Olympia and then in the kitchens of the Trocadero and the teashop on Queen Victoria Street. He had always found time to speak to those he encountered, to hear their stories and try and understand their problems.

Up till now, it had been enough to focus on his work at Lyons. A quiet manager, esteemed by his peers and respected by his staff, Isidore believed that if you kept your head down, worked hard and loved your country, you would be rewarded in return – no matter your class, your country of birth or even your religion. After all, wasn't that the story of his own family? But something new was happening in Great Britain – something sinister, distasteful. A rising tide of anti-immigrant feeling was sweeping the country. Jewish refugees, in particular, were being blamed for society's ills.

The recent influx of Jewish immigrants to Britain had started in the early 1880s, following a wave of brutal pogroms in Russia and Ukraine. Whilst many of them found refuge in communities across the country, including Manchester, Leeds, and Liverpool, most settled in London. By 1905, more than 140,000 Jews lived in the capital, the vast majority of them in an area of three square kilometres around

Whitechapel, Aldgate, Stepney and Bethnal Green – precisely the neighbourhood where the Salmons and Glucksteins had settled sixty years earlier.

Accommodation for these newly arrived refugees was shockingly overcrowded, poorly heated and lacking basic sanitation. Clothes and leather workshops were often located in basements, garrets, old sheds and garages, which were dimly lit, unventilated and polluted with toxic fumes. A large percentage of the population relied on charities to provide them with food; many of the children worked, instead of attending school; and infant mortality was 50 per cent higher here than in the rest of the capital.

The sudden influx of European Jewish families had caused great alarm amongst the residents of east London. Some blamed rising levels of crime and disease on the new arrivals, while those living in other parts of the capital shunned Whitechapel and Stepney, as places of prostitution and vice. Meanwhile newspapers ran editorials calling for immigration controls and deportations. On 19 April 1905, the *Manchester Evening Chronicle* described the Jewish refugees as 'dirty, destitute, diseased, verminous and criminal', whilst in an article on 'The Alien Question' on 9 May the *Birmingham Daily Gazette* talked of 'undesirables'.

Taking advantage of this hysteria, the MP for Stepney, Major Evans-Gordon, formed an anti-immigrant organisation called the British Brothers' League, which soon boasted more than 45,000 members. In the spring of 1905, the League organised protests through the streets of east London, with chants such as 'England for the English'. Next, seeing a chance to gain electoral advantage, Evans-Gordon and a handful of other populist politicians proposed legislation that would clamp down on immigration.

On 2 May 1905, a debate was held in the House of Commons on a so-called 'Aliens Bill'. Gordon now told his colleagues that 1.5 million humans beings were 'on the move from the South and East of Europe pressing towards the West'; that the 'Jewish emigrants do form a very large part of the whole'; and that 'it is the poorest and the least fit of these people who move, and it is the residuum of these again who come to, or are left in, this country'. He then declared that not only were immigrants taking jobs away from the British, but they were bringing crime and disease with them: 'I will only say that smallpox and scarlet fever have unquestionably been introduced by aliens within the past few months.'

Such arguments were not limited to the political fringe. In this same debate, Herbert Asquith, MP for East Fife, who seven months later would become Chancellor of the Exchequer, said, 'there is undoubtedly an excessive percentage of crime among the immigrant alien population in this country as compared with the indigenous population'. The Conservative prime minister, Arthur Balfour, was at pains, however, to say that the Aliens Bill had 'nothing whatever to do' with the Jewish people. Indeed, he added, 'the treatment of the race has been a disgrace to Christendom, a disgrace which tarnishes the fair fame of Christianity even at this moment'. Instead, he continued, this was a question of sovereignty. 'Every individual country has or has not the right to decide who is to be added to its community from outside, and under what conditions. That, I think, is a final and indestructible right of every free community.'

The bill was passed with a large majority. This is how the Aliens Act of 1905 came into force, Great Britain's first ever legislation aimed at limiting immigration. Despite its vague name, and the protestations of the prime minister, it was widely understood by the press and the public that its passage was a direct response to the influx of Jewish refugees.

Reading about the debate in the newspaper the following day, Isidore Salmon was sickened by this obviously anti-Semitic legislation. He wanted to challenge the populist sentiment that was currently gripping British politics. The solution was clear to him: he would become a politician. His first task would be to persuade his relatives at the next meeting of the Fund, an effort not without its own risks.

No matter the qualifications, achievements or rank of its members, nobody in the Fund was immune from teasing or bullying. In particular, a dim view was taken of any perceived slowness of cognitive skills. So when he stood up at the next meeting of the Fund at the Trocadero, Isidore was nervous. He had an announcement, he told them: he wanted to get involved in politics. The leg-pulling was immediate. One cantankerous uncle cried out, 'You're a nice man Isidore ...' and his sentence was completed by a cousin, '... but do you have the brains for politics?' This was met with laughter.

Isidore pressed on, explaining that he wanted to run for office in the London County Council as a member of the Municipal Reform Party, a group that focused on local elections and was allied to the Conservatives. What about his work for Lyons? he was asked, more seriously this time. It was a part-time position, he said, and he would of course continue with his current business responsibilities. After a short discussion, he received the Fund's approval, and the group moved on to other matters.

So it was that in early 1907, Isidore put down his name for the West Islington constituency. Several weeks later, the *Islington Gazette* provided a review of the new candidate. After listing Isidore's job experience – director and managing director of Lyons, responsible for more than 8,000 staff – it said that he was 'a young man of charming personality, there are not many who could boast of similar business experience'. As an example, they pointed to his recent organising of a gargantuan banquet in Aberdeen for more than 2,000 people. 'His practical experience of organisation,' they continued, 'must be of the utmost value in solving the difficult problems of municipal government.'

To enter politics was to enter public life. It meant putting one's head above the parapet; it meant exposure to approbation as well as ridicule. 'He loved meeting people and knowing everybody,' his nephew, Geoffrey Salmon, later recalled, 'and unlike most of his generation he thoroughly enjoyed the limelight.' What Isidore didn't have, however, was a formal education. He was also painfully aware of his cockney accent, inherited from his parents. To address this, he sought elocution lessons.

As he walked around his prospective constituency, Isidore discovered that local politics had little in common with what he read in the national newspapers. Whilst in Westminster the Liberal government ushered through educational reforms (providing free meals to school children), celebrated the opening of the Piccadilly Line (from Finsbury Park in the north to Hammersmith in the south, a few steps from Cadby Hall and Isidore's home), and provoked Germany by launching HMS *Dreadnought* (the world's fastest and best-armed battleship), the people he met on the doorstep complained about their noisy neighbours, the landlord who failed to fix the plumbing, and problems of feral dogs in the streets. Ever the administrator, Isidore took good notes and promised he would look into it.

He had to give speeches and attend long luncheons with local business groups; he had to go door-to-door to meet the voters; and he participated in public forums with the other candidates. His younger brother Harry helped run his campaign and managed security. The campaign trail was physically hard work. It was also expensive. Signs, flyers and banners had to be printed, halls and community rooms paid for. As the election was not related to Lyons, the business could not reimburse him; and because Isidore had not asked for money from the Fund, he and Kitty had to pay all the campaign bills. These were not insubstantial, as well as off-the-book expenses, to be distributed to local leaders who could assure a good turnout on election day. Once all these invoices were satisfied, Kitty found it hard to pay her domestic bills at the week's end. Sometimes she had to choose between paying the domestic staff or her husband's campaign costs.

At the previous election the district's two seats were both won by the Progressive Party. Eager to retain power, and clearly worried about Isidore's candidacy and the local paper's endorsement, the Progressive Party now came after him, circulating a pamphlet declaring that Isidore did not wish to bring the tram system to Islington. Worse, they accused him of overseeing dangerous and unhealthy work conditions at Lyons and, in a thinly veiled anti-Semitic accusation, of making a profit from those less advantaged. Finally they sent hooligans to disrupt Isidore's meetings, resulting in arguments and even violent skirmishes.

The stress of the campaign, along with its financial burden, proved difficult for Kitty. A shy person, unused to the public eye, she struggled to cope with the busy social calendar and the intrusion of the newspapers. At the end of one long day's canvassing, Isidore returned home to find his wife in bed with the lights off and the curtains drawn. Anxious that Kitty was seriously sick – there were reports of a meningitis epidemic in Scotland – he called the doctor. After a quiet word with Kitty, the physician told Isidore that his wife was suffering from a nervous breakdown. On hearing of her condition, uncle Monte insisted that she move into 14 Kensington Gardens with him and Tilly, at least until the end of the campaign. There Kitty was nursed and kept company by Tilly, who made sure that she slept and ate well.

One evening, Kitty found an envelope by her bedside. Inside was £200, along with a note from Monte that she should use the money to purchase the household necessities she had been unable to afford. She was deeply moved both by his support and by his tact. A week later, Kitty returned home, feeling rested and less anxious. She brought with her Monte's gift, which she handed to Isidore. But her husband insisted that Kitty keep it for herself. According to Mimi, 'Because of this [generosity] I.S. went up in Father's estimation.'

Just before election day, Isidore and the other candidates gathered for a last public meeting. There was a Mr Clarke, who was also a member of the Municipal Party, and the two Progressive Party candidates: Mr Lambert, a barrister, and Mr Mundella, who was once a member of the London School Board. In front of a packed audience at the Caledonian Road Baths, they took it in turns to share their manifestos.

When it was his turn to speak, Isidore said he was pleased to see that his opponent's supporters were present – a statement that was greeted partially by applause and partially by jeers. He went on to say that he would ensure that the London County Council provided electricity to Islington, which was met with cheers; and then indignantly denied that he had ever opposed the tram system. From the audience, someone shouted, 'More extravagance!', which was met with laughter. The LCC, Isidore pushed on, had failed to invest adequately in public transport, refusing to raise funds through local taxation. 'A lie!' someone else shouted. Drawing the event to a close, Isidore encouraged all to vote that Saturday, stating emphatically that he was confident of victory.

Finally, after what seemed like a long campaign, election day arrived and, after the ballets were counted, Isidore learned that he had won easily. He was the first family member to enter public life. However, if he thought being in office would be easier than campaigning, he was wrong.

The week after the election, Isidore attended a meeting at Drovers Hall, an enormous brown-brick building overlooking the Metropolitan Cattle Market on Caledonian Road in Islington. Proceedings were soon interrupted by a young man who stood up, waving one of the

Progressive Party's scurrilous pamphlets, and with a German accent accused Isidore of poor work conditions. According to the *Islington Gazette*, when the man and his supporters refused to be silent, Harry Salmon told his 'stalwarts' to evict the troublemakers. They then roughly grabbed 'the pugnacious Teuton' by the coat and manhandled him outside. 'The loud-mouthed emissary of the Fatherland and his allies discovered to their surprise,' added the paper, 'that the Englishman has a summary way of dismissing an adventurer on mischief bent.'

Two weeks later, Harry found himself in the dock in Camberwell magistrates court. Isidore sat behind him in support. The *Gazette* summed up the situation as follows: the plaintiff was an 'alien' who had the 'impudence' to lecture 'English commercial men as to how they should conduct their business'. The magistrate appeared to agree. When questioning the plaintiff, the justice asked, if he was so unhappy with labour conditions in England, why didn't he return to his own country? When no reply was forthcoming, he dismissed the case.

The distinction of nationality had not gone unnoticed. Harry and Isidore Salmon – whose grandfather had been born in Rheinberg and spoke with a German accent throughout his life – had been given preference in a London court, as men of England.

As a newly elected politician, Isidore had to respond to key issues of the day. One of these was women's suffrage. In 1903, Emmeline Pankhurst had founded the Women's Social and Political Union, calling for women to be given the vote. Over the next five years there was hardly a day when the suffragette movement was not in the newspapers. Women disrupted political meetings up and down the country and this drew considerable press attention, partly because political meetings were typically attended only by men, but also because interrupting them was considered ill-mannered. Scores of suffragettes were arrested and incarcerated in Holloway Prison, attracting further coverage and public interest. The protestors next used physical objects, tying themselves to railings and throwing rocks at high-value targets, such as the windows of 10 Downing Street. In June 1908, more than half a million women and men attended a rally in Hyde Park in support of women's suffrage. At the time it was thought to be the largest demonstration ever held in the UK.

This was the context to a meeting Isidore attended on the afternoon of Tuesday, 3 November 1908. On the surface, it could not have been quainter. His job was to welcome everyone to the annual Universal Cookery and Food exhibition that was being held at the Royal Horticultural Hall in London. There were 200 visitors standing in the main foyer, all eager to explore the latest kitchen wares and appliances inside the hall. After a brief introduction from Isidore, it was the turn of Charles Wynn-Carington, a government minister and member of the Cabinet. Lord Carrington was a few sentences into his address when a female voice shouted, 'What about Mrs Pankhurst and the other women in Holloway?' Ignoring the heckler, Carrington raised his voice and ploughed on, 'I have no satisfaction ...' but was interrupted again. 'You'll have no satisfaction till women get the vote!' A policeman rushed over to the heckler, placed a hand over her mouth and half-pulled, half-carried her out of the hall. While he was waiting for the audience to settle down, Carrington quipped that sometimes 'too many cooks can spoil the broth', which evoked a roar of laughter.

He started again, but then another woman cried out, 'Why don't you give women who pay rates and taxes the vote?' The audience groaned in protest. Then another woman shouted, 'We will have votes!' A third yelled, 'Taxation without representation is tyranny!' Realising that it was no use continuing, Carrington sat down. As the women were being expelled, the event organiser declared, 'even if women might be in the right to demand the vote, they are going about it in the wrong way'. This comment was received with great applause.

Seeing an opportunity to wrap things up, Isidore quickly stood and, without reference to the protest, announced that any surplus monies generated by the exhibition would be donated to a charity that 'instructed the poor on the art of cooking'. Without further ado, the exhibition was opened. Isidore shook the minister's hand, the doors swung open and visitors streamed into the hall.

From his words, nobody in the room would have concluded that Isidore supported the protestors, or their calls for women's rights. Yet ever since managing the Lyons teashop on Queen Victoria Street, Isidore had valued women's labour and shown little tolerance for those who believed women to be inferior to men in any respect. 'The woman who has a living to earn has no time to be temperamental,' he once said. 'I do not think a woman goes off at the deep end any more than a man does.'

When it came to his own family, however, Isidore had a traditional view of the sexual division of labour. It was, he believed, his wife's, nieces' and female cousins' task to bring up the children, manage the domestic staff and host social events. None of the Salmon and Gluckstein women of Isidore's generation went out to work. Indeed, employment would have been considered not only unseemly, but a step backwards. For one of the chief aspirations of the family – at least for its male members – was that women would not have to take up paid employment. True, his mother Lena had played a crucial role in the early years of the cigar-making business, but that was before they had amassed wealth following the sale of the tobacco company. If challenged, Isidore would say that he valued not only the company of his female relatives, but also their counsel.

Outside the Royal Horticultural Hall, the ejected women were dusting themselves off and discussing what had just happened. Some of them would have bruises tomorrow, but they were pleased with what they had achieved and with the press attention that was sure to follow. They were surrounded by supporters, who clapped and cheered. One woman, it was later reported in the *Votes for Women* newsletter, congratulated the protestors and said they should be upbeat, because 'You will win in the end'.

Chapter 18

1909

By the end of the first decade of the twentieth century, three social phenomena were taking place simultaneously in England and Wales. For those of little means, life was getting harder. According to a report in *The Economist*, poverty in England and Wales was on the increase, with more than 800,000 paupers, out of a population of thirty-five million. At the same time, according to an inquiry by the Board of Trade, rents and wages were consistent across the country, the exception being London, where rents and wages were 'remarkably higher'. Rents in the capital were twice as high as those in Blackburn, for instance, and three times as high as Macclesfield. Thirdly, and perhaps most importantly for J. Lyons, the middle class was expanding fast, particularly in London, with large numbers of families finding they had a surplus at the end of each week and looking for new and interesting ways to spend it.

Isidore and his relatives discussed how to make the most of this trend. If the Trocadero was for the wealthy and aristocratic, and the teashops were for the working man and woman who fancied a properly brewed cup of tea and a well-baked cake (at an affordable price), what of the middle class? Their solution was a consumer complex that could seat more than 2,000 people at one time – a single building encompassing venues where customers could eat, shop and even purchase theatre tickets. As the *Globe* suggested, 'The idea seems to be to cater to that immense class who, although of modest pocket, like things served well.' The family called this new complex the 'Corner House'.

The Corner House would be neither a single teashop nor a restaurant. The company's objective was to provide an array of shops and eateries that could cater to different tastes at different times of the day. Particularly targeted were those who attended matinees or early-evening performances, as the building would be located in the heart of theatre-land. Critical to the roll-out was the physical branding. For the Corner House would be exactly that: a large four-storey building on the corner of Coventry Street and Rupert Street, just a few metres from Piccadilly Circus.

On New Year's Day, 1 January 1909, Lyons took out displays in all the major newspapers. The *Morning Post* was typical of many:

The 'Corner House' just erected by J Lyons. Another marvellous advance in popular catering. It is the most magnificent and comfortable light refreshment house in Europe. Light meals. Light charges. Bright music.

Before sunrise on 3 January, Isidore and the rest of the board arrived at the site. Waiting outside the bronze-framed doors of the Corner House stood a queue of inquisitive shoppers. By the time the staff were filing in, the line stretched around the block. Finally, at 9 a.m., the doors were opened and the public surged forward. They were welcomed by members of the Salmon and Gluckstein families, along with members of the senior staff.

Inside, the public found a large marble colonnade that led into a collection of shops: one sold chocolates, another cooked meats, a third exotic cheeses and fine wines. In addition there was a shoe-shine parlour, a hair salon and a telephone bureau. Up the white marble stairs, shoppers were presented with an assortment of restaurants, including a grill, a bar and a teashop.

Coventry Street Corner House

Soon the cafés and restaurants of the Corner House were full, and the family began discussing the purchase of the next-door building, so that the facilities could be doubled to more than 4,000 seats. Over the next few years Isidore and his cousins would roll out two more Corner Houses, one on Oxford Street (at the corner of Tottenham Court Road) and the other on the Strand (between Charing Cross station and Trafalgar Square). As with the Lyons teashops, the Corner Houses would become a national icon.

At the time of the original Corner House launch, Lyons was already managing more than 130 teashops. They were efficient, bureaucratic businesses, in which each transaction was carefully tracked and every receipt was forwarded to the clerks at the headquarters in Cadby Hall. The business produced all of its own cakes, tea and breads, delivering the fresh products by van to the growing archipelago of eateries. Given the strength of the brand, the obvious next step was to move into the production and selling of consumer products: starting with tea.

It had been Monte's idea, again. For some time customers had been able to buy loose tea at the Lyons teashops. The tea had been purchased at the London auction house, distributed under the 'Maharajah' label and then sold in small quantities over the counter. Monte's question was: why not sell packet tea to grocers across the nation, just as Salmon & Gluckstein had sold tobacco through tobacconist shops?

Monte called Isidore in for a meeting and, after discussing his idea, asked him to create a new tea department, from scratch. They would need to build a tea-blending and packaging plant at Cadby Hall. They would need to hire or train a team of expert tea-tasters. They would also need to recruit an army of salespeople. Above all, they would need a top manager to design, build and grow the new department. Isidore said that he happened to know just the right person – the man's name was George Pollard.

Five years earlier Isidore had sat across from Pollard during a difficult catering contract negotiation. Pollard was at the time running the Salvation Army's international congress at the Crystal Palace and had driven a hard bargain. Isidore had been impressed by his organising ability and negotiating skills. With Monte's approval, Isidore went off to persuade Pollard.

Monte's timing was, as usual, impeccable. A century earlier the consumer market for tea in Great Britain had been restricted to the most affluent parts of society. At that time, China had a monopoly over tea production and its authorities had severely limited its export. Then, in the 1830s, the East India Company – which had a virtual monopoly on trade with India – began cultivating tea production in Assam, Punjab, Bengal and parts of South India. Once the leaf tea arrived in London, Manchester, Dublin and Edinburgh, its cost was high and its quality variable. Given its value, there was a temptation for wholesalers to mix higher-grade product with those of lesser quality, or even to sell the leaf underweight, leading to complaints of mis-selling.

To counter these concerns, a number of suppliers had begun to package tea, distributing the leaf under their own brand names. Early labels included John Horniman, Brooke Bond, Thomas Lipton and Mazawattee. As production in India improved and other plantations began to be cultivated outside India – for instance, in Ceylon (now Sri Lanka) – prices fell, making tea affordable to the general public for the first time. As a result, between 1841 and 1909 the amount of tea consumed in the United Kingdom quadrupled from 1½ lbs (0.7 kilos) to 6 lbs (2.7 kilos) per person per year. Monte and Isidore saw no reason why this trend should not continue.

Now Isidore, as general manager, and Pollard, as his deputy, worked together to build the new tea department Vast quantities of tea were purchased at the London auction house, then transported to the new Lyons factory in Cadby Hall where it was unpacked, checked for quality, blended and packaged, ready to be sold. The first tea was known as 'White Label'. Later there would be a range of products: Orange Label, of moderate quality and the cheapest; Green Label, the best leaf and therefore the most expensive; and Red Label in between.

Launching a national product would not be easy. The market was already saturated, with more than twenty other companies competing for sales. At this time the vast majority of retailers were one-person operations that purchased their stock from a field of agents who travelled the country on foot, on bicycle and in horse-drawn carriage. These agents, in turn, acquired their products from the wholesalers. At each stage of this chain the relationships were personal, with loyalty long-earned. Any attempt to shift allegiances would require a significant incentive.

Guided by Monte, and making use of the lessons learned during the Tobacco Wars, Isidore now designed their strategy. The plan was threefold. First, he and Pollard recruited more than 200 seasoned salesmen (by offering wages above the going rate), who arrived with their own personal contacts, which gave them an instant network of more than 15,000 agents. Next, they instructed their salesmen to offer Lyons' White Label at a significantly reduced price, compared to their competitors. They hoped that the dual attraction of cost-cutting and brand recognition would persuade even the most hardened agent to take on their product. Finally, they told the salesman to inform the agents, and therefore the retailers, that they would back the product with a massive national marketing campaign, which would not only run today, but would continue for years to come.

The launch of White Label was a huge success. By 1910, Lyons was selling 3,500 chests per week, making it the third-biggest supplier of tea to the British public. And the company was true to its word. The marketing campaign continued month in, month out. One advertisement that ran at this time featured a packet of tea wearing pin-striped trousers and holding out a top hat, declaring:

Good morning, I am Lyons Tea. I won my way into public esteem on my intrinsic merits. My richness, purity and exquisite favour appeals to all tastes. I first came to notice by being sold at the modest price of 2d per cup. Today I am the only tea exclusively used in millions of homes and I am sold in nearly a million packets every day. I am the tea of the millionaire and the mill-worker, the peer and the peasant, the duchess and the dairymaid. I please everybody.

Given the success of their tea in the UK, Isidore now suggested that they export their products first to France, Germany and Scandinavia, then to countries across the British Empire. What had started as a side-business was set to become one of Lyons' major departments. This was soon followed by the next great enterprise: hotels.

Until the end of the nineteenth century travellers, businessmen and tourists had to choose between the basic but affordable accommodation offered by guest houses and the more expensive but often squalid hotels built near railway stations. In London, for instance, there were a handful of boutique hotels in Knightsbridge and Mayfair, upper-class establishments, but these were out of the price range of all but the wealthiest guest. Then, in the 1880s and 1890s, a new wave of large, well-appointed hotels was opened: the Royal Kensington Palace, the Carlton, the Savoy, the Hyde Park and Claridge's. Each of these proved popular, driven in part by their lower cost and superior quality, and in part by the recent improvements in transport links.

Given their management, catering and real-estate expertise, it seemed perhaps inevitable that J. Lyons could be successful hoteliers. Monte, however, was protective of the family's good name and so, after discussions with the Fund, he set up a new company called Strand Hotel Ltd. The directors included himself, Joe Lyons, his brother Izzy and his nephew Alfred Salmon. The concept, according to the prospectus they would release, was to build a hotel that was 'to be the last word in luxury' and was aimed at the traveller 'not born rich in America or made rich in South Africa'. Having secured a parcel of land on the Strand a short walk from Trafalgar Square, they set about construction.

Ten storeys high, the Strand Palace Hotel covered more than 18,000 square metres of floor space and boasted more than 470 rooms. Each suite had a sink with running hot and cold water, an unusual feature at this time, with adjoining private sitting rooms, if required. There was also a public dining room, a writing room, a billiard room and a winter garden, where high tea could be enjoyed surrounded by exotic plants and natural lighting.

Isidore was one of the family members who helped Monte with the launch of the hotel. At one meeting to discuss the redecoration of the Strand Palace, the architect, Oliver Bernard, produced some designs of which Isidore did not approve and he announced, 'It looks like a brothel, Bernard', to which Bernard answered, in the tone of one always ready to learn from someone else's experience, 'Does it, Isidore?'

Strand Palace Hotel

The Strand Palace Hotel opened on 14 September 1909 and was run by Julius Salmon, Isidore's youngest brother. The tariff was priced in the middle range. A single room, with an electric light, a bath, 'boots' (a person who cleaned shoes) and breakfast went for six shillings per night – half the cost of staying at the Savoy or Claridge's. As ever, Monte eschewed publicity, so the opening was led by Joe Lyons, who told the assembled press that the hotel had stopped taking reservations as they were already fully booked for the entire first month. By the year's end, the hotel had made more than £40,000 profit, which was impressive, given the surfeit of new hotels in London at this time. Buoyed by the success of the Strand Palace, Monte said they should build more hotels, starting with the Royal Palace next to Piccadilly Circus.

Some in the press were bemused by the Salmons and Glucksteins, their sudden rise, their accumulation of power and wealth. 'London went to sleep one night and awoke the next morning to find the philanthropic Salmon and the benevolent Gluckstein ready in almost every street,' wrote the *Bystander*. 'London dozed again and with the dawn the white and gold of Lyons' teashops could be seen north, east, south and west. In the development of the business there is something uncanny, something savouring of the magician's wand.'

Monte the magician, however, was nowhere to be seen. He had kept to his promise to remain in the shadows, leaving it to others to stand in the public gaze. So it was that, on 22 February 1911, it was Joe Lyons, and not Monte Gluckstein, who received a knighthood from the King. According to the notice published in the *Gazette*, this honour was in acknowledgement of his public services. Given that Joe Lyons was not the powerhouse behind the catering company, this was surprising to many. If anyone was to receive recognition, should it not be one of the Salmons or Glucksteins? It was soon widely rumoured that, like so many others in royal circles, Joe had purchased his honour.

A few days after receiving the news from the palace, Joe asked Monte whether he would like his own knighthood, saying that he could arrange it. Still smarting from the Olympia court case, Monte was horrified by the suggestion. He told Joe that 'the next generation would be more suited to carry this honour'. Later, he confided to his daughter Mimi, 'We don't need titles as our honour is established', adding that 'too many Jews with titles might lead to jealousy'.

Being Jewish, what that stood for – its religious rituals and its philosophy – was at this time very much on Monte's mind. He strongly believed that the practice of his faith was in need of radical modernisation. The problem was that the rest of the family did not share his opinion.

Chapter 19

1911

Monte considered the family synagogue in Bayswater to be old-fashioned. Its practices were based on antiquated customs that had been brought out of Germany and Russia. He thought it hypocritical, for instance, that up and down the country his family's teashops and restaurants sold bacon and eggs for breakfast, ham sandwiches for lunch and pork chops for dinner, yet in their own dining rooms they were adamant about keeping kosher.

He had read in the Jewish papers about communities in Europe who were experimenting with their rituals. In northern Germany there were congregations who were conducting services in their native language, as opposed to Hebrew, while others incorporated choral music, a practice shunned by traditionalists. Frustratingly for Monte, the only liturgy available to the Jews of London, was that of the Orthodox and Reform synagogue, which had not changed, it seemed, for decades.

Monte started attending a group committed to modernising Jewish worship in Britain. Led by the charismatic Lily Montagu, daughter of the Member of Parliament Samuel Montagu, with whom the family had worked during the Whitechapel murders, this group was attempting to drag Judaism into the twentieth century. Services should be held on Saturday afternoons and Sunday mornings, they said, so that the working man or woman could participate. They should be shorter, to allow busy families to be included; and, perhaps most controversially, men and women should sit together.

Lily Montagu

By early 1911, Lily Montagu, Monte Gluckstein and the other members of the group believed there was sufficient support to set up their own synagogue. They secured the lease to an old chapel in St John's Wood, in north-west London, which had previously served the Mount Zion Baptist community, cleaned it up, and then told the press that a new congregation would soon be opened. It was to be called the Liberal Jewish Synagogue (LJS).

Early in the afternoon of Saturday, 17 June 1911, a shiny black landau pulled up outside the new synagogue. Out of the carriage climbed Monte, Tilly and their three children. Having waved goodbye to the driver, they walked up the short flight of steps and into the newly consecrated synagogue. Inside the sanctuary they found rows of wooden benches, which could seat up to 230 people. Another 200 could sit in the gallery above. They were now faced with a revolutionary decision. In the past, Mimi and her mother would sit in the women's gallery. But not today. The family chose a bench and sat together.

At the rear of the sanctuary stood a large mahogany Ark draped with a thin curtain. On a table on either side of the Ark sat a seven-stemmed candelabrum, each stem filled with candles burning brightly. Between the Ark and the seats was a *bimah*, or raised platform, where Rabbi Israel Mattuck – recently arrived from New Jersey – was now conducting the service. The congregation recited prayers in English, sometimes out loud, sometimes in silence, occasionally disturbed by the sound of shunting engines, for the building backed onto a railway goods yard. Then the rabbi delivered a sermon. According to a reviewer from the *Jewish Chronicle*, his voice 'filled the building and held the congregation spellbound'. Monte enjoyed the rabbi's passion and the modernity of the service. He was pleased that he had supported the creation of the new synagogue.

In this, as far the family went, he was alone. When he tried to persuade his relatives to join the synagogue, his cousins, nephews and nieces resisted vehemently. By moving to the new synagogue, Monte's relatives now asked, wasn't he – the very person who had been so unyielding about family unity – splitting the family up? Weddings in one synagogue, *bar mitzvahs* in another. And what about when it came to burying the dead? Surely the new synagogue would have its own cemetery, away from the family plot in Willesden. This would break the rule that Monte had always argued for: family comes first.

Amongst those most upset was Isidore. The new congregation's rituals were just too strange. Speaking in English, sitting with the wives, Sunday services – he didn't care for it. Not only was he a firm believer in the orthodox rituals, but he was also a member of the Bayswater Synagogue's council. Voices were raised. Feelings were hurt. For the first time in a generation, the family was faced with real discord.

The Salmons and Glucksteins were not alone in this schism. Other families were also struggling with the formation of the new synagogue. Parents forbade their children to attend the Liberal Jewish Synagogue. The elders of the orthodox community ruled that no rabbi or Jewish official could attend Liberal meetings. Supporters of the Liberal project were forced to resign from their existing posts with other communities, such as the Bayswater Synagogue, and were accused of being 'traitors' and 'heretics'. Lily Montagu's father, Samuel, was so outraged by her role in the new synagogue that he refused to speak to her ever again. 'Family squabbles were not infrequent,' she later wrote with understatement, 'and they were fraught with genuine pain.'

In late 1913, Monte was invited to join the new synagogue's founding council. This was perhaps unsurprising, given that he ran one of the largest companies in the Empire, bringing with him reputation, contacts and management skills. By the end of the year, 120 members belonged to the Liberal synagogue. The following spring, there were sixty more. Anxious that they would soon run out of seats, Monte was asked to chair the congregation's first building committee, whose task was to find new premises. Deploying the skills he had learned during the early days of J. Lyons, he now set about scouting locations in north-west London.

Meanwhile he worked with the council to find a technical solution to the funeral problem. At the next family meeting, Monte explained that the Liberal synagogue had acquired a burial ground in Willesden, adjacent to the orthodox cemetery that the family had been using for more than thirty years. This meant that, in death, the relatives could now remain united. And although there would be a brick wall between the two cemeteries, a gate would be installed to allow easy passage. In effect, Monte argued, they would all be together, and it would be easy for visitors to pay their respects to those buried in both the 'old' and 'new' cemeteries. This was enough for most of the family. Alfred Salmon now joined the Liberal Jewish Synagogue along with his son Barney, as did Monte's brother Joseph, his wife and their two children, Louis and Gluck. Monte's other brother, Izzy, also joined his family, but said that when the time came, he wanted to be buried in the orthodox cemetery in Willesden.

The choice was more complicated for Monte's other nephew, Isidore. As a member of the synagogue council, Isidore still felt a commitment to the Bayswater congregation. Moreover, he was accustomed to, and liked, its orthodox service. Yet he hated the idea of splitting up the family, and especially of creating any disunity with his uncle Monte. He wasn't sure what to do: for himself and Kitty and, more importantly, for his two sons, Sam and Julian.

Whereas Isidore Salmon had grown up in a small flat above a tobacconist shop on the Edgware Road, and had left school at eleven to work in the family's cigar workshop, his children's childhoods were coloured by luxury. Sam and his younger brother, Julian, enjoyed long holidays in France and Switzerland, lavish birthday parties and a constant round of visits for breakfast, lunch, tea and dinner at the family's many teashops and restaurants. They were waited on by maids, their food was prepared by a full-time cook and they were driven to school and back by a chauffeur. The boys saw little of their father, given Isidore's busy workload at Lyons and the LCC; or of their mother, who was similarly occupied by charitable engagements;

but they were surrounded by family members offering attention and affection, and there were more than enough events to fill their social calendar.

Sam attended Colet Court school in Hammersmith, where the headmaster was pleased with his efforts, describing him as an 'industrious boy' and saying that he had 'come on well in all subjects'. He was a happy, sociable child, who was neither nervous nor shy. The headmaster was, however, worried about the limiting impact of the boy's worsening eyesight, adding the caveat that Sam's achievements were accomplished 'in spite of his drawbacks'. Given the principal's concerns, Kitty took Sam to see an optometrist in London. Having concluded the examination, the doctor said that the boy was likely to experience a total loss of vision by the time he reached seventeen years old. There was nothing that could be done, and he advised the family to prepare for Sam's transition towards blindness.

Over the next few days and weeks, Kitty tried to find a boarding school that worked with poorly sighted children. Eventually she found a school in Hampshire that was based on a farm. Students fed the animals, worked in the fields and made pottery – all touch-based activities. She liked the sound of that. They also said that their poorly sighted pupils wrote on green paper, which was easier to read than white paper; and, if necessary, they taught the use of Braille.

When Sam heard about the new school he was excited. He was thrilled by the idea of living in the country and, while he would miss his family, he was looking forward to the new adventure. Now that he had turned thirteen, however, and before he went to the new school, he had to perform his *bar mitzvah*. The question was: where?

Ever since Monte had moved to the Liberal Jewish Synagogue, Isidore had been wrestling with which congregation to belong to. The matter was still bubbling away when, on 11 October 1913, he attended the orthodox Bayswater Synagogue for the morning service of Yom Kippur, the Day of Atonement. For the first time in his life he was not sitting next to his uncles, Monte, Izzy and Joseph, during this most holy of days. As he sat reading the ancient prayers, his stomach rumbling from lack of food, he thought about his predicament. To join the new Liberal synagogue felt like a betrayal to his ancestors. The rituals had remained the same for thousands of years; they had been performed by great-grandfather Lehmann in Germany and by grandfather Samuel in London. Why the need to change? Yet to remain at Bayswater meant a break with his uncles. It felt like an impossible choice. Isidore decided to postpone the decision.

Two weeks later the issue came to a head over dinner at 30 Holland Villas Road. It was just the four family members, Isidore, Kitty, Sam and Julian. They were in the formal dining room, white linen tablecloth covering the long oak table, their plates filled with rich food, two candles lit, a maid waiting in the next-door room, alert for the call for service, and they were discussing the arrangements for Sam's *bar mitzvah*. Who should be invited? Where should they hold the reception? What presents would he like?

They looked at Sam. He was silent for a moment, and then he said that he didn't actually want a *bar mitzvah*. This came as quite a shock. Every male member of the Salmon and Gluckstein families had up to this point taken part in a *bar mitzvah*. Sam's cousin, Louis Gluckstein, had completed his just two years before. When asked to explain himself, Sam said, rather forcibly, that he didn't care for the fuddy-duddy ways of the Bayswater Synagogue and wanted to join uncle Monte's more modern congregation instead. He wasn't even sure if he believed in God (after all, if the Almighty was so powerful, why would he let bad things happen, like grandmother Lena losing six children?) and he didn't see why, if you had a nice carriage like Father's, you couldn't use it to drive to synagogue on *Shabbat* (which was forbidden by orthodox Jews). Most importantly, how was it right that he was expected to take part in a service held in Hebrew

– a language that almost nobody, and certainly not him, could understand? The Liberal synagogue didn't offer *bar mitzvahs*, he said; instead he could take part in a 'confirmation' at the age of sixteen, in English.

Riled by his son's impertinence, Isidore said that the reason the boys and girls of the Liberal Jewish Synagogue were made to wait until sixteen was because the founders of the new synagogue – rather patronisingly, he thought – did not believe teenagers were mature enough to make a choice about their religion until that age. Sam shot back that if his father believed a thirteen-year-old was old enough to make a contract with God, then surely he was old enough to choose which congregation he should belong to. This last comment was met with anger. Sam would remain at Bayswater, because the family would remain at Bayswater, and he *would* take part in a *bar mitzvah*. If the issue was one of linguistic understanding, Isidore added, then Hebrew lessons would be arranged. The conversation was over, the decision made. Sam bowed to his father's will.

A few months later, on a warm Saturday spring morning, Sam was getting dressed in his room. A starched white shirt, a tie and a new dark suit had been laid out for him, along with a pair of black socks and gleaming patent-leather shoes. He brushed his short-cropped brown hair and checked himself in the mirror. His large nose and thick-glassed spectacles did not make him the most handsome of boys. Any physical deficiencies, though, were more than made up for by his superior suit. His parents had paid for Sam to be tailored at the very best of outfitters.

A few minutes later, Sam, his parents and brother walked out of the front door and set off on foot to the Bayswater Synagogue. Thirty minutes later they arrived at the entrance, where they were greeted by relatives. Uncle Monte and aunty Tilly were there, as were Sam's cousins Barney, Louis and Gluck, along with a horde of other uncles and aunts, second cousins and third cousins. Inside the hall, Sam wrapped his shoulders in his *tallis*, a blue-and-white prayer shawl, and covered his head with a *kippah*. Then it was time. His father proudly stood to let him by and, with a deep breath, Sam walked up to the stage and began to sing, in Hebrew.

In the eyes of his family, Sam was now a man. Yet he understood that he was not in control of his life. One day he would be able to make his own decisions, he told himself, away from the shadow of his father. For now, he was looking forward to getting away and starting at his new boarding school.

Chapter 20

1914

On the eve of the Great War, the British Empire was by far the largest, most powerful, most productive force on the planet. Stretching across five continents and covering a quarter of the Earth's land mass, including Canada, Australia and large swathes of south-east Asia and Africa, the Empire contained more than a quarter of the world's population, with more than 425 million people.

Such power had resulted in tremendous wealth flowing from the colonies and dominions into Britain: cotton, tea and jute from India, gold and diamonds from South Africa, coffee from the plantations of East Africa, sugar from the Caribbean. Goods went the other way as well. By 1914, 60 per cent of all Indian imports came from Britain. Meanwhile London was the centre of world financing, with 50 per cent of global capital investment raised in the city. Whilst much of this prosperity was captured by the top 1 per cent of the population, much also rolled down to the other classes. In consequence, the British standard of living had risen sharply between 1870 and 1914. The wages of craftsmen and their helpers, for instance, doubled during this period, whilst the cost of living increased by only 28 per cent. With wealth came education. In 1850s Britain, 50 per cent of women and 30 per cent of men were illiterate, but by 1914 this was close to zero for both genders. For the vast majority of those living in Britain, therefore, the Empire was both a source of pride and of much gratitude.

By the second decade of the twentieth century, however, it was clear that Britain's hegemony was increasingly being challenged by its European rivals. Germany in particular was outpacing Britain in terms of economic and military strength. Whereas Britain's GDP had been 40 per cent larger than Germany's in 1870, it was now 6 per cent smaller. Similarly, between 1880 and 1914 Britain's share of global industrial production fell to 14 per cent whilst Germany's rose from 8 to 23 per cent. Remarkably, the German army was now far larger than Britain's, with 4.5 million well-armed men, compared to a little over 700,000 British soldiers.

As the spring of 1914 turned to summer, there was increasing talk of war in the British newspapers. Germany was arming at a prodigious rate. The Austro-Hungarian Empire was threatening Serbia, and Russia was publicly declaring its support for Serbia. France and Britain, meanwhile, announced that their armies were ready for any threat that came their way.

Then, on 28 June 1914, the Austrian Archduke Franz Ferdinand and his wife were assassinated by a Serbian nationalist. In the following days the press was full of editorials predicting imminent armed conflict. When, on 2 August, Germany threatened to invade Belgium, it triggered a treaty that forced Britain to come to Belgium's aid. Once Germany ignored Prime Minister Herbert Asquith's demand that they withdraw their forces, conflict was inevitable. In its editorial, *The Times* said, 'This day will be momentous in the history of our time', adding that 'We have one duty before us. We must strike with the full force of the Empire for the small nation that has asked for our protection ... we must suffer much, but we shall know how to suffer for the great name of England and for all her high ideals, as our fathers did before us.'

On the morning of 5 August 1914, Isidore Salmon walked down the stairs at 30 Holland Villas Road, across the oak-floored hallway and entered the dining room, where breakfast had been laid out, along-side a carefully ironed copy of *The Times*. He picked it up. The news, though distressing, did not surprise him: Britain had declared war on Germany. This pronouncement impacted not only on the residents of London, Manchester, Edinburgh and Cardiff; it also changed the lives of all the Empire's citizens. In addition to those living in the British Isles, 50 million Africans and 250 million Indians were also now at war with Germany.

Later that day, members of the Fund met to discuss the news. The government had declared that all men between the ages of nineteen and thirty who were physically fit would be encouraged to enlist. Those with previous military experience up to the age of forty-two would also be accepted. This would of course have a dramatic impact on the Lyons workforce. The solution was agreed: they would have to rely on older workers as best they could, and recruit others to take up the slack, and these would most likely be women.

The outbreak of war would also affect the family. At thirty-eight years old, Isidore was too old to serve with the armed forces. Indeed, he had already received a letter from the War Office conscripting him to work at the Department of the Food Controller, where he would help to coordinate the army's supplies. He would have the rank of captain. This would be a part-time position, allowing him to continue his duties at Lyons. At fourteen and eleven years of age respectively, Sam and Julian were too young to enlist and would remain at school.

There were many in the family, though, who were of fighting age. Amongst them were Alfred's son Barney, Monte's sons S.M.G. and Dore, as well as Joseph's son, Louis. Having said goodbye to their parents and siblings, each of these young men set off for army training camp.

Sixty-year-old Monte Gluckstein, meanwhile, offered his company's services to the government. He also helped personally in quieter ways. As soon as war was declared, Belgian refugees began arriving in London. In response to a call for help, Tilly invited a family to come and live with them in Addison Gardens. She provided them with fresh clothes and food and helped the children to enrol with local schools. Monte's compassion was not, however, without its limits.

On one occasion, with his daughter Mimi standing next to him, Monte welcomed a newly arrived Belgian husband, his wife and their children to his house. There in the hallway the group found themselves facing a pretty picture of a semi-naked woman beneath a tree. The husband's first words were, 'That picture must go, I do not want my daughters to live with it.' When Monte asked if it made him uncomfortable, the refugee made no comment. Three days later the Belgian family was moved to another home.

The onset of war brought about a wave of anti-German sentiment in Britain. Employees with roots in Germany and Austria were sacked from their jobs. German shops were attacked and looted. The newspapers ran stories about people being accused of spying for Germany. The name for the German Shepherd dog was even changed to 'Alsatian'. This fear soon spread to the food and drink industries.

On 21 August 1914, seventeen days after Britain declared war on Germany, J.S. Smith, the head of Lipton's tea department at City Road in London, sent out a letter to his 100-plus tea agents. In his letter, Smith encouraged the agents not to purchase J. Lyons tea because the family was made up of 'German Jews'.

Before he put the letter in the mail, Smith asked his clerk if he thought any of the Lyons directors were actually German. When his junior replied that he did not know, Smith said, 'It is alright, I know they are.' Over the next few days, each of the agents sent receipts that they had received Smith's letter. One of the Lipton agents wrote back to Smith requesting posters that he could give to shops, stating that the family who owned Lyons were German Jews. Another salesman approached a shop owner in south Wales and told him, 'Why throw up Lipton to deal with the Germans?'

When they heard from retailers about Lipton's underhand tactics, Isidore and Monte were furious. They hired a private detective to find out what had happened and offered a £1,000 reward for information. A few days later, two of Lipton's employees came forward and told them about J.S. Smith and his letter to the agents. Monte and Isidore decided to sue.

Within the week they had secured an interim injunction from a judge restraining Lipton Limited, its agents and servants from speaking or publishing anything to suggest that J. Lyons & Company, or its directors, was composed of Germans, or that by purchasing their commodities the public was assisting the enemies of Great Britain. Lyons then took out an advertisement in *The Times*, which announced the details of the injunction and stated:

J. LYONS & CO
(by appointment to his Majesty the King)
is an ALL-BRITISH COMPANY
with ALL BRITISH DIRECTORS
has 14,000 ALL BRITISH SHAREHOLDERS
and 160,000 ALL BRITISH SHOPKEEPERS
selling LYONS TEA

Several months later the case was heard before Mr Justice Darling of the High Court. When the judge asked if any settlement had been agreed, the lawyer representing Lipton's said that indeed it had. The libellous statements that had been uttered by their employees were utterly untrue and unjustifiable, he said, but they had been made without the knowledge of the directors. His client, Thomas Lipton, was willing to offer an unqualified apology, along with payment to cover any costs (amounting to £15,000). The judge then turned to the barrister representing J. Lyons, who confirmed that he had a letter from the board saying that the offer was acceptable.

With the matter apparently solved, Justice Darling joked, 'They are all friends now?' To which the lawyer for Lyons replied, 'Universal friendship now prevails.' When the judge responded, 'Perhaps they might have a tea party at which they could mutually consume each other's commodities', the court erupted in laughter.

What the Lyons lawyer did not say was that the board's acceptance had not been unanimous. Indeed, while a draft of the acceptance letter included the line 'with the full assent of my colleagues', by the time it was sent out, these words had been removed. For Isidore had been outraged by the anti-Semitic and xenophobic comments circulated by Lipton Limited. It was both a professional and a personal affront. After all, the company's owner, Thomas Lipton, and his wife had attended his and Kitty's wedding. Yet with Monte's encouragement, Isidore had allowed the letter to be written. This was not the time to place personal interests ahead of the business, let alone ahead of one's country.

The war was already having a significant impact on the tea business. Before that summer, Lyons had handled 10 per cent of all the tea imported into the country for home consumption. Now, with a large part of his workforce enlisting, Isidore was struggling to fulfil the weekly orders. In Leeds, for instance, of the eight salesmen who had previously managed the area's agents, only two remained. The rest were now fighting in France. This allowed other tea companies, such as Brooke Bond, to muscle in on the Lyons territories. To make matters worse, the government imposed a series of controls on the manufacture of tea. Tea was now deemed to be a luxury item and was added to the list of restricted foods, reducing supply and increasing costs. When consumers complained that tea was becoming unaffordable, the Food Controller declared that tea must be sold at a fixed price, reducing the profit margin still further. For the first time in its history, Lyons was faced with over-capacity: workers and machines standing idle, horses and carts remaining in their sheds, agents being courted by the opposition. All of this posed a real threat to the business.

During an emergency board meeting it was agreed that rather than make a large number of people unemployed, which would have damaged both the bottom line and morale, the best solution was immediate growth. To deliver this, Isidore proposed that Lyons take over two of the country's most well-established tea companies: Horniman's, which had a strong presence in Lancashire, and Black & Green, which dominated the Manchester market. By taking such steps, the board hoped the tea business would survive the war.

Chapter 21

1915

On 17 January 1915, fourteen-year-old Sam Salmon took a train from Waterloo to Petersfield, arriving at the station there at 5.23 p.m. He was picked up and driven up Bell Hill, along Church Road and into a yard that looked more like a farm than a school. He was starting at Bedales boarding school.

Established in 1893 by John Badley, a lifelong socialist, with the support of his suffragist wife Laura, Bedales was far more progressive than the more established schools of Eton, Winchester and Rugby. It was also England's first co-educational boarding school, with an equal number of girls and boys, and was one of the few to accept Jewish pupils. Sam was not the only scion of a well-known family to attend Bedales, for his contemporaries included Josiah and Camilla Wedgwood, of the pottery family; Eileen Rutherford, the daughter of the 'father of physics', Ernest Rutherford; and Alister and John MacDonald, sons of the leader of the Labour Party, Ramsay MacDonald.

To chronicle his time at the school, Sam started a diary, a small black-cased leather book, with pockets at either end to insert additional items. He began with the basics: 'Size of gloves 7.5. Collar

14. Size of boots 8. Weight 7 stone 13.5 pounds. Height 5 feet 1.75 inches.'

Many of Sam's diary entries related to indoor activities. There were frequent mentions of 'Hebrew lessons' – his father had made good on his threat – along with 'ordinary work', 'elocution', 'letter from father', 'listened to Casey's gramophone' and 'prayers'. But he also described spending considerable time outdoors. He gathered apples in the orchard with his classmates and later pressed them into cider. He spent some afternoons 'levelling' the playing field next to the sheep pen with a pickaxe and shovel, and others riding a horse along the steep wooded bridleways surrounding Bedales. His greatest joy, however, was taking a swim in the school pond.

Early each morning he snuck out of the 'boys flat' and hurried over to the pond next to the headmaster's house. When he arrived, the dew was often still on the grass, the mist hanging over the water's surface, the ducks just out for the day's first venture through the bulrushes and wild irises. No matter the weather or the time of year, he jumped in. Away from his parents and the wider family, whom he loved but found overbearing, Sam relished the calm of the pond and its quiet, cool waters. Most of all he liked being alone, free to do as he pleased.

In February 1915, Sam returned to his parents' house in London for half-term. There he played tennis, had tea at the Trocadero, saw David Copperfield at the theatre ('which was very good') and played cards with his aunt Mimi. But his time in the capital was not all pleasant.

While Sam was in London, Lyons was caught up in a scandal that was widely covered by the papers. As part of their efforts to help the war effort, J. Lyons supplied beef to the Imperial Kitchens in White City, which fed more than 10,000 Indian troops. The contract was managed by Henry Apfel, who was married to one of Sam's cousins. A few days before Sam's arrival, a soldier based in White City had noticed that some of the meat was discoloured and emitted a bad smell. He referred the matter to the police, who then seized the delivery, and J. Lyons was charged with gross negligence.

At the ensuing hearing, the defence and prosecution barristers made their arguments to the court. Once they had rested their cases, the magistrate turned to Henry Apfel. 'Are you German?' he asked. Henry said he was not, and that he, his father and his wife were all born in England. The magistrate pressed him further. 'Are you registered as an alien?' Henry again assured the court that he was not. Still unpersuaded, the magistrate turned to his judgment. He declared that J. Lyons should have ensured that bad food was not served 'to the gallant soldiers who had abandoned their homes and those most dear to them in order to uphold the honour and safety of their country', and he fined the company for 'gross negligence'. All of this was widely reported, under provocative headlines such as 'ARMY MEAT SCANDAL' and 'MEAT FOR TROOPS. CONVICTION OF MESSRS. LYONS AND COMPANY'. Once again the family was accused of profiteering, and their loyalty and patriotism were questioned. All of which was especially sensitive during wartime.

When he asked his father about the scandal, Sam was told that J. Lyons had done nothing wrong. The meat was fine, Isidore said; their competitors were using the war to gain commercial advantage. Although they had lost that contract, they had many others. They would, therefore, be providing additional staff training and putting up educational notices to ensure quality and safety. Appearances mattered, he said. One had to be seen doing the right thing.

The war was never far away from Sam's life. In an entry on 28 February 1915, he wrote: 'Hear that Wilson died. Address by Mr Williams on "service".' Robert Wilson was a former pupil who had graduated from Bedales just months earlier. He had wanted to become an architect, but had instead joined an army medical training camp and, just weeks before being deployed, had contracted meningitis and died. He was the first war-related fatality known to Sam. Then, on 7 May, there was another entry, equally brief. 'Had a glorious bathe at lunch time. The Lusitania was torpedoed.' The *Lusitania* passenger ship had been sunk by a German submarine off the coast of Ireland, with the loss of 1,198 lives, including 128 Americans.

Although he was fiercely patriotic, Sam was well aware of his German roots. He was therefore greatly alarmed when, in the days following the sinking of the *Lusitania*, he learned that anti-German riots had erupted across Britain. In Liverpool alone, 200 German-owned premises were smashed. In Birkenhead, a crowd of more than 2,000 roamed the streets, invading German family homes and setting fire to their furniture. The army was called out in Southend, but was unable to stop the rioting. Meanwhile in London more than 150 shops were wrecked. The rioting was particularly serious in east London, according to *The Times*, and a 'considerable number of people, including several constables, were injured'.

Not content with smashing windows and doors, thousands of rioters marched from shop to shop and house to house, hacking staircases apart and tearing down walls and ceilings. Even the homes and businesses of naturalised Germans were attacked. One of those wrecked belonged to a tobacconist; another was a baker who had run his shop for thirty-two years. In Cardiff a notice was issued declaring that Germans and Austrians, even if naturalised British citizens, were banned from using the Corn Exchange. The popular *Daily Sketch*, which claimed a readership of more than a million, devoted four pages to the disturbances, filled mostly with pictures of jubilant rioters. 'In the City and in working class districts there is but one opinion expressed,' the paper said. 'We will not have any Germans in England unless they are under lock and key.'

Anti-German protest, *Daily Sketch*

Two days after the riots, Prime Minister Herbert Asquith announced that all German men of fighting age would be interned, unless naturalised, with the result that more than 30,000 people were rounded up and put in camps. Sam felt thankful that his father and grandfather had been born in England.

Two weeks later, on 29 May 1915, Sam reported happier news in his diary. That afternoon, while the boys and girls of Bedales were playing outside during a break, Royal Flying Corps pilot Harry King Goode had landed his biplane on the football field. His official reason was 'engine trouble threatening', but everyone knew that the Old Bedalian just wanted to show off his aircraft to his former school chums. In his diary, Sam wrote simply that an 'aeroplane came to see us. Took a photo.'

After tea at the school – the plane was left in the charge of a constable, to make sure the machine was not tampered with – Goode made ready to leave. The headmaster, John Badley, described his departure:

> Then it was time to go and after the trial of the engine it was started, at first slowly, like a great wounded moth fluttering along the ground, then moving faster and faster, until, not far from the furthest fence it rose gracefully, and after circling overhead with hand-waving in acknowledgment of our cheers shot away towards Butser [Hill] and was soon out of sight.

Keen to avoid a 'militaristic spirit' in the school, and hopeful that the war would soon be over, the headmaster had resisted starting a

Plane lands at Bedales school, 1915

training corps for the students. Now, with the end to the conflict no closer, he decided it was necessary 'to give them as much as possible of the requisite training', given that many of the boys would soon see active service. The following term, accordingly, forty boys began military exercises three afternoons a week.

Sam was amongst those who took part in drilling practice, though he was a terrible shot. One diary entry read: 'shooting, shot very badly'. Given his appalling eyesight, he was told that enlistment was impossible, which greatly disappointed him. Nevertheless he continued to turn up for the drills, keen to show his solidarity with the boys who would be called up.

Sam dreaded morning assembly when John Badley read out the list of those who had recently died. About once a week Sam learned about the death of another young man. Given the school's small size, he knew many of these former pupils, who were often only one, two or three years ahead of him and had only recently graduated. Though deeply shaken by the many deaths, Sam believed that he must keep control of his emotions. He never cried. Nevertheless, the news had a profound effect. Wishing that he could have been on the field of battle with his friends, he experienced a survivor's guilt. He was, after all, an enthusiastic supporter of the British Empire and believed that the war was morally justified. Most of all, the young men's deaths reinforced his commitment to duty. For without a belief in playing one's part for the greater good, it was hard to justify the sacrifice of all these young men. From this point on, disloyalty to the Crown and a failure to do one's duty became anathema to Sam.

In the spring of 1915, Sam received a wedding invitation at school: his aunt Mimi was getting married to his uncle Julius Salmon. Sam was eager to attend. On Tuesday, 1 June, he was given leave to take the day off school for the special family occasion. 'Went up to town by 9.37,' he reported in his diary. 'Miss Band met me went to get some gloves.' After lunch at home, he walked with his parents and brother to the Liberal Jewish Synagogue in St John's Wood, where the wedding was being conducted. Following the service, a modest reception was held at Monte and Tilly's house in Kensington. It had been agreed that, given the fighting, a large society event would be tasteless. Sam now took the chance to catch up with his relatives and find out the latest war news.

He heard about Monte's son Dore, who, after taking part in the Officers' Training Corps, had joined the 10th Battalion, London Regiment and expected to be posted to France sometime soon. Meanwhile Monte's eldest son, S.M.G., had returned from the trenches, having suffered acute intestinal pain, and was recovering from stomach surgery. Alfred's son Barney was serving with the 17th Battalion, London Regiment in Palestine and had been promoted to captain. As for Louis Gluckstein, Joseph's son, he had completed a stint working behind a desk for the Intelligence Corps and, to his great delight, was now transporting cipher books from London to Padua by boat and train.

As for the war itself, the news sounded horrendous on all fronts. German airships were dropping bombs on Paris. There were reports of liquid fire being deployed against the British and French troops and, shockingly, of chemicals being used at Verdun. The war had now spread beyond Europe, to Egypt, Greece, southern Africa, Russia and further, with appalling casualties. Reports were also coming in of a terrible massacre of Armenians by Ottoman government forces.

The following morning, Sam caught the train back to school, frustrated that, unlike his cousins and because of his poor sight, even when he came of age, he would be unable to fight for King and country.

Ten days after Mimi and Julius' wedding, on 12 June 1915, J. Lyons held its first ever wartime shareholders' meeting. As always, the assembly was held in the ballroom of the Trocadero on Shaftesbury

Avenue in central London. At the front, sitting behind a long table covered in a white cloth, were Monte Gluckstein, Isidore and Alfred Salmon. Also present was Joe Lyons, who when he stood appeared old and frail. He had been ill for some time and had taken little interest in the firm's day-to-day business. His speech, as ever, had been written for him by Monte and carefully reviewed by the other board members. It would be printed in full in *The Times, The Economist* and other outlets, and therefore had to be just right.

At the previous year's meeting, Joe had presented the outlook as having 'no cloud on the horizon'. Now things looked very different, he said, given the 'tremendous struggle which our country and Allies entered in August last'. Despite this, he was pleased to announce that the company's profit had reduced by only £54,000. This, though, barely reflected the difficulties the company faced. 'Large numbers of our staff who had become experts in their respective departments after years of training have joined His Majesty's forces, and their places have been filled by those who with even the best will in the world are less efficient labour.' By 'those', Joe meant women.

Since the declaration of war, 1,300 Lyons men had been deployed to France, Belgium and the Middle East. And although the teashops were staffed by women, the majority of those who had been working for Lyons before the war – in the factories, driving the vans and in the administration offices – were men. To cope with the labour shortfall, the company had taken on thousands of women. Now it was women who lifted the heavy sacks into the massive coffee-grinders, pushed the carts from the flour store to the bakery, loaded the crates of cakes, bread and tea into the vans, which were also driven by women.

Meanwhile, Joe said, the managers at J. Lyons & Company had kept in touch with the dependants of enlisted men, topping up the government allowance, ensuring they were in as good a position financially as they had been before leaving, and guaranteeing that their jobs would

Women producing coffee, Lyons factory, WWI

be open upon their return. They were also sending the men 'small comforts', such as cigarettes, cocoa and chocolate. Labour shortages, Joe continued, were not the only problem that the company faced. The price of sugar had risen by 88 per cent, flour by 71 per cent and butter by 24 per cent. While one option would be to pass these additional costs on to their customers, the board had agreed this would be improper. Their customers had difficulty as it was in making ends meet.

Joe then moved on to a subject that many in the audience wished to hear about, the so-called 'White City meat scandal'. Using words carefully chosen and scripted by Monte, the Lyons chairman declared 'I am not in a position to say more about it than what occurred was in the nature of a pure accident, which might happen at any of our homes. I could say a great deal more, but will not.'

That didn't stop him from adding, 'Success always makes enemies and the personal element has an unhappy faculty of intruding itself in these matters.' After twenty-one years of being in business, he said, the company's reputation would continue to withstand the 'evil breath of calumny'.

Joe sat down and Monte then took his place at the front of the room. He had worked at the company since its inception twenty-one years earlier, he said, and, because of the war, the work was 'if possible, more strenuous than it had ever been before'. He added that he was afraid there were 'anxious times' before them as long as the war lasted but, whether the times were good or bad 'the best service of my colleagues and myself will be given to the company'.

His comments met with loud applause. The shareholders remained confident in J. Lyons and in the men who ran it. But if Monte and his relatives believed that anti-German sentiment would end with the accusations of war profiteering, not to mention the Liverpool, Birkenhead and London riots, they were wrong. It now became even more personal.

On 18 October 1916, an open-air meeting was held in Putney, close to the River Thames, under the auspices of the British Workers National League. The League had been formed earlier that year, following a division within the Socialist and Labour movement over whether to support Britain's involvement in the war. With support from well-known people such as the writer H.G. Wells, the League was both xenophobic and pro-Empire, airing its prejudice in a news-paper called the *Empire Citizen*.

At the Putney meeting a tense exchange took place between a Mr Pittman, a speaker for the British Workers National League, and a member of the audience:

Pittman: Why did Lyons give preference to so many Germans in their employ? Gluckstein is German, where did he come from?

Audience member: You had better make further enquiries as you will find he is not German.

Pittman: We have tackled Lyons over and over whenever we have been at their places, whether it be at the Crystal Palace, or Highbury Corner, or Cadby Hall, we have always found their places streaming with Germans. What did [Monte] Gluckstein say when I phoned him up: 'What about those Germans Mr Gluckstein?' And he would say 'Who are you?' I sometimes used my wife's maiden name when I phoned up and then I would say 'my wife will have no tea as you are Germans.'

Receiving reports of this encounter can only have added to the strain Monte was feeling. Yet what options did he have? There was a war to fight, troops to feed, his family's health and well-being to maintain. He kept his head down and waited for news about his sons.

Chapter 22

1917

At the war's start, Germany had deployed its fleet of submarines to the North Sea in an attempt to prevent Britain importing food and other supplies from its colonies. They were partially successful; by the start of 1917, the Germans were destroying 300,000 tonnes of shipping cargo each month. In February alone, they sank more than 230 vessels. To counter the German blockade, the Royal Navy deployed a flotilla of destroyers, providing just enough cover for the ships to make it to Britain's shores.

Meanwhile politicians reassured the public that the vast majority of shipping vessels were making it safely past the German submarines. In a statement to the House of Commons on 21 February 1917, the First Lord of the Admiralty, Sir Edward Carson, said that 6,976 ships had arrived in British ports over the previous eighteen days.

At first the British government responded to the German blockade by imposing voluntary rationing. Citizens were asked to limit their weekly consumption to 1.8 kilograms of bread, cakes and pudding and 1.1 kilos of meat. To encourage moderation, the government launched a mass marketing campaign. 'Save Wheat, Help the Fleet, Eat Less Bread,' proclaimed one poster produced

Women pack tea at Lyons factory, WWI

by the Ministry of Information. As the conflict progressed, and with German submarines increasingly disrupting the British fleet, new restrictions were announced. One of them was that fresh bread could not be sold. The thinking was that stale bread was less appetising, which would lead to a decline in sales. Surprisingly, perhaps, with strict price restrictions on raw materials and few, if any, new businesses entering the market, Lyons' profits from bread sales actually rose during the war.

Meanwhile, with flour, butter, eggs and sugar increasingly in short supply, Lyons struggled to maintain pre-war production levels of baked goods. In response, the teashops and other restaurants now shifted away from desserts, focusing more on savoury fare. There was some concern, however, when the government announced that it was illegal for customers to eat more than a two-course meal at lunch or three courses for dinner. Thankfully, this had little impact on Lyons' teashops, hotels and Corner Houses, because few people felt inclined to dine lavishly by this point in the war.

Of all their wartime efforts, Lyons found tea production to be the most challenging – not because of shortages, though there were plenty of those, but because government policy kept changing. At the start of the conflict, and anxious not to upset a public that considered tea its national drink, the government had allowed the free market to continue. Following the German blockade, it then added tea to the list of luxury foodstuffs and drinks. Next, in early 1917, it rescinded this decision, and awarded licences to manufacturers according to their pre-war sales. Even this wasn't the end of it. In the corridors of Whitehall, Isidore was picking up talk that the government would soon nationalise the industry. If true, then all tea would be sold under a single brand: 'National Tea'. This would be the end of Lyons' White, Red and Green Labels.

All the British tea companies faced similar uncertainty, yet Lyons struggled more than most. Between 1913 and 1917, British consumption of tea fell by 15 per cent, but during this same period Lyons' production of tea collapsed by 40 per cent. Perhaps their poor performance was because Isidore, and other key individuals in the tea department, spent increasing amounts of their time advising the army. Or maybe the other companies were more agile because they focused on just one trade (rather than also having to run teashops, hotels and restaurants). Whatever the cause, by the spring of 1917 the future of the Lyons tea division looked uncertain.

Meanwhile, from a personal point of view, Isidore was having, as they say, a 'good war'. After working for a time at the Navy and

Army Canteen Board, he had supervised the army's female kitchen employees, proving himself to be both an excellent manager and a reliable officer – a man who followed orders and executed commands efficiently. Deploying the lessons acquired in the teashops, Isidore soon had the canteens working efficiently. His success was such that his superior officer lobbied for him to be given a more senior rank, so that he could be even more effective. Indeed, on 4 April 1917, a letter was sent to the War Office urging that Isidore be promoted to major 'as quickly as possible'.

As part of the vetting process, Isidore now had to fill in an MT 393 form or, as it was also known, 'An application for the appointment to a temporary commission in the regular army for the period of the war'. He gave his birthday as 9 February 1876, which was odd because he was born a day later. To question 4, 'Whether of pure European descent', he said yes. To question 7, 'Occupation of father', he replied 'Director of Public Company', which while technically true, omitted that fact that Barnett had been dead for close on two decades. To question 10, 'School or schools at which educated', and clearly not wanting to reveal his lack of formal study, he wrote 'privately'.

Irrespective of his lack of candour, Isidore was granted the temporary title of major, which he deployed to cajole his seniors to release more resources to support the Navy and Army Canteen Board and to impress his juniors to work still harder. Although he had worked part-time as a politician for the LCC, and had taken part in various boards and committees, Isidore's army service provided him with his first taste of working at the national level outside the family. He relished it: the fast-paced nature of the job, the technical challenge of the logistics, the scale of the impact.

On 22 June 1917, shortly after his promotion, Isidore attended the next annual general meeting of J. Lyons at the Trocadero. Instead of Joe Lyons starting the proceedings, Isidore was shocked to see that it was his uncle who stood up before the assembled shareholders.

Monte Gluckstein said that he had some bad news: the chairman of the company and his good friend, Joe Lyons, was gravely ill with Bright's disease, a chronic and painful inflammation of the kidneys.

'You will readily understand when I tell you that my brother and I have worked with him in perfect amity and affection throughout the past thirty years in the building up of this business,' Monte told the shareholders, 'and every member of the board, old and young, loves him and has cooperated with him at all times in perfect harmony. It is a great boast to us to be able to make that never, during the whole course of our and all our colleagues working together, have we had a really acrimonious business discussion.' He then added, 'I am sure you share our fervent hopes that, with God's blessing, Sir Joseph may take a turn for the better and that his life may be prolonged.'

Alas, it was not to be. Later that evening Joe Lyons died at his flat in the Hyde Park Hotel. Without any children, his assets would return to the Salmon and Gluckstein families. His bequest would be of a more cultural nature. The following day, the newspapers were unanimously effusive, enshrining the legend that Joe Lyons was the man behind the Lyons empire. 'He was the founder of the popular restaurants bearing his name,' stated *The New York Times*. The *Manchester Evening News* called him the 'Prince of Caterers' and 'probably the greatest caterer alive'. the *Scotsman* called him 'the founder and chairman of J. Lyons'. In its lengthy obituary, and under the headline 'THE MAN WHO REVOLUTIONIZED THE TEASHOP,' the *Pall Mall Gazette* wrote that Joe Lyons 'probably did more to improve the amenities of London life than any man of his day'. It went on:

> There was a time when good and cleanly service of pleasantly prepared food was accessible only to the comparatively rich, and when the idea that a well-served meal of several courses could be secured in a palace

and eaten to the strains of a string band for something less than half a crown would have been scorned by caterers as the delirious imagining of a lunatic. Sir Joseph Lyons, however, had the wit to see that in catering for the great middle-class there was a field of enterprise presenting almost unlimited possibilities.

This was, of course, an accurate description of the impact and achievements of the company of J. Lyons, but not perhaps of the man, Joe Lyons, whose greatest skill was self-promotion.

Almost fifty years later, in an unpublished but authorised history of J. Lyons & Company, David John Richardson would describe the man Joe Lyons somewhat differently: 'He was by no means an entrepreneur in the classic mold, neither was he a particularly shrewd businessman.' Richardson added that where 'Lyons had imagination, Montague Gluckstein had vision, supported by planning ability and administrative skill'.

In another authorised but unpublished family biography, the journalist Charles Lyte wrote about Joe Lyons as follows: 'An ebullient character, part showman and part salesman, Joe had great flair and energy. He was the perfect man to front the business which would be backed by the money and commercial genius of the Salmons and the Glucksteins.' In other words, Lyons wowed and impressed, while the family and the rest of the staff did all the work.

Of the original six founding directors of J. Lyons, there were now only three remaining: Monte and his brothers Izzy and Joseph. As the *de facto* senior member, Monte took on the role of chairman, although he remained reclusive and stayed in the background, allowing his nephews Alfred and Isidore to represent Lyons at social and business events. As the family mourned the loss of Joe Lyons, they yearned for word on their sons and brothers on active duty.

The autumn of 1917 brought mixed news from the frontlines. In Western Europe, the tide seemed to be turning in the Allies' favour, with American troops arriving in large numbers following their declaration of war against Germany. Meanwhile in the Middle East, British, Arab and Indian troops were racking up victories against the German and Ottoman forces, taking Baghdad, Aqaba and then Jerusalem. In eastern and southern Europe, however, Britain and her allies were faring less well. In the first week of November, Austro-German forces pushed through the Alps at the Twelfth Battle of the Isonzo, with Italy suffering more than 300,000 losses. And on 15 December, following the Bolshevik Revolution in Russia, Lenin declared a unilateral ceasefire, allowing Germany to focus its forces on the Western Front.

It was at this point, at the end of 1917, that Monte and Tilly heard that their son Dore's tour was over. He had spent eight months in France, where he had faced the horror of the trenches. He had been badly wounded, but Monte and Tilly were relieved to hear that he was alive and would soon be coming home.

There was also news about S.M.G. After recovering from stomach surgery, their eldest had returned to Dunkirk, where he had been overseeing the unloading of supplies to be transported to the front. His parents now read in the *London Gazette* that he, too, had received minor injuries. During an air raid S.M.G. and his colleagues were in a shelter when a bomb hit the docks, causing three massive explosions. Without thinking about the consequences, S.M.G. had run out of the dugout with another soldier, grabbed some buckets of water and managed to put out the fires. Later his commanding officer, Major Leslie Herbert, had commended him in dispatches. S.M.G. was awarded the Military Cross 'for conspicuous gallantry and devotion to duty'. He was one of only 140 British Jewish soldiers to receive the medal during the Great War. Monte and Tilly felt both terror at what their son had experienced and extraordinary pride at his bravery.

Monte's younger brother, Joseph, was in correspondence with his son Louis, who was still running messages for British intelligence in

Italy. Though he was far from the frontline, his parents were of course concerned for his safety. In one letter, Louis' mother described her belief 'in the good guidance of the Almighty, who always seems to save us from the greatest disasters and troubles at the right moment and when we have suffered enough to deeply appreciate his help and deliverance'. Shortly after receiving this letter, Louis contracted a severe fever and was confined to an abandoned farmhouse, where he was cared for by his loyal batman. This was where Louis remained, a long way from home, hallucinatory, but well cared for.

The war of Dore, S.M.G. and Louis was fairly typical. The war of Louis' sister Gluck was not.

At the start of the war, and contrary to her father Joseph's wishes, Gluck had enrolled in art school at St John's Wood in London. She had met a female student who invited her to Cornwall for a month, where Gluck saw for the first time the possibility of an alternative life. On her return, she told her parents that she needed to get away from London, from the war, from the clawing and oppressive Salmon and Gluckstein families. Joseph tried to meet her halfway. He would build Gluck a professional studio in the house, he said; he would support her career. They argued, sometimes violently and then, halfway through the war, she ran away.

Gluck rented a small cottage in Cornwall and moved in with her girlfriend, Craig. 'I am flourishing in a new garb,' she wrote to her brother Louis. 'Intensely exciting. Everybody likes it. It is all black though I can wear a coloured tie if I like and consists of a long black coat, like a bluecoat boy's with a narrow dark leather belt. It was designed by yours truly and carried out by a mad dressmaker. Utterly loony ... I hope you like it because I intend to wear that sort of thing always.'

In February 1918, Gluck heard some welcome news. After years of protests, Parliament had given the vote to more than eight million women. Gluck would not be amongst them, however, for the new law limited the franchise to those who were thirty years old and above. Having been born in 1895, Gluck was just twenty-three. She would have to wait another seven years to cast her ballot in a general election.

That summer, as the newspapers became increasingly full of upbeat stories about British and American military successes in France and North Africa, and rumours were rife about the war's imminent end, Gluck ventured up to London with more frequency. She was seen around town, dressed like a boy with short-cropped hair, walking arm-in-arm with her female lover and smoking a pipe.

This was too much for Joseph. On 3 July 1918, he wrote to Louis, who was still recuperating in Italy, about the split with Gluck. His wretchedness was, he said, 'sometimes too strong for philosophy':

> I don't think she will ever return permanently and that will always remain a cancer to me and however I try to forget, I really shall never be able to. Your dear mother is very brave and I believe she suffers in silence to save me pain. She says her temperament is different to mine, but when she talks of you, her temperament is mine. I certainly do admire her bravery in the other case. Perhaps she is wiser than me. Anyhow, we can never tell and I shall always hope for the best because one cannot live without hope.

This was far more than simply a scandal for Joseph, his brother Monte and the rest of the family. It went much deeper, for ever since their father's terrible court case, they had promised to stay together, come what may. To look past petty irritations – even if these challenged their core beliefs, and what was proper – for the sake of the family. After all, their motto was 'Unity makes strength'. Gluck's behaviour went against all they had been working for. Perhaps it was down to the strains of war; they hoped so. If this was true, they feared things might get worse before they got better, since the economy was starting to buckle.

In response to the government's rationing policy, Bedales headmaster John Badley had set about reducing the school's consumption. Coal was rationed. Petrol for the school's small fleet of vehicles and tractors was severely restricted. Even the purchase of stationery was limited. Badley announced that, as part of the war effort, the pupils must produce more of their own food.

Throughout the year Sam spent as much time in the fields, orchards and barns as he did in the classroom. This suited him fine. Though he had not, as once feared, lost his vision completely, his eyesight remained extremely poor. The lenses in his glasses were 3mm thick and to read he had to hold a book 5cm from his eyes. Unable to serve in the army, the least he could do was help on the domestic front. Often the first to be at work and the last to leave, Sam laboured with the other staff and students to gather the wheat.

Their efforts paid off for, in August 1918, the harvest was one of the best the school had ever seen. 'The introduction of rations and the greatly restricted quantity and range of food supplies of all kinds,' the headmaster wrote in his end of year report, 'have made the Housekeeper's task one of constant anxiety that has needed great skill and forethought and untiring effort on her part; without our own farm produce the task would be almost impossible.'

With the rest of his year conscripted into the army, Sam was one of only three eighteen-year-old boys remaining at the school. He was pleased, therefore, when Badley announced that Sam would be the next head boy. They now spent considerable time together, the headmaster appreciating the young man's leadership skills and embracing of the school's values, and Sam enjoying Badley's wisdom and common touch. Tall, bearded and charismatic, the headmaster – or the 'chief', as he was known – talked about social justice and equality, staying close to nature and of the benefits of socialism and 'doing our utmost'.

On 4 November 1918, just as the war was coming to a close, Sam and his peers were confronted with one last tragedy. Early that morning, an eighteen-year-old Bedales student named Harold Woollacott closed the door to his dormitory room and sat down on his bed. About to graduate, Woollacott was desperate to avoid conscription, but couldn't see a way out. After a few moments' pause the boy lifted the pistol in his hand and shot himself in the head.

A few days later, Sam Salmon and five other boys lined up to carry Harold's coffin from the school to the local church. On the head-master's signal, the pall-bearers lifted the coffin onto their shoulders and slowly walked the 200 metres to the small Norman-era church nearby. Following a brief service, Harold Woollacott was buried in the church's cemetery overlooking the South Downs.

By the end of 1918, 70 per cent of those who had been through Bedales were reported as having 'served in some capacity', and sixty of the 400 boys who had attended the school since its foundation in 1893 had died. Not all were British soldiers. One of the fallen was Ferenc Békássy, who had joined the 5th Hussars of the Hungarian army before dying in the trenches.

In his annual report to the pupils and parents, the headmaster noted that in Békássy, 'though he died fighting for our enemies' cause, we have lost one of our truest sons and one from whom had he lived we expected great things'. Badley saw each of his pupils as a human being, irrespective of their loyalties or their country of birth. It was highly unusual, however, for the headmaster of any British private school to speak kindly about the death of an adversary's soldier. His message to Sam and the other pupils was clear: Do what it is right, not what is expected.

Chapter 23

1918

———————

On 11 November 1918, the war was finally declared over. It had lasted for more than four years. Four years in which families had been separated. Four years in which the country's highly charged expectations about honour and empire had turned to disillusionment and exhaustion. Four years in which J. Lyons & Company had to cope with rationing, labour shortages and, worst of all, human loss. At the final count, more than 4,300 of Lyons' employees had enlisted in the armed services. Of these, 239 had died in combat and hundreds had been injured.

For years now, Monte had remained out of the limelight. The war's end changed all that. As head of the family, he felt it was his task to make some sense of what had happened publicly, on behalf of the company. To acknowledge the pain, while at the same time offering a way forward. It was vital that, after such a profound trauma, he brought people together. The moment he chose was the next shareholders' meeting. Once again the event was held at the Trocadero and the hall was filled with a large number of staff (who owned shares), investors, journalists and, of course, family members. Monte had never had to do something like this before and feared he would say the wrong thing, use the wrong tone. He stood up.

'Ladies and Gentlemen,' he began, 'this being our first annual meeting since the Armistice was signed we may congratulate each other upon the glorious victory achieved by us and our allies in stamping out, as I hope for ever, the peril to which we were exposed of becoming slaves to our enemy.' He took a brief pause, then continued. 'Before entering into the details of the company's figures for the year, I feel that we must all pay a tribute to the thousands of our valiant members of staff who so nobly did their share in this greatest and most terrible of wars. Unhappily our records show that more than 200 men made the great sacrifice with their precious lives, and there is a vast number who we have not, and probably never will have, any records of.'

After another pause, he went on, 'Many hundreds are also badly maimed, and a large number will require time and care to bring them back to their former vitality and health. You and we can have nothing but admiration and pride for such a body of heroes.' This was received with long applause and cries of 'Hear, hear'. Monte then continued, 'We are busy now with the still more grateful task of reinstating them as fast as they are demobilised,' adding that the returning veterans had 'first call' on job openings, and that no new staff members would be taken on until all the returning soldiers had been accounted for.

Nothing, however, was said about the more than 2,000 women who had taken up the labour shortfall, the majority of whom would now find it hard to obtain employment. In the vast majority of cases, these women would return to their families and take care of domestic duties, even if they preferred being employed by Lyons.

Monte then reviewed the financial state of the company, which was, unsurprisingly, unimpressive. During the previous few years growth had been 'arrested' and profits had been affected by 'shortages in supplies and other adverse conditions arising out of the war'. Yet since the signing of the armistice, the chairman continued on a more positive note, 'the business of the company had considerably increased'. He was extremely hopeful about the future – the next few months would see a significant growth in the company's activities.

Following the shareholders' meeting, Monte put his words into action by announcing a major investment in the tea division. Of all Lyons' products during the war, tea had been the hardest hit. The number of tea chests produced each week had fallen from 6,000 in 1914 to 4,000 in 1918 – equivalent to the production of 1909. To tackle this slump, Monte said they were moving tea manufacturing to Greenford, west London, where they would build a state-of-the art production facility. It would be the largest tea-packing plant in the world.

In a second announcement, Monte reported that he had invited Dr Leslie Lampitt to set up a food laboratory at Cadby Hall. If they were to stay ahead of their competition, he said, they had to invent new products; and to achieve this, they needed to work at the intersection of food and science. Dr Lampitt had a PhD in chemistry and an MSc in malting and brewing. He had also worked with Monte's son S.M.G. in Dunkirk during the war. A new purpose-built lab was planned, extending more than 3,500 square metres across four floors. It would be the first of its kind in Europe.

With these and other initiatives, the family hoped to pull Lyons out of the lean war years and into the more productive 1920s.

On 4 February 1919, Isidore Salmon received a letter from the War Office telling him that his commission with the Navy and Army Canteen Board was now relinquished. It added that he had 'permission to retain the rank of major, a notification of which will appear in an early *Gazette*'. Now forty-two, Isidore plunged back into civilian life with full force.

Isidore Salmon

He had found his wartime post rewarding and wished to continue his public work. So in the spring of 1919 Isidore campaigned for, and successfully regained, his seat on the London County Council. Soon he was selected to head a group that was lobbying for the decimalisation of the British pound, and another that examined housing shortages in the nation's capital. He sat on the board of the London Polytechnic and of the Prison Commission. He chaired the London War Pensions Committee and the Public Accounts Committee. He also founded the Westminster Technical School, which trained boys as chefs and waiters. But of all these public bodies, Isidore was most excited about his work for the Board of Deputies of British Jews.

The Board of Deputies represented the Jewish population not only of Great Britain but also of its empire. Some called it 'the Jewish Parliament'. Its origins could be traced back to 1760, when the *Deputados* (representing Jews from Portugal and Spain) and the 'Secret Committee for Public Affairs' (representing Jews from Germany and central Europe) began holding joint meetings. By 1919 the Board comprised more than 300 deputies, representing more than 100 synagogues, 100 provincial congregations, twelve congregations of the British dominions and sixteen Jewish institutions. For some years Isidore had represented Bayswater Synagogue on the Board of Deputies, and now he was elected to the position of vice-president, along with the banker and Member of Parliament Lionel Walter de Rothschild. In addition to dealing with domestic matters, such as marriages and Jewish law, the vice-chairmen would lobby and liaise with the British government. Most importantly, they would represent the Jewish population's views on international relations on the Empire's newest territory, Palestine.

One of the lasting consequences of the First World War was both the mental and physical redrawing of the map of the British Empire. Following the Treaty of Versailles, signed in June 1919, many of the countries that had previously been managed by Germany and the Ottoman Empire were handed over to Britain to be run as mandates. As a result, almost one-third of the globe was now controlled by London, with the new possessions including Togo, parts of Cameroon, Tanganyika (now Tanzania) and the oil-rich region of Mesopotamia, which was divided into Syria and Iraq. Britain was also given responsibility for Palestine, which had until that time been governed by the Ottoman Empire.

The government's policy towards Palestine had been set by the Conservative Foreign Secretary, Arthur Balfour. On 2 November 1917, he had written to Isidore's new colleague, Lionel Walter de Rothschild, stating that 'His majesty's government view with favour the establishment in Palestine of a national home for the Jewish people and will use their best endeavours to facilitate the achievement of this objective.' Significantly, Balfour then added, 'nothing shall be done which may prejudice the civil and religious rights of existing non-Jewish communities in Palestine'.

The Anglo-Jewish community of the day found itself divided over the question of whether Palestine should become a Jewish state. As vice-president of the Board of Deputies, Isidore actively campaigned *against* Palestine becoming a home for the Jews. He firmly believed that if Jews had their own country, then Europeans would consider them to be foreigners, which would encourage their persecution. He was also anxious that increased Jewish settlement in the Holy Land would create tensions with their Arab neighbours.

Such fears were not entirely unfounded. Indeed, in his desk drawer Isidore kept a copy of a letter written in 1919 to the Prime Minister, Lloyd George, from the spy and military strategist Richard Meinertzhagen, in which Meinertzhagen prophesied that 'in fifty years time, both Jew and Arab will be obsessed by Nationalism [...] The Jew, if his immigrant programme succeeds, must expand, and that can only be accomplished at the expense of the Arab who will do his utmost to check the growth and power of the Jewish Palestine. That means bloodshed.'

Anxious to avert such a disaster, Isidore threw himself into study. He read as many books as he could find on the history of the region and discussed the various options with his friends and colleagues, readying himself for the debate that he knew must surely come.

The post-war era also ushered in a new start for Isidore's son Sam. In the first week of October 1919, Sam was driven up to Cambridge by his father's chauffeur. After checking in with the porter at the front lodge of Jesus College, he carried his belongings up to a small, damp room at the top of a winding stone staircase, just a few hundred metres from the city centre.

His generation was the first in the family to attend school all the way up to the age of eighteen. He was now one of four boys studying at Cambridge, while his cousin Louis – recently demobbed and returned from Italy – was reading law in Oxford. They were the first Salmons or Glucksteins to attend university. At this, Monte, Tilly and the other uncles and aunts were delighted, not just for the boys themselves, but also because it was proof, as they saw it, of the family's cognitive health despite decades of intermarriage.

The next morning Sam attended his first lecture on agriculture, his main subject. He would supplement this with classes in history, chemistry and modern languages. Along with the other students, he took meals in the main hall, a high-ceilinged room along whose length ran four dark-wood tables, at the end of which stood High Table, which was reserved for the Fellows and the head of the college. Sometimes Sam turned up for classes with his tutors, but often he slept in. Remarkably, nobody seemed to care. For the first time in his life, Sam was living away from home. He was out from under the shadow of his father and the wider family who monitored his every move. It was liberating.

He soon discovered that he enjoyed the good things in life – staying up late, drinking fine wines, smoking cigars, dancing – all of which were offered by a drinking club called The Roosters. Officially the debating society of Jesus College, The Roosters had been established in 1907, but only truly gained momentum after the war. According to its by-laws, the club was 'a monarchiko-oligarchiko democracy and a Parliament of ffowls' [sic] whose objectives were to 'study, practice, maintain & extend the art, craft, science and mystery of Roosting'. In practice, the club was a chance to be silly and to drink vast quantities of alcohol. During one debate it was agreed that cleanliness was not next to godliness. At another that all bicycles should have square wheels. In a joint debate with Newnham, an all-girls college, it was agreed that life on a desert island offered less scope for self-expression than life at Cambridge. In his second year, Sam was elected president of The Roosters. At the end of his tenure he was given a wreath made out of vegetables, though the club secretary noted that 'the gift had lost some of its freshness owing to a week's postponement'.

Besides attending an occasional lecture and his time with The Roosters, Sam busied himself with rowing. Like horseriding and swimming, rowing was one of the few sports that did not require hand–eye coordination, which made his near-blindness no handicap. By the end of the second year he was good enough to represent Jesus in the inter-college races known as the 'Bumps'. At 73 kilograms, Sam was the heaviest member of the crew and was therefore seated at the third position in the so-called 'engine room' of the boat. There he followed the timing of the stroke, who sat two seats in front of him, and the orders barked out by the small cox perched at the stern. To the delight of their college colleagues, who cycled along the rocky towpath shouting encouragement and narrowly avoiding pedestrians, in 1921 the Jesus College crew 'bumped' Emmanuel, Trinity Hall, Christ's and Queens' colleges, making them sixth overall in the university.

Indeed, Sam's efforts were so impressive that the following spring he was selected for the Cambridge University team to row against Oxford. The one condition, he was told, was that he would have to remain in Cambridge during the Christmas holidays to train with the rest of the crew. When Sam told his father that he would be rowing for the Blue Boat – the name for the best Cambridge rowing team – Isidore was furious, for Sam was expected to work for J. Lyons during the holidays. How could he let the family down? his father asked. Shortly afterwards, Sam informed the Blues' coach that he would not be able to train with them after all. His new-found independence would stretch only so far.

Expectations for the young women in the family were very different. Daughters were encouraged to perform communal or charity work and not to idle. Taking a job was not countenanced.

When the time was right, typically in their early twenties, a match would be found that was both suitable and fortuitous for the family. This was Kitty and Mimi's life, as it was for their female sisters and cousins.

Not, so far, for young Sam. After three years of study and quite a bit of cavorting, he graduated from Cambridge with a second-class degree. Returning to London, he moved in with his parents, who were now living at 51 Mount Street, a three-storey Georgian building located in the heart of Mayfair, one of the capital's most exclusive districts. Soon Sam and Isidore were discussing his next steps. He had two choices. He could become a professional, preferably a lawyer (always helpful for the family), like his cousins Louis Gluckstein and Cyril Salmon. Or he could work at J. Lyons – his father's preference.

Sam was twenty-one when he started working at the Trocadero, almost twice the age that his father had been when he, Isidore, began at the cigar factory. In two years' time, when he was twenty-three, Sam would become a full member of the Fund and, as such, would receive as much income as his father, who was the managing director of Lyons. He would also be eligible for a chauffeur-driven car and, when he was ready, a house of his own.

He spent his first day at work in the noise and steam of the kitchens, washing dishes and learning how the system worked. Two weeks later he was promoted to waiter, taking orders and bussing plates back and forth in the Grill Room. The next month he was given the job of purchasing meat and vegetables at the market place. After that, he was learning how to cook *haute cuisine* under a French chef at the Coventry Street Corner House. This was the family's informal training scheme, an obligatory passage for all the young family members who joined the company. If asked, Sam would have said that he was enjoying his time in the kitchens. In truth, he missed the quiet of the countryside. Afternoons next to the River Cam in

Cambridge. Walking through the water meadows filled with wild-flowers next to Granchester. Yet he knew the path that he was expected to tread, and he moved forward willingly.

At the summer's end, Sam was invited for a chat with his father. After briefly talking about his experiences in the training scheme, Isidore asked where Sam would like to work next. Sam said that he would like to work with uncle Harry Salmon in the baked-goods division. It was Harry who had managed Isidore's first LCC campaign and, after beating up a heckler, had managed to avoid sanction by the court. Five years younger than Isidore, Harry was a good-looking man with a powerful presence. He was prone to excitement over small issues but, when faced with a true crisis, he remained completely calm. He was widely regarded within the family as a rising talent. Indeed, Monte had picked him out as a possible future leader of the company.

The following week, Sam began work under his uncle, learning how bread was made, about purchase orders and delivery schedules. How to package, store and transport the loaves to best maintain freshness. How to deal with staff issues and double-entry book-keeping. There was a lot of information to absorb and few oppor-tunities for sleep. It was his job to stay up all night to supervise the bread baking for the morning's first batch. He didn't much like the work: it was noisy, dirty and, worst of all, tedious. It also cut into his bar time. More often than not, he had to turn down his affluent Rooster friends who invited him out for a drink. He had to work, Sam would tell them.

Every morning he rose early, breakfasted with his family and then walked to Cadby Hall with his father. When they arrived they would find Isidore's brother Alfred standing at the entrance, gold watch in hand, making sure that everyone arrived punctually. Once inside the administration building, Sam settled down at his desk. In the rooms around him sat more than twenty of his close relatives, young and old, checking invoices, writing memos, sampling products, in meetings with staff. He vowed that he would not let his family down.

The Salmons and Glucksteins had come a long way in just two generations, not only in terms of money (though there was plenty of that), but also in social standing. They were keenly aware, therefore, that there was a ladder up which one could climb, and the same ladder down which one could quickly fall.

Chapter 24

1921

As Sam was energetically learning the ropes in the bakery department, the head of the family was finding it increasingly hard to muster the strength to go to work.

Now sixty-eight years old, Monte was frequently woken by pains in his chest. His doctors suggested a tour to one of the European spas, but he had tried these before, and though the hospitality was impressive, his symptoms never seemed to improve. He now spent most days at 38 Hyde Park Gate, his and Tilly's new home, which gave him plenty of time to think back on all that the family had accomplished, and about what more could be achieved.

His daughter, Mimi, had just given birth to her third child, Neil, and Monte was enjoying being a grandfather. That summer of 1921 he sent a message to J. Lyons' marketing department. They were fast approaching the twenty-fifth anniversary of the opening of the Trocadero and they should celebrate. He instructed them to book a four-page advertisement in the *Daily Mail*. Out of a total of sixteen pages, it would take up a full quarter of one day's issue.

He then sat down to write his own 1,000-word contribution. Monte began by saying that he preferred not to boast about the company's successes, as that was 'not our way, not our habit of mind'. There were always other ideas, he continued, each better than the last, and while every idea must 'necessarily pass the common-sense business test, we do in our way push on towards an ideal, beyond the pound, shilling and pence of trading, and strive for something more than the commercial objective'. He went on to explain his philosophy:

> The foundation of our business was the realisation of what the Public desired, we judged symptoms and, so to speak, prescribed; but our ideal nowadays is to get in front of the public and present them with something better than they had thought of, so that, we hope, they may say 'The very idea! Glad they thought of it – just what we wanted'.

When the J. Lyons special anniversary supplement was published in the *Daily Mail* on 5 October 1921, it was, according to its editor, the largest marketing campaign ever placed with the paper. Next to Monte's company history, there was a hagiography from Jerome K. Jerome, along with a telegram from Alfred Charles William Harmsworth, also known as Lord Northcliffe, owner of the *Daily Mail*. 'It will give me utmost pleasure,' he had written from on board his yacht, 'to drink your health at sea between Australia and Japan on 5 October. Sincere congratulations on your triumph over difficulties and your attention to detail and great public service rendered.'

Beneath was an article by Lady Angela Forbes, an entertainer and women's rights campaigner who had been nominated as the first 'British Forces sweetheart'. Forbes wrote about the impact of the Lyons teashops on women:

It may seem at first sight a somewhat far-fetched statement, but I have no hesitation in saying that the opening of the Lyons teashops in the city marked the beginning of a new era. Here was for the first time a place where business women might take their midday meals. City men had their chop houses; now women had at least a restaurant of their own. It seems a little thing, that first step towards a distant ideal, but its influence was far reaching. Conditions have altered, as was economically inevitable, for the better, but there is still much to be done. Equal rights for women is still an ideal not a fait accompli. In such matters, the first step is all important. Today the girls who crowd the teashops at midday no longer need the protection of a room reserved for their sex alone. They share a table with men as naturally as they take a seat in tram or train. Nothing, perhaps, has had a greater influence towards the sensible and natural intermingling of the sexes than the management – the revolutionary management as it was once regarded – of the Lyons teashops.

As the country's first mass-circulation newspaper, and with a readership of more than one million, the *Daily Mail* cemented Lyons' position as an essential part of Britain's cultural fabric.

In late September 1922, Sam received a message at Cadby Hall. Monte was gravely ill and was asking to see each of his relatives. Sam immediately went over to his uncle and aunt's house. There he found Mimi, who told him what had happened. Monte had suffered a heart attack. The doctors said he had only a few days to live.

Sam went in to see his uncle, who was lying in his bedroom. Monte looked frail and colourless. In a voice barely more than a whisper, he reminded Sam of the values that he held most dear –

loyalty, integrity, unity – and of the importance that the family be protected at all costs. After a few minutes the dying man was exhausted, and Sam took his leave.

On 7 October, Mimi spent the day with her father. After talking about his condition for a while, Monte dictated a letter for her to give to his son, S.M.G., after his death. In this letter he left a small gift of money to various female relatives. In jest, Mimi said, 'What about me?' After a while Monte replied, 'You are a Salmon and Gluckstein, a born member of the family. You cannot have any wants. To be an S and G is all-sufficient.' Mimi explained that she had not been serious, which appeared to please him.

Later that evening, surrounded by his wife and three children, Monte lost consciousness. He died during the night.

Two days later, on Tuesday, 9 October, a cortège set off from 38 Hyde Park Gate and rolled slowly along the southern edge of the park. At the front of the procession was a black motor hearse bearing a black-shrouded coffin. Behind, sixty motor cars followed, conveying family and friends. The hearse headed west along Kensington High Street, through Notting Hill and up to Kensal Rise.

The procession was supervised by fifty policemen and several inspectors, keeping the route clear of traffic. Word quickly spread that the hearse carried the founder of the much-beloved J. Lyons. As it passed by, men and women stopped what they were doing, removed their hats and witnessed the passing of the procession in silence. After forty-five minutes, the hearse crept through the gates of the Liberal cemetery in Willesden, crunching along the gravel of the turning circle, before pulling up in front of the red-brick mortuary hall. The rear doors were then opened by a funeral director and Monte's coffin was carried by Isidore, Harry, Dore, S.M.G. and two other family members towards the open grave. Around them stood a crowd of more than 1,000 people.

SILK-HATTED MOURNERS AT MR. GLUCKSTEIN'S FUNERAL.

Monte's funeral

It had been just eight years since the Liberal Jewish Synagogue had opened this cemetery, and ever since Monte had been clear that this was where he wanted to be buried. The only question was exactly where. The choice was his: in the centre of the neatly cut lawn? Next to the stone memorial commemorating the fallen heroes of the Great War? Near the front gate, so that everyone would see him as they arrived? In the end he said that he wanted to be as close as possible to his relatives who were buried in the adjacent orthodox cemetery: his sister Lena and his brother-in-law, Barnett; his other sisters, Clara and Sarah; his brothers Izzy and Henry and their wives, along with twenty others. This is why the mourners now gathered around a six-foot hole next to the brick wall that separated the two cemeteries. As the crow flies, Monte would be less than 200 metres from his brothers and sisters.

According to the *Financial Times*, the *Pall Mall Gazette* and the *Jewish Guardian*, the 'chief mourners' for Monte's funeral included his brother Joseph, his sons S.M.G. and Dore, along with his nephews Isidore and Alfred Salmon and his great-nephews Sam and Louis. Each wore top hat and tails.

The names of Tilly and Mimi were not mentioned by the papers. Nor were Kitty, Gluck or Monte's other nieces and female cousins. For, following the customs of Victorian England, the women of wealthy families (or those aspiring to such status) were not invited to funerals. The reasons for this exclusion were summarised in *Cassell's Household Guide ... A Complete Encyclopaedia of Domestic and Social Economy*:

> It sometimes happens among the poorer classes that the female relatives attend the funeral; but this custom is by no means to be recommended, since in these cases it but too frequently happens that, being unable to restrain their emotions, they interrupt and destroy the solemnity of the ceremony with their sobs, and even by fainting.

The timing of the interment had been arranged with careful precision. After a brief prayer by Israel Mattuck, rabbi for the Liberal Jewish Synagogue, the unadorned coffin was lowered into the ground. At exactly the same time, a two-minute silence was observed across the Lyons enterprise. The machines at Cadby Hall were stopped. Teashop waitresses and restaurant chefs put down their tools. Delivery vehicles idled. Men and women removed their caps, berets, cloches, derbys and toppers. Each, for a few precious moments, was remembering Montague Gluckstein, son of Samuel and Ann, family man and restaurant magnate.

'There is always a risk that a prominent figure becomes, in the course of time, invested with legendary qualities,' Monte's nephew Geoffrey Salmon later recalled. 'I was fourteen when he died and although I knew him and remember him, I certainly did not appreciate his stature then, but I heard too much testimony from those who did know him, for there to be any doubt. Montague Gluckstein is the outstanding figure in our history.'

Monte Gluckstein, who lifted his family out of the squalor of Whitechapel when it was being terrorised by a serial killer. Monte Gluckstein, the driving force behind J. Lyons, the company that had made eating out available to the masses. Monte Gluckstein, who provided jobs to hundreds of thousands of married women. Monte Gluckstein, the man whom few people now remember.

As for who would run J. Lyons, planning for the succession had long been in place. The position of head of the company would fall to the next-oldest male relations: Alfred Salmon, followed by his brother Isidore.

PART IV

ISIDORE

'Your thoughts span the heavens and the earth, why should your achievements be limited to the days. Think of each day as part of time and the 'waste' of this day will have no more meaning for you.'

Gluck

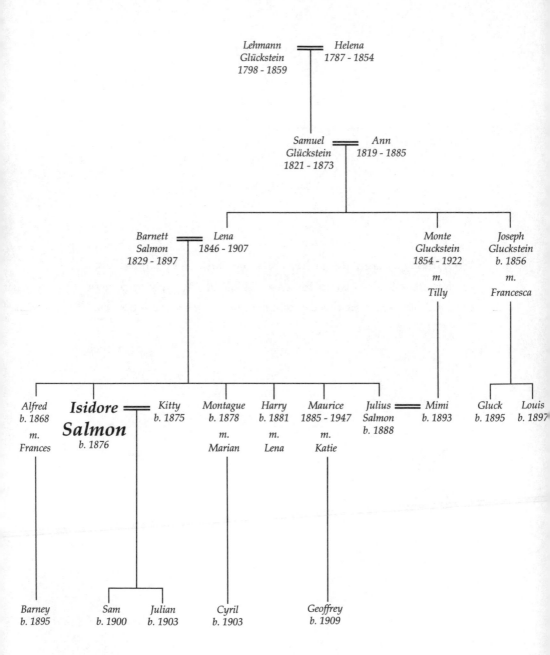

Lehmann
Glückstein
1798 - 1859

Helena
1787 - 1854

Samuel
Glückstein
1821 - 1873

Ann
1819 - 1885

Barnett
Salmon
1829 - 1897

Lena
1846 - 1907

Monte
Gluckstein
1854 - 1922

m.

Tilly

Joseph
Gluckstein
b. 1856

m.

Francesca

Alfred
b. 1868

m.

Frances

Isidore
Salmon
b. 1876

Kitty
b. 1875

Montague
b. 1878

m.

Marian

Harry
b. 1881

m.

Lena

Maurice
1885 - 1947

m.

Katie

Julius
Salmon
b. 1888

Mimi
b. 1893

Gluck
b. 1895

Louis
b. 1897

Barney
b. 1895

Sam
b. 1900

Julian
b. 1903

Cyril
b. 1903

Geoffrey
b. 1909

Chapter 25

1923

Isidore Salmon (far right) gives tour to King (next to Isidore) and
Queen (in furs)

On the morning of 27 February 1923, King George V and Queen
Mary toured the new Lyons factory at Greenford in west London.
It was, as had been anticipated, the largest tea-packing plant in the
world. As the first-ever visit by the Crown to a Lyons factory, it was

not only a tremendous honour for the family and staff, but also provided a superb publicity opportunity for the company.

Stepping out of their large box-shaped Daimler, the King and Queen were warmly greeted by Isidore Salmon, who then introduced the guests to the welcoming party. Amongst them was his brother Alfred who, although company chairman, would take a secondary role that day as he was feeling unwell. Isidore went on to introduce his wife Kitty and other family members. It was bitterly cold and the men wore long, dark wool coats and bowler hats. The women were dressed in mink coats and hats, their hands being kept warm by fur muffs, their shoulders draped with red fox. Each carried an umbrella, with the exception of Isidore, who held a walking stick, and the King, who presumably would be sheltered by another person. After a few moments Isidore's seven-year-old niece, Joan, walked forward, curtsied precisely and handed the Queen a bouquet of carnations and fresh lilies-of-the-valley.

Isidore explained that the construction of Greenford had started in 1919 and was completed just in time for the royal visit. The floor space of the various buildings, warehouses and storage sheds comprised more than 50,000 square metres. Within the boundaries of the 12-hectare property was a canal dock, along with four kilometres of railway lines. In addition to tea, Greenford also manufactured coffee, cocoa and other confectionery.

When Isidore suggested that he show the royal couple how a carton of tea was prepared for the consumer, the King and Queen nodded their approval. They set off, past the canal dock, where wooden crates were being unloaded from a line of barges, and into the warehouse, where a line of tea-tasters dressed in long white coats awaited the royal presence. It can take five years to develop the skills to differentiate between different harvests and the way they are cured, packed and transported, Isidore explained and, much like wine-tasting, it was a critical job for this industry. Then, following a gesture from Isidore, a tea-taster took a large metal spoon and dipped it into one of a long line of brews that had been prepared previously. In a somewhat dramatic gesture, he loudly sucked the liquid into his mouth, waited for the flavour to pass over his tongue and spat the liquid back out into a spittoon. Having noted down the quality of the flavour, leaf colour, size and shape, he then moved on to the next sample.

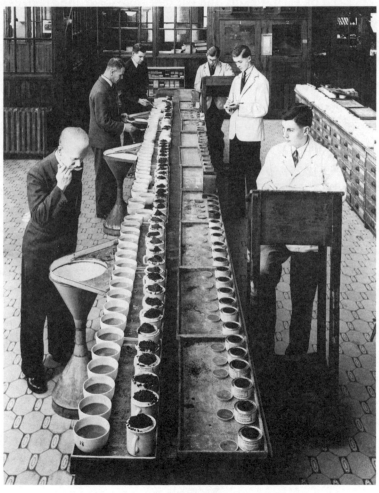

Tea Tasting, Lyons factory, Greenford

The group continued their tour, and next saw how the leaf was poured into a shredder, to be cut down to size, before being funnelled past a powerful magnet, which removed any stray nails or other bits of metal. To the amazement of the King and Queen, though overseen by men and women in white coats and caps, most of the work was performed by whirring and clunking machines. The leaf continued on, to be blended and then packed into waiting paper packets, with a label placed on each. Finally the packets were loaded into boxes and hefted into a line of lorries and waiting goods trains. In this manner, more than five million packets of tea were produced each week.

Photographs taken that day capture Isidore looking animated, confident and charming, walking at the head of the pack with the King as if they were out on a summer stroll. In another image, Alfred can be seen speaking seriously to an unsmiling, almost scowling Queen, while his younger brother is with the King, scratching his jaw with his thumb, a cheeky smile on his face. In a third, a peak-capped lorry driver talks to a clearly fascinated King, overseen by Isidore, who looks on like a proud father. In every picture Isidore appears engaged, strong, youthful and smiling – as if he is enjoying himself.

Shortly before lunch, more than 3,000 Greenford workers lined up outside to see them off, cheering and waving as the royal party motored away. At the head of the crowd was Isidore Salmon. For with the death of his uncle Monte the year before, and the ill health of his elder brother, the occasion had made public what the workers already knew: Isidore was now in charge.

Soon after Greenford's opening, Lyons' bread and coffee divisions also moved there, liberating the manufacturing capacity at Cadby Hall. After some discussion, the family agreed to develop an exciting new product line: ice-cream.

Until the start of the twentieth century ice-cream was made by churning a number of ingredients (sugar, milk and eggs) together with an array of flavourings (strawberry, chocolate, vanilla) in a metal container that was packed with crushed ice and salt. Natural ice was rarely available in England, so had to be imported from Norway or Sweden, making production expensive. Quality ice-cream was made on the premises and sold in small quantities by high-end retailers such as Harry Selfridge's store on Oxford Street. Mass-market ice-cream, such as that sold by Italian vendors in Hyde Park, was of dubious quality, comprising shards of crunchy ice mixed with lumps of undissolved sugar. These 'penny-licks' were sold in little green glasses, which were poorly washed and then reused, leading to various illnesses, such as tuberculosis.

Making ice-cream bricks, Lyons factory

The production and distribution of ice-cream would require someone both imaginative and entrepreneurial at its head. Thankfully, the family had such a person. This was another of Isidore's brothers, Maurice Salmon. A small, determined man, with a pronounced speech impediment, nervous manner and introvert personality, Maurice loved solving puzzles. Many of his relatives considered him to be a genius. Like his cousins, he had trained in the Trocadero and had since worked in the bakery division. In developing ice-cream, he would be assisted by his nephew, Sam Salmon, who was a self-confessed glutton for the frozen delight.

The first problem was manufacture. This was a matter of engineering. Already Lyons had proved it could operate at scale, with its Greenford tea-packing and bread-baking divisions. Work soon commenced in R Block at Cadby Hall. A series of huge electric pasteurisers was constructed, along with a grid of giant mixers and wrapping and labelling machines. In between was strung a web of belts that would carry the products to and fro. An entire floor was devoted to the fabrication of block ice, and another to the production of compressed ammonia, which was the principal freezing agent employed in the process. One key innovation was the addition of air to the mixture during the freezing process, resulting in ice-cream that was lighter and more consistent in texture. It had the extra advantage that, when eaten, it felt less cold on the tongue. A second innovation was to compress the ice-cream into standard-shaped bricks, which would allow for more efficient storage. According to *Ice and Cold Storage* magazine, Lyons' new facility was the 'largest ice-cream plant in Europe'.

Emphasis was placed on hygiene, simplicity and automation. 'Of course like the merry go rounds they have to be attended to by minders,' wrote one wide-eyed journalist who was invited to inspect the process, 'but I hope these young ladies with snow white dresses and caps and strawberry and cream complexions won't be offended if I observe that their duties appeared to me to consist mainly of starting and stopping the machines'.

The next problem was transportation. After the end of the war, the sausage-makers T. Wall & Sons had opened a factory in Acton and had started selling ice-cream from ice-boxes carried by tricycles. To attract customers, one Wall's employee developed the slogan 'Stop Me and Buy One'. In their first three years of business, sales increased from £13,719 to £444,000.

While Lyons did not have a fleet of tricycles, it did have a garage full of steam-powered and electric lorries, and relationships with more than 200,000 grocers around the country. The difficulty was to find a way to sell ice-cream year-round, direct from their shops. This was no easy task, not least because affordable electric refrigerators were yet to be invented. To solve this, Maurice had an ambitious plan: they would persuade shop owners to install ice-chests in their shops, at Lyons' expense. Sam would supervise a nationwide army of men who would deliver ice every few hours to these retailers, so that their boxes could be 'iced up'.

Now Maurice and Sam asked themselves: what ice-cream should they make? Up to this point, ice-cream in Britain was only eaten during the summer time and was available in a limited number of flavours. They were looking for something that would attract customers – something new and exciting. And of course, as with all other Lyons products, it had to be of good quality and affordable. To track down this confectioner's Holy Grail, Sam took a train to Southampton and then boarded a boat. He was off to the centre of modern food-processing: America.

This was Sam's first trip to the USA. Arriving in New York, he was astonished by the height of the buildings, the mad rush of the busy streets, the friendly staff who greeted him at the front desk of the hotel where he was staying. From New York, he took a train to Boston, Massachusetts. There he was picked up by car and driven to

Charlestown and on to one of the city's greatest treasures, the Schrafft factory. In many ways, Schrafft's was the nearest equivalent to J. Lyons in the USA. They both produced chocolate, confectionery and cake, and both ran a network of shops and restaurants. Most importantly, like Lyons, Schrafft's was still run and controlled by the family of its founder.

It was here in Charlestown that Sam had his first taste of Schrafft chocolate ice-cream. He was astounded: unlike Italian ice-cream, it was rich, creamy and smooth; and unlike Selfridges' ice-cream, it could be produced in bulk. Wishing to share his discovery as soon as possible, Sam booked the next boat home. He wanted to take a sample back with him, but how was this possible? He commissioned a local firm to build a custom-made metal container that could be filled with ice-cream, packed with dry ice and contained in a box stuffed with wool to add further insulation. With good weather, the trip should take just under a week and Sam hoped the ice-cream would not have melted by the time he arrived.

Five days later, Sam was standing in the board room of Cadby Hall. He had not stopped at home to wash, and had even left his suitcase in the car, in the rush from the train station. In front of him on the table was the metal container, along with a line of spoons and napkins that had been prepared in advance of his arrival. He was surrounded by family members and senior staff, eager to try the American ice-cream. Sam opened the lid – he had not dared to do so until now, for fear of letting warm air in. To his relief, the ice-cream was still frozen. Then each of the men was handed a spoon laden with chocolate ice-cream. They were impressed; it was truly a new taste. Now the question was: could they replicate it?

This was the final problem. Maurice handed it over to Dr Lampitt, who was in charge of the laboratory at Cadby Hall. Within a short time, Dr Lampitt and his team of scientists managed to duplicate the Americans' chocolate ice-cream recipe, and soon they were producing it at the Cadby Hall factory. The product was then tested with a focus group that had been gathered from the nearby Hammersmith population, and was put into production. It was a smash hit.

Maurice and Sam now set about developing other ice-cream products: vanilla ice-cream, made from real vanilla beans; strawberry ice-cream, from fresh strawberries and not from essence that had been stored in bottles. By the end of spring 1923, Cadby Hall was producing more than 12,000 gallons (54,000 litres) of ice-cream each day.

To build a market for it, Lyons rolled out a campaign to promote their new products. Amongst this was an essay written by the author and journalist Thomas Crosland, which was published in a full-page advert in *The Times* on 21 June 1923. 'Next to the man who invented sleep,' Crosland began, 'no person in history would seem to be entitled to so liberal an allocation of human gratitude as the man who invented ice-cream.' After several hyper-inflated references to Cleopatra, Pliny and Plutarch, Crosland wrote that Lyons:

> have laid themselves out to create – create is the absolute word for it – not only a standard ice-cream of a quality and purity which cannot be surpassed, but methods of package and supply which enable the consumer to handle and carry it as readily as any ordinary commodity and relieve him of the old-time necessity of going out to eat it. At first blush, the fact may not appear of wild and exciting importance but in the long run it is pretty sure to bring ices into their proper position in the national dietary scale and may even place us in a position of equality with the Americans as an ice-consuming people.

This was heady stuffy, given that at this time less than 1 per cent of the British population ate ice-cream on a regular basis.

Over the next few years Sam and Maurice oversaw a massive expansion in ice-cream production. By the mid-1920s, Cadby Hall was producing 80,000 ice-cream bricks each day. This enormous volume was supported by a national advertising campaign, which promoted year-round consumption, both on the street and at home. After Wall's, Lyons was now the second-largest ice-cream maker in Britain.

Lyons workers load ice-cream at Cadby Hall, 1920s

Three months after the royal visit to Greenford, the government announced that it would hold an exhibition to celebrate the British Empire. According to the planning documents, the official objective of the 'British Empire Exhibition' was to 'stimulate trade, strengthen bonds that bind mother Country to her Sister States and Daughters, to bring into closer contact the one with each other, to enable all who owe allegiance to the British flag to meet on common ground and learn to know each other'. The unofficial reason was to raise the country's morale after a series of appalling and catastrophic errors.

Four years earlier, in April 1919, a British commander had ordered troops to fire on a crowd of non-violent protestors in the Indian town of Amritsar, killing as many as 1,000 people and wounding up to 1,500 others, to the outrage of the world's headline-writers. Then, in 1922, the Irish Free State had been established, following a gruelling two-year guerrilla war in Ireland, during which Britain was responsible for the summary execution of at least 100 republicans and the internment of 4,000 others. The result had been a torrent of negative publicity. Finally, that same year, after protracted but inconclusive negotiations with Britain, Egypt had unilaterally declared its independence, raising the possibility that other colonies might soon be lost. What was needed was a celebration, it was thought by Prime Minster Stanley Baldwin – a morale boost for the Empire.

An 88-hectare site was chosen at Wembley in west London, where an enormous complex of buildings, stadia and pavilions soon began to rise. Fifty-eight British colonies or dominions agreed to host exhibitions, each with its own purpose-built hall erected at the respective colony's or dominion's expense. More than 2,000 men were employed in the construction, 71 per cent of whom the organisers boasted had served in the First World War.

An early question for the organisers was who would provide the catering? For each of the exhibition halls would boast at least one restaurant, offering food and drink from that country. This matter was quickly resolved when the scale of the endeavour was realised. The largest catering contract in history should be awarded to the most capable caterer in the Empire. Which is why, on 30 October 1923, Isidore Salmon sat at a table in the Westminster offices of the 'British Empire Exhibition' and signed the 'sole and exclusive' concessions contract.

With more than 100 restaurants, bars and grills to run, preparing for the exhibition's spring inauguration in 1924 would take an enormous effort. The arrangements were too large to fall on any one person's shoulders. Sam, Maurice, Julius, Harry and many other family members were now sucked into the project. They would have to work day and night to be ready in time.

Over the next seven months Isidore and his team consulted directly with each colony's or dominion's staff. Each had specific catering needs. At one meeting, for instance, Isidore met a Mr Kendal from the Indian viceroy's office, along with a Major Mason from the 'British Empire Exhibition'. After a lengthy conversation, Isidore agreed to employ Indian cooks and waiters, not his own staff. Similarly the Cyprus authorities made it clear that they must approve all wines that were to be served by Lyons, while the New Zealand commissioner insisted that Isidore's team 'must consult with the official architect' with regard to the decorating of their restaurant.

With the menus agreed, Isidore and his staff set about hiring the more than 5,000 waiters and waitresses they would need for the exhibition. To each of these was handed a ten-page guide entitled 'General Rules and Regulations'. The dress code, it said, would be white tie, white waistcoat, smart light black boots or shoes, and staff 'would not be allowed to work unless perfectly clean'. Customers must be treated with 'utmost courtesy and promptness', and soliciting for tips would be 'severely dealt with'. Moreover, conversations with other staff were strictly forbidden during service – 'especially in a foreign language' – and all waiters' cloths had to be carried over the left arm and not in pockets or under arms. When a customer spoke, the waiter was never to put his hand on the table or the back of their chair.

It was an intensely busy few months, but finally the arrangements were complete: all the cooks and waiting staff were hired and trained, the restaurants and other eateries decorated according to the local custom, the menus printed, the food prepared and the tables laid. They were, they hoped, ready.

At the opening ceremony on St George's Day, 23 April 1924, Isidore and Kitty chatted with various dignitaries in the VIP box at the newly built Wembley Stadium in north-west London. Around them more than 100,000 people eagerly waited for the spectacle to commence. At exactly 2 p.m. the royal procession arrived, led by King George V in military regalia, riding in an open black-lacquered carriage drawn by six black horses. Next came a battalion of Horse Guards wearing shiny silver helmets, followed by the Duke of York and the Prince of Wales, also in open carriages, with their wives and children.

As the crowd clapped and cheered, the King pulled up in front of the royal enclosure, disembarked and walked over to a podium on which was attached a large microphone. After a few seconds he began to speak, in halting, drawn-out sentences that echoed round the stadium. He congratulated the event co-ordinators for their 'marvellous organisation and industry' and for overcoming 'numerous adverse circumstances including the exceptionally unfavourable weather'. He then welcomed the guests from across the Empire and wished the event immense success. As he finished, thousands of troops marched around the arena while eight biplanes flew overhead. Finally the Bishop of London recited the Lord's Prayer, then Edward Elgar conducted a mass choir in a performance of 'Land of Hope and Glory' and 'Jerusalem'.

Later Isidore took Kitty around the exhibits, checking to see what was on display, as well as ensuring that the Lyons catering operations were running smoothly. To her delight, many of the buildings were constructed in their native styles. To enter the Burma pavilion, for instance, one walked across a wooden bridge based upon Mandalay's Arakan Pagoda, while the Hong Kong exhibit featured a Chinese street along which tradesmen sold silks and ivory statuettes. Within the West Africa pavilion there was a circle of thatched huts, where people from Nigeria, the Gold Coast and Sierra Leone demonstrated weaving and the cultivation of cocoa and rubber. Inside the Palestine building, visitors were invited to sample Jaffa oranges, previously unavailable in England; while the India pavilion was most impressive, an enormous white building modelled on the Jama Masjid mosque in Delhi and the Taj Mahal in Agra, containing twenty-seven courts, each celebrating a province in India. Perhaps most extraordinary was the Canadian exhibit, which contained a life-size refrigerated butter sculpture of the Prince of Wales and his horse.

Hong Kong pavillion at British Empire exhibition

With the opening of the 'British Empire Exhibition', and Lyons managers in place to run the colonies' and dominions' restaurants, Isidore was able to turn his attention to the family's core business, particularly the tea trade. Top of the pile was a classified memorandum

from a surveyor named Colonel W.G.B. Dickson. He was proposing
that Lyons purchase a tea plantation in Africa.

Over the previous few years, the British public's thirst for tea had
continued to grow. By 1924 each person in the UK was consuming
on average 4 kilos per year, up from 2.7 kilos in 1909. Building on
this, Lyons was selling 9,500 tea chests per week in 1924, up from
4,000 in 1918. Most of the leaf tea that Lyons used in their blending
processes came from the London auction rooms on Mincing Lane,
while the remainder was obtained direct from agents in Calcutta and
Colombo. If Lyons produced its own supply in India, South America
or Africa, it would be able to control the supply chain and protect
itself from the volatilities of the open market. Colonel Dickson had
travelled to central Africa on behalf of Lyons to evaluate the potential purchase of the Lujeri Estate tea plantation in Nyasaland (now
Malawi).

A landlocked country in southern Africa, Nyasaland had until the
middle of the nineteenth century escaped European colonialism.
Following the arrival of British explorer David Livingstone, mission-
aries arrived in the area, then colonial soldiers and, finally, bureaucrats.
Since 1891, Nyasaland had been a British protectorate run by a British
commissioner. It was his task, with the help of ten European staff,
a small military force and 150 Punjabi and Zanzibar assistants, to
oversee a landmass of more than 90,000 square kilometres and more
than 1.5 million people. By 1924, close to 15 per cent of the country's
land had been distributed to British companies, comprising 27 per
cent of the cultivatable land. These private estates were home to
about 10 per cent of the local population. The commissioner, and
his superiors in London, supported the further acquisition of land
by British-based companies.

The Lujeri Estate that Colonel Dickson was recommending was a
block of almost 3,300 hectares situated at the southern base of the
Mulanje Mountain, which rose to an elevation of 3,000 metres. The

estate in question lay just north of the province of Mozambique, where 'very cheap' labour was available, and a few kilometres east of the Mulanje Tea District, which Dickson was 'confident will develop into one of the finest tea producing countries in the world, obtaining prices equal to the average of Ceylon on the London Market'. He added that, 'Under proper organisation and liberal treatment, all the labour required will probably be obtainable.'

The purchase of Lujeri was discussed at the next meeting of the Fund. Maurice, Julius and some of the others were concerned that the family had no experience of growing tea. It was a highly technical endeavour, and Nyasaland had not yet established a strong record in tea production. Others worried that the plantation would be difficult to manage from England, that the politics of the country were unknown and the risks high. Eventually a vote was taken and it was agreed to move forward with the acquisition, pending an inspection. A few weeks later, Isidore's younger brother, Harry Salmon – who had recently become head of the tea division – travelled to Nyasaland to visit the plantation.

Following months of negotiations, Harry acquired the Lujeri Estate from a Mr Alberto Sabatini for £25,000. Next he hired a manager from Ceylon with previous experience of running a tea plantation. This manager would be responsible for all local matters, including the employment of labour. Much of the property was still undeveloped, with large areas of bush and forest that had to be cut back before tea-planting could commence. As electricity was not available, the local river was dammed to provide power. Seedlings were planted and nurtured until the trees became productive. The young leaf was picked and laid out in large drying lofts, before being weighed and boxed into tea chests, for transport to the coast by railway and onward by freighter to the UK.

A year after the purchase, Harry visited the plantation again. In a letter to the family, he reported that a small hospital had been built for the benefit of all Europeans and the 'Natives'. In addition there were now three 'Native Stores', a public market that supplied the 'needs of the Natives', while a 'European Store' catered for the wishes of the white population. A 'Native School' had also been built, which was 'carried on' by the white farmers. In addition, the plantation manager had employed a police squad of ten men to maintain law and order. Harry was told by the manager that 'everything was being done to encourage the Natives to settle as a contented and permanent community', which would 'ensure the supply of labour to the Estate and protection of the Natives'.

Harry Salmon

A few days later, Harry sent a second letter back to the board. 'My dear family,' he wrote, 'the nurseries and plantations look very healthy from a layman's point of view.' In another letter he wrote, 'Yesterday afternoon we had a native dance with music. It was most amusing. Hundreds and hundreds of them came to watch. At the end of the performance, we chucked sweets amongst them and it was a real fine scramble.'

He also visited the governor's mansion, a round-trip journey of 400 kilometres, which he described as being 'no nosh' – meaning difficult – after which he visited the previous owner, 'our good friend Sabatini, who has a house built like a castle'. While visiting Sabatini, Harry learned that despite the family's investment – in the land as well as in the community – many in the local population were distressed that a foreign company had purchased the Lujeri Estate.

Indeed at this time there was a growing nationalist movement in Nyasaland. Protests were organised by the African churches and through so-called 'native associations'. Anti-colonial activity, however, could prove dangerous. Less than a decade earlier, in 1915, a failed revolt against a tobacco plantation in Nyasaland led by Baptist minister John Chilembwe had resulted in the execution of forty insurgents and the imprisonment of 300 others. One proposal that was proving popular amongst the nationalists was to end the *thangata* system, in which agricultural labourers worked their landlord's fields without pay, in lieu of rent. Another idea gaining traction was to take 10 per cent of the land owned by Europeans and redistribute it to the local population. This would apply to parcels over 12,000 hectares owned by a single entity.

Hearing about this last proposal, and worried about the possibility of losing part of the Lujeri Estate, Harry sent an urgent note via the Eastern Telegraph Company to his family back in London. In this cable, Harry suggested that they split the plantation into seven parts, each smaller than 12,000 hectares and owned by a separate

Hep Hep anti–Semitic riot in Germany in 1819,
from engraving by Johann Michael Voltz (Alamy)

Jack the Ripper murder scene, Whitechapel, 1880s (Getty)

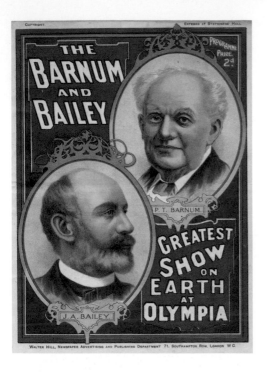

Barnum and Bailey circus, 1889 (V&A)

Venice in London exhibition, 1891
(Look and Learn)

Lord Kitchener S&G cigarette
card, 1901 (author copy)

Lord Roberts S&G cigarette
card, 1901 (author copy)

THE BIGGEST BANQUET SCOTLAND EVER SAW

Dining 2,500 Guests at Aberdeen from London.

Aberdeen banquet overseen by Isidore Salmon, 1906
(Mary Evans)

Lyons tea truck (London Metropolitan Archives, City of London)

Nippies at work at Lyons Corner House (Topfoto)

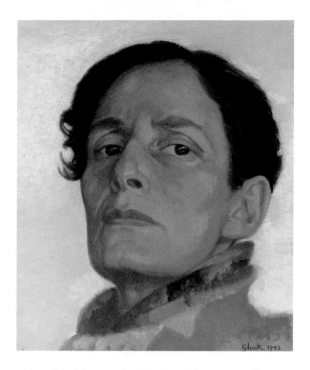

Isidore Salmon as seen by
Fred May, 1934 (*Sketch*)

Gluck self-portrait (National Portrait Gallery)

Boycott of German goods protest, London, 1934
(Board of Deputies of British Jews/London Metropolitan Archives,
City of London)

Lyons teashop in 1930s (General Photographic Agency)

Lyons ice-cream poster, 1950s
(Salmon and Gluckstein
family archive)

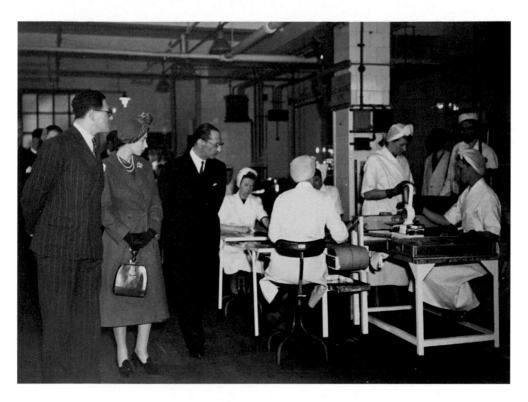

Sam Salmon gives Queen Elizabeth II a tour of the Lyons factory in
Greenford, 1950s (Salmon and Gluckstein family archive)

Wimpy bar, Old Compton Road, London (London Picture Archive)

Sam Salmon with Leo computer team, 1967
(Salmon and Gluckstein family archive)

Salmon and Gluckstein family members gather at
Hackney cemetery, 2019 (Ken Robinson)

company. Two days later he received a response from Cadby Hall. It was in code, each character being written by pencil and in a capital letter:

FGZYNGUCFA DEMELUGCEG ULPGEUBEFD RYFHKMYDAB AKYOVFIMKA UKKIBISKCO OJTYPBIZYS FORTHICRIC ANTIDOTE TUGNYVUSAP UBBDFVORAJ WUSELPIPEB EMORKJYONK

Harry consulted his cipher book. Above each word he wrote the translation in black ink. After twenty minutes he had deciphered the message. 'After further consideration of your telegram,' it started, 'think suggestion so obvious an evasion that it would probably call forth immediate antidote.' His relatives were telling Harry that his clever scheme might trigger a backlash. 'We suggest waiting your return,' it continued tersely, 'to discuss matter.'

When he returned to London, Harry suggested an alternative solution. With Isidore and the rest of the board's permission, he joined forces with other European settlers, calling for greater powers to be given to landowners. In response to their lobbying, the British-appointed governor announced a compromise solution. On the one hand, landlords in Nyasaland were encouraged to pay their tenants in cash, and unused land would be redistributed to the local population. On the other hand, male children would lose their automatic right to live on estates once they turned sixteen, and plantation owners would be able to expel up to 10 per cent of the locals living on their land, without cause.

It would take a few years for this decision to be enacted as legislation. When it was, little changed in practice. The vast majority of estates continued with the *thangata* system, including Lujeri, whilst few – if any – local tenants were moved off the land. Although the discontent continued, it was too poorly organised to pose a threat to the white settlers. For now, at least, the Lyons tea plantation was safe.

Lyons tea estate workers, Lujeri, Nyasaland

Chapter 26

1924

_____

While Harry was occupied with the Lujeri Estate and with developing the tea division, Isidore was turning his eye towards national British politics. With three general elections in two years, it had been – even in historical terms – chaotic.

The first general election was held on 22 November 1922 and was won by the Conservatives, led by Andrew Bonar Law. In May the following year, after just 209 days in office, Bonar Law stepped down, due to illness, to be replaced as prime minster by his Chancellor of the Exchequer, Stanley Baldwin. When Baldwin appointed Neville Chamberlain to the post of Chancellor of the Exchequer, Isidore wrote him a letter of congratulation. They may previously have met, at a Conservative Party function perhaps or at the London County Council, but from the formal tone of the letter, it appears they were at this stage no more than acquaintances:

28 August 1923

Dear Mr Chamberlain

I expect you are inundated with congratulations on the particularly well merited honour which like the rest of the nation I am so glad to see announced this morning but feel I must join with the others. Hoping you may long be spared to administrate the affairs of the country with the success I am certain your efforts will meet.

Believe me, yours sincerely,

Isidore Salmon

The second general election has been called a few months later, after Baldwin decided he wanted to win a personal mandate from the electorate. He had greatly miscalculated. After the votes were cast on 6 December 1923, the Conservatives had lost eighty-six seats, resulting in a hung parliament. In the days that followed, the head of the Labour Party, Ramsay MacDonald, joined with the Liberals to form a minority government – making MacDonald Britain's first Labour prime minister. He, too, would not last long.

In September 1924, after less than eight months in power, MacDonald lost a vote of no confidence in the House of Commons. This had come after a series of mis-steps. First, he had formally recognised the Soviet Union (in contravention of previous governments' policy). Then he had proposed that Britain should forgive old debts with the Soviets and negotiate a new trade treaty with the Bolshevik nation. Finally, he had refused to prosecute a communist who had incited mutiny in the British army. The vote of no confidence triggered the third general election in two years.

This, Isidore believed, was his chance. For while he had enjoyed his fifteen years at the LCC, he felt that his opportunities for growth were limited. He had just been appointed vice-chairman of the LCC, which meant that the following year he would automatically become chairman, but after that, there was nowhere else to go. He wanted to have more impact, which meant working at the national level. His time with the Board of Deputies had given him an opportunity to work directly with a number of parliamentarians, so he had the contacts to step onto a larger stage. To do so, however, he would once again need the backing of his family.

After lunch at the next meeting of the Fund, an update was given on the Fund's finances, and then various family members took the opportunity to raise the usual personal concerns – someone had an outstanding medical bill that needed to be paid; another discussed the budget for their daughter's upcoming wedding; a third asked about how much of their recent trip oversees would be covered by the Fund.

When there was a break in the discussion, Isidore took his chance to speak. The 'British Empire Exhibition' was due to finish at the end of October, he said, and had been a huge success for the firm. In the two years since it had been opened, more than twenty-seven million people had attended. With an overall budget in excess of £12 million, it had been the largest exhibition ever held in the world. That Lyons provided meals for more than eight million people in that period had cemented its reputation as the premier catering company in the country – and, indeed, the Empire. With its closing, Isidore continued, he would have time and energy to spend elsewhere. While he would remain managing director of Lyons, he would like their support to become a Member of Parliament for the Conservative Party.

The Fund members immediately backed him. If he was able to succeed at national politics, it could only be good for the family and the firm. Moreover, they were concerned about the socialist leanings of the MacDonald government and were eager to bolster the Conservative Party in any way they could. As a sign of their support,

Isidore was offered £1,000 per annum towards his campaign expenses. When asked which seat he had his eye on, he said Harrow in north London, which was about to be vacated by a man called Oswald Mosley.

Six years earlier, Oswald Mosley had won the Harrow seat for the Conservative Party. Over the next few years, however, he had become disgusted with his party and switched to being an independent candidate. He had lambasted Bonar Law and then Baldwin for their 'wildcat schemes of adventures in all parts of the world', for the way they had 'financed the luxuries of Arab princes by starving physically and mentally the people of this country' and for their tax cuts for the rich, which had been paid for 'by squeezing the poor'.

Such populist rhetoric had won Mosley his seat as an independent at both the 1922 and 1923 general elections, though his majority had steadily decreased. For this new election, in 1924, he had joined the Labour Party, attracted by the 'dynamism' of its leader and first-ever prime minister, Ramsay MacDonald. It came as a surprise to many, therefore, when just weeks before the general election, Mosley announced that he was giving up his Harrow seat and would instead be running in Birmingham's Ladywood constituency. It would be a symbolic fight in which he would take on one of the Conservative heavyweights, Neville Chamberlain.

This was why, in early August 1924, Isidore was standing in a windy church hall before a row of dour-looking men who made up the selection committee for the Harrow Conservative Party. As part of the so-called 'singing competition', he was first required to demonstrate his oratory skills. Given his previous experience as a member of the LCC, this was relatively easy. He gave them part of a speech that he had given before. Then he was asked a series of pointed and intricate questions about Britain and the British Empire. Again, this proved to be no trouble. Next he was interrogated about the party platform. Once more, this was a simple task. He had memorised the manifesto and knew all the policies by heart. Finally they asked: why should he be chosen as the candidate? This was a reasonable question. Harrow was now considered a safe Conservative seat and there were six others vying for the place. He had the financial backing of his family and company, Isidore replied, along with that of the tens of thousands of staff who lived in the constituency.

The following day, 15 August, the papers reported on the selection committee's decision. The *Leeds Mercury*, for instance, stated that the 'Harrow Conservative Association last night decided to adopt Major Isidore Salmon as prospective Conservative candidate for Harrow'. They called him 'Mr O. Mosley's Successor'.

The next few weeks were spent canvassing in Harrow's streets and squares, at public meetings and on private doorsteps. The cornerstone of Isidore's campaign was the Conservative manifesto, a document that he handed out to anyone who asked for it. He fully supported each of the party's twenty action points, four of which focused on the British Empire, including the statement that 'To strengthen and develop the Empire by every possible means is, indeed, the first and dominant item in our policy.'

Once again, Isidore was assisted by his brother Harry – who had taken some time away from his work at the tea division – as well as by other family members. He was also helped by the local branch of the Imperial Federation League, whose objective was to promote closer union within the British Empire. Volunteers from both the adult and junior branches of the League assisted with the campaign, organising events, distributing printed materials and getting out the voters.

The race was not without its difficulties. Isidore's main competitor was the twenty-six-year-old Labour candidate, Kenneth Lindsay. Energetic and articulate, he already had campaign experience. Just four months earlier he had fought and lost a by-election in Oxford, gaining 13 per cent of the vote, which was considered respectable, given that it was his first outing. In his election flyer, Lindsay asked voters to support the sitting Labour prime minister, Ramsay MacDonald, whom he described as running 'the first non-class government'. Lindsay added that he and Oswald Mosley stood 'absolutely and entirely for the same causes'.

Isidore's other rival was Sir Robert Blair, a former teacher and educational officer at the LCC. In his flyer, Blair reached out to potential female voters. 'Of those I have seen, a good number have told me that they will not vote because they don't understand politics,' he said. 'Vote for me in order to secure that I have the best opportunity of continuing to work for the good of you and your children.' Blair was the Liberal candidate.

On 25 October 1924, four days before the election, the *Daily Mail* published a letter supposedly written by Grigory Zinoviev, President of the Communist International, to the British representative on the Comintern executive. In this letter Zinoviev urged Labour members to support Ramsay MacDonald's détente with the Soviet Union and thus 'assist in the revolutionising of the international and British proletariat ... make it possible for us to extend and develop the ideas of Leninism in England and the Colonies'. While historians would later cast doubt on the authenticity of the letter, at the time many believed that it turned voters away from Labour.

Election day fell on Wednesday, 29 October. In the early hours of the next morning, when the votes had finally been counted, Isidore found himself standing in line with the other party candidates at Harrow town hall, waiting for the declaration. In the assembled crowd were his wife Kitty, sons Sam and Julian, as well as a host of League and other supporters. Finally the counts were announced. As was the custom, they were given in alphabetical order. 'Blair, Sir Robert (Liberal),' declared the returning officer, '4,302 votes.' He looked down at his notes. 'Lindsay, Kenneth (Labour), 9,507.' Another quick look at the notes. 'Salmon, Isidore (Conservative), 16,526.' A loud cheer went up from Isidore's supporters. 'A majority of 7,019,' continued the official. This was 2,000 more votes than Mosley had won at the previous election. 'I declare Isidore Salmon the Member of Parliament for Harrow.'

Nationwide the Conservatives had also done well. Stanley Baldwin had won a landslide victory, increasing the number of their seats by 154 and giving his party a majority of 209 – more than enough to run a stable and long-lasting government. He quickly appointed his Cabinet, including Winston Churchill as Chancellor of the Exchequer and Neville Chamberlain as Minister of Health. Supporting the new Cabinet from the back benches would be the new MP Isidore Salmon.

Ever since the Glucksteins had been chased out of Prussia a century before, they had yearned to belong, to be in control of their fate. Now, for the first time, a family member was a representative in the national Parliament.

Chapter 27

1925

One year later, on 20 October 1925, a small parcel arrived at Isidore and Kitty's home in Holland Villas. Wrapped in brown paper, it came with a note from Joseph Gluckstein, Monte's brother and Louis and Gluck's father. At sixty-nine years old, Joseph no longer worked for the family business and so he had time to spend on genealogical research. 'I am sending you a complete set of the family tree,' Joseph wrote. 'You should feel free from time to time to add to the appropriate trees any event that requires a recording so as to keep your set up to date.' To make this easier, he provided six sheets of blank paper. The letter ended: 'with the hope that they will prove as interesting as the compilation has been to me'.

The only item printed on the book's dark-green cover was a golden bundle of sticks, under which was written the family motto: '*L'Union fait la force*'. The title, found on the spine, was simple and to the point: *Family Trees*. On the inside cover, Isidore found a summary of the bundle-of-sticks story and then a facsimile of Lehmann Glückstein's handwritten notes that he had made in the back of his *Lexicon*. 'Many and varied thoughts have passed through my mind as I looked up records and wrote the names,' Joseph wrote in his foreword to the book. 'I thought of the loves and hopes of the mothers for their children, the struggles of the fathers for their education and support and the devotion of dear brothers and sisters.' He then added, 'There must be many disappointments in life, but I pray that those whose names will be added will endeavour to continue the good work in the same spirit of mutual devotion and family unity.'

Then came a series of family trees, starting with the Glucksteins, the Salmons and the various related branches that were created when daughters had married outside the family – the Josephs, the Abrahams, the Cohens and six others. In all, more than 300 people were listed, each with his or her own dates of birth, marriage and, where appropriate, death. Joseph had printed more than fifty copies of *Family Trees* and circulated them to the heads of each family branch.

If Lehmann's list of key family names and dates scratched into the back of his favourite book had been an optimistic claim on the future, this was more a declaration of clan, lineage and familial bond. If you were listed on these pages you were part of the in-group, included in one of the country's most affluent, most powerful and most significant families. On receiving his copy, one relative commented that 'it tells us where we came from, but it doesn't tell us where we are going to'. The answer to that would have to be provided by the current generation.

The delivery of Joseph's book coincided with the Lyons brand becoming a cultural icon. Journalists wrote effervescent articles praising the Corner Houses' sumptuous French-inspired decor and the quality of their artwork, commissioned from the period's best-known painters. Novelists and playwrights featured the teashops in their books and plays, while directors featured the smoke-filled establishments in their silent movies. Society columnists mentioned which star or celebrity had been seen entering the family's Regent Palace and Strand Palace hotels, and on whose arm. Lyons now became synonymous with the best of British values: consistency, prudence, quality, fairness, good taste. Nowhere was this truer than of the Trocadero.

London was at this time in the middle of the so-called 'Roaring Twenties'. Women's short skirts and bobbed hair had replaced long dresses and buns. For the men, lounge jackets and bow-ties had taken the place of top hats and tail coats. Music was faster, the dancing racier, the comedy more risqué, and the appetite for live entertainment enormous. To meet this demand, Isidore and Alfred now hired Charles Cochran, a flamboyant American impresario, to host a daily show at the Troc, and they asked their cousin, Major Monte Gluckstein (nephew to the first Monte Gluckstein), to work with him. In turn, Cochran and Major Monte recruited London's hottest acts.

On Thursdays the audience was wooed by Nina Mae McKinney, an African American singer from the USA, who was supported by a troupe of dancers dressed in top hats and tails, and whose heads were zipped into 'African' rubber masks. On Fridays they were charmed by the comedy duo 'Mr Flotsam and Mr Jetsam' and sang along with the banjo-playing Will Van Allen. During the weekend they came to see the singer George Robey and the music-hall favourites the Western Brothers. Within six months of Cochran opening his show, the Troc had become a West End sensation.

In February 1926, Cochran and Major Monte went one step further and produced a show that would run for weeks. Called *Supper Time*, this was a history of dancing that included roller-skating and the scantily clad and high-stepping Dodge Sisters. It too met with instant success. Later that year they launched *Merry-Go-Round*, featuring the starlet Florita Fey. This last proved such a triumph that Fey was featured dressed as a jockey on the cover of the *Illustrated Sporting and Dramatic News*. A critic from *Tatler* described another of Cochran's shows, *Bon Ton*, as 'perhaps the most attractive cabaret in town', but complained that the show was so 'tantalizing' that the eating of food became problematic. 'The stage gets in the way of the dinner or the dinner in the way of the stage.' Worse, he continued, was that 'not content with giving us a wonderful dancing cabaret show, a procession of lovely creatures leaves the stage at one moment to promenade amongst the diners. No wonder the soup gets cold!'

The Cochran shows proved so cutting-edge that soon some of the most avant-garde were attending. Young women known as 'flappers' flocked to see the entertainment. As did women dressed as men, and men dressed as women. Sometimes they were accompanied by their beaux, and sometimes they went, scandalously, alone.

One of those now attracted to the Troc was Joseph's daughter Gluck. Since the war's end, she had been spending more time in the capital. She had rented a flat on Finchley Road in north London, where she stayed with her girlfriend Craig; as well as an artist's studio in Earls Court. Gluck felt at home with the colourful characters who filled the Troc's cramped dressing rooms and dimly lit corridors. In a series of paintings, she captured life backstage. In one, the ballet dancer Léonide Massine is seen dressed in red trousers and green jacket, his long hair tied in a pigtail as he waits in the wings; holding his hand is a rake-thin waistcoated man, on whose head sits a fedora. In another, entitled *Three Nifty Nats*, a trio of men in black suits and boaters strut across the boards, their movements perfectly synchronised. In a third, a beanpole-thin man dressed in tails stands in front of an orange stage curtain and looks to his left, as if hoping for a signal; later in the show he would appear in drag. Gluck called this picture *Ernest Thesiger waiting for his turn*. These pictures were admired by the performers as well as by Gluck's artist friends and she began to receive calls from gallery owners.

In spite of her growing success, Gluck's behaviour and attire still did not sit well with her parents. Her mother Francesca – who was busy with public causes and social events – gave Gluck little attention and said that her girlfriend, Craig, was 'pernicious' and had a 'kink in the brain', while her father, Joseph, found it hard to speak to her. This was not helped by Gluck's perennial umbrage over her personal financial arrangements. Joseph had set up a trust in her name, into which the Fund had put £6,500, which produced a steady income of more than £6 per week. The amount more than covered her expenses, affording her a good standard of living, and for this Gluck was grateful. The problem, for Gluck, was that she was unable to spend the capital, and all payments had to be approved by her father. This was not only humiliating and annoying, but also meant that she could not access significant sums if she wanted, say, to purchase a house or build a studio to her own design.

Yet not everyone in the wider family was antagonised by Gluck. Neither Isidore nor his son Sam seemed to mind her unusual habits; indeed, they were both keenly fond of her. And so apparently was Mimi, who was pregnant once again. Mimi hoped that her youngest child, Neil, who was now four years old, would respond well to the new baby. All Mimi would say of her cousin Gluck was that 'she was very good company', and she made no judgement that she 'dressed in a masculine way'.

Indeed, the family was seen as being unusually accepting of those pushed to the fringes of society. The Corner House on the Strand, for instance, had become the unofficial centre for London's male gay community. It was known as the 'Lilypond' because of its lily-themed wallpaper, and a section of the restaurant was unofficially reserved for gay customers. Gay men of all classes stood in line waiting for hours so that they could eat and drink without harassment and enjoy the day's musical entertainment.

This is not to say that the Salmons and Glucksteins had eschewed their conservative principles. Far from it. The family guarded its unblemished reputation jealously. For theirs was a business known for its dignity, propriety and relentless profits.

Keen to attract not just colourful characters to the Troc, and determined that they would not return to the early days when the balconies were occupied by 'strange ladies', Isidore and Alfred launched a new marketing campaign. In the national papers they ran an advertisement that portrayed a suited father and son eating at a table, under which was written: 'When you are expected to give the boy a holiday treat, remember the Trocadero Grill Room. Its gay, bright atmosphere and cheerful music will delight and amuse him.' It then noted that the current featured act was Trini, 'the most beautiful girl in the world'.

Family unity was important, but so was the protection of the business.

In March 1926, Stanley Baldwin's government announced radical changes to the coal industry. Over the previous two years the price of coal had collapsed, following Churchill's reintroduction of the gold standard and Germany's increasing export of cheap coal. In a speech to Parliament, Baldwin said that coal miners' wages would be decreased by 13.5 per cent. In response, the miners laid down their tools, and sympathy actions spread to other industries. When negotiations between the government and the Miners' Federation of Great Britain broke down, the Trade Union Congress called for a general strike, starting at one minute before midnight on 3 May.

As managing director of J. Lyons, which now employed more than 30,000 people, Isidore knew that the strike would hit them hard. Even if every one of their own staff turned up for work – which he hoped would be the case, given the loyalty they had shown over the years – other critical parts of the supply chain were bound to collapse, most importantly their coal deliveries and the rail networks.

To evaluate the situation, Isidore asked his son Sam to provide a report on staff attendance. The following day Sam stood by the entrance to Cadby Hall, welcoming the staff and keeping an eye out for any picketing. He saw no groups or protests on the street, but he did pick up grumblings from many of the workers, who complained about the government's harsh tactics. Later Sam met the heads of divisions to assess who had, and had not, turned up for work. To his own and his father's relief, all staff had arrived for work on Tuesday, 4 May, and again on Wednesday, 5 May. Perhaps they would see this through.

That evening the members of the Fund gathered for their weekly meeting at the Trocadero. The atmosphere was unusually tense. There was a long and heated discussion about the strike and what action, if any, the company should take. Isidore counselled patience. Others judged him naïve. A strike could hit Cadby Hall, the Greenford factory or any of the teashops or other depots at any time. What was needed was a back-up plan and measures to ensure security for the staff who did work. Sam expressed sympathy for the miners and their fight for equality. Perhaps influenced by the egalitarianism of his former Bedales headmaster, he was concerned that they might be hearing only one side of the argument in the establishment newspapers. Isidore's older brother Alfred remained quiet throughout the discussion. Though technically still chairman of Lyons, and with an equal voice to the other members of the Fund, he was happy to take a back seat. He had found these last few months tiring and would accept the decision of the younger generation.

In the end, a compromise was reached. The employees would be warned of the consequences of strike action, and the police would be asked for protection in case of trouble. In case of a major walk-out, 600 volunteers would be drafted to staff the bakeries, on which numerous hospitals and schools depended. At the same time a communication channel would be established with the unions, to ensure misunderstandings were avoided.

When he arrived at Cadby Hall the following morning, Isidore was disappointed to find a large crowd blocking his way. Most were warehouse workers, although some were bakers. Almost all were men, wearing flat caps and jackets. A troop of mounted policemen was on the scene, maintaining order. Having gained access through a back entrance, Isidore spoke with the head of personnel, who told him that more than 1,000 male and female employees had failed to report for work. The Trade Union Congress had discovered that Lyons was using its vans to deliver coke to its restaurants and had called for an immediate stoppage. The good news was that, with the help of the fresh recruits, all deliveries had been sent out on time.

Isidore next called in the head of publicity and told him to issue a statement to the press: all members of staff who failed to report to work by noon on Saturday would be 'deemed to have left work and their places will be filled'. To make things absolutely clear, he ordered a large sign to be printed and hung over the main entrance overlooking Hammersmith Road. 'Food is essential,' read the sign in bold letters, 'permanent staff required to pack and deliver foodstuffs. Support your country and the constitution!' According to one journalist, by lunchtime some of the strikers were 'already regretting their hastiness'.

On Saturday the walk-out was called off and each of the strikers was accepted back to work. In appreciation of their loyalty, the staff at fifty-eight of the teashops – none of whom had gone on strike – were given a day off.

On 12 May, eight days after it had begun and following a meeting with the prime minister, the Trade Union Congress called an end to the general strike. In all, almost two million workers had refused to turn up for work, sending shockwaves through government, business and the media. The industrial dispute in the coalfields, however, rumbled on for months without resolution. By the year's end, most miners had returned to work, despite their hours being increased and their wages cut.

In spite of the disruption, Isidore's Conservative Party came out of the strike stronger and more united. The following year Parliament

General Strike, Cadby Hall, 1926

passed legislation that banned sympathy strikes and mass picketing. Companies like Lyons now felt better protected from the uncertainty of industrial action. Meanwhile in the union and labour movements, a debate roiled as to whether the 1926 strike – the only general strike in British history – had been a success.

At the next meeting of the shareholders, which took place on 23 June 1927 at the Trocadero, Alfred Salmon rose to give the chairman's speech. Sitting next to him was his younger brother Isidore, who muttered encouraging noises. As in previous years, the text had been a group effort: drafted and redrafted, checked for spelling mistakes, factual inaccuracies and, most crucially, anything that might offend. It was Alfred's job to project authority, confidence and strength. None of this was easy, given the turbulence of the previous months and his declining health.

In as strong a voice as he could muster, Alfred admitted that J. Lyons & Company had experienced losses as a result of the general strike and the coal stoppage that followed. The industrial action had caused considerable out-of-pocket expenses that had impacted on profits. 'One does not want to labour this matter too much,' he said, 'those responsible have on the whole, I think, admitted that it was a mistake, and therefore the less we say about it the better.'

On the positive side, he continued, the Corner House on Coventry Street had been expanded so that it could now seat 4,500 people at any one time. Open all night, it served 60,000 meals in a twenty-four-hour period. In addition, land had been acquired overlooking Marble Arch on which would be constructed a new hotel and cinema. Meanwhile, tea, coffee and baked-goods manufacturing at the Greenford factory was going well.

Finally Alfred took a moment to praise the efforts of the female staff who worked at the Lyons teashops. It was upon their diligence, efficiency and hard work that the Lyons food empire had been built. Then, on a lighter note, he added that it was interesting how words became household names. This was no truer than of the name Lyons used to describe their female waiting staff – a word that had entered current speech as a generic name for all waitresses: the Nippy.

Nippies at work, Lyons teashop

It is unclear when the word 'Nippy' was first applied to the waitresses working at the Lyons teashops, but by the mid-1920s the two were synonymous. Their uniform consisted of a stark black dress, black stockings, white apron and white tiara. The ideal Nippy behaviour was published in a copy of the in-house magazine, *Lyons Mail*. 'Be ready to smile,' it said, with a spotless uniform, clean nails, brushed teeth and hair 'combed nicely' and 'no body odour'. The white towel should be draped over the forearm (never under it). Rouge and lipstick should be used 'sparingly'.

By 1924 the word 'Nippy' held such value that Lyons registered it as a trademark. Indeed, the word was so prevalent that it was recorded in the *Oxford English Dictionary*: 'A waitress in a Lyons restaurant – Nippy'. A little later, a Nippy appeared as a character in one of Dorothy Sayers' mysteries, *Unnatural Death*. Soon afterwards, a musical opened at London's Prince Edward Theatre called *Nippy*, with heart-throb Binnie Hale playing a Corner House waitress whose love for a drunken youth is unrequited until she becomes a film star, by which time it is too late. The show rehearsed some of society's current preoccupations: social mobility, female empowerment and dopey men lost to the winds of change. 'We hardly look for originality in musical comedy,' wrote the theatre critic for *The Times*. 'The purveyors of entertainment of this sort prefer rather continuity – the continuity of that which has proved its worth elsewhere.' Yet the reviewer did find something noteworthy about this show. 'But a piece that is these days unashamedly English at least deserves to be called unusual. In humour, sentiment and setting, *Nippy* is English.'

Partly to promote the well-being of their staff and partly to attract press coverage, Lyons now hosted an annual Miss Lyons beauty pageant at the company's sports fields in Sudbury, west London. In a typical affair, twenty young female employees sashayed around the swimming pool, each in a tight-fitting Jantzen bathing suit and heels, all projecting their most brilliant smiles. To the left stood the audience, clapping and cheering. To the right were the judges, clipboards in hand, taking notes. On one occasion, for instance, the judges included the movie stars Anne Crawford and John McCallum, along with Isidore Salmon's son Sam. The following day the tabloids reported the name of the winner of the Lyons 'Loveliest Girl' contest, along with photographs and a brief biography. If she was lucky, she was soon taken on by a talent agent.

Not unaware of the Nippy's potential to grab attention, the family worked hard to develop a range of publicity opportunities. Photographers were invited to take pictures of Nippies practising shooting rifles on the roof of Cadby Hall or riding their bicycles round a track. Each year a ball was thrown for more than 1,000 Nippies at London's Opera House. Such events were well covered by

Nippies pose on roof of Cadby Hall

the press, who reported on the exotic fancy dress worn by attendees. Under the headline 'THE PRETTIEST GIRLS IN COVENT GARDEN', one paper reported that 'The girls looked just as charming and far more natural than many of the international cabaret stars of Park Lane.'

Nell Bacon, who was in overall charge of the Nippies, placed great emphasis on creating a 'family atmosphere' amongst the waitresses. Loyalty, honesty and punctuality were demanded, in return for security and concern for personal welfare. She was determined that promotion was possible for her staff. But there were limits. For there were very few management positions available to female employees working at Lyons. None of the divisions – tea or ice-cream, Corner Houses or hotels, outdoor catering or teashops – were run by women. None of the senior managers or board members were women.

Indeed, this point had been raised at a Lyons annual general meeting a decade earlier. When one of the shareholders, a Mrs Samson, had suggested it was time that a woman be made a board member, Monte had replied that such a suggestion did not come as a 'shock' to him or the other directors and that they had a 'very broad mind'. He added that he didn't think 'the day was far distant when they would see ladies on many boards' and that 'nothing would give the directors more pleasure than to make such an appointment'.

Yet there had still been no women appointed to the board – an omission that would remain unchanged throughout the history of J. Lyons.

Chapter 28

1928

———————

Equality at work was hotly debated at this time. The issue was taken up by unions as well as by women's rights activists. The Six Point Group, for instance, called for reform in six areas, including equal opportunities for men and women in the Civil Service and equal pay for male and female teachers. The other key issue on the minds of many was women's right to vote.

The issue came to a head on 29 March 1928, when a second reading of the Equal Franchise Bill came before Parliament. It had been ten years since women had first won suffrage in Great Britain, but this right had been limited to women over thirty years of age who met minimum property qualifications. If approved, this new bill would add five million women to the electoral rolls.

For more than a decade the issue had divided the Salmon and Gluckstein families. On one side were the traditionalists who believed that women should be kept out of the public sphere, away from the hurly-burly of commerce and politics. This group's view had become entrenched when a group of suffragettes had thrown stones at one of the Salmon & Gluckstein tobacconist shops, smashing its windows. Any hope that this was a rogue element had been dashed when the organisers of the protest, the Women's Social and Political Union, released a statement saying, 'We are going to prove our love and gratitude to our comrades by continuing the use of the stone as an argument in the further protests that we have to make. Does not the breaking of glass produce more effect upon the Government?'

On the other side were family members who were pushing for greater gender equality. Amongst these supporters were Gluck, Kitty and Mimi. Isidore was split on the issue. When it came to female participation and religion, he had always been a conservative. To him, it felt wrong that men and women sat together at the Liberal Jewish Synagogue, and when women had recently started to lead that congregation's service, he found it even more disturbing. Yet he did believe in fairness and equality. After all, this is why he had become a Member of Parliament. He would listen to the parliamentary debate, he decided, then make up his mind.

In a packed chamber, Isidore Salmon, MP sat on one of the narrow green back benches, waiting for the debate to start. The Home Secretary stood and provided the background to the bill. He explained how gradually, over the previous hundred years, the franchise had been extended, starting at 16 per cent of the adult population in 1832, up to 48 per cent today. It was no longer tenable, he continued, to treat men and women differently, and those who either feared the women's vote or believed women unfit to take their share in political work needed to step aside. If the bill was approved, he added, and following the loss of so many men in the First World War, there would be two million more female voters than male.

This prompted an angry intervention from one of the backbenchers. 'Women voters will become the determining factor in the polities of the count!' shouted Brigadier-General Sir George Cockerill, former Director of Special Intelligence during the First World War and now Conservative member for Reigate in Surrey. 'Unless you redress that balance by some means,' he added, 'you are going to get a position where women will have absolute supremacy at the polls.' To this, the first female Member of Parliament, Viscountess Nancy Astor, called out gleefully, 'Hear, hear!' But the veteran was not done. Having pronounced that men were the 'highest organism', he suggested a solution to removing the inequality of numbers. 'One way, which I do not advocate, would be, of course, to murder the women innocents.' From the back benches Isidore and many others cried out, 'Shame! Shame!'

Another opponent of the bill stood up. 'I do not believe the women want it,' declared Colonel Reginald Applin, the Conservative MP for Enfield and a pioneer of the machine gun. 'I am certain that the women of the country realise, as many of the older women do, that a franchise on equal terms with men carries with it equal duties. Hitherto, men have done all the heavy work in this country.' To this Ellen Wilkinson, the Labour MP for Middlesbrough East and a former suffragette, shook her head and shouted, 'Oh, really! Good gracious!'

It was now the turn of Gwendolen Guinness, the newly elected Conservative MP for Southend. First, she pointed out that perhaps there were more female infants than male because of the law of survival of the fittest. This was received with much laughter. She then pointed out that young women were not 'irresponsible and addicted only to pleasure' – as many had argued – but hard-working and serious as proved by the part they had played during the Great War.

Next to stand up in support of the bill was Margaret Bondfield who, under Ramsay MacDonald, had become the first-ever female British government minister. 'Since I have been able to vote at all, I have never felt the same enthusiasm because the vote was the consequence of possessing property rather than the consequence of being a human being,' she declared in a clipped tone. 'This Bill does lay down for the first time that a vote is conferred not merely because women are women and men are men, but at last we are established on that equitable footing because we are human beings and part of society as a whole.' Isidore was not alone in finding this statement powerfully moving. The parliamentarians around him stood up, waved their ballot papers and cried out, 'Hear, hear!'

With the debate over, the Speaker of the House called out, 'Division. Clear the Lobby!' The division bell was rung: it was time to make a decision. If Isidore had thought it hard at the start of the debate, the choice was now simple. He joined a large body of members who walked towards the 'Aye' lobby.

Once inside, the teller noted which way he and the others in the room were voting. A few minutes later Isidore was back in the chamber, waiting for the result to be announced. After a brief pause, the total votes were read out: '387 for the Ayes,' called one of the tellers; '10 for the Nos,' said the other. 'The Ayes have it,' declared the Speaker. The room erupted in cheers.

Four months later, on 2 July 1928, the bill became law. For the first time in British history, women had the same franchise as men.

Like his father, Sam Salmon was becoming increasingly interested in the world beyond the family, though for different reasons. While Isidore was driven to improve the lot of those around him, and to give back, Sam was impacted more by curiosity; he wanted to explore the world, to find and enjoy the good things in life.

As part of his Lyons management training, and then later through his work in the bakery and ice-cream departments, Sam had traversed London and then travelled around Great Britain. As he went, he had been introduced to the company's various restaurants and hotels, staff and tradesmen and customers, and he had noticed the differences in people's health, education and wealth. All of this had come to a head during the general strike of 1926, when he had come face-to-face with organised labour and their legitimate complaints about inequality.

Now aged twenty-eight, Sam wanted to travel overseas. Top of the list was the world's first communist country: the Soviet Union.

Sam spoke with his uncle Harry and persuaded him that they should go together. The family might learn something from the socialist experiment. After all, large-scale catering enterprises should have much in common, irrespective of whether they were state or privately owned. The Soviet Union also offered hope of a different, perhaps even fairer, way of organising money and labour, which was of interest to Sam, for the socialist ideal of equitable distribution echoed many of the values he had learned from John Badley at Bedales. This ideal was also not so very different from that of the family's Fund.

Only a decade after the October Revolution in which the Tsarist regime had been replaced by the Bolshevik government, the Soviet Union was still beset by instability and uncertainty. Vladimir Lenin had died four years earlier, and Joseph Stalin was attempting to consolidate his power. Just six months before Sam's departure, Stalin had banished his main rival, Leon Trotsky, to Siberia. That very month, Sam had read in *The Times* about the 'Donetz Trial', in which a group of German engineers and fitters were accused of sabotaging a coal mine in the Donetz basin of the Ukraine by means of arson, flooding and explosion. This 'Western plot' had been uncovered by OGPU, the Soviet secret police, and five of the engineers had been found guilty and executed. 'Stalin insists on a policy of violence,' *The Times* had written, 'in order to retain the sympathies of the extreme.'

If Sam was at all anxious about his travel plans, it was not recorded in the detailed diary he kept throughout his month-long trip. In his first entry, dated Friday, 20 July 1928, he noted that he and uncle Harry set out by train from Berlin at 7.30 p.m., heading for Riga, and then on to Moscow and 'St Petersburg' (he chose not to use the city's new name, 'Leningrad'). His hotel accommodations were 'marvellous', he noted, and of 'great style'.

Arriving in St Petersburg, Sam and Harry visited the Hermitage museum and the opera. Next they drove 40 kilometres south to Catherine I's enormous rococo palace at Tsarskoe Selo, which the Empress had used as a summer residence. Touring around the ornate rooms, whose displays had been re-created since the Soviet revolution, Sam noted that the 'propaganda' was 'very clever'. In one room, for instance, the uniforms of two noblemen had been mounted next to a sign explaining that the average worker could ill-afford such clothes. In another, a picture had been posted of King George V wearing his coronation robes at Westminster Abbey, 'showing that even in modern times such folly still exists'.

In Moscow, Sam observed long lines of people queuing in the rain outside Lenin's tomb, 'a marvellous but morbid sight'. Later he saw a government propaganda film, which was a year old and 'very bad'. From its anti-capitalist content Sam understood that free-market enterprise would soon be 'definitely stopped'. In another diary entry he recorded the new society's apparent contradictions: 'We dined at midnight at the hotel where there was dancing and every sign of wealth, yet 90 per cent of people present were Russian.'

At one stop along the way, they visited a factory that employed more than 11,000 people. There they were invited to taste the caviar, borscht soup and pork chops served for the 'special workers' – presumably senior managers – which Sam found to be 'excellent', whilst noting that such fare was not offered to the ordinary worker. Elsewhere, they toured a soup kitchen that served 12,000 meals daily. With his professional eye, Sam observed that the kitchen was over-staffed, but the service was under-staffed. And while he and the other guests were made to wear white coats, the factory itself was 'filthy dirty'.

Yet amongst the Moscow-based British officials and journalists with whom he lunched and dined, Sam heard numerous concerns, even panic. One contact told him that Russia was now 'in a very bad way'. Summarising his own findings, Sam wrote that 'The basic ideals [of the revolution] are good' and that 'The preaching of the religion of state ownership is upmost in everyone's mind. Nothing has been well done but everything has been attempted.' And he went on:

The Russians are Asiatics and must not be judged on Western standards. There are two opinions as to whether the worker is better off now than before the Revolution. Today at least the worker and the peasant have hope. In spite of all their muddles they try to be helpful and mean well. Russia today is full of dishonesty and trickery, although allowances must be allowed for the present system which is hit and miss. They are still nowhere near Socialism. Stalin is the real head of affairs and is likely to remain so for some considerable time.

With the Jewish New Year falling that year on 15 September, Sam and his uncle walked through Moscow in search of a synagogue. Down a narrow back street, they discovered a 'beautifully decorated synagogue full to overflowing and a congregation extremely noisy and unpleasant'. Sam was surprised at the large number of young people present, singing Hebrew prayers, bowing towards the Ark. He was moved by the determined survival of the Jewish population, despite the prevailing communist anti-religious propaganda.

By the end of the second week of September, Sam had had enough. In his diary he noted that he was very tired and 'fed up with Harry'. He was ready to return home. The following day they set off by train for England, by way of Kiev, Budapest and Vienna. It had been a grand adventure, illuminating and not a little scary.

Back in London, Sam returned to his parents' house at 51 Mount Street in Mayfair. While Isidore and Kitty were clearly pleased to see him, it was soon obvious that something was wrong. After putting down his luggage and taking off his coat, they told him that his uncle Alfred was doing poorly. Though nominally chairman of Lyons since

Monte's death, Isidore's brother had suffered acute stomach pain for some time and had done little work for the company. While Sam had been away, his condition had grown far worse. He had been rushed to hospital and had undergone two emergency operations. He was now recovering at home in Kensington, but the prognosis was not good.

Two weeks later, on 11 October, the phone rang. Isidore took the call and listened in silence. It was bad news. His eldest brother Alfred had died at his home in Kensington. He was only sixty years old. The obituaries written about him over the next few days were kind, and none more so than that in the *East London Observer*, which having pointed out Alfred's connection to Whitechapel, wrote that his death 'removes a merchant prince who was typical of what can be done in England by hard work, foresight and faith in personal effort'. Two days after his death, Alfred was buried in the Liberal cemetery in Willesden, next to his uncle, Monte Gluckstein.

Two weeks after Alfred's death, on 29 October 1929, the stock market in New York crashed. The impact on Britain was both immediate and devastating. With the collapse of the American economy, Britain lost one of its biggest consumers. At the same time American banks, which had loaned millions of pounds to British industry since the end of the Great War, called in their loans. By the end of 1930, unemployment in Britain rose from one million to 2.5 million – almost 20 per cent of the workforce. Meanwhile British exports fell by more than 50 per cent. The hardest-hit regions were those associated with extraction and manufacture in northern England, Scotland and Wales.

The Great Depression, as it was now being called, posed significant challenges to the directors of J. Lyons. Reports began arriving in

Cadby Hall of reduced trade across the country. By this point Lyons had seven teashops in Manchester and Liverpool, five in Birmingham, two in Sheffield and Leeds, along with fifty other locations outside London. They also owned a chain of high-end restaurants, such as the Maison Lyons restaurant complex in Liverpool and the Popular Café in Manchester, along with a provincial bakery in Liverpool and another in Glasgow.

Isidore, Harry and the rest of the board met to discuss how to respond. With such high unemployment, they were confident that the next year or two would see lower staff turnover than usual. After all, why would someone leave, if they believed it difficult to find a job elsewhere? This would mean they could cap wage increases and save money on recruitment and training. To boost sales, though, they would need to reduce prices. This, they hoped, would make the Lyons teashop a place of daily necessity, not luxury. Having agreed their strategy, the board instructed their division managers to put their plan into action.

While Lyons was organising a swift and robust response to the economic crisis, the British government struggled to do the same. Ramsay MacDonald's Labour government could not agree on whether to cut or increase public spending. Whether to pay benefits to those unemployed according to contributions paid in, or according to need. Torn apart by accusations of incompetence and class disloyalty, the Labour government fell into disarray, leading to a general election in October 1931.

For Labour, the result was catastrophic, losing 80 per cent of their seats in Parliament. Meanwhile, the Conservative Party won a landslide, increasing their seats from 260 to 470. With the country still in economic turmoil, King George V encouraged the head of the Conservative Party, Stanley Baldwin, to form a National Government with the Liberals. Then, to the shock of his own party, the Labour politician Ramsay MacDonald agreed to stay on as prime minster, for the sake of the national interest. He was called a traitor by his Labour colleagues and was ejected from the party.

For Isidore Salmon, the 1931 election was a happy one. With the tide turning in favour of the Conservatives, he easily kept his Harrow seat, increasing his vote to 48,068, up from 23,466 at the previous election. With his party in the ascendant, Isidore was looking forward to his role in the next cycle of government.

Chapter 29

1932

On the evening of 9 November 1932, Gluck – as everyone now called her, even the press – stood at the entrance to the Fine Arts Society at 148 New Bond Street in Mayfair, just a few steps from Isidore and Kitty's house.

Wearing a crisp white shirt, navy blue suit, and a spotted silk cravat, and sporting her trademark close-cropped hair (shaped at Truefitt & Hill's, barbers to the King), she greeted guests as they arrived for her 'Diverse Paintings' exhibition. In all, twenty-nine pictures had been hung on the whitewashed walls, including two theatrical paintings – *Three Nifty Nats* and *Ernest Thesiger waiting for his turn* – an oil painting of her mother, and a variety of flower still-lifes, including one of a vase of tulips.

Despite Gluck's ongoing feud with her father, despite her mother's failure to understand her choice of fashion, haircut or lovers, despite her relatives' aversion to scandal, in the end the family came first. Her parents, her brother and his wife arrived early, as did various uncles and aunts and cousins, including Mimi, Isidore and Sam. Also present were various society grandees, such as the fashion designer Cecil Beaton and the architect Oliver Hill. The socialite Nesta

Gluck, Fine Arts Society exhibition

Obermer made an appearance and then, to everyone's delight, Queen Mary arrived.

As she walked around the exhibition, the Queen conversed with Gluck. 'I would give a lot to know,' wrote a columnist for the *Portsmouth Evening News*, whether Queen Mary 'addressed her as "Miss Gluck" or as "Gluck". For Gluck is an artist of the Bohemian kind, wears an Eton crop, affects a masculine type of dress, and tells you she dislikes the prefix "Miss" and prefers plain "Gluck".' The Queen remained for thirty minutes to review the twenty-nine pictures on display (she said she wouldn't mind being given *Tulips*) and then left.

The event was well covered in the papers. *The Times* said that the show was 'remarkable chiefly for its suavity of workmanship and unusual effects of colour'. The *Scotsman* wrote that 'Gluck's subjects are well chosen and full of variety.' The *Lady* reported that 'No one who loves painting should miss this exhibition.' The *Belfast News* was less complimentary, describing the paintings as 'caricatures' and 'ludicrous'. For the most part, however, the exhibition was well received, and the gallery encouraged Gluck to return for another show as soon as she was ready.

Somehow the family had managed to square the circle of respectability, gender-fluidity and art. Part of this stemmed from a commitment to unity above all things. And it surely did not hurt that Gluck benefited from a trust in her name, whose coffers were regularly filled by the Fund and which, although managed – to her annoyance – by her father, paid for a fine three-storey building in Hampstead and a well-equipped studio, allowing her to live an independent lifestyle.

In June 1932, J. Lyons held its annual shareholders' meeting. Isidore was pleased to report that despite the economic downturn, the company was able to increase slightly its profit from the year before.

They had achieved this by reducing prices, which led to increased demand. During the year 1930–31 Lyons had served more than 160,000 million meals, 20 per cent more than the previous year. At the same time they maintained sales of packed tea, coffee, cocoa and other products to retailers, amounting to 76,000 tonnes per year.

And Gluck was not the only family member to be recognised by the royal family. In the New Year's honours list it was announced that Isidore Salmon would be receiving a knighthood, in recognition of his political and public service. This was partly an acknowledgement of his work as vice-president of the Board of Deputies of British Jews. It was also a nod to his many other civic activities, such as his leadership of the organisation that argued for the decimalisation of the British pound, and his chairing of the Home Secretary's committee on the employment of released prisoners.

Early one morning in January 1933, Isidore and Kitty were driven by car to Buckingham Palace for the accolade. Once inside the royal gates, Isidore and the other honourees followed a footman through a series of plushly appointed corridors and into a gold-encrusted hall. In the line with him, waiting to be called, was the former editor of *Punch* magazine, Owen Seaman (whose former assistant was A.A. Milne, who may have based Eeyore's gloominess on his boss's sour personality), the art dealer Joseph Duveen, along with Rennell Rodd, Britain's ambassador to Italy during the First World War.

When it was his turn, Isidore took three paces forward, bowed stiffly, then walked forward a few more steps and knelt on the red-cushioned knighting stool. After a brief pause, King George lowered a heavy sword towards him, gently dubbing the flat side of the blade on the right shoulder, then over his head, to tap the other one. Not only was Isidore the first member of the family to have been elected a Member of Parliament, but he was now the first to be addressed by the honorific 'Sir'. Kitty would be addressed as 'Lady Salmon'.

Meanwhile, as a member of the Foreign Affairs Committee of the Board of Deputies of British Jews, Isidore had been closely following political events in Germany. In particular, he had kept a keen eye on the rise of the right-wing National Socialist German Workers' Party, or Nazi Party, led by Adolf Hitler. The national election that was held in November 1932 had resulted in no one party having a majority in the Reichstag, the German parliament, although the National Socialists had won the largest number of seats, with 33 per cent of the vote. Unable to find an alternative, the German president, Paul von Hindenburg, had reluctantly appointed Hitler as Chancellor of Germany on 30 January 1933. The election had been extensively covered by the British media, including Hitler's frequent attacks on

The newly knighted, including Isidore Salmon (top right), *Bystander* magazine

international Jewry. In response to the rise of the National Socialists, a growing number of Jewish and non-Jewish organisations in Britain were calling for a boycott of German goods.

The idea for a boycott was picked up by the British media. On 24 March, the *Daily Express* ran a front-page article about the campaign, under the headline 'JUDEA DECLARES WAR ON GERMANY'. 'Sectional differences and antagonisms have been submerged,' it wrote, 'in one common aim to stand by the 600,000 Jews of Germany who are terrorised by Hitlerist anti-Semitism.' By the end of the month, hundreds of British businesses had announced they were no longer purchasing German goods, whilst flyers were circulated listing German products that consumers should not purchase, including rubber sheets, pencil sharpeners, Christmas crackers, ladies' and girls' fleecy underwear, photograph films and soft flannel toys.

The Board of Deputies was inundated with calls to support the boycott. The issue was referred to the Joint Foreign Affairs Committee, of which Isidore was a member, but it was split on its response. Some argued that the Board should join the campaign, that they must publicly demonstrate the strength of their outrage. Others said that a British boycott might provoke Hitler to take his anger out on the Jews in Germany, and they must avoid this at all costs. They added that a boycott could also trigger a backlash in Britain, and could lead to right-wing groups accusing the Jews of meddling in foreign affairs. Any demonstration or criticism should be left to non-Jews, they said, who could argue their case for them. It was best, as always, to keep their collective heads below the parapet. A third group, including Isidore Salmon, said that the situation in Germany was hard to verify. What they really needed was more information. For now, the Board of Deputies agreed to take a neutral position on the boycott. An invitation to speak in Hyde Park was declined (too political), as was a request for funding (they had no surplus to distribute), while press requests were answered with a polite 'No comment'.

Over the next few weeks, Isidore was kept informed of the situation in Germany by a variety of secret and confidential sources. He was given access to witness statements from refugees who had just arrived in London, letters from family members in Berlin, as well as cables from diplomats across Europe. He received a copy of a speech by Joseph Goebbels, Hitler's Minister for Propaganda, in which he had declared that the German government's policy was the 'entire destruction of the Jews'. He read a report of a 'blood libel' case in Czechoslovakia in which two Jews were accused of having drawn blood for ritual purposes from the arms of two Christian schoolchildren. And he saw a pamphlet put together by the SA (the Nazi Party's paramilitary organisation), which told its members, 'When Jewish blood spurts from the knife wounds, yes, then everything will be good.'

At the end of March, the Board of Deputies' fears of retaliation were realised. Blaming the Jews of Britain and the USA for boycotting German goods, Hitler called for a boycott of Jewish businesses in Germany. On 1 April 1933, thousands of Jewish shops and businesses were attacked in Berlin and around the country. Windows were smashed. Slogans reading 'Dirty Jews' and 'Jews are our misfortune' were painted on doors and walls. These shocking events in Germany were widely reported by the British newspapers. The question was how should the Board respond? Isidore still strongly believed that maintaining a low public profile was the best approach.

On 10 April, just nine days after the anti-Jewish attacks in Germany, the full Board of Deputies gathered for a closed-door session at Woburn House in central London. There was a febrile, nervous atmosphere in the room. Isidore sat behind a long white table at the front of the hall, next to the president and the other vice-president. Before them sat the assembled deputies – more than 200 men, all keen to hear the latest news from Germany and to share their opinions. The floor was open and members were invited to speak.

A deputy from Romania stood up and said that the Joint Committee on Foreign Affairs had failed to give leadership to the masses and that 'running after non-Jewish opinion' was enough to 'make them think we are a second-class people'. Another from Nairobi added that 'If we must go down, we should at least go down fighting. Perhaps there is little we can do but for God's sake let the elected representatives of the Jewish community issue a call and show their indignation.' When a member of the audience said that it was 'not fair' to criticise the Joint Committee on Foreign Affairs, someone else shouted out, 'Why?' To this, a deputy from east London jumped up and declared, 'Let us show the world a united front.'

Then Joseph Gluckstein's son Louis rose to speak. As a director of the Liberal Jewish Synagogue, Louis had joined the Board of Deputies the year before. From the front of the hall, Isidore was curious to hear what his cousin would say. Louis declared that he 'deplored immoderate statements'. The country had two simple choices, he said: either put diplomatic pressure on Germany or 'employ some form of war, economic or military'. Louis favoured a boycott. A vote was called and, to Isidore's relief, the Board decided not to support the boycott. His cousin Louis was less pleased.

Flyer, 1933

While Isidore and Louis were engaged in debates about international diplomacy, their cousin Mimi was preoccupied with rearing the next generation.

Throughout the summer and autumn of 1933 she engaged in a lengthy correspondence with her twelve-year-old son, Neil, who was attending Malvern College, a private school in Worcestershire. A precocious boy with a good head for numbers, Neil also had a keen interest in the family business. On 30 June, for instance, he wrote that he had read in the papers that J. Lyons had made a net profit of £30,000, 'in spite of father's grumbling about the business last year'. In another letter, Neil asked to have cream with his porridge for breakfast. Fourteen other boys had it, he said, and he would pay for the cost by not taking carpentry lessons. He also thanked his mother for sending a mathematical proof, which was 'very interesting', and asked that she take care of his two dogs, Squib and Mussolini.

It is clear from his letters that Neil felt compassion for others. In one letter, he talked about a boy named Brian Johnson who 'had a bitter bereavement' after his father collapsed and died while playing golf. The boy, said Neil, 'was a great friend'. In another missive, Neil said that he had seen a film about the Battle of the Somme, which 'was very good – in parts it was rather sad.'

In early 1934, the correspondence returned to the theme of food. The school had been informed that they would no longer be able to purchase cakes at a heavy discount from Lyons. This caused great alarm amongst Neil's peers. 'As a special favour,' Neil pleaded with his mother, 'could you avert the disaster, otherwise I will come home like a rake. The other boys will pull my leg saying how rotten Lyons grub is; but they think they would prefer it to nothing; and have placed all their hopes in you.' A few days later, the head of supplies at Malvern was informed that deliveries of Lyons cakes would resume.

At the end of the summer term 1934, Mimi and her husband Julius received a letter from the school congratulating them on Neil's intellect and leadership skills. 'It would certainly be a good thing if he could go to university I fancy,' wrote the headmaster, 'he undoubtedly has good brains.'

Mimi Salmon

Meanwhile, by the summer of 1934, the Board of Deputies' unwillingness to take a public stand against Germany had angered many in the wider Jewish community. In the wake of this inaction, a 'Jewish Representative Council for the Organisation of the Boycott' was formed, made up of an array of synagogues, trade unions, textile traders and other groups. Some in the Council questioned the motives of the Board. They suggested that several members had conflicts of interests because they ran companies that traded with Germany and were buying products 'dripped in Jewish blood'.

As pressure mounted over the next few weeks for the Board of Deputies to take action, its president, Neville Laski, was in constant correspondence with Isidore. Addressing him variously as 'Dear Salmon' and 'Sir Isidore', Laski conferred on the course of action. Should they respond to journalist enquiries? Best to answer with 'No comment', Isidore said, for now. Should an aggressive letter be sent to Members of Parliament, urging them to criticise Hitler? Again, let's wait and see. Should they forward to the press a letter received from the Home Secretary about the Board of Deputies? Best not to.

Laski also shared the latest intelligence from Germany. Sometimes the information was out of date, or Isidore had seen it before. On other occasions it provided only a partial picture, which was confusing. On 5 July 1934, for instance, Laski sent Isidore a copy of a cable from the American Jewish Committee in Paris, along with a note that it was 'of the greatest interest':

> Berlin recent occurrences which argue great improvement situation coreligionists. Believe Nazis subjugated permanently. Fuehrer now window-dressing controlled by Army Conservatives. Advisable Everybody Rabbis Press restrained comment.

On first look, this seemed like very good news. 'Coreligionists' meant the Jewish community of Germany. 'Nazis subjugated permanently' – if true – sounded excellent. 'Fuehrer ... controlled by the army' suggested that Adolf Hitler was now in the hands of the anti-fascist generals. The 'restrained comment' meant that, as always, the Jewish community in Britain should keep a low profile.

After reading the cable a second time, it appeared that a raft of senior Nazi leaders, including Hitler, had been arrested in Berlin, which would be very positive indeed. But a few days later, Isidore and Laski learned that far from being a reversal of fortune, the cable had instead described a purging of Nazi opposition, in what would later become known as the 'Night of the Long Knives'. Hitler was not weakened; he was more powerful than ever.

At 5 p.m. on 25 October 1934, a meeting was convened between the two rival Jewish groups at the Ben Uri Hall in Woburn House near Euston, London. The objective was to calm emotions and agree on a unified public position. Six members of the Board of Deputies were present, including Isidore, along with six members of the Jewish Representative Council. They embarked on a three-hour discussion in which they repeated the arguments they had all heard before. The difference now, though, was that with every passing day Hitler and the National Socialists were gaining power, and the threat to the Jews in Germany was increasing. It was clear to Isidore and everyone present, therefore, that, despite their instincts, they had to put their head above the parapet and show leadership on behalf of the British Jewish community.

Finally a compromise was agreed and a joint statement was released to the press: 'That in view of the continued anti-Jewish policy in Germany, no self-respecting Jew will handle German goods or utilise German services for so long as this policy endures.' At last the Board of Deputies had come off the fence.

With hostilities within the British Jewish community becalmed, Isidore turned his attention to a threat closer to home.

Chapter 30

1933

For some months memos marked 'completely confidential' had been arriving at Isidore's home in Mayfair. These had been prepared by the staff at the Board of Deputies and detailed the rise of Oswald Mosley's new organisation, the British Union of Fascists.

'For the first time in British history,' stated one memo, 'anti-Semitism is being used as the official policy of a political movement.' At speeches in London, Liverpool and Manchester, Mosley had accused the Jews of 'aiming at world domination ... of controlling the city of London and the press, and of crippling industry with their sweatshops'. He had also described the Jews as 'sweepings of the ghettos' and 'hordes subsidised by Moscow gold'.

'In general,' continued the memo, Mosley's aim was the 'absolute dictatorship by the Fascist organisation, to English conditions'. The fundamental difference between the British Union of Fascists (BUF) and other political organisations in Britain was that it was a 'drilled and disciplined fighting machine under the absolute control of THE LEADER.' Their uniform comprised a black shirt, black trousers, black belt (made of aluminium, and useful in the fray) and black shoes. The BUF national headquarters were located at 33 King's Road in Chelsea,

Londons, where Mosley claimed that '700 members work and in addition 500 S.S. men, whom we call Defence Force, are quartered'.

Another memo gave a brief history of Mosley's recent rise to power. After losing the election against Neville Chamberlain in Birmingham, he had twice won the Staffordshire seat for Labour, before falling out with Ramsay MacDonald and the Labour leadership and forming his own party, the New Party. Following a dismal performance at the 1931 general election in which the New Party failed to win a single seat, receiving less than half the votes gained by the Communist Party, Mosley had looked increasingly to European politics as a way forward. In January 1932, he had travelled to Rome, where he enjoyed an inspirational meeting with Benito Mussolini. Speaking in French and discussing politics at length, Mosley liked his host and found him easy to get on with. During this meeting Mussolini had advised Mosley to bring fascism to Britain. Upon his return, Mosley had written an enthusiastic article about Mussolini for the *Daily Mail*, declaring that 'the Great Italian represents the first emergence of the modern man to power'. Eight months later, on 30 September that same year, the British Union of Fascists was launched with fifteen members, including Mosley himself. His second-in-command and head of organisation was Dr Robert Forgan, a Scottish-born former Member of Parliament and physician, who was godfather to Mosley's son. Mosley's new fascist policies and philosophies were laid out in his book *Greater Britain*, which had been published in October 1932, and was amplified in the movement's weekly newspaper, the *Blackshirt*.

Mosley had issued his first anti-Semitic remark in public on 24 October 1932, less than a month after the launch of the BUF. It was during a speech that he was giving at the Congregational Memorial Hall in Farringdon, central London, when he called a group of hecklers at the meeting 'three warriors of the class war – all from Jerusalem'. Then he started using the slogan 'Britain for the British'. Very quickly

Mosley made clear that anti-Semitism and xenophobia would be central to his new movement's ideology. Early supporters of the BUF included the journalist G.K. Chesterton, Vivienne Haigh-Wood (writer and wife of T.S. Eliot) and William Joyce (who later became infamous for his Lord Haw-Haw wartime radio broadcasts from Berlin).

Oswald Mosley was now attacking the British Jews for their boycott of German goods, saying that they had in effect 'declared war on Germany'. He would come to say that 'our quarrel with the Jewish interests is that they have set the interests of their co-racialists at home and abroad above the interest of the British state'. This questioning of patriotism felt very familiar to Isidore and to the family.

As Isidore went through his mail each day, he came across increasingly disturbing reports. One correspondent described the 'violent anti-Semitic activity of the Blackshirts' that was taking place in Bethnal Green, east London, and begged that her name not be published or 'the Blackshirts will finish me off quick as lightning'. Another letter reported seeing a poster stuck on a wall in east London:

Warning to Jews
We give you till Friday April 24th
to clear from London, or fight us.
Black Shirts

Isidore had heard about the 'Hep-Hep' riots in Rheinberg from his grandfather and grandmother. The similarities were obvious: false accusations. Encouragement to leave. Threats of violence. Fear of identifying yourself. Then things became even more personal.

On 30 April 1933, seven members of the British Union of Fascists gathered outside the Lyons Corner House on Coventry Street near Piccadilly Circus. Wearing the organisation's uniform, they sold copies of the *Blackshirt* and harassed members of the public. A fight soon broke out on the street between the fascists and two Jews who happened to be passing by. They were all arrested. At the court hearing the following day, the magistrate dismissed the defendants with a stern warning. The only instruction to the fascists was to avoid Coventry Street, 'owing to the Jewish attitude towards them'. A week later, another fight broke out in front of the Corner House, and this time eight were charged with disorderly conduct. Two were sentenced to prison; both were Jewish.

The fascists' anger towards the chairman of J. Lyons & Company was mirrored in the pages of the *Blackshirt*. One article began with the headline 'IS ISIDORE SALMON A JEW?' The piece went on to say that Jews 'have made themselves objectionable in more ways than one way' and called on Londoners 'never to be deceived by their methods or be hoodwinked by their cringing under the British flag'. In another front-page article, a writer 'blushes to admit' that he was taking tea at one of the Lyons Corner Houses, played a game of 'spot the gentile', and was surprised that some of the waiters were 'mere Aryans'.

And still the movement grew.

While the mounting threat of British fascism absorbed considerable emotional energy, Isidore and the rest of the family were working all hours of the day managing their business. One of the chief causes of their heightened activity was the opening of their long-planned-for property opposite Marble Arch, the Cumberland Hotel.

With 1,000 bedrooms, 1,000 bathrooms and more than 2,000 staff, the Cumberland Hotel was the Salmons and the Glucksteins' most ambitious project yet. Encased within its walls were 15,000 tonnes of steelwork, 45,000 metres of carpet and £200,000 worth of furniture. In the run-up to the launch, Lyons' marketing department unleashed a familiar avalanche of display advertisements in the newspapers. A half-page display in the *Western Daily Press*, for instance, declared that each of the hotel's bedrooms had its own private toilet and bathroom, came with a fitted wardrobe, baggage hall and telephone, and with individually regulated heat. As a result of this campaign, the *Daily Express* declared the hotel 'famous before its doors are opened'.

Two weeks before Christmas 1933, and two days before the public opening, the first visitors arrived. In the marble-floored vestibule they were met by Isidore, who introduced them to his brother Harry and son Sam. None of the staff knew that a tour had been arranged, and they were surprised when they looked up from their labours – polishing the cutlery, laying the beds, stocking the bar, checking the 'silent lifts' and 'maid-finder' buzzers – to see the King and Queen.

When the visitors arrived at the massive kitchens, filled with the latest stainless-steel cabinets and work surfaces, Isidore introduced the head chef, a Monsieur Brégon. 'Do you know Monsieur Cédard, my chef at Buckingham Palace?' asked the King in French. The head chef said that yes, indeed he did; they belonged to the same culinary society. Isidore then explained that Brégon was one of France's most-respected chefs and had received the *Chevalier du Mérite agricole*. After an hour's tour, the party made their way back to the front desk. Were the reception clerks able to deal with non-English speaking visitors? enquired the Queen. To her delight, the women said they could speak three languages. As he climbed back into his car, the King complimented Isidore on his new project. 'I call it a creation, and worthy of the company's organisation.'

The following day, a luncheon was given in the hotel's Banqueting Room for more than 300 guests. In attendance were a number of press barons, politicians and heads of industry. Standing in front of a packed room, Isidore declared that the Cumberland was a unique offering, providing what he called 'super-luxury' to the public at a reasonable price. He then gave a tribute to the newspapers. 'No one appreciates more than my company the press as an advertising medium,' he gushed, 'and everyone connected with industry recognises that if he has a good article it pays to advertise.' Looking at the room in front on him, full of well-dressed guests, Isidore added with a smile, 'we must confess there has been a remarkable response to our announcements in the press'. This was received with loud chuckles and some clapping from his audience.

Once the chairman of Lyons had finished, the man next to him stood up. It was Viscount Rothermere, the owner of the *Daily Mail*, which had the largest newspaper circulation in Britain. A head taller than Isidore and younger-faced, with slicked-back hair and a charismatic smile, Rothermere first gave thanks for the luncheon and then declared his appreciation for the new hotel's astonishing decor and superbly attentive staff. This was met with more clapping.

He then lifted his glass of champagne and said, 'Industries such as the great company of which Sir Isidore is the head are the backbone of the country.' He proposed a toast: 'Sir Isidore,' he cried. To which 300 guests retorted loudly, 'Sir Isidore'.

Isidore Salmon (right) next to Viscount Rothermere, opening Cumberland Hotel

J. Lyons & Company, however, was not the only venture supported by the newspaper proprietor. On 22 January 1934, less than a month after he had toasted Isidore at the Cumberland Hotel, Viscount Rothermere wrote articles for the *Daily Mail* and *Daily Mirror* under the respective headlines 'HURRAH FOR THE BLACKSHIRTS' and 'GIVE THE BLACKSHIRTS A HELPING HAND'.

Britain's survival, Rothermere argued, depended on the 'existence of a Great Party of the Right with the same directness of purpose and energy of method as Hitler and Mussolini have displayed.' He added, 'The socialists who jeer at the principles and uniform of the Blackshirt being of foreign origin forget that the founder and High Priest of their own creed was the German Jew Karl Marx.' Rothermere, it seemed, feared the rise of socialism and saw the militancy of the British Union of Fascists as a bulwark against the left.

The support of Rothermere was a major boost for Oswald Mosley. It was also a huge disappointment for Isidore Salmon. Not only did he count the press baron a personal friend, but he believed that Lyons' marketing budget guaranteed neutrality, if not support, when it came to the Jewish cause. Just over a decade earlier, Monte had purchased a quarter of one day's issue of the *Daily Mail* to celebrate the twenty-fifth anniversary of the Trocadero. Since then, Lyons had spent hundreds of thousands of pounds on advertising in it and associated papers.

With Mosley's increasingly populist rhetoric, inflamed by coverage in Rothermere's papers, membership of the BUF now swelled to more than 50,000 people. According to a report from Special Branch, which was closely monitoring the union, the new recruits included generals, admirals, businessmen and young women 'with Union Jacks around their lily-white shoulders who probably saw just one side of it, the patriotic side'. Britain's fascist movement was becoming respectable.

Daily Mail, 22 January 1934

Late in the afternoon of 7 June 1934, Isidore Salmon was working at his desk on the fourth floor of the WX block of Cadby Hall when he was disturbed by shouting and raucous singing. He walked to the window to see what was going on. Outside on Blythe Road, the narrow street that ran between Cadby Hall and Olympia, was gathered an enormous crowd. From the black clothes they were wearing and the signs they were holding, he could see that they were connected to the BUF. They appeared to be heading towards the exhibition hall. Here, on the street in front of him, were tens of thousands of people calling for attacks on Jews, for immigrants to be deported from the country, for a fascist state to be created in Britain. It was terrifying.

From newspaper reports, Isidore knew that Oswald Mosley had been planning to hold an event at Olympia that evening, but there had been no warning that it would draw such a large crowd. The most recent BUF mass rally had taken place at London's Albert Hall three months earlier and had passed without violence, so there was no reason, Isidore had thought, to be concerned. Yet now that he saw the crowd's size, he would have to telephone Kitty and tell her that he would be late for dinner. It was probably a good idea to stay, in any case. More than 6,000 people worked at Cadby Hall and while the majority had left by now, many were still involved in the overnight manufacture of baked goods. His son Sam was also in the building, as were a number of the other directors.

Back at his desk, he sent a message to the night managers to warn the staff of the trouble, and another to the night watchmen to secure the premises as best they could. He would remain with them all and would monitor events from his office. He hoped that none of his off-duty employees would get caught up in the evening's activities and that any fracas did not spill over into the grounds of Cadby Hall.

By 8 p.m. the situation had worsened. There were now more than 16,000 people milling around the streets outside Olympia. The vast majority were BUF supporters, but there were also thousands of counter-demonstrators, many of whom were Jewish and had marched from Whitechapel and other parts of east London, a distance of more than 10 kilometres. The mood was tense, with parts of the crowd singing old English airs, whilst others sang 'The Red Flag' and the 'Internationale'. Some of those gathered were seen carrying knuckledusters, knives and wooden batons. When the main hall at Olympia was full to capacity, the doors were closed and more than 3,000 people were left outside in the streets – 1,000 fascists and 2,000 anti-fascists. Hundreds of mounted and foot-police were also present, having been barred from entering the building by the event organisers.

Inside the exhibition hall there were now 12,500 BUF supporters and 500 counter-demonstrators. At 8.35 p.m., thirty-five minutes late, a trumpet sounded and four powerful spotlights arced through the darkened hall, searching the crowd until they landed on a slender figure sporting a tidy moustache and slicked-back dark hair, striding down the aisle surrounded by a phalanx of black-shirted guards carrying Union Jacks. The hall erupted in cheers as Oswald Mosley marched onto the stage and took the podium. After long applause, the leader gave a stiff 'fascist salute', and started his speech. 'This meeting,' he began, 'is the culmination of a great national campaign ...'

Oswald Mosley, Olympia

'Fascism means murder,' shouted a heckler. 'Down with Mosley,' screamed another. The protestors were swiftly grabbed by uniformed stewards and hustled out of the hall. Mosley restarted his speech, but was once again interrupted. The protestor was picked out by a search-light, surrounded by twenty stewards and, while he was manhandled out, the crowd chanted, 'We want Mosley! We want Mosley!' Once the man had been evicted, Mosley told the crowd that 'we are very grateful to those who are interrupting. They illustrate how necessary a Fascist defence force is to defend freedom of speech in Great Britain.'

He resumed his speech, but was interrupted a third time, then a fourth and a fifth. It was becoming clear that this was a well-organised protest. When he noticed that one of the protestors was a woman, he added, 'It is typical of the red cowards to send a woman to do the job they dare not do themselves.'

Over the next one and a half hours, scores of protestors were roughly escorted out by the stewards. As time went on, the violence escalated. The interrupters were dragged out of view by mobs of uniformed Blackshirts, into darkened corridors and stairwells, where they were thrown onto the ground and brutally beaten. 'Several men were bleeding profusely,' police sergeant Rogers later wrote, 'almost every person bore some mark of violence and was in a state of semi-collapse.'

In the streets and alleys around Olympia, the boisterous but peaceful gathering of fascists and anti-fascists now descended into a brutal melee. The police made sporadic efforts to intervene, arresting nineteen men and two women in the process, but for the most part the fighting continued unabated. While one group shouted, 'Come on, comrades' and 'Down with Mosley', the others yelled, 'Get the Reds!' and 'Stinking Jews!'

Much of the violence could be seen from Cadby Hall's WX block. 'Leaving the building by the Blythe Road entrance,' reported one witness, 'I saw a man being half carried, half dragged, by eight men in black shirts to the gates. Here they stopped, stripped him of his trousers, and assaulted him in a way that made him scream with agony. Then they threw him into the road.' It was the worst violence seen on the London streets in a generation. When Isidore and Sam finally managed to return home, they discussed what had happened with Kitty and Julian. Sam urged his father to write to the papers and describe what happened, to use his position as head of Lyons and vice-president of the Board of Deputies. Isidore, as ever, cautioned restraint. Nothing was agreed. They all retired to bed deeply anxious.

In the press the following day Mosley was severely criticised for encouraging the violence and not allowing the police inside the hall. *The Times* quoted an independent eyewitness who said, 'the force used in ejecting people was much more than was required to get them out'. In a letter to the same paper, Mr G. Lloyd – a Member of Parliament who had been curious to hear Mosley speak – said that in 'case after case' he saw protestors being surrounded and beaten up by six or more Blackshirts. 'It was a deeply shocking thing for an Englishman to see in London. The Blackshirts behaved like bullies and cads.'

In a series of interviews Oswald Mosley shot back that scores of his followers had been stabbed and suffered head injuries, and that the counter-demonstrators had long planned to hijack the event using violence. He blamed the communists and the Jews; he demanded police protection; he said that the Olympia event proved the need for a robust response to left-wing agitation. But few listened.

With public opinion turning against the fascists, Isidore decided it was time to take action. He tracked down Viscount Rothermere and made it clear that he had to make a choice: either support the Blackshirts or protect his business. According to Mosley's colleague William Joyce, Rothermere later 'admitted in private that Sir Isidore Salmon had told him that continued support of the British Union of Fascists would mean the withdrawal of all Lyons' advertisements from the *Daily Mail*, as well as any other financial inconveniences which could be arranged'.

Mosley himself confirmed the story. 'I went to see [Rothermere] in a hotel he frequented,' he wrote in his autobiography. 'He was in trouble with certain advertisers who had not liked his support of the Blackshirts.' When Mosley said that Rothermere should fight back, declaring that 'Jews threaten British press', Rothermere demurred. 'He felt that I was asking him to risk too much, not only for himself, but for others who depended on him.' The encounter was also noted by the German attaché in London in a memo sent to his bosses back in Berlin. The German diplomat was informed by 'reliable sources' that 'the Jews threatened to remove their advertisements'. He then mentioned the name 'Lyons'. Another person to endorse this account was Randolph Churchill, who worked as a journalist for Rothermere and was the son of Winston Churchill. His boss' newspaper abandoned its support of Oswald Mosley, Randolph later recalled, 'under the pressure of Jewish advertisers'.

Within days of the meeting at the hotel, the *Daily Mail* pulled its support from Mosley, starving him of publicity and severely diminishing Britain's leading fascist movement. 'Thus a multi-millionaire and a man of very strong character was compelled to bow down to the dictate of Jewry,' Joyce later recalled, adding that 'there could be no graver stigma on the so-called freedom of expression said to prevail in Britain than that a body of Englishmen should be prevented from expressing their views by an Oriental confectioner.'

The animus towards J. Lyons & Company didn't seem to stop the leader of the British Union of Fascists from enjoying their establishments. Shortly after Viscount Rothermere's decision to withdraw his support, the *Bystander* published a sketch of Oswald Mosley sitting at a white-clothed table, in a black shirt and black tie, in front of a glass and a bottle of wine – at the Trocadero. Perhaps he was there to drown his sorrows.

On 12 June 1934, five days after the street-fighting around Olympia, Isidore stood up to give the chairman's speech at J. Lyons & Company's fortieth annual shareholders' meeting. The country's economy was generally healthy, he reported, after years of stagnation. Various industrial innovations were under way, and morale in the company was high. Lyons' profit was similarly on the increase, he continued, and this past year it would exceed £1 million. As a share of GDP, this would be equivalent today to a profit of £461 million.

Under previous leaders – Joseph Lyons, Monte or even Alfred – the chairman's report would have been upbeat, even enthusiastic. This, however, was not Isidore's style. The business, he said, had 'some tendency for improvement'. A few moments later, in case his caution had been overlooked, he repeated the same phrase: 'some tendency for improvement'. More important to Isidore, though, than the company's recent successes, or his fiduciary duties as chairman, was the election to the board, for his son Sam was being appointed director for the first time.

Tradition dictated that each of the Salmon and Gluckstein men was elected to the Lyons board. It was a question of lineage and seniority, not talent. This did not prevent Isidore being proud. 'This event is particularly gratifying to me as he is my elder son,' he said. 'In common with the rest of us he has been thoroughly trained in this business and is imbued with that spirit of devotion to its interests and knowledge of its technicalities which are the first requisite for the position he has obtained.'

In its two-and-a-half-column verbatim coverage of the meeting the following day, *The Times* said that the chairman's report was approved by the shareholders both with applause and with acclaim. Isidore was determined to redouble his efforts. He did not want to let anyone down. His body, however, refused to cooperate.

On Christmas Eve 1934, Kitty wrote to Neville Laski, the head of the Board of Deputies, informing him that her husband had been struck by acute abdominal pain, had undergone an emergency operation to remove a kidney stone and was now resting at the London Clinic in Marylebone. It appeared there were limits, after all. Isidore's efforts to run J. Lyons, perform his duties as a Member of Parliament, whilst also trying to curtail the rise of Oswald Mosley, had come at a cost.

A few days later, Laski wrote to Isidore from New York, where he was on a business trip: 'It gives me infinite distress and anxiety to hear that you had suddenly become ill', adding, 'I beg you to believe that you have been very much in my thoughts throughout my absence.' Over the Christmas holiday, Kitty worried about her husband's health and the crushing responsibilities he shouldered.

While Isidore lay in his sickbed, the business of government continued. Three issues in particular dominated Parliament at this time: the economy, India and rearmament.

The Chancellor of the Exchequer, Neville Chamberlain, announced that, following years of contraction, the country's economy was at last improving. 'Broadly speaking,' he said to his colleagues in the House of Commons, 'we may say that we have recovered 80 per cent of our prosperity.' The problem was that while the economy in the south was indeed improving, large swathes of the country, particularly in northern England, Wales and Scotland, continued to suffer from high rates of unemployment. In some towns, such as Jarrow, more than two-thirds of the male population were out of work. This rising inequality threatened to reduce the popularity of the National Government, which was dominated by the Conservative Party.

At the same time India was taking up an increasing amount of Parliament's time. A nationalist movement, led by Mahatma Gandhi, was calling for independence. After three round-table meetings with Prime Minister Ramsay MacDonald and his *de facto* deputy, Stanley Baldwin, Gandhi was telling journalists that victory was in sight. This had prompted a strong reaction from Conservatives, including Winston Churchill, who established the Indian Defence League, which vowed to retain India's dominion status and, in so doing, defend the Empire. The result of this debate was the Government of

India Act, introduced in late 1934 and enacted into law the following year, which granted a degree of autonomy to India, but retained ultimate control for the British Parliament.

The third issue that roiled below the surface of day-to-day politics was the question of rearmament. It was only seventeen years since the end of the Great War, and there continued to be great debate about its cause. Those on the right – the Conservatives, business leaders, army chiefs and the aristocracy – blamed Germany and Austria–Hungary for their imperial obsessions. Those on the left – including Labour, the Liberals, the unions and the communists – accused the upper classes of driving the country to conflict. The war, they said, resulted from capitalism and was waged to benefit the arms manufacturers. Indeed, on 30 July 1934, Labour had tried, and failed, to censure the government because of its planned expansion of the Royal Air Force. Its leader, Clement Atlee, had said, 'We deny the need for increased air arms … and we reject altogether the claim of parity.'

The spring of 1935 provided Isidore and the rest of the country with a moment of reflection for, on 6 May, King George V celebrated his jubilee. Many of the papers compared his first twenty-five years on the throne with those of his grandmother, Victoria. *The Times* published a twenty-eight-page special supplement, describing the epoch that had unfolded since the King's ascension. It was reticent, however, to draw too many conclusions. 'It is beyond the power of a contemporary to bring his own times to a strict balance,' the editor wrote, 'but the unbiased witness will find more for his notebook than some animadversions.' One example of progress the newspaper did provide was the 'levelling up opportunities' between classes and sexes. Another was the increased participation of the electorate, which ushered in an era of 'bread and butter' politics and provided a bulwark against the 'usurpation of extremists'.

On 7 June, Ramsay MacDonald stepped down as prime minister due to ill health and was replaced by Stanley Baldwin. There was now increasing talk – in the House of Commons tearoom, in the press, at union meetings and over dinner tables across the country – that a general election would probably be held that autumn.

Such was the political context in early summer 1935. Now, with his strength returned and despite Kitty's concerns, Isidore announced that he was ready to go back to work. He had no choice, he told his wife. With a general election soon to be called, he had to prepare his political campaign. This looked likely to be his toughest election yet. With more than 16 per cent of the workforce still unemployed, and rising concern that the Conservative prime minister Stanley Baldwin was not up to tackling the problem, support for Labour was growing fast. Isidore decided that his best strategy was to keep his distance from Westminster and appeal directly to the public. To achieve this, he would need press coverage. And to get press coverage one had to make a splash.

He took his chance at the next Lyons annual shareholder gathering, which took place on 13 June. It was a smart choice. He knew that the press would be in attendance and that his every word would be recorded, and he knew, without having to say it, that they would connect his words as the head of the country's favourite catering company to his ambitions to win at the next election.

Isidore started by lambasting the 'archaic licensing' laws that not only hampered business, but were an annoyance to overseas visitors. The background to his argument was that in 1914, fearing inebriation would disrupt the war effort, the government had limited the sale of alcohol to lunchtime (12–2.40 p.m.) and dinner time (6.30–10.30 p.m.). These restrictions had been temporarily lifted during King George V's anniversary celebrations, but two weeks ago they had snapped back into place.

'The Jubilee we have just been celebrating has shown,' Isidore declared to the assembled shareholders and journalists, 'that we are not the "dull dogs" our Continental friends sometimes call us, nor are we so childishly irresponsible, when allowed a little extra freedom, as our legislators seem to think.' He then continued: 'If only we could induce our rulers to see what this indicates we might yet bring about such a relaxation of the present restrictions as would make our country an attractive resort for Continental holiday-makers.' This was met with a loud 'Hear Hear' from the assembled audience. 'For I am convinced it is not our much-maligned climate, nor our resorts, not our hotels and restaurants, but our law-imposed dullness which does most to keep them away. Perhaps something could be done by appointing a Minister of Pleasure – the post would not be hard to fill.'

This idea of a Minister of Pleasure was happily picked up by the press. So while the *Daily Express* reported how the 'King of Catering' had called for an end to 'petty and annoying restrictions', the *Daily Mail* commented that 'Our national reputation for a funeral sense of whoopee is beginning to crumble; quite a lot of it crumbled under the pungent comments of Sir Isidore Salmon.' The paper went on to suggest some remedies: the total abolition of crooners; central heating in railway waiting rooms; cabarets in the British Museum; compulsory second helpings of dessert; and the barring of boarding-house aspidistras, lace curtains and plush sofas.

Bedecked with all this publicity, Isidore cruised to victory yet again when the general election took place on 15 November 1935. And although the Conservatives lost eighty-five seats, they retained a majority and Stanley Baldwin remained prime minister. Once he returned to the House of Commons, Isidore was keen to take advantage of his celebrity and to foster relations with a new political friend, Neville Chamberlain.

Isidore and Neville's first contact had been in August 1923, when the former had rather formally congratulated the latter on being appointed

Chancellor of the Exchequer. Since then they had frequently crossed paths in Parliament, as both sat on the Conservative benches.

Despite their different beliefs – Isidore an orthodox Jew, Chamberlain showing no interest in organised religion – they had much in common. Chamberlain's grandfather was from east London, as was Isidore's. Both their fathers ran manufacturing companies (Chamberlain's managed a large metal-screw business in Birmingham); both had commercial experience before entering politics (Chamberlain had run a company making metal ship berths); and like Isidore, Chamberlain had started in local politics before the First World War. Perhaps most importantly, they shared a commitment to fighting the growing threat of fascism.

Now, thirteen years after their first encounter, Chamberlain was Chancellor of the Exchequer and Isidore was a member of the all-important Public Accounts Committee. In the second week of April 1936, Chamberlain asked Isidore to help win support for his budget in Parliament, which, controversially, called for a dramatic increase in military spending. The budget debate would take place within the context of growing international tension. Just that month Germany had remilitarised the Rhineland (in contravention of the Treaty of Versailles) and had rebuffed France's demand to withdraw its troops; Italy had bombed the ancient walled city of Harar in Ethiopia; the Soviet Union and Mongolia had signed a treaty of mutual assistance to counter Japan's growing power in the Far East; and eleven Jews had been killed in Palestine during anti-Jewish riots.

At 3.28 p.m. on the afternoon of 22 April, the budget debate started in Parliament. After six hours of raucous statements and counter-statements, Isidore stepped in, as agreed, to intervene. 'The only way in which we can ensure the existing buoyancy of our trade is by having security at home and security abroad,' he boomed, 'and I believe that the system of strengthening our armed defences is the best means of ensuring the peace of the world.' The hall erupted in shouts and protest. 'Protected against what?' bellowed David Logan, a Labour MP from Liverpool. 'Against aggression,' replied Isidore. 'We have to get down to reality. We tried for years to get disarmament. We not only preached it, but we practised it.' Over a few cries of 'No!', Isidore continued, 'The Honorary Gentlemen may say "No," but facts speak better than their statements, and the fact can easily be proved that we did more than any country in the world to reduce our armaments. What has been the effect? The rest of the world went on increasing armaments, and we reached a time when it became dangerous for this country.' The government had adopted a policy of rearmament, he said, so that the world knew Britain was prepared to meet emergencies, should it be called upon to do so. 'It seems to me,' he concluded, 'that a large number of the Members of the Labour party are not realists.'

Unable to contain himself any further, Logan jumped up. 'I cannot say that I listened with pleasure to the remarks of the last honourable Gentleman,' he said, sounding disgusted. 'He told us that Labour men are not realists. If a little of the realism of the North country could be shown to him perhaps he would better understand the realism that exists,' he continued. 'The kind of realism to which I can point shows the instance of a widow woman in the City of Liverpool, 65 years of age, lying dead upon the floor with rats running over her body and eating it. Surely it cannot be said that the party to which the honorary gentleman belongs stands for the class to which I refer.'

Isidore did not like that. 'Does the honourable member suggest that other Members of the House do not also represent those people?' Taking the bait, and in a barely veiled attack on Isidore's party and his religion, Logan responded. 'What I am saying is that in a land that preaches Christian ethics,' he yelled, 'I am able to find in my division a woman dying of starvation in a cellar.' Then to make clear to everyone what he was talking about, he added, 'Money and

Mammon are the only things we hear about. We ought to pay more attention to the living men and women who have helped to make the greatness of this Empire.' Everyone in the room knew that 'Mammon', which was the Hebrew for money, was an age-old slur against the Jews. After stuttering for a few more sentences, and realising what he had said, Logan sat down, humiliated.

It was time for Chamberlain to step in. Isidore gave way to his friend. 'The sacrifices to which I was referring,' proclaimed Chamberlain, 'were those to which I was asking the country to submit this year. I did not commit myself as to what I shall do in future years.' As the debate then drifted on to other, more arcane aspects of the budget, the Chancellor gave Isidore a nod. The anger of the opposition had been lanced. According to the Whip, they had enough votes to pass the bill. With the support of Parliament, Chamberlain could then give the armed forces, particularly the RAF, the funds needed to rearm rapidly. Isidore had done his bit for the party. He would be thanked later, once the debate was concluded. He was a team player.

His public association with Chamberlain, however, had put him more in the spotlight than ever — something that was noted with interest in Berlin.

Chapter 31

1936

Sam Salmon

As a director of Lyons, Sam was given his own office on the fourth floor of Cadby Hall and a secretary who, like the rest of the employees, addressed him as 'Mr Sam'. To have called him 'Mr Salmon' would have been confusing. As a member of the Fund, Sam also attended the long weekly lunches at the Trocadero. It was at these meetings that the real decisions were made, which were then reported back to the formal Lyons board meetings that took place the next day, on Thursdays, and which were attended by non-family members.

Sam now worked under his uncle Harry, who still ran the company's tea department. Sam's brother Julian and his cousins Douglas and Kenneth also worked for Harry. In addition to tea, coffee and cocoa, they produced and sold a number of other experimental products, known as 'special lines'. By 1936, Lyons was selling twice as much Bev (a liquid coffee) as dried coffee, and as much custard powder as cocoa. Other products were less successful, such as Jersey Lily Tomato Sauce and the cream powder Kookal.

The sale of tea, however, continued to be Lyons' main product. Its chief competitors were Brooke Bond and Typhoo. The latter had recently launched a budget tea that could be purchased using discount stamps, while Brooke Bond produced 'Pre-Gest-Tee', a tea that supposedly helped the digestion, although, after a legal complaint challenging this claim, it was renamed 'PG Tips'. Harry's team, however, eschewed such gimmicks. Their focus was on maintaining quality, keeping prices steady and constant investment in marketing. By the start of 1936, Lyons had increased its tea production to 11,000 chests each week, up from 9,500 in 1924.

At thirty-six, Sam was quite old to be a bachelor. His father had wed at twenty-three. His uncles had also married in their twenties: Alfred at twenty-six, Maurice at twenty-five, Harry at twenty-two. Even his younger brother, Julian, had tied the knot. But married life was not for Sam. The truth was that he enjoyed the opportunity to, as his relatives called it, 'play the field'. For this he was constantly teased, asked about his latest dalliance, told that he would never settle down. But if the cost of keeping his independence was a bit of banter, he was willing to pay the price.

By day, Sam worked diligently at Lyons. By night, he dated the leading artistes of the day. First there was one of the country's biggest film stars, Anna Neagle. Then there was Hélène Cordet, an actress who was just catching Hollywood's eye. And there were many others, all impressed by the good manners, fine suits and gleaming black Bentley of this scion of Lyons. He would take the young women out for dinner and a dance at the Trocadero, returning them home in the early hours of the morning.

Sam described himself as a 'stage-door Johnny', someone who stood by a theatre's door with flowers in hand, waiting to greet an exiting star. 'I could take women out who my mother expected,' Sam would say, 'and I could take women out who were unsuitable. Then there was a third type of woman, who I would allow myself to fall in love with.' Flirtation was okay, he concluded, but 'you had to know when to stop'. Beneath everything, his attitude to romantic relationships was guided by a profound sense of duty and respect for tradition. This is why he was so angry when, in November 1936, he read in the newspapers about King Edward VIII's marital intentions.

Edward VIII had ascended the throne earlier that year, following the death of his father, George V. The Salmons and Glucksteins had been greatly saddened by the death of the King, whose health had been failing for some time. Lyons was by now not only the official baker to the royal family, but also catered for the garden parties held each summer at Buckingham Palace, along with the tennis championship at Wimbledon, which George and his wife Mary had long attended. They had also given the couple private tours around many of Lyons' facilities. As a result, Isidore, Harry, Sam and others in the family had regular contact with the royal family and their staff.

Now, ten months after taking the throne, Edward had created consternation by announcing that he intended to marry Wallace Simpson, an American divorcee. The problem was that, as King, he was head of the Church of England, which vehemently opposed remarriage. Which is why on 16 November, Prime Minister Stanley Baldwin told Edward that the marriage would be unacceptable to the vast majority of his subjects, not only in Britain, but across the Empire. This view was strongly supported by Sam and the rest of the family.

Divorce was virtually unheard of within the Salmon and Gluckstein clan. The marriage bond was considered inviolable, held almost in as high esteem as loyalty to the family. There had been a couple of annulments – discreetly taken care of with a contract and a small purse – and one 'unpleasantness'. According to Mimi, her father had discovered that an American who had been courting one of the family's daughters was already married. 'You are a bogus man!' Monte had screamed at the dupe. 'There is no truth in what you told us, you scoundrel. Clear out, and stay out!' The American was duly dispatched back across the Atlantic.

Sam was therefore relieved when, on 10 December, Edward VIII signed the abdication papers, to be replaced by his younger brother, George VI. The better man, Sam believed, had become King. He also admired George VI's wife, Elizabeth, whom he had met during a recent tour of Cadby Hall. Sam respected George both for finding someone he loved and whom his family would accept.

In the days following the abdication, Sam thought more about his own romantic life. Perhaps his relatives were right: it was time he settled down. Time to find the 'third type of woman' and allow himself to fall in love.

Sam was not the only family member to be thinking about true love.

Gluck first met Nesta in 1932 at a dinner party in Hampshire. A charismatic and glamorous society woman, sometime playwright and reader of poems on BBC Radio, Nesta travelled in the same refined artistic and literary circles as Gluck. Both in their forties, they immediately formed a strong connection. The problem was that Nesta was married to an elderly American named Seymour Obermer. Yet even this did not stop them. Knowing, furtive glances were exchanged across dinner tables. Romantic letters were swapped, read and reread. They kissed behind closed doors and, despite the looks of disapproval, boldly sat next to each other in public at society events, such as Glyndebourne, where they were swept up by the passion of *Don Giovanni*. They were inseparable, fused, in love. So they made a commitment to be with each other, for ever. Although a wedding between two women was not sanctioned by the state, their 'marriage', as Gluck called it, took place on 25 May 1936. In a private ceremony between the two of them, vows were uttered and wedding bands exchanged. Officially, Nesta remained married to her husband, Seymour.

'My darling wife,' Gluck wrote soon afterwards. 'My divine sweetheart, my love, my life. I felt so much I could hardly be said to feel at all … I am interested now only in you and my work, a vast interest really and it doesn't leave time or energy for anything else.' To celebrate their union, Gluck painted the two of them, heads close, looking to their right, out of the picture frame. Nesta eyes wide-open, powerful, her blonde hair streaming back. Gluck in front, looking lower down, more contemplative. She called the picture *Medallion* and also *YouWe*, and hung it in her studio in Hampstead.

Yet despite their acknowledged mutual affection, Nesta also kept up her old life, travelling to the USA and around Europe – to Venice, St Moritz, Paris. When they were apart, they wrote frequently to each other, sometimes as often as three times a day. Even then, Gluck was lovesick. 'You see darling,' she wrote, 'when you are near or with me, it's like a warmth that keeps me from analyzing and retro-

Nesta and Gluck in "Medallion"

spection and gradually I melt and feel human and creative and happy.'
Keen for resolution, Gluck pressured Nesta to leave her husband.
Nesta, in turn, promised to visit soon.

Feeling despondent, Gluck purchased barbiturates on the black
market. These softened the emotional blow of Nesta's distance, but
also made it harder to be productive. Nevertheless, she persevered
with her art. Much of her work was taken up with portraits of
friends, landscapes and street scenes. But the majority of her paintings were now of vases of flowers: lilies, tulips, orchids, nasturtiums.
She was particularly attracted to blooms of white, their leaves succu-
lent, wide open and inviting.

Now forty years old, Gluck continued to receive a sizeable monthly allowance from the Fund, but her relationship with her parents had improved little. Most of all, she wished to be seen achieving success on her own terms, apart from the Salmons and Glucksteins. Just weeks before her next exhibition, again held at the Fine Arts Society in London, Gluck wrote to her mother Francesca. 'For at least a year,' she began, 'I have tried to show you how vital it seemed to me to avoid, especially in my exhibition, any connection whatsoever with the family.' She then asked that both Francesca and other members of the family ensure that they didn't use her given name 'Hannah'. Gluck also asked her mother not to invite any members of the crown. 'My paintings have nothing to do with royal patronage, but a good deal to do with Time!' she wrote. 'And Time is a dignified affair and does not truckle with temporary things.'

Once more, Gluck's exhibition attracted considerable press attention and praise. Some of her new paintings were included, such as *They Also Serve*, a picture of crowds and soldiers waiting during George VI's coronation, which Gluck had painted from a room on the fifth floor of the family's Cumberland Hotel. Various celebrities attended the opening, along with family members, art critics and friends, such as Nesta and her husband, who hosted a celebratory lunch at Claridge's. Those who signed the visitors' book included, to the painter's chagrin, members of the royal family. Later it was learned that the King's mother particularly liked *They Also Serve*. Hearing of the sovereign's interest, Francesca, in cahoots with Nesta (they had built a close relationship), purchased the picture without Gluck's permission and presented it to Her Majesty as a gift, which when she found out caused Gluck immense displeasure.

After the exhibition's end, Gluck returned to her studio, 'furious' (at her mother's betrayal) and exhausted. Meanwhile Nesta continued to travel with her husband, but promised to visit soon, which she did from time to time – a dog show at Olympia, a weekend with friends, skiing in St Moritz – until she left again. And so Gluck waited. For Nesta to leave her husband; for the time when they could live together as the 'real thing'; for her darling wife.

It was around this time that Gluck's cousin, Sam Salmon, met Wendy Benjamin, the woman who would become his wife. Wendy was nineteen years old, slender, dark-haired and so beautiful that people stopped talking when she entered the room.

Wendy's family was firmly from the middle class, far poorer than the Salmons, who now considered themselves very much part of Britain's elite. Not quite in the top echelon perhaps but, given their immigrant and Jewish backgrounds, as close as they might ever come. Wendy's mother, Hannah, was a feisty, ambitious, intelligent woman who had emigrated a decade earlier from Australia to England. She had been introduced to the Salmons and Glucksteins through a mutual friend, and before long was playing bridge with Sam's mother Kitty. It was at one of these card games, in the drawing room of their house in Mayfair, that Sam first saw Wendy. He was smitten. He had to be with Wendy, for the rest of his life.

Wendy's mother was pleased by Sam's interest in her daughter, and all the benefits that such a high-society match might bring. Wendy, however, was not that interested in Sam. He was sweet, but a little on the boring side. But she would do what her mother wanted. Sam's father was also less than enamoured by the prospect. Upon discreet enquiries, Isidore learned that Wendy's mother had won an annulment from her first husband (claiming they had failed to consummate the marriage) and that her second husband (Wendy's father), had worked in the shabby and inglorious rag trade of east

London. Three years earlier he had died in the bath, following a bout of rheumatic fever and much domestic squabbling, leaving his wife with few assets and even fewer connections.

When Sam spoke to his father about his new sweetheart, Isidore was direct. Where was the profit in marrying this girl? But Sam was insistent. When the question of their age difference came up – seventeen years – Sam reminded his father that it was the same as that between his grandparents, Barnett and Lena. There were many stormy conversations. Yet it was clear that Sam was determined, more so than he had ever been.

Over the next several months Sam set about courting Wendy. Slowly, gradually, she warmed to her new beau. He took her to lunch at the Troc and introduced her to his uncles, aunts and cousins. They listened to the BBC radio broadcast of the Berlin Olympics, and marvelled at the brilliance of the sprinter Jesse Owens. He took her riding in Hyde Park and though Wendy was a little afraid of the horse, she enjoyed dressing up in the formal attire: the black wool jacket, tight-fitting jodhpurs and tall leather boots. Sam learned that she was well read and had an interest in world events. They talked about the news: Roosevelt winning the presidential election in America; the civil war in Spain, made worse by the bombing of Madrid by German planes; and the fire at Crystal Palace, which totally destroyed the exhibition hall, and the orange-red glow of which could be seen all the way to Mayfair. Finally, over the New Year, Sam asked Wendy to marry him. Happily, Wendy said yes.

To share the good news, Sam went to see his father, who was working in his study in Mount Street. He talked excitedly about his wedding plans. They needed to make a guest list and send out invitations. They needed to book the rabbi. They needed to make arrangements at the Trocadero for the reception. Seeing that he had no choice, Isidore relented and gave his blessing. With one condition: the wedding must take place at the orthodox synagogue in Bayswater.

This upset Sam, for he wanted the wedding to take place at the Liberal Jewish Synagogue. If Mimi had her wedding there, why couldn't he? Isidore was unbending. Since Wendy's mother could clearly not afford to pay for the wedding expenses – which would be considerable, given the press and the public's expectations – these would have to be covered by the Fund. And the Fund would only pay if Isidore gave his blessing, which he would not, unless the event took place in Bayswater. This was yet another reminder to Sam, as if he needed it, that he owned no assets. He could not have paid for the wedding, even if he wanted to. Any disbursements that he wished to make had to be approved by members of the Fund. For although he was thirty-seven, Sam was not in control of his own purse strings. As for Kitty, she was thrilled by the news. Whenever she saw Wendy, she poked her in the stomach and said, 'Any news, dear?'

The day before the wedding, Wendy practised her part with her brother, Peter, who was to give her away. He took her arm and guided her along the corridor that ran through their family's small home at 19 Alvanley Gardens in north London. Both had a hard time taking the moment seriously, Peter later recalled, having to constantly stop as they fell into bouts of giggling. Wendy was just a teenager, two years off being able to vote and still very much interested in other boys. Could she really be marrying into the world-famous Lyons family?

So it was that on Thursday, 29 April 1937, Sam waited under the embroidered *chuppah* canopy in front of the Ark at the orthodox Bayswater Synagogue. Standing next to him were his mother, father and brother, as well as the Chief Rabbi, Joseph Hertz. Behind him sat more than 600 friends and family members. Looking around, Sam saw that the hall was full of white flowers – hydrangeas, lilies, daisies, irises and lilacs. Then the music started.

Wendy appeared at the back of the hall, resplendent. She wore an Empire-line gown of white satin – its bodice ended just below the chest, giving the impression of a high waist – embroidered with pearls and a tulle veil held in place by a pearl tiara. Holding her arm was Peter, who had hired a slightly ill-fitting morning suit from Moss Bros. Behind Wendy flowed a long train embroidered in a delicate leaf design of pearls and silver thread, which was carried by three bridesmaids, each with a dress of similar design. Given the scale of the occasion and their nerves, neither the bride nor the groom remembered much about the ceremony. The following morning, the couple embarked on their honeymoon, a two-week-long motor tour abroad in Europe.

The nuptial festivities were covered by both national and international newspapers, their stories typically being upbeat and sentimental. The exception was a column carried by the *News Chronicle*: 'The impression carried away is one of a solid basis, founded for the two young lives it is designed to support,' wrote the society reporter. 'There is an atmosphere of practical determination. The ceremony and the ritual make no reference to those transports of physical love which are the mainsprings alone of so many unions, destined, alas, to snap in so short a while.'

The reporter was correct that there was little 'physical love' between the newlyweds, at least as far as Wendy was concerned. She had married into the Salmon and Gluckstein clan, as her mother had urged her to do, but that didn't mean she would be monogamous. Young, attractive and with a sexual appetite, she had no intention of remaining at home while her husband worked late at the office. Where the journalist was wrong, however, was that the union was liable to snap. For Wendy had no intention of wrecking her financial advantage, and Sam was a man steeped in tradition. He took his wedding vows seriously.

Wendy and Sam

Eleven months after the wedding, on 10 March 1938, Wendy gave birth to a baby girl, named Belinda. The sixth generation had begun.

The following day, a Friday, Isidore and Kitty were in the dining room taking breakfast. Isidore picked up his copy of *The Times* to make sure his new granddaughter's birth notice had been printed correctly. It had. While looking through the paper, however, he saw that the Chancellor of Austria had called for a referendum to be held that Sunday to affirm the country's independence from Germany. This, he knew, could pose a major problem. If the Austrian government went ahead with its plans, Adolf Hitler would take it as a direct attack on his power. If Austria was not very careful, it could mean war. Isidore excused himself, discarding the newspaper on his way out; he had urgent business to attend to at the House of Commons.

Chapter 32

1938

———————

Early on Saturday, 12 March 1938, Germany's 8th Army crossed the border into Austria. Later that day, accompanied by more than 4,000 soldiers, Hitler drove through Braunau am Inn, the town of his birth, and on to Linz, the third-largest city in Austria. Along the way he was welcomed by crowds of local residents waving swastikas and German flags. At a rally, Hitler announced the annexation of Austria, or *Anschluss*.

On Monday morning, Isidore was once more back in the House of Commons, this time to hear the government's response, following the weekend's turbulent events. To loud cheers and calls of support, Neville Chamberlain – who was now prime minister – said he was 'shocked' by Hitler's actions, but this was not the moment for hasty decisions or careless words.

After a few restrained words from the leader of the opposition, the Speaker of the House called on Winston Churchill. Sitting on the back benches, far from power, the short, bulldog-faced man from Woodstock was considered by many a 'has-been' – left out of the Cabinet, known for his incendiary criticisms of the government's appeasement policy. Now, in a booming, gravelly voice, Churchill declared that Europe was being confronted by a programme of aggression and 'the countries concerned must either submit or take measures to ward off the danger'. To this, the prime minster replied that the government had determined there was an urgent need to assess the British Empire's readiness for war and so 'we have decided to make a fresh review' of the county's defence programmes.

As part of this review, Chamberlain now asked Isidore Salmon to assess the army's catering procedures. This was an unsurprising choice, given his experience in the previous war and his role as managing director of Lyons. As part of his brief, he was asked to evaluate the current situation, make recommendations for improvements and, potentially, oversee their implementation. This was a colossal task. Not only would it impact upon every part of the British army, but it would also carry over to the colonial forces, including those in India. Isidore's title was 'honorary catering advisor', and the post had a rank equivalent to general. The army chiefs had clearly not forgotten his impressive work in reorganising the army's canteens during the First World War.

Until this point, cooks in the British army had been seen as the lowest form of soldier – ill-trained and seriously under-resourced. Indeed, Isidore described the cookhouse as the 'Cinderella of the army'. It was a well-known fact, he would tell his colleagues, that 'an army cook is of little use in civilian life'. Put more plainly, army cooks were dreadfully unskilled. This was significant, Isidore believed, not only for culinary and health reasons, but also for matters of overall military strategy. For Isidore agreed with both Frederick the Great and Napoleon Bonaparte that 'an army marches on its stomach'.

Driven by the prospect of war, Isidore began a gruelling three-month tour of the army's catering facilities and mess halls. He was appalled by the lack of equipment in the kitchens. The same pots were being used for making meat stock and boiling vegetables, preparing porridge and custard, as well as for brewing tea. He interviewed food suppliers, transport workers, cooks and kitchen staff. It was clear they were overworked, underpaid and hardly noticed, let alone appreciated. He visited the training school in Aldershot and discovered that not only was there no curriculum, but the teachers themselves were not trained cooks. He ate meals with the soldiers and, while he tried not to grimace, asked for their feedback.

As part of his investigation, Isidore sat down with the Secretary of State for War and the Quartermaster-General. To his relief, they were supportive of his efforts. They discussed why the army's catering was in such an appalling state. At the heart of the problem, the army's catering was decentralised, so each regiment ran its own cooking according to its own policies and standards, or lack thereof. They encouraged him to complete his review as soon as possible.

On the evening of 5 April 1938, Isidore and Kitty entered the Grosvenor House Hotel, located across the street from Hyde Park and just a few steps from their flat on Mount Street in Mayfair. Kitty was wearing a modest short-sleeved black dress, pearl necklace and white evening gloves that reached to her upper arms. Isidore, like all the men that evening, was in tails, white shirt, ivory waistcoat and white bow-tie. This was the annual gala event hosted by the Chancellor of the Exchequer.

From the lobby, they walked into an enormous ballroom, which was filled with more than 400 guests, and were ushered to a white linen-covered table in the centre of the room. There they were greeted by the prime minister, Neville Chamberlain, and his wife Anne, who was dressed in a silvery gown and a sparkling tiara and carried in her hand a long silver feather. Also at their table was the Chancellor of the Exchequer, Sir John Simon, and his diminutive wife Kathleen, the renowned abolitionist, who was wearing a black dress and had a white fox over her shoulders.

Over dinner, Isidore discussed his findings with the prime minister and Chancellor of the Exchequer. With war looking increasingly likely, there was an urgent need to modernise the training of the army kitchen staff, Isidore explained, as well as to update the way that food was procured, transported, cooked and served. Put simply, what was needed was a total overhaul of one of the army's core functions. This would, unfortunately, not only require enormous amounts of money, but would also take considerable time.

That night's gala was featured in the next issue of *Life* magazine. Under the headline 'LIFE GOES TO THE PARTY: SIR ISIDORE TO MEET THE PRIME MINISTER', America's best-selling magazine depicted the various luminaries present for the occasion, including eighty-year-old Henry Selfridge, whom they said was 'the most energetic diner-out in London'. The four-page article went on to describe Isidore Salmon and his company, J. Lyons: This 'most famous restaurant chain in

Kitty and Isidore at Chancellor's banquet, 1938

Europe' not only ran 257 teashops and four hotels, employing more than 43,000 staff and serving more than 400,000 meals a day, but provided 'sandwiches and Claret for garden parties at Buckingham Palace'. The journalist from *Life* then added, 'To the humble Englishman who does not wear white tie for dinner, no guest was more important than Sir Isidore Salmon' – the man in charge of 'the largest restaurant business in the world'.

Over the next three weeks, politicians debated the upcoming budget. Would an increase in military spending trigger retaliation from Berlin? If they didn't prepare for war, did that make them more vulnerable to attack? And, crucially, how much time did they need to rearm properly? These questions dominated the newspapers' front pages. In public, Chamberlain trod a fine line between appeasement and belligerence. In private, he directed John Simon to spend even more money on the military.

On 26 April, the Chancellor of the Exchequer stood up in Parliament and announced that year's budget. It included £234 million for military spending, in addition to the £90 million agreed earlier in the year. As a percentage of GDP, the government would be spending three times more on defence than they had just three years before. Such funds would cover the costs of any necessary changes to the army's catering.

On 3 June 1938, Isidore submitted his findings to the British army. 'I should like to stress that where my views may appear somewhat critical,' he began, carefully, 'they are directed towards the system that has grown up, and not towards the loyal and frequently overworked personnel who have been striving to attain an adequate standard under conditions rendered extremely difficult by lack of facilities, training and equipment.' Nevertheless, he continued, what was needed was a fundamental change of perspective: 'Men should be engaged in this work first, and be soldiers afterwards.'

Then, having itemised the shocking state of affairs, he summarised his radical recommendations. The entire catering service needed to be centralised under one organisation. An additional 2,700 cooks, caterers and kitchen porters needed to be recruited. The army needed a new training school in England, he said, and another in Egypt. Pay should be increased, and seven permanent civilian advisors with professional catering experience should be hired. Overall, the cost of implementation would be £700,000 capital, plus an additional £750,000 per year. Considering that the average army pay was between one-third and a half a pound a day, this was an enormous amount of money.

On 1 July 1938, a civil servant at the War Office responded to what was quickly becoming known as the 'Salmon Report'. 'I confess that I do not think that it will have an easy passage with the Treasury.' To his surprise, the Secretary to the Treasury was enthusiastic. 'Good food, well cooked and properly served, makes for health and contentment,' he wrote, 'and should prove a very real and permanent attraction to Army life.' The recommendations contained with the Salmon Report were approved.

But just when Isidore thought the policy had the go-ahead, it ran off the rails. Apparently, unwilling to lose control of his local catering staff, the Indian High Commissioner was not supportive. As the Quartermaster-General noted on 4 July, 'you may wish to modify the draft accordingly or if you prefer it we can omit the Indian commitment at this stage'. Isidore was adamant that the changes must be made across the Empire. The army chiefs said they should move ahead, regardless. The policy was now in limbo.

During the night of 9 November 1938, more than 400 synagogues were destroyed in Germany. Some were burned to the ground, others were looted, their precious scrolls wrecked, their sacred Arks smashed. That same night, thousands of Jewish businesses were attacked, anti-Semitic slogans painted on their walls and windows. The following day, 10 November, more than 2,000 Jewish men were brutally dragged out of their homes in Berlin, marched through the streets and imprisoned in a concentration camp called Sachsenhausen. Later this pogrom would be called *Kristallnacht* – the Night of Broken Glass.

This was not an isolated attack by a group of fascists who could be dismissed as 'one-offs' or 'bad apples'. Nor was it an involved and arcane debate about the virtues of economic boycotts, which could be finessed through closed-door meetings and artful rhetoric. This was an open, violent, coordinated attack on a religious minority. If it was no longer safe for Jews to live in Germany, where could they go?

Two weeks after *Kristallnacht*, on 21 November 1938, Isidore was sitting in the House of Commons waiting for another debate to begin. It was late in the evening and he was in his usual green-leather seat towards the back of the chamber. With the rise of anti-Jewish attacks in Germany, the opposition was calling for more Jewish immigrants to be accepted into Britain. The government's position was that Jewish refugees should instead travel to Palestine, even though only a few entry permits for the British mandate were available.

Isidore had long been an ally of Neville Chamberlain. He had supported the prime minister's dual policy of increased military spending while trying to negotiate with Adolf Hitler. Like most of his colleagues in the House, he had cheered when, just weeks before, Chamberlain had returned from Munich declaring 'Peace for our time'. Isidore's unquestioning support had lasted until he had heard about the shocking anti-Jewish pogroms in Germany. During the previous eleven days, he and his colleagues from the Board of Deputies had lobbied the government to open its doors to Jewish refugees from Europe.

At 10 p.m. the proceedings were started by a Labour MP, Philip Noel-Baker, who provided a brief history of the Nazi regime's rise to power, its leaders and its growing litany of human-rights abuses. Then it was the turn of the Home Secretary, Sir Samuel Hoare. Rather than speaking of the dangers of immigration, and how it would threaten the British way of life, Hoare spoke of Albion's long tradition of protecting the underdog, of providing safe haven to those in need. It appeared that, seeing the strength of opposition, the government had changed its mind: it would welcome Jewish children from across Europe.

The Home Secretary now explained how earlier that day he had met a refugee committee, which had told him they were ready to transport thousands of Jewish children from Germany and Austria to London. These children would travel without their parents, and their maintenance would be guaranteed either by their own family's funds or by generous individuals. 'The Home Office would certainly be prepared to provide facilities of that kind,' he announced to the Commons, 'and I venture tonight to take the opportunity of commending this effort to my fellow countrymen in general. Here is a chance of taking the young generation of a great people, here is a chance of mitigating to some extent the terrible sufferings of their parents and their friends.' Hearing these words, Isidore and his colleagues waved their ballot papers in the air and called out 'hear, hear.'

Four days later, one of Britain's highest-profile Jews, the High Commissioner for Palestine, Viscount Herbert Samuel, spoke on BBC Radio. He explained that thousands of refugee children would shortly arrive in Britain and appealed for people to provide foster homes for their care. Hearing this, the women of the Salmon and Gluckstein families decided they had to help.

The following day, Kitty, Mimi and Lena (Harry Salmon's wife) gathered outside a drab little building in Kentish Town, north

London. It was owned by the family, having previously been a Lyons teashop, until a larger depot had been opened nearby. Inside, they found the rooms to be full of broken furniture and rusting kitchen equipment. Over the next three weeks they worked with staff commandeered from Cadby Hall to fix up the place. Having removed the debris and cleaned and mopped, they painted the ceilings, doors and walls in bright, happy colours. Next, they filled the upstairs rooms with thirty child-sized beds, cupboards, chairs and desks. A room downstairs was set aside for dining, large enough for everyone to eat their meals together. Next to it was a room with sofas and comfy chairs, a place to read a book perhaps or play board games. With the building ready, they discussed what to call it: the 'Children's Space' perhaps, or 'Rainbows'? In the end they selected a name that captured what they hoped the children would feel when they arrived: 'The Haven'.

A few weeks later, Lena, Kitty and Mimi stood at Liverpool Street station waiting for a train to arrive. It was early in the morning and freezing cold. When the steam engine wheezed to a halt, the doors were flung open and a cascade of children poured onto the platform. It took some time to manage the paperwork, but before long they had under their care twenty-three terrified-looking children of varying ages, sexes and sizes.

After struggling with their introductions – the new arrivals could not speak English, and the three Salmon ladies had long forgotten any German they might have picked up from the elder generations – they managed to marshal their wards into a line of waiting cars. Then, once their bags were loaded, they drove through the streets of north London to The Haven. In all, more than 10,000 unaccompanied Jewish children would arrive in Britain from Germany, Austria, Czechoslovakia and other countries terrorised by the Nazis. Later the programme for rescuing these young refugees would become known as the *Kindertransport*.

Once inside The Haven, each child was shown to his or her dormitory. A basket of clothes sat next to each of the beds, along with an eiderdown and a stuffed dog. Breakfast, the children were told, would consist of kippers and porridge, which provoked a number of puzzled expressions. In a few days' time they would start school, and boys and girls would be separated. Tomorrow they would be taken to Cadby Hall, for a tour of the factory and a haircut.

Later, Traute Morgenstern, one of the children who lived at The Haven, wrote about the reception that she and her brother received from the Salmon and Gluckstein families. 'As luck would have it,' she recalled, we came under the wing of J. Lyons & Company. 'We say "luck"', she continued, 'not from a financial point of view, which must have been a factor, but because of the extraordinary, never-failing kindness, attention and generosity.'

The family had taken care of Belgian refugees in the last war, and now it was time to help these poor German children.

On 4 April 1939, the King finally signed a royal warrant confirming the creation of Isidore's new cookery organisation, including a training school in Aldershot. It would be called the Army Catering Corps.

Two days later, Britain and France agreed on a mutual-assistance pact with Poland, pledging to come to Poland's aid in the event of a German attack. With Hitler's growing belligerence being reported daily in the newspapers, Isidore's recommendations were now extended across the Empire, to India, Burma, the West Indies, Egypt and beyond. In a final move towards professionalism, Isidore recruited thirty-six-year-old Richard Byford to become the army's first Chief Inspector of Army Catering. Byford had trained under Isidore at Lyons' Regent Palace Hotel.

Not everyone was happy with Isidore's work to improve catering in the military. Volunteers from the British Union of Fascists now printed up flyers denouncing the elevation of British Jews to positions of power in the army, and left them on train and bus seats around the country:

> Who is the head of the army? A Jew, Hore-Belisha.
> Who clothes the army? A Jew, Montague Burton.
> Who feeds the army? A Jew, Isidore Salmon.
> Better join the Navy.

Though such sentiments reflected a significant and growing anti-Semitism amongst the British public, which was both disheartening and not a little upsetting for Isidore, they were not going to stop him fighting on behalf of the Jewish community.

Three weeks after the royal warrant, Isidore was once again sitting in the House of Commons, readying himself for another important ballot. This time the party Whip was encouraging him to support the government's policy on Palestine. In particular Chamberlain was keen to reduce the number of Jewish immigrants who could enter Palestine. To the prime minister, this was a matter of geopolitics. He did not want to annoy the Arabs, whose support – and, more critically, oil supplies – would be crucial if war broke out with Germany. When the count was taken, Chamberlain's policy was supported by a clear majority. Isidore Salmon was one of six Jewish MPs who voted in favour.

For Isidore, the vote had been personal. Despite his experience with the Blackshirts and his growing concern about the Nazis, he remained convinced that the creation of a Jewish homeland would only help the fascists. At the heart of Hitler's and Mosley's ideology, Jews were considered an ethnic group, tied by blood, not culture. This was anathema to him. Like his father, grandfather and great-grandfather before him, Isidore believed Judaism to be, above all, a religion; a collection of mores, rituals and traditions. That involved a community of like-minded people, bound by rites of passage and spiritual beliefs.

In Germany, the family had been viewed only as Jews. The same had happened in Arnhem, Amsterdam, Antwerp and then Whitechapel. It was only when they had made it to Kensington, and then finally to Mayfair, that the perspective had changed. Isidore believed that the family was now part of the in-group. Londoners, born and raised. Owners of a British company, with British employees, selling British goods to British people. He was, without question, loyal to the King, his Empire and all that it stood for. His religion was Judaism, but he was British, through and through.

Chapter 33

1939

_____

On 1 September 1939, just five months after the creation of the Army Catering Corps, Hitler's forces invaded Poland. In response, the British government called on Germany to cease military operations or it would be forced to come to Poland's aid. When this ultimatum was ignored, Britain declared war against Germany on 3 September, followed by its independent dominions, Australia, South Africa, New Zealand and Canada. Its other territories, such as India, Egypt and Nyasaland, were obliged to fight as part of the Imperial Army.

And so began the Second World War.

The declaration of war was discussed at the next meeting of the Fund, which, as usual, took place in Room 14 at the Trocadero. At sixty-three years of age, Isidore was the most senior member, followed by his brothers Harry, Maurice and Julius. Next came Sam's generation, including his brother Julian and his cousins Louis and Barney. There was also a cohort of young men present, including Mimi's sons, Tony, Brian and Neil.

Having just turned eighteen, Neil was a relative newcomer to the Fund meetings. As was the custom, there had been no ceremony for his induction. In five years' time, when he reached the age of twenty-three, he would be allowed to vote. But from the start he was encouraged not only to listen, but to take part. Which he did. For if Isidore was like his mother, Lena, and was happy in the background, and Sam was like his great-grandfather, Lehmann, curious about the unknown and enjoying the moment, then Neil was more like his great-grandfather, Samuel – opinionated, quick to anger and never satisfied with what was in hand. Interestingly, nobody was yet to match the creative genius of Monte, who had balanced the yearning for a better tomorrow with an appreciation of what he had in front of him.

Today, the most urgent issue before the group was war: who would be signing up for military service, and how the business could be run in the meantime. Julian said he would work in the army and air-force catering corps, as did two of his cousins. Tony said he was eager to see some action, so he would enlist as a foot soldier. Neil wanted to join the Intelligence Corps, though it was not clear how he would make this happen. Would the military spooks take the great-grandson of a German refugee?

At thirty-nine years old, Sam was too old to serve and would instead work under his uncles Maurice and Harry at Cadby Hall. The others would also remain in London, to manage the business and contribute in whatever way they could to the war effort. It was agreed that they would try and avoid making major decisions whilst the young men were absent. Not be outdone, the elder women of the family held their own meeting – in Room 12 of the Trocadero. Led by Mimi, the session focused on the organising of support for the German refugee children and discussions on how best to support the families of employees who went off to war.

Gluck, meanwhile, responded to the declaration of war in private. On 3 September, she made a simple diary entry: 'War declared'. A few weeks later, she rented a country house nestled into the side of the South Downs of East Sussex, from where she wrote long, tortured letters to Nesta, who still refused to leave her husband. As the German army churned through Western Europe with extraordinary speed, Gluck appeared more interested in matters of the heart than in matters of war.

In early April 1940, Germany invaded Denmark and then Norway. In an attempt to show support to the Norwegian people, Chamberlain's War Cabinet hastily sent a small armed force to the coast of Norway, which, following the threat of capture, was soon recalled.

A few days later, on 7 May, this clumsily organised mission triggered a discussion in Parliament. What started as a routine debate about military strategy morphed into a referendum on Chamberlain's government. Over the next two days the deliberations became increasingly fraught, ending with the Labour Party demanding a vote of no confidence in the prime minister.

Isidore was devastated for his friend Neville Chamberlain, who he believed was being unfairly blamed for Britain's entry into the war. After all, the prime minister had successfully delayed the start of war through his ongoing peace talks with Hitler, giving the country sufficient time to rearm. The final speaker now rose to talk. It was Winston Churchill, who spoke enthusiastically in support of Chamberlain and the government. 'Let pre-war feuds die,' he declared to a great waving of ballot papers and cheers from the Conservative benches. 'Let personal quarrels be forgotten, and let us keep our hatreds for the common enemy.'

A vote was called. Isidore and Churchill cast their ballot in favour of the government, along with 279 others. The number voting against was 200. Although Chamberlain had won, sixty Conservatives had abstained, and forty-one MPs who normally supported the government had voted against him. This was seen as disastrous, both by Members of Parliament and the press. As the government was thrown into crisis, the war outside was accelerating.

Early on 10 May, Germany invaded France and the Low Countries. During an emergency Cabinet later that day, Chamberlain proposed that he should step down, triggering a debate as to who should replace him. Some argued that it should be his Foreign Secretary, Viscount Halifax. Others believed that Churchill was the best man for the job.

That evening, Chamberlain met the King and, after offering his resignation, suggested that Churchill lead the next government. Just before 3 p.m. the following Monday, Churchill stood up for the first time in Parliament as prime minister. An hour later, a vote was called in support of the question 'this House welcomes the formation of a Government representing the united and inflexible resolve of the nation to prosecute the war with Germany to a victorious conclusion'. Isidore voted in favour, as did Chamberlain and every other Member of Parliament. Churchill had the support of the House.

Four weeks later, at 5.30 a.m. on 14 June, German advance troops drove into Paris. They took the city without a fight. A swastika hung on the Arc de Triomphe. That afternoon Isidore was once again in the House of Commons, this time to hear the new prime minister's reaction to the fall of Paris. Churchill rose and proclaimed that upon the outcome of the fight 'depends our own British life and the long continuity of our institutions and our Empire ... if the British Empire and its Commonwealth last for a thousand years, men will still say, "this was our finest hour"'. He then added that the Battle of France was over. 'I expect that the Battle of Britain is about to begin.'

Hitler was indeed preparing for the invasion of Britain.

From their experience during the occupation of other countries, the Nazis had learned that the swift arrest of key individuals was critical to success. The names would be handed over to the Gestapo, who had proven so effective in eliminating opposition in Germany.

Reinhard Heydrich, head of the Reich Main Security Office, now asked General Walter Schellenberg to prepare a list of those to be rounded up. It would be Schellenberg who would run the British arm of the Gestapo after the invasion. Its headquarters would be based in Birmingham.

To compile the list, Schellenberg and his team used newspaper articles and telephone directories, along with pre-war intelligence reports. Once compiled, alphabetically, it ran to 104 pages and contained 2,820 names, and had 'Secret' printed on its cover. First were the political and military leaders, such as Winston Churchill, the Cabinet and the army chiefs. Then obvious opponents, such as members of the Fabian Society (such as Beatrice Webb), women's rights activists (such as Sylvia Pankhurst) and those who had fled to Great Britain (for instance, Charles de Gaulle, Sigmund Freud and Stefan Zweig). Next came newspaper owners (John Astor, owner of *The Times*, was mentioned, though not Viscount Rothermere, owner of the *Daily Mail*) and left-leaning writers such as E.M. Forster, Virginia Woolf and Bertrand Russell. Along with the names came the following instructions: '*Sämtliche in der Sonderfahndungsliste G.B. aufgeführten Personen sind festzunehmen*' – 'All persons mentioned in the Special Wanted List Great Britain are to be arrested.'

Also included in the list were the leaders of the Jewish community: Joseph Hertz, the Chief Rabbi; Neville Laski, the president of the Board of Deputies of British Jews; his vice-chairman, Lionel de Rothschild; and, on page 181, the other vice-chairman:

Salmon, Sir Isidore. 1876. London. W. 51 Mount Street. RSHA II B2.

Decoded, this meant that Isidore and his colleagues would be dealt with by Heinrich Himmler's Reich Main Security Office department of Jewish affairs. Ironically, given his determination to be seen as British above all things, Isidore was listed because he was Jewish.

Before arresting British citizens, however, Germany had to seize British territory. This was more than simply a theoretical threat.

The island of Jersey was part of the British Isles and sat just 350 kilometres south of the English coast. It was only a six-hour ride by boat to Southampton. The Germans saw Jersey as a stepping stone to their occupation of Great Britain. On 30 June 1940, a Junkers transport plane landed at the island's airport, disgorging a platoon of German troops. By the day's end, they were in control of the island.

A few days later, a German patrol arrived at the large red front door of Sun Works, Lyons' tea factory on the island. Sun Works took in tea from India, Ceylon and Nyasaland, blended and packed the leaves and then exported the boxes around the world. Most of the managers had already fled to London, but a core staff remained in place to protect the plant. The supervisor was told that the entire stock was being confiscated by the occupying forces and the factory was now under German management. Before handing over the keys, he sent an urgent cable to Cadby Hall: 'The Lyons tea factory in Jersey has been seized by the Nazis.'

If the Germans could take Jersey, how long would it be until they crossed the English Channel, deployed their security units and started rounding up people in Britain?

The following month, July 1940, Hitler launched an air assault against Britain. His intention was to secure control of the skies, which would provide cover for his invasion force. With victory now certain, he hoped that Churchill would be forced to surrender, as the French had in Paris.

Each side had approximately 2,000 aeroplanes at their disposal and, even though Britain was assisted by crews from Australia and other colonies, critically the Germans had access to a larger pool of trained pilots. In addition, many in the Luftwaffe had combat experience, having taking part in battles during the Spanish Civil War. The Royal Air Force, however, had the advantage of motivation, for its pilots were fighting to protect their homeland. For the next few weeks British Hurricanes and Spitfires chased Messerschmitts and Heinkels across the sky.

As the fighting intensified during the summer of 1940, Isidore and Kitty anxiously followed the news reports on the radio. From the broadcasts, it was not always clear who was losing and who was winning. With round-the-clock fighting, over open water for the most part, the casualties on both sides were devastating. Within weeks the British had lost more than 1,500 air crew and the Germans more than 2,500. By the end of August it was clear that Germany had failed to gain air superiority over the English Channel.

Hitler now changed strategy. He ordered the German air force to launch an aerial bombing campaign upon towns and cities in England and Scotland. On 7 September, close to 400 German bombers and more than 600 fighters attacked the docks of the East End of London. Six days later, a bomb fell on the north side of Berkeley Square – 300 metres from Kitty and Isidore's home – destroying a row of houses and setting fire to many others on the southern end. On 26 October, a block of flats on Curzon Street received a direct hit, again just 300 metres from their house, killing dozens of people. The attacks were relentless. Whenever the air-raid sirens sounded, mostly at night, the family grabbed their coats, ran outside and joined their neighbours in the nearby Underground station at Hyde Park Corner.

Throughout this time, Isidore continued his role as chief catering advisor to the War Office, ensuring that the Army Catering Corps had all the necessary resources. He also kept up his responsibilities at J. Lyons. Key items, such as tea, coffee and bread, were considered vital to the economy, and Isidore and the rest of the board worked tirelessly to ensure production levels were maintained. With little time for rest or sleep, and already feeling weak, Isidore's health now deteriorated. Yet he was firm in his resolve that he must do his part for his country, and rejected Kitty's suggestions that he slow down.

Isidore's friend, Neville Chamberlain, was also suffering from ill health. That autumn, having been diagnosed with terminal bowel cancer, he stepped down as head of the Conservative Party. Isidore immediately dashed off a letter. 'My dear Chamberlain,' he wrote on 7 October 1940, 'I have hesitated to write to you earlier – not wishing to add to the avalanche of letters you must have received – but I do wish to express my deep feeling of regret that the state of your health has made it necessary for you to resign.' Having stated that it was a 'privilege' and 'a great pleasure' to work under his leadership, Isidore said that he hoped his friend would be quickly restored to health 'under the loving care of your dear wife'. He then added, 'The Country owes much to you, and history will confirm the wisdom of your policy which prevented the earlier outbreak of hostilities when our position would have been most serious.'

Sadly, Neville Chamberlain did not recover. On 9 November, he died at home in Hampshire. Three days later, his wife Anne received the following telegram: 'Please accept our heartiest sympathy in your irreparable loss = Isidore and Kate Salmon.'

The next few weeks were some of grimmest yet for the residents of England. Night after night, the bombing raids continued. One neighbourhood was struck and then another. Christmas and New Year came and went, with little good cheer, as people hunkered down, in the Tube tunnels, in basements and in air-raid shelters.

Then, almost inevitably, disaster struck. During the night of 17 April 1941, the Luftwaffe dropped more than 151,000 explosives on London. The strike was sufficiently heavy in Mayfair for Winston Churchill's Assistant Private Secretary, John Colville, to note that the area had 'suffered badly'. The west front of the Catholic church at 114 Mount Street was wrecked, as were numbers 105–8 Mount Street and 12–17 Mount Street. Also hit was number 51, where Isidore and Kitty lived, and it was totally destroyed. Fortunately, neither was at home at the time.

Isidore and Kitty's street hit during Blitz

Isidore was determined not to let the loss slow him down. He was consumed with reinventing the Army Catering Corps. He had to stay in London. But to find a place to live was not an easy task, given the destruction wrought by the German bombing. Many families had been forced to move in with relatives or friends, in cramped and unfamiliar conditions that made the constant bombardment even harder to deal with. Kitty and Isidore were fortunate. They were allocated a serviced apartment at the family's Cumberland Hotel, opposite Marble Arch. Their maid, Rose Pratt, would live down the corridor in a modest bed-sitting room. The day after their home was flattened, Isidore was back at work.

With the Blitz terrorising the capital, Sam and Wendy decided it was time to move to the countryside. After a brief search, they found a four-bedroom house called Foxhill, just outside Marlborough, a market town 100 kilometres west of London.

Sam would have liked to remain in the country, away from the crowds and chaos of the capital, his days spent fishing on one of Wiltshire's chalk streams, but he felt the pull of duty. With his wife and daughter now rehoused, Sam returned to London, where he assisted his uncle Maurice Salmon in the running of the cake and bread divisions in Cadby Hall. This was not a simple task, considering the shortage of labour and supplies. Following Germany's attempt to operate a sea blockade against Britain, deploying hundreds of boats and submarines in the North Sea, the government had introduced mandatory rationing. At first, only petrol was restricted, but soon this was followed by sugar, butter and bacon, margarine and then tea.

The restriction on tea affected Lyons' core business. Each household was now allowed to purchase only 2 ounces (57 grams) of loose tea per week. To buoy the public mood, the Minister of Food appeared on the BBC with a wartime slogan, 'One [teaspoon] per person and none for the pot!' The family's main competitors, Typhoo and Brooke Bond, responded by producing a brand of tea that was blended from different-quality leaves. But compromising on quality was not something any of the Salmons and Glucksteins could contemplate. They would not dilute their premier brand, Green Label tea, with leaf of lower quality. When insufficient tea was available, which was often, they were forced to sell their lower-grade brand, Yellow Label, which proved unpopular. In wartime, perhaps counter-intuitively, British households preferred buying higher-grade products, which they trusted to last longer.

Desperate to avoid shortages of bread, which was considered a key part of the British diet, the government had also passed a series of measures to support the baking industry. Lyons now received a subsidy towards its bread-baking, which offset the increased price of raw materials such as flour. In return, they sold their loaves at the fixed price of eightpence. Moreover, worried about the possible impact of the Blitz on bread production, the government had established an Emergency Bread Scheme, which coordinated the response, in case of disruption. Luckily, Cadby Hall had so far not been hit. Meanwhile, the production of sweet goods was significantly reduced. The few cakes that were made had their ingredients changed. Margarine was replaced with oil, for instance, and the use of sugar was significantly limited. In this way, Sam and his employees worked hard to meet the new conditions ushered in by war.

When his daytime duties were over, Sam had a quick bite to eat and then donned his Air Raid Precaution (ARP) uniform. He spent his nights distributing gas masks to civilians, encouraging residents to maintain the blackout and – once bombs had been dropped – liaising with the ambulance and fire services. Sometimes he was able to rescue people from the ruins; often all he could do was recover bodies. With his ARP responsibilities complete, and after a few hours' sleep on a cot set up for him at Cadby Hall, Sam would then trudge over to his office for another day's work.

One morning, as he walked through Hammersmith, he found a woman standing outside the smoking ruins of her house. It had been destroyed by a bomb the previous night. Sam knew her to work at Cadby Hall. Recognising him as a Lyons director, the woman said,

'Hello, sir, I'm going to be late for work today.' Sam marvelled at the woman's stoicism and her resolve to fulfil her duties and obligations.

Wendy enlisted with the Women's Voluntary Service (WVS), driving British, American and Canadian soldiers who were billeted at the nearby military bases. Soon soldiers began appearing and staying late at Foxhill. Wendy tried to be discreet about these romantic interludes, as she didn't want to upset her husband or attract attention from the neighbours.

While they were apart, Wendy wrote to Sam almost every day. Most of the letters focused on the routine. In one she wrote that, 'The floods around here are awful, the river has overflowed.' In another she reported, 'Baker [the chauffeur] has a cold and spent today in bed.' In a third, she wrote that their daughter Belinda 'sends daddy a hug, kiss and tight squeeze, as do I.' In others, the loneliness was more evident, and Wendy told of her desire to move back to London. 'My own Darling one,' began one letter on blue note paper, 'I am coming home again, air raids or no air raids, I can't bear being away from you.'

One weekend at the start of the summer, Sam was at home in the country with his wife and daughter when the phone rang. Picking up the receiver, Sam listened to the person on the other end of the line. He looked profoundly worried, his daughter Belinda later remembered, and then, seeing her watching him, he quickly shifted back to his normal equanimity. After a few moments Sam thanked the caller and put down the phone. 'Our flat in London has been blitzed. Many of its windows have been blown out but it's all fine,' he said to his daughter. 'Don't worry about it, the war will end soon.'

But the war was not even close to being over.

By the end of the summer of 1941, Sam's father was struggling with his health. After months of bombing and years of overwork, Isidore was running out of steam. In the mornings, he found it difficult to get out of bed. Walking upstairs, he was quickly out of breath. His mind had lost its sharpness. And yet still he worked. He discussed the allocation of resources at Lyons' board meetings. He worked with the War Office to ensure that his catering reforms were being properly implemented. And he continued his political duties. At one event held in the town hall of his Harrow constituency, for instance, he gave a speech urging Britain to be self-sufficient. 'The first thing is to assist ourselves,' he said, 'recognise our own responsibilities and if we do we shall have no cause to be pessimistic.' This was met with loud applause.

Nippies prepare teashop for air attack

But his symptoms worsened. He found it increasingly difficult to breathe, he felt nauseous and his ankles and legs swelled up. Kitty told him that he had to take some time off work, which he did. When he showed no signs of improvement, the doctor said that Isidore required twenty-four-hour care. This was when Kitty moved him into The London Clinic on Devonshire Place in Marylebone.

Still he would not stop. From his hospital bed, Isidore sent a letter to the Ministry of Food asking if it was possible to improve conditions for 'women war workers', who found that everyday goods such as eggs and milk were in short supply. In his response to Isidore, the secretary said that distribution would be improved so that there would be 'no necessity for anyone to form a queue to obtain rationed food'. That afternoon, Isidore underwent an operation to remove one of his kidneys. Later that day, Lyons released a statement to the press that their chairman was making 'satisfactory progress'.

Alas, it was not to be. Three weeks later, he had a stroke and then his remaining kidney failed. On 16 September 1941, with Kitty, Sam and Julian at his bedside at The London Clinic, sixty-five-year-old Isidore Salmon finally ran out of energy. Though he had been poorly for some time, his wife and sons had believed that, with some rest, he would bounce back and get back to work, like he always had. Isidore's death, therefore, came as a total shock.

More than 500 letters of condolence arrived for Kitty via the mailroom of the Cumberland Hotel: from the head of the Civil Service, to the Chief of the Imperial General Staff (the country's most senior soldier); from the General of the Salvation Army, to the Soviet ambassador. All spoke of Isidore's extraordinary work ethic and public service. 'The army will mourn the loss of the man who had their interests so greatly at heart,' wrote General Richard Talbot Snowden-Smith, head of supplies at the War Office. 'They know that it was their welfare that caused Sir Isidore to continue his arduous duties, when he should have rested, and that he laid down his life in devotion to duty.' The chairman of the Conservative Party Association, Douglas Hacker, echoed these sentiments: 'I hope it may be some small comfort to you and to his family to know how much his great efforts were appreciated. If ever there was a man who died in service of his country, he did. He never spared himself for one moment.' Meanwhile, in the days following his death, obituaries recounting Isidore's life and achievements were published in more than fifty British newspapers.

Kitty, Sam and Julian discussed the funeral arrangements. Given Isidore's long-term service to the orthodox community, they agreed that he should be buried at the Jewish cemetery in Willesden, on the other side of the brick wall from his uncle Monte and brother Alfred. A few days later, on Wednesday, 24 September 1941, 800 mourners gathered at the Bayswater Synagogue in west London. It was an especially dark moment for the family and the country for, in addition to Isidore's death, the previous week had seen Hitler taking Kiev (capturing half a million Ukrainian troops), the flight of the Greek royal family to London and the sinking of the SS *Portsdown* passenger ferry off the Isle of Wight, with the loss of twenty-three lives.

Inside the synagogue hall were more than fifty members of the Salmon and Gluckstein families. Sam, Julian, Maurice, Harry, Louis and the rest of the men sat in the rows facing the Ark. Upstairs in the balcony sat the women, including Kitty, Mimi and Wendy (Gluck was not present). When it was time, Rabbi Ephraim Levine walked across the red carpet at the front of the hall and up to the *bimah* – a raised platform carved in gilded wood, alabaster and marble. Above him burned an enormous rose-shaped stained-glass window.

'From birth to death, man is haunted all the time with the fear that life is all a tragedy or a mockery,' began the rabbi. 'Man can either become submerged under this burden of existence and pass his days like the animal eating and working and sleeping without any satisfaction to himself but the performance of his daily routine. Or he can rise above the mood of resignation and seek and find the purpose of life in adding to the total of the world's achievements.' This, it seemed, was not some recycled speech. Isidore had been on the synagogue's governing board for years and was well known and loved by Ephraim Levine. 'In brief,' continued the rabbi, 'the secret of living is labour and love. Our beloved friend, Isidore Salmon, whose early passing has created such a void in our hearts, was the very embodiment of these truths. No man of our generation worked with greater zeal or with greater diligence, and no man could have found greater joy in his work.' When the time came to assess his wartime efforts, concluded the minister, 'the name of Sir Isidore Salmon will be valued and honoured'.

Curiously, none of those trying to establish Isidore's legacy – the journalists, his friends and colleagues, his rabbi, his relatives – mentioned what was perhaps his greatest achievement: the thwarting of Oswald Mosley and the British Union of Fascists. Thanks to its ambiguity, the October 1941 issue of *Food & Cookery Review* perhaps came closest. 'To live in the hearts of those we love is not to die,' it declared, 'and it may safely be said that there are literally thousands of hearts that must have missed a beat when the dire news was first heard. No monument will be necessary to preserve the treasured memory of Sir Isidore Salmon!'

PART V

SAM

'One of the fundamental values of the Fund is that the strong should look after the weak, the high earners contributing to the standards of the low earners so that all members of a given age have approximately the same standard of living. And departure from this however small would destroy the basic concept of the Fund.'

Neil Salmon

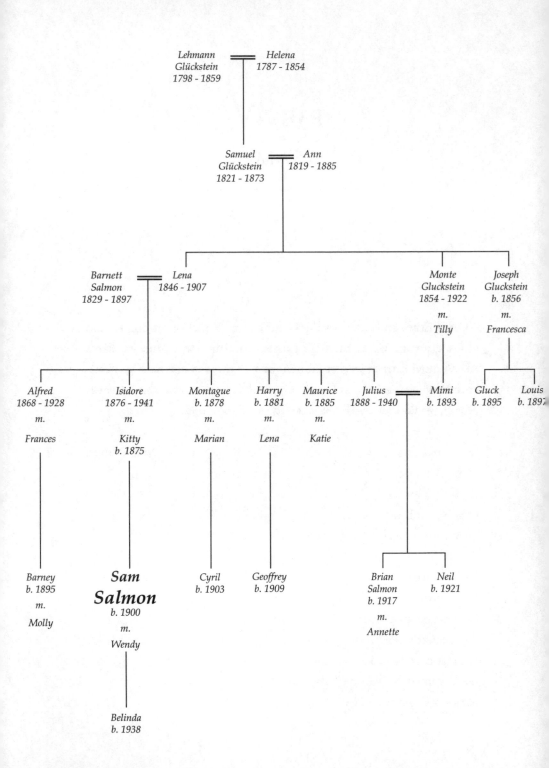

Lehmann
Glückstein
1798 - 1859
═══
Helena
1787 - 1854

Samuel
Glückstein
1821 - 1873
═══
Ann
1819 - 1885

Barnett
Salmon
1829 - 1897
═══
Lena
1846 - 1907

Monte
Gluckstein
1854 - 1922

m.

Tilly

Joseph
Gluckstein
b. 1856

m.

Francesca

Alfred
1868 - 1928

m.

Frances

Isidore
1876 - 1941

m.

Kitty
b. 1875

Montague
b. 1878

m.

Marian

Harry
b. 1881

m.

Lena

Maurice
b. 1885

m.

Katie

Julius
1888 - 1940
═══
Mimi
b. 1893

Gluck
b. 1895

Louis
b. 1897

Barney
b. 1895

m.

Molly

**Sam
Salmon**
b. 1900

m.

Wendy

Cyril
b. 1903

Geoffrey
b. 1909

Brian
Salmon
b. 1917

m.

Annette

Neil
b. 1921

Belinda
b. 1938

Chapter 34

1941

As the autumn of 1941 darkened to winter, Adolf Hitler and his allies appeared to be in the ascendant. Germany now occupied most of Western Europe, from France in the west to Denmark in the north and Bulgaria and Greece in the south. It also controlled much of North Africa, an enormous swathe of land stretching from Egypt to Libya. In Eastern Europe, the Wehrmacht and the SS killing squads, the *Einsatzgruppen*, had pushed far into the Soviet Union, with the result that hundreds of thousands had perished in the fierce battles around Leningrad, Kiev, Minsk and Smolensk. By October 1941, German forces were closing in on Moscow.

Meanwhile, in an attempt to destroy Germany's industrial base and dampen its population's morale, British planes began dropping bombs on the cities of Hamburg and Cologne, along with other key targets. On 7 November alone, 160 British bombers were sent over to Berlin. Due to poor weather, however, little damage was done, and twenty-one planes were lost to anti-aircraft fire. The following week, a British aircraft carrier was torpedoed near Gibraltar and two British warships were sunk off the coast of Singapore. For the listeners and readers back in London, bad news had become a near daily occurrence.

Then, on 7 December, Japanese planes attacked the American naval base in Pearl Harbor, killing 2,403 American sailors, airmen and Marines and sinking eighteen ships. Within twenty-four hours the USA had declared war against both Germany and Japan. In the week that followed, Britain declared war on Finland, China declared war on Japan, Hungary and Bulgaria declared war on the USA, while military campaigns commenced in Thailand, Malaysia, Hong Kong and Burma. The conflict now involved more than 100 countries across four continents. It was the largest global conflagration in history.

With war gathering pace, and the needs of the country foremost in their minds, there was little time for the family to mourn the passing of Isidore Salmon. His brother, Harry, now stepped up and took on the mantle of chairman of J. Lyons. In practice, this changed little, as Harry had been in charge of the company while Isidore focused on the Army Catering Corps. There were bread orders to fulfil, tea to blend, pack and box, workers to train and pay, teashops to stock, staff and manage. The wheels of industry kept turning.

Of those away fighting there was only occasional news. Bruce Gluckstein, Monte's grandson, was headed for the frontline in Italy. Sam's brother Julian was assigned to the RAF, where he was busy helping with their catering corps. Mimi's eldest son, Tony, had returned from the infantry regiment because of a gastric ulcer and was put in charge of Lyons' laundry subsidiary, James Hayes & Sons. Then there were those about whom little was known. Neil Salmon, for instance, was attached to the Intelligence Corps, but his mother Mimi had not heard from him in months, while Edna Gluckstein, the wife of one of Izzy's grandsons, was working in Bletchley Park, a secretive government location on the south coast of England.

Nearby but not in contact was Gluck, who was still living in East Sussex. Given the financial constraints of the war, she had been forced (by her brother Louis) to sell her house in London and then her studio in Cornwall. After finally realising that she would never be with Nesta, and suffering a breakdown, she had moved in with her friend, the journalist Edith Heald. There Gluck remained, holed up away from the London art scene and her family, rarely painting and feeling bereft, cut off from the war.

It was now, in late 1941, that a request arrived at the fourth floor of Cadby Hall, marked 'Top Secret'. The War Office wished to have a meeting with the managers of J. Lyons. The subject of the meeting was curiously anodyne: 'Operation and maintenance of a filling factory'.

A few days later, Sam and Maurice Salmon were driven over to a nondescript building in Whitehall, where they were ushered into a windowless room in the basement. Sitting across from them was a man who introduced himself as Mr Bedford from the Ministry of Supply. Maurice, who was known for his plain talking, wanted to know why he had been dragged away from Cadby Hall, where he was busy feeding the nation at war. And what was all this about a filling factory? The British government, said the civil servant, requested that J. Lyons build and manage a secret factory – not to produce food for the army, or bread or tea, but instead to make bombs. The Salmons were taken aback. They had no idea this was coming. What did they know about armaments?

Lyons was not alone in receiving such a 'request'. By this time Churchill's government was desperate for help from the private sector, as the War Office was simply unable to supply all the munitions and armaments that the country needed. In all, ninety-seven companies had been approached, including well-known names such as Cadbury's and Schweppes. Some were asked to manufacture tanks and rocket-launchers, others military uniforms and rations. Together they were tasked with managing 160 of these so-called 'filling factories'. Many in the military questioned the merits of subcontracting the production of munitions to companies known for making household products. But the government said it had no choice. If they were to catch up with German production, they had to move along with the plan – and fast.

Back at Cadby Hall, Maurice called an emergency meeting with his managers. It was a puzzle, but Maurice liked solving puzzles. The questions they needed to answer were: how, where, what and who? 'How' referred to the science of bomb-making. Luckily, the chemistry was relatively well known, and the government would lend them experts who could help with the finer points. More worrying was safety. Mixing highly volatile substances was a delicate task, and they would have to develop strict protocols that the workers would need to closely follow. 'Where?' was also relatively straightforward. The civil servants had identified a site near Elstow, a Bedfordshire town some 70 kilometres north of London. It had good transport connections and was close to a number of airfields.

The next problem of 'what?' was trickier. A year into a global war, the appetite for ordnance was colossal. So what would they need in order to produce the volume of munitions in the time required? Over the next few weeks, and after lengthy discussions with architects, engineers and other planners, the Lyons team decided that the factory's design called for the construction of 250 separate buildings, 20 kilometres of fencing, 10 kilometres of roads and a new rail system, enabling supplies and products to be shipped in and out efficiently. The complex would be constructed in phases, allowing for production to start as soon as possible. Once the budgets were written and approved, all of this would be funded by the government.

Finally came the problem of 'who?' Given the shortage of male workers due to conscription, women would have to staff the factory. Only a very few would have any experience of the manufacture of bombs, so a robust four-week training programme had to be created. Letters were exchanged with the War Office in which Lyons was told that, according to the convention of the day, the women's wages would be 75 per cent of those of their male counterparts. On 23 January 1942, for example, Lyons received a letter from a Mr Ekins saying that a male machine operator working at Elstow was to be paid £72 per month, whilst a woman was to be paid £50. When the factory reached full capacity, more than 3,000 workers would have to be recruited, trained and organised into shifts working at the factory.

When Sam relayed their plans to the War Office, he was informed there was another issue that needed to be solved: security. This was a major concern for the army, he was told. They were worried about German intelligence-gathering operations. Even sabotage. Just a few months earlier, two Germans had been dropped off by seaplane next to the Scottish coast. Fortunately, an alert railway-station worker spotted one of these men acting suspiciously, checking and rechecking a train timetable, and notified a policeman. On looking into the traveller's bag, the officer discovered radio equipment, a pistol and a large sum of English money. The Germans were found guilty of spying and, on 6 August 1941, were executed at Wandsworth prison in London.

To deal with the threat of foreign espionage, the Elstow factory would be known as a 'Lyons Enterprise', rather than a government munitions depot, and workers would tell their friends that Lyons was operating an industrial laundry at the site. It would also not feature on any maps. Private policemen would be hired, and all staff would have to sign a form stating that they would comply with the Official Secrets Act.

In early February 1942, the first buildings were complete and the Lyons factory swung into production. At first they concentrated on assembling two-inch trench mortar bombs, which were relatively straightforward. To start with, a team mixed eighty parts of ammonium nitrate to twenty parts of TNT. This was then carted in wooden boxes to the next section, which carefully divided up the mixture by precise weight. A third unit then slowly poured the mixture into metal casings, which were tamped down using a screw press, leaving a small hole into which was placed an explosive capsule and fuse. Finally, a stencil was painted on the exterior of the bomb, which was packed, along with others, to be transported to the front. Within a few weeks the factory was producing more than 6,000 mortar bombs per week.

To run the factory, Maurice established a management office at Elstow. This was staffed by Lyons employees, provided for free by the company. The management office supervised all the departments, including those associated with production, such as engineering, electrical and construction departments, as well as personnel, catering and security. There was also an onsite ambulance service and a fire brigade, both of whose staff comprised almost entirely women. In addition, Maurice created what he called a Planning Office, whose task was to maximise production in the most efficient and economic fashion. At first this had only one employee, but soon it grew to nine. It was the creative hub of the enterprise, experimenting with better and safer ways of building munitions. The management office now focused on increasing production rates as well as producing other types of munitions, such as depth charges to blow up submarines, and shells for the navy's quick-firing guns.

Most of the factory workers came from the surrounding area, but to find the necessary numbers, Lyons had to recruit additional staff from Ireland, who were billeted in the nearby town of Bedford. They knew the risks of the work, yet turned up every day. Despite the volatility of the explosive materials being handled, and the limited training received by the workers, the factory's safety record was exemplary. Remarkably, only one worker died during the course of the war, having incorrectly mixed a batch of chemicals, causing a massive explosion.

The impact of Elstow on the local population was twofold. For those who worked at the factory, it provided employment and a great sense of purpose. To others, it was known as 'Chimney Corner', owing to the volume of smoke it produced, and it remained a mystery, a subject of much conversation and conjecture over pints at the local pubs. To the Salmons and Glucksteins, Elstow was partly a massive distraction from the day-to-day business of running J. Lyons & Company, which in itself was a colossal undertaking. But Elstow was also something much more. For the family knew how many bombs were made each week and that these were delivered to the army, navy and air force, to be used day in, day out in the bloody struggle against the most terrible foe Britain had ever faced. And as Jews, they knew what was at stake, for them, if they lost the war.

Making munitions at 'Filling Factory'

Starting in May 1942, the British newspapers began reporting that the Nazis were carrying out appalling atrocities in Eastern Europe. On 25 June 1942, *The Daily Telegraph* published a story that 'more than 700,000 Polish Jews had been slaughtered by the Germans in the greatest massacre in the world's history', and to do this they were using 'travelling gas chambers'. Though the article was published on the fifth page of a six-page issue, it was widely circulated amongst London's Jewish community.

Then, on 11 December, *The Times* and many other papers reported that the Polish government in exile had given a sixteen-page note to the British, Soviet and American governments, which stated that 'The German authorities aim with systematic deliberation at the systematic extermination of the Jewish population of Poland', and although it was not possible to know the exact number of Jews exterminated, of the three million Jews who had lived in Poland at the war's start, 'over one third have perished during the last three years'.

Seven days later the Foreign Secretary, Anthony Eden, rose in the House of Commons and denounced the Nazi killings. He concluded by saying, 'Such events can only strengthen the resolve of all freedom-loving peoples to overthrow the barbarous Hitlerite tyranny. [We] reaffirm [our] solemn resolution to ensure that those responsible for these crimes shall not escape retribution, and to press on with the necessary practical measures to this end.'

Like the rest of Britain's Jewish community, the family was horrified by the reports coming out of Poland. In private, the Chief Rabbi of Britain, Joseph Hertz, who had conducted Sam and Wendy's marriage, was frantically urging the British government to find a way to stop the mass killings. In response, Churchill said that the best way to stop the Nazis killing Jews was to defeat Hitler. All their efforts, therefore, would be focused on winning the war.

With fighting in 1942 and then 1943 taking place on so many fronts – from North Africa to the Pacific Islands, to southern and

Eastern Europe – it was easy to become lost in the alphabet soup of names, ranging from hard-to-pronounce cities in the Soviet Union to tricky-to-locate towns in the Philippines. The list was overwhelming to much of the British public, especially given that many of the names were in a foreign language. To short-circuit this, the press resorted to nicknames. Soldiers, for instance, were given easy-to-remember monikers such as the 'Red Devils', 'Tojos' and 'Desert Rats'. Journalists also invented names for ships. Two of these, the *Scharnhorst* and *Gneisenau*, became known as 'Salmon and Gluckstein'.

The *Scharnhorst* and the *Gneisenau* were the two German battleships that the Allied High Command most sought to destroy. Built before the war, and with displacements of 26,000 tonnes, a crew of almost 2,000 men, and armed with nine 11-inch guns, twelve 5.9-inch guns and an array of smaller firepower, they were at the time of their launch the two largest and most powerful vessels in the German fleet. Their names were also, to the English tongue, impossible to pronounce.

On 27 December 1943, British newspapers reported that a fleet of German ships had attacked a convoy in the North Sea heading for Russia. In the ensuing fierce exchange, the *Scharnhorst* was repeatedly hit by British ships and sunk. Of the 1,968 officers and enlisted men, only thirty-six survived. The editors reminded their readers that the *Gneisenau* had been mortally damaged the year before. But instead of calling the ships by their German names, the papers used a phrase that tripped off the tongue more easily: 'Salmon and Gluckstein'. Not once, but again and again and again.

This was difficult for Sam and his relatives to read. It left a bitter taste in their mouths. Reputation had always been critical to the family. Samuel had won it on the streets of London, building his customer base one cigar at a time, only to squander it during the court case in 1870. Monte had fought to win it back, through his brilliant showmanship, his quality products and his reasonable prices. And when he too had slipped, over the Olympia scandal, he had stepped back to protect the family's good name. Since then, Isidore, Harry, Maurice and the others had hardly put a foot wrong. They had produced a number of household names: the Nippies, Corner Houses and Lyons teashops, to name but a few. Isidore, in particular, had been extraordinarily careful in his work as a Member of Parliament and as vice-chairman of the Board of Deputies, always insisting that he put country first, before family, before faith. Yet here they were, once again being seen as non-British.

For almost a hundred years they had sought to persuade their fellow countrymen that their allegiance was to England. Sam's father had striven to become more British than the British: he sent his son to Cambridge, wore tails and a top hat, served drinks to the Queen at her summer garden parties, and feigned a posh accent. Yet here they were, once more being linked to Germany and, at least in the public imagination, their loyalty questioned.

Yet in another way the reputation of J. Lyons – and by extension the family – was never greater than at this moment. Despite the labour shortages, the restrictions on raw materials, government rationing, the Blitz and the many other difficulties of war, they had somehow managed to keep their business going. Above all, and perhaps most importantly, they continued their production, distribution and serving of the national drink: tea. According to Richard Dimbleby, the BBC journalist who reported throughout the war, 'To many of us, I believe, it became more than just a warming drink. It was the outward mark of security and comfort when these qualities were sadly lacking.' By keeping the teashops open and the teapots flowing, Lyons played a key role in buttressing the morale of the British people at its time of greatest peril.

J. Lyons was also of course playing another, far less public role: with its 'filling factory' in Elstow.

★

On 19 November 1943, more than 400 Avro Lancasters rumbled through the skies of France, Belgium and western Germany and, on arriving above Berlin, dropped their massive payloads on the population below. They returned the next day, and the day after that. By 17 December, a quarter of the capital's housing had been destroyed. This signalled the start of a new phase of the war: the mass bombardment of German civilian targets. By the New Year, Hamburg, Cologne, Frankfurt, Dortmund, Dresden, Munich and scores of other cities and towns were experiencing the unrelenting terror of daily aerial bombardment.

To supply this avalanche of TNT, the munitions workers at the Lyons factory in Elstow were working in three shifts around the clock. They were now producing a range of items, from the smaller 200-kilo and 500-kilo bombs, to the massive 2,000-kilo, 4,000-kilo and even 10,000-kilo varieties. These larger munitions were known as 'blockbusters' and were capable of destroying an entire street or a large building. Once packed and stencilled, they were transported to the RAF to be used in their missions over Germany.

As the Allies launched their D-Day naval offensive in June 1944, enabling British, American and other troops to land on the Normandy coast, and push into France, the Lyons factory in Elstow ramped up its supply of ammunitions. Each month, more than 1,200 tonnes of TNT were now being made. Efficiency was such that they could produce more than 130,000 two-inch trench mortar bombs per week. Between July 1943 and the end of 1944, Elstow delivered some five million two-inch trench mortar bombs to the army. Lyons had met the government's request.

The country was now seeing significant change in its military prospects, partly as a result of the escalating capacity to bomb German positions. Hitler was on the retreat. For once, workers at the factory truly believed the end of the war was on the horizon.

Chapter 35

1945

At the start of 1945, the Allied forces advanced eastwards across France, then into Belgium and Holland, and Hitler's forces pulled back into Germany, blowing up bridges as they went. In response, the Allies erected Bailey bridges to span the otherwise uncrossable streams and rivers. The hardware of these temporary bridges came from various sources, including the Lyons Elstow factory, which made the kingpins that bolted together the ironwork.

Meanwhile the bombing of German cities intensified. While Allied tanks rumbled through western Germany, and as Soviet forces approached from the east, the aerial bombardment of Berlin, Dresden, Leipzig and other cities continued. Finally, in April 1945, Soviet forces rolled into Berlin and, with Adolf Hitler committing suicide in his bunker, the Luftwaffe and Wehrmacht capitulated.

When the tally was complete, Elstow had supplied 96,488 tonnes of bombs to the RAF. By April 1945, the J. Lyons factory in Bedfordshire had contributed one-seventh of all the high explosive dropped by Bomber Command on Germany. With the help of the Salmons and Glucksteins, and their thousands of hard-working staff, Germany had been bludgeoned into defeat.

On 8 May 1945, after almost six years of combat in which at least fifty million people had lost their lives, war in Europe finally came to an end. Britain's economy was in tatters, its people exhausted and grieving.

Two months later, on Monday, 9 July, Sam walked from his house at Hyde Park Place in Mayfair to the Trocadero near Piccadilly. It was the first peacetime shareholders' meeting since 1939. Like the rest of the country, Sam was emotionally and physically drained, but as one of the company's directors, he had no choice but to turn up. The country was at that moment in limbo. A general election had been held the previous Thursday, but the results were still to be announced. The victorious wartime leader, Winston Churchill, had campaigned hard to retain the premiership, but Clement Atlee had argued that his Labour Party was better placed to rebuild the country. According to *The Times*, 'the only thing that all seem to agree is that never was it more difficult to predict the probable outcome of the election'.

At exactly 10 a.m., Sam's uncle and Lyons chairman, Harry Salmon, stood up at the front of the hall and called the meeting to order. He started by saying that he hoped the shareholders would consider the financial report 'satisfactory', given the 'continued limitation of supplies and other controls which the country's war effort necessarily imposed'. Throughout the conflict the company had been able to pay out dividends, and Harry said they should 'consider themselves fortunate'. As for the production of foodstuffs suspended during wartime, 'we know that far from being any early relief in that respect the position is worse'.

The chairman now took the opportunity to tell his investors that during the previous six years the company had done more than produce tea, coffee and bread. To the surprise of those assembled, he said that they had also been responsible for the secret bomb-making factory in Elstow. In addition to their production of munitions, he continued, they had built thousands of special bodies for military service vehicles and had packed millions of composite rations for troops in Europe and the Far East.

Despite their achievements, it was impossible to disguise the fact that the war had had a terrible impact on the company. Many of Lyons' products had lost market share during the war years, with the tea business hardest hit. Between 1939 and 1945, tea production had collapsed from 11,000 to 6,000 chests per week. It had dropped from second to fourth place as a seller of tea, behind Brooke Bond, Tetley and Typhoo.

The Lyons teashops had had a mixed time. On the positive side, the depots had maintained a profit throughout the war. For although raw materials had been restricted and the government had imposed limits on the menu, demand had remained high and the company had reduced its wage costs by introducing self-service to many of its outlets. On the other hand, seventy of its teashops had been destroyed during the Blitz, an enormous financial burden for the company.

Worst of all had been the war's human cost. The final numbers were as yet unknown, but it appeared that as many as 242 Lyons workers had died in the fighting and thousands more had been injured. As his uncle Monte had before him, at the end of the previous conflict, Harry promised that as soon as the veterans returned home, their pre-war jobs would be waiting for them.

As for the women who had filled in during the men's absence (and again just as with the previous war), they would be expected to relinquish their positions. Those who remained would be paid at lower rates than their male counterparts, according to the J. Lyons office manual. While men working at Grade D, for instance, would be paid 80 shillings, women would receive 77.6 shillings. Equally, men working at level F3 would be paid £650, while women would receive £500. In this era of rationing there were, however, some advantages afforded to the female employees.

According to the same office manual, female clerks with between three and ten years' unbroken service would be given upon marriage a wedding cake whose retail value was £2. If the bridegroom also worked for Lyons, they would be provided with a two-tiered cake worth £4.

Harry did not discuss the wartime experience of his own family: Isidore Salmon, who had transformed the army's catering, and who, according to the War Office, had died during active service. Or Sam's first cousin, Peter Salmon, who had died at the age of twenty-two in a Japanese prisoner-of-war camp. Or Bruce Gluckstein, Monte's grandson, who was killed aged twenty-two while defending the beach-head at Anzio on the Italian coast. Many in the family had served heroically. Some the family knew about, others they didn't. Edna Gluckstein, for instance, had served with the secretive Special Operations Executive (SOE) and had been dropped behind enemy lines. She was safely back home, but was tight-lipped about her wartime activities. Meanwhile Mimi's son Neil was still with the Intelligence Corps and was currently somewhere in Europe.

It had been a long, brutal war. For most, it would be impossible to 'get over it', 'move on' or 'get back to normal'. How could you get over the loss of a husband or brother, wife or daughter, mother or father? But they would do their best and, with that in mind, peacetime operations began once again. With the war ended, the task was to reboot the business of J. Lyons. If the family enterprise was to hold on to its status as the Empire's leading catering company, it would have to maintain its one historical advantage: developing products before anybody else. As Monte Gluckstein had once said, they needed people to yell, 'Glad they thought of it – just what we wanted!'

Yet with rationing continuing, it would be challenging to excite the public about new products. There was, however, one luxury food item that had not been rationed, and it was upon this that the family would now focus considerable energy: ice-cream.

The production of ice-cream had been outlawed in Britain since October 1942. While the government had blamed the restriction on scarce transportation resources, its real motive had almost certainly been that the eating of ice-cream was considered too much of a luxury, and bad for morale at a time when men and women were risking their lives overseas.

It had been with some jubilation, therefore, when at the start of 1945 the nation heard that ice-cream could once again be produced. Sam Salmon was now put in charge of the ice-cream division. The use of milk products and sugar was still restricted, so Sam asked his scientists to come up with another solution. Lyons now installed the most up-to-date equipment and set about recruiting the country's best young scientists. One of these was Margaret Hilda Roberts, who had just graduated with a degree in chemistry from Oxford. After she was married she would be known as Margaret Thatcher.

This new cadre of motivated scientists worked at the Lyons' laboratory, trying to crack the secrets of ice-cream production. The key to a smooth and consistent product, they knew, was to prevent the milk fat separating from the water. To guarantee this, they introduced an emulsifier that would stabilise the mixture. Their next breakthrough occurred when they discovered that, through the dextrinisation of flour (during which starches were broken down by the application of heat), they could produce various sugar substitutes. Next they experimented with sugar replacements with names such as 'Swefat' and 'Malogel'. Finally, instead of cream they used margarine – which had also not been rationed – and later vegetable oils, ushering in a decades-long period during which Lyons (followed soon afterwards by other manufactures) was making 'ice-cream' without using any milk products at all.

Margaret Hilda (later Thatcher) at work, J. Lyons

Emboldened by such successes, Sam encouraged the scientists to innovate still further. While considerable energy was channelled into coming up with new products, much of the thinking went into designing novel manufacturing processes. One development to come out of the lab was 'ribbon extrusion', in which ice-cream that had been channelled out of a nozzle was cut into slices, making it creamier and stiffer, and 'enrobed' – in which ice-cream blocks were coated in a thin layer of chocolate. Perhaps the most important innovation was a process known as 'continuing mixing', where engineers constructed complicated automated pneumatic valves, which controlled the ingredients as they flowed into enormous vats and pans. The Lyons ice-cream plant at Greenford was now the world's first automated one and, like his father before him, Sam was soon giving tours of the plant to Princess Elizabeth and other members of the royal family.

Lyons was now once again the second-largest ice-cream maker in the UK, after Wall's. By the early 1950s, Wall's sold 30 per cent of Britain's ice-cream, while Lyons' share was 15 per cent. If Isidore had been the King of Catering, Sam was now the Prince of Ice-Cream.

Sam and his family were now living at 12 Hyde Park Place, only a few steps from Speakers' Corner and the Cumberland Hotel. Theirs was an enormous flat with a large hall, four reception rooms, a dining room that could sit twenty people, a drawing room filled with antique French furniture, and four bedrooms. Sam and Wendy occupied the master bedroom with a view over Hyde Park. Eight-year-old Belinda slept in the dressing room, and the new baby, Jonathan, was in the nursery overlooking the tennis court to the rear.

The family employed a cook, a housemaid, a nanny, two chauffeurs and a charlady. The staff had their own living quarters on the top floor and in the basement, with their own kitchens, bathrooms and separate entrance. It was made clear that the staff worked for the adults, not the children. One day, for instance, Belinda left her Mary Janes out to be cleaned. Seeing what her daughter had done, Wendy said curtly, 'the chauffeur polishes my shoes not yours'.

Although Wendy didn't like to cook, the large kitchen had been fitted out with all the latest appliances and had its own walk-in pantry. In the walls of each room was hidden an electronic button, which the Salmons could use to call the servants. Yet despite the luxury, the flat was a gloomy, sombre place, its floors covered with Persian rugs and its tall windows draped with thick paisley-patterned curtains.

Sam was a stickler for routine. Each weekday morning he woke at 7.30 a.m. First he dressed, his clothes having been laid out for him by the chauffeur, Baker. Next he ate breakfast, the same each day (two slices of white toast and a cup of coffee), and then, promptly, at 8 a.m., with his black trilby on his head, two handkerchiefs in his pockets (a shower and a blower), he grabbed his coat and walking stick and joined Baker who was by now waiting outside. If she wanted a lift, Belinda had to be ready with her satchel packed, coat on and waiting by the front door, Sam told her, or he would leave without her. Nervous that he would carry out his threat, she was never late. Having dropped Belinda at school, Baker then took Sam to work.

Sam's weeks were regulated. Mondays and Tuesdays he worked in the ice-cream department, meeting the managers, discussing new products and resolving personnel issues. Wednesdays were busy with the Fund, lunch at the Trocadero, then a meeting with his male relatives. Louis, his cousin, was almost always there, as were Mimi's sons, Brian, Tony and Christopher. His uncle Maurice and cousin Barney usually attended, as did the high-court judge Cyril Salmon, though he kept his counsel to himself. Sometimes a few of the teenagers were present – not yet inducted, but eager to see how it all worked. In all, there were usually around twenty men at these meetings.

On Thursdays it was the Lyons board meeting, which entailed another long lunch in the directors' dining room, followed by an excruciatingly boring discussion, involving endless presentations, cashflow forecasts, balance sheets and bottomless reports, all of which were empty of tension, because all the key decisions had already been agreed at the previous day's meeting of the Fund. On Fridays, Sam gratefully returned to the ice-cream department.

At the end of most afternoons he would visit his mother, Kitty, who was now living in a suite of rooms on the sixth floor of Claridge's Hotel in central London, then he would play an hour's bridge at the Hamilton Club. Finally he would arrive home, where he would join his family for dinner, taken at exactly 7.45 p.m. After the meal, and having read a few pages to Belinda – typically from one of Charles Dickens' novels – Sam retired alone to his study, where he lit his pipe, filled with Three Nuns tobacco, and commenced an endless game of Patience until it was time for bed.

Sam's favourite hours of the week, however, were Saturday and Sunday mornings. Waking early and having put on his riding gear – baggy jodhpurs, checked shirt, thin tie, tweed jacket, stringed gloves, flat hat, whip – he quietly closed the apartment door and walked to the stables behind the building. There he saddled a large mare measuring sixteen hands and guided the horse across Park Lane to Hyde Park, where, on the other side of a large wrought-iron gate, was Rotten Row, a 1.5-kilometre stretch of sand that ran in a straight line along the bottom edge of the park.

A strong rider, Sam moved smoothly from a walk to a trot to a canter. This was as fast as he was allowed to go, for galloping was forbidden in Hyde Park. But it was fast enough for him. This was where he wanted to be. Not in the board room reviewing spread-sheets, or at the Trocadero for one of those dreadful family meetings, or at home with his unfriendly wife and noisy children. But here, in the unfettered open. As he had been when he was a boy swimming in the school pond, and then at university on the River Cam, he was in his element, outside and alone.

Seventeen years younger than her husband, Wendy was uninter-ested in ice-cream production, horse riding or Patience. Instead she was looking for fun and attention that Sam was simply unable, or unwilling, to provide. After all, she had been pushed into the marriage and had never felt she had truly consented to the arrangement. Sam, by contrast, truly loved Wendy and was deeply disappointed by his wife's coldness. Yet he remained, above all, a loyal man, and considered it his duty to stand by his wife, even if their relationship lacked passion.

It was around this time that Sam and Wendy took their children on holiday to Saint-Tropez on the French Riviera. There, on the beach one day, they met Pierre and Lucille Lazard: he a tall, good-looking Frenchman who worked for a leading advertising company, and she a charming woman with short blonde hair and a slim figure. Liking each other, and not without a little flirting, the couples spent time together and, when the holiday ended, promised to stay in touch. Which is exactly what Pierre and Wendy did, their initial correspondence blossoming into something more serious.

Chapter 36

1947

Neil Salmon

Unlike Sam Salmon who had remained in England managing Cadby Hall and the Elstow bomb factory, his cousin Neil had spent almost the entire war overseas with the army. He had rarely been given leave, although enough to marry his girlfriend, Yvonne (his brother Tony's wife's sister), and get her pregnant (she gave birth to a boy, whom they named Roger). When, a year after Victory in Europe Day, Neil finally returned home from Germany, Harry suggested that he work in the ice-cream department under Sam.

Neil, who was by now twenty-five years old and was rarely seen without a cigar or a pipe in his mouth, spoke little about what he had been up to overseas – his time with 31 Field Security Section in the UK, with 108 Wireless Intercept Section in North Africa and later with the Intelligence Corps 'Depot' in north-west Europe. What he did talk about, over and over again, to Sam and other relatives at the weekly Fund meetings was the urgent need to modernise J. Lyons. The family could not possibly run the company forever, he said. They should bring in qualified managers. If, and when, family members did join Lyons, they should first receive training from outside the company. In addition Lyons needed to incorporate new ideas from other countries, particularly America. There had been advances in retailing and food manufacturing, which Lyons needed to catch up with. Clarence Birdseye, for instance, had found a way to freeze fish and vegetables, enabling such items to be transported across long distances whilst remaining fresh. Equally, retailers such as Kroger and Safeway had grown into nationwide chains of self-service grocery shops, known as supermarkets, selling uniform products at discount prices. Why couldn't such innovations happen in England?

Neil's elders listened respectfully to such ideas, but they were committed to the old ways: each generation being trained in the kitchens of the Trocadero; reserving the Lyons management board to those called Salmon or Gluckstein; keeping the business held tightly within the family. It had worked in the past, they argued; indeed, it had worked so well that they had survived two world wars, so why change things now?

Neil was grateful that he had been brought into the senior management of Lyons, especially as he had been away for almost six years at war, but he was deeply frustrated by his relatives' intransigence. He believed that radical change was inevitable. He could smell it. But if his uncles and cousins were not yet ready, all he could do was wait for the right moment to present itself.

Luckily, he didn't have to wait long. In the spring of 1947, John Simmons approached the board with an idea. Simmons was the company's comptroller, in charge of all administration. His proposal was to send two of his assistants to the USA to investigate recent developments in clerical machines, in particular to visit an electronic prototype being developed at the University of Pennsylvania. They were calling it a 'computer'. At this time there was no commercial application for computers; indeed, the world of computers was very much in its infancy. Encouraged by Neil and other young family members, the board approved the research trip and asked for a comprehensive report on their return.

On 20 October 1947, Simmons submitted his staff's findings to Sam, Harry and the rest of the board. In a cover note he wrote that the Pennsylvania computer had 'incredible speed', could potentially 'have a profound effect on the way clerical work (at least) is performed' and that 'what effect such a machine could have on the semi-repetitive work of the office needs only the slightest imagination'. Simmons recommended that J. Lyons create a machine to meet its own needs, starting with an investment in Cambridge University, where a team was attempting to build Britain's first computer.

At first glance, this does appear an extraordinary suggestion. J. Lyons was, after all, a catering company, not an incubator for new technologies. Yet Lyons had long been at the forefront of clerical innovation. Sam's father, Isidore, had vigorously promoted the use of decimalisation, first in the family business and later in the country as a whole. The company had also been early adopters of counting machines to assist with the payroll and staff schedules. In addition they had used an early form of microfilm to capture and process customer orders. Every aspect of the production process was tightly monitored and calibrated, from the thickness of the jam in their Swiss rolls to the time allocated to pack a chest of tea. Simmons himself was considered a leader in the field of administration, and was currently chairman of the Office Management Association.

Following a long discussion, the board agreed to donate £3,000 to the team in Cambridge who were developing the computer prototype and, if that worked, up to an additional £60,000 to build a machine that could take on Lyon's clerical work. In return for their contribution, it was agreed that the university would assist Lyons in the development of their computer, if and when a decision was made to move forward.

The team of engineers immediately set to work. Based in the mathematics laboratory in Cambridge, they built a series of tall racks that housed 3,000 valves, thirty-two mercury delay lines and a tangle of cables and wires. Once complete, the computer was smaller than the one in Pennsylvania, yet the room was cramped, with little room to move around in. To operate the apparatus, an engineer keyed instructions using a typewriter that, instead of printing characters on paper, punched holes in a card, which were then converted into electrical signals read by the computer. The engineers devised a language that used binary codes (based on 1s and 0s), allowing the machine to carry out simple addition and subtraction. The question remained: would it work? On 6 May 1949, they ran a test, asking the computer to provide the squares of all the numbers between 0 and 99. To the excitement of the engineers, the machine began spitting out correct answers on a printer. It worked. In all, it took just two minutes and thirty-five seconds to complete the task. The engineers called their machine EDSAC, or Electronic Delay Storage Automatic Calculator.

Simmons now informed the board of J. Lyons about the success in Cambridge and requested approval to build their own computer. On behalf of the board, Harry Salmon sent Simmons a note in response. 'Yes', he wrote, they could proceed with the project. With the board's support, Simmons set about building a dedicated computer department. This was called Lyons Electronics Office, or LEO for short.

Simmons and his team worked around the clock to build the Lyons computer. A 250-square-metre area was set aside on the second floor of the administration block in Cadby Hall, two floors below the executive level, where Sam and the other directors worked. With a staff of six engineers, and support from Cambridge University, they constructed the hardware, piece by piece, made up of banks of valves, memory batteries, tape drives and card punchers, all standing on a suspended floor under which ran data cables. It would be an enormous machine. Simmons said it would take a year to build, maybe more.

It was at around this time that Neil took on most of the day-to-day responsibilities of the ice-cream division. Neil worked with the geniuses of the ice-cream department to design a range of innovative products. First came Orange Maid, the so-called 'drink on the stick', made from puréed fruit. Next was the Mivvi, a water-ice shell with an ice-cream core, one of the world's first split confections. To Neil's delight, and that of the board, sales of both new ice-creams were brisk. In one year, sales of Orange Maid rose by 400 percent.

Neil's success freed Sam to pursue activities beyond J.Lyons. Like his father, Sam found himself attracted to politics. As a boy, Sam had grown up in close proximity to Members of Parliament, their campaign managers and aides. From watching his father, he understood how to write a manifesto, and the importance of knocking on doors. It was therefore relatively straightforward to have his name placed on the list of Conservative Party candidates running for the three Cities of London and Westminster seats of the London County Council. The councillor position was part-time, allowing him to continue his duties at J. Lyons. The election was held on 7 April 1949, and Sam and the other two Conservatives won 18,000 more votes than the three Labour candidates. Soon Sam was taking part in committee meetings on the capital's transport and sewage systems. The LCC also introduced him to another, entirely more secretive world.

One evening after working at his office on the banks of the Thames, Sam said goodnight to his secretary and took the lift down-stairs. Instead of getting out at the ground floor and being met by his chauffeur, he exited in the basement and headed towards a room that he had never previously visited. There, in an anteroom, he was met by Albert Bernard Kennedy, a Labour representative from the London borough of Southwark. After greeting each other, Albert told Sam to place his bowler hat, briefcase and umbrella in a nearby locker. Then he instructed Sam to roll up his left trouser leg and to unbutton his shirt, revealing his left breast. Albert then placed a black mask over Sam's eyes, and around his neck a noose made of coarse rope.

His charge now ready, Albert escorted Sam to a large oak door and gave three long knocks. From the other side of the door Sam heard someone announce, 'There is a report.' The door swung open and Sam sensed that he was now facing a large room where a group of men awaited. The door-opener then asked for the 'candidate' to be named. 'Mr Salmon,' Albert replied, 'a poor candidate in a state of darkness who has been well and worthily recommended, regularly proposed and approved in open Lodge, and now comes, of his own free will.'

After these words were repeated around the room, a man with an elderly but firm voice said, 'Then let him be admitted in due form', at which point Sam felt the prick of a small blade against his naked left breast. 'Do you feel anything?' he was asked, to which he replied that he did. Someone then took Sam by his right hand and led him a few paces forward, before whispering to him to kneel. Sam was then asked if he was more than twenty-one years of age. 'I am,' he replied, a little bewildered.

Suddenly a gavel was banged loudly, which was startling, and then two men walked alongside Sam, each holding something about his head – long sticks perhaps. Next the elderly man told Sam to kneel on his left knee, with his right foot forming a square, and asked him, 'Are you therefore willing to take a solemn obligation, founded on the principles I have stated?' Sam affirmed his commitment. The elderly man then asked, 'Having been kept for a considerable time in a state of darkness, what, in your present situation, is the predominant wish of your heart?', to which Sam said, 'Light.' Again, a gavel was banged, this time followed by a new sound, as the congregation clapped their hands once. At this point Albert removed the mask from Sam's face. It took a few seconds for his eyes to adjust to the light, but soon Sam recognised many of the men in the room, each a member of the LCC and all wearing white gloves and a turquoise apron over their suits. 'Rise, newly obligated Brother,' said the elderly man, who was a senior member of the Conservative Party.

A few weeks later, a parcel arrived at his office wrapped in paper. Opening the package, Sam found a brown leather case on which were emblazoned his initials, 'S.I.S.' Inside was his own turquoise apron, from which hung a number of silver balls, with a similarly coloured band around the waist, on which was pinned an oval white badge stamped with 'London County Council Lodge No. 2603'. Also in the case were a pair of white gloves and a small black book that provided the service for the 'Nigerian Ritual'.

Sam was now a Freemason. The grandson of Barnett Salmon, who grew up in a poor house in east London, and great-grandson of Samuel, who had fled Holland after being found guilty of fraud, had joined one of Britain's most clandestine inner sanctums. If ever there was a symbol that Sam had assimilated into British life, this was it.

In early 1950, while he was learning the ropes at County Hall, Sam received some bad news. His uncle Harry had suffered a heart attack and needed to step away from his duties as managing director of Lyons. Like almost every other member of the family, Harry was a heavy smoker and the years of inhaling nicotine were catching up with him.

As his health deteriorated over the summer, Harry attended fewer and fewer meetings of either the board or the Fund, and then stopped altogether. In July, he somehow found the strength to give the chairman's address at the company's annual meeting, but the effort exhausted him. On 13 October, as he was being driven to his house in the Kent countryside, Harry suffered a fatal heart attack.

The chairmanship of J. Lyons now went to the next in line: Izzy Gluckstein's son, Major Monte Gluckstein, who had worked with Charles Cochran back in the 1930s and was in charge of the teashops. His ascension was met with some concern amongst his relatives, especially Neil and the family's younger members. Though respected and well liked, Monte was not seen as a forward-thinking leader. An aficionado of theatrical music, for sure, and good with market ideas, but perhaps not someone who could lead one of the world's largest catering companies into the 1960s. The transition left the family feeling a bit uncertain about their future.

Beyond a little chatter around the edges of the weekly meeting of the Fund, however, there was no challenge to Major Monte's leadership. The economy was picking up, consumer confidence was rising and the family could see little real threat on the horizon. Following the rules that had worked well in the past made common sense.

One year after Harry's death, Simmons announced that LEO was ready. They had conducted numerous tests, and he believed that the computer could now take over one of the company's clerical tasks. So it was that, on the evening of Thursday, 30 November 1951, LEO began to process the weekly stock calculation for the bakery department. Once complete, this so-called 'Bakery Valuation' was delivered to the board at the following week's meeting. According to the results, LEO had been a 100 per cent success.

The directors were delighted that LEO would save time and money, and proud that they had supported the building of the groundbreaking machine. LEO was not only one of just three computers in Britain at this time, it was also the world's first computer to perform a regular routine office job.

Chapter 37

1953

On 2 June 1953, Sam, Wendy and the rest of the family peered over the balcony at the front of the Cumberland Hotel, whose railings were bedecked with red, white and blue bunting. They were surrounded by a host of relatives and staff. In the road below they could see tens of thousands of people, to the left all the way down Oxford Street and ahead down Park Lane, all eagerly awaiting the arrival of the royal procession. For today was the coronation of Elizabeth II.

First came a lead car to clear the way, followed by a marching band playing trumpets, French horns, trombones and huge drums. Next came the Horse Guards in red coats and tall brass helmets, followed by a troop of cavalry, with white pith helmets and swords held aloft. Behind them strode line upon line of soldiers – Scots Guards, Welsh Guards, men and women, navy, army and air force – stiffly marching, rifles swishing up and down on their shoulders. With each new group the crowd roared with approval, caught up in the excitement of the occasion.

As part of the coronation, Lyons was providing catering for the troops who were participating in the parades. That morning, breakfast had been served to thousands of soldiers billeted at Olympia. Across the capital, Lyons teashops featured cakes and desserts with royal themes. The windows of its oldest store, at 213 Piccadilly, were festooned with Elizabeth Regina II decorations. And to commemorate the day, the company had produced a special 'Coronation cup' ice-cream.

Lyons teashop decorated for coronation, Piccadilly, 1953

Finally, marked by a roar from the crowd, the royal party approached. As the procession turned the corner round Marble Arch, Sam, Wendy and the children could look directly into the golden carriage in which sat the bejewelled Queen Elizabeth and the handsomely dressed Prince Philip. Seeing two hands waving through the window, the crowd cheered again, the children eagerly fluttering their Union Jack flags as the carriages trundled on down Oxford Street.

In all the procession was 3.2 kilometres long, comprising more than 29,000 service personnel from Britain and the Commonwealth. It had taken more than forty-five minutes to pass by. When it was finally over, exhilarated by all the jubilation but ready to get away from the noise, the family turned back into the Cumberland Hotel, where a grand luncheon awaited.

Just seven years since the war's end, and with rationing still in place and much of the country's infrastructure still unrepaired, the nation was ready for an emotional uplift. Sam hoped this would be a turning point, and that the Queen would usher in a new era of peace and prosperity, both for the country and for the family.

Shortly after the coronation, a book arrived at the family's flat on Hyde Park Place. It was addressed to Sam, and was from his cousin Louis. It had been twenty-nine years since Louis' father, Joseph, had circulated the *Family Trees*, and now it was time for an update. Though twice the size of the original, the book's cover was the same dark green, embossed with just the family crest and motto.

It had been Louis' labour of love. In addition to extending and filling in the main branches of the Salmon and Gluckstein family trees and updating the dates for births, marriages and deaths, Louis had also included new family lines that had been added through marriage. More ambitiously, he had included a pull-out sheet entitled 'Some of the civic, military and academic honours gained by the family since 1907'.

Sam quickly checked to see if his name was mentioned; it was: University of Cambridge (1922) and Member London County Council (1949). He noted that for the first time various female relatives were recorded, including Louis' mother, for her work helping refugees during the First World War (though there was no mention of his sister Gluck, despite her wide acclaim). Sam's father, Isidore, was listed in five spots (which made him proud), topped only by Louis himself, who had found seven ways to enter his name: Member of Parliament, King's Counsel, London County Council, Territorial Decoration, Mentioned in Dispatches (1918), Deputy Lieutenant for County of London (1952) and University of Oxford.

In his foreword Louis explained that he had 'tried faithfully to set out the many changes that have occurred' since his father's edition. 'My father expressed the hope that our family might continue to work together,' Louis wrote. 'He would rejoice to know that the ideal of family unity embodied in our crest remains the foundation upon which the family fortunes stand. Long may it continue to be.'

Since the invention of the LEO computer, the board had discussed what to do with the technology. It was successfully managing the 'Bakery Valuation' and it was hoped that it would soon have the capacity to take on other clerical tasks, such as the company payroll. The question was: should the computer be sold to outside companies? For this to be successful, Lyons would have to make an even larger investment, to improve its capability and reliability.

Over the summer of 1954, the debate reached boiling point. On one side were those who believed that the computer department should serve only the needs of Lyons. 'Leave the development of computing to computing companies,' they argued. Sam, Major Monte and the older family members were amongst those pushing this line of argument. Then there were those who said that Lyons had to move beyond catering. It was now the leader in this new computer technology, whose market potential was enormous, and it would be a huge mistake not to take advantage of this opportunity. Neil and his brothers, Tony and Brian, were the leaders of this group, supported by John Simmons and his staff. In the end, a compromise was agreed. They would continue to focus on the needs of J. Lyons, but would announce LEO's arrival to the public and see if there was any interest from outside groups.

Over the next two years Lyons invested an additional £150,000 into the development of LEO. Its capacity was improved, its operation made more reliable. In February 1954, it took over the company's payroll. A week later, Lyons introduced LEO to the press. Most were impressed by the speed of what they called the 'electronic brain', though some worried that automation might lead to the loss of clerical jobs. The publicity attracted considerable interest, and soon Sam and the other directors were guiding tours around the LEO laboratory. Potential clients included government departments along with commercial companies, both of which were keen to understand the computer's potential to handle administrative tasks.

Finally the decision was made to spin off the project into its own company. In the spirit of Monte Gluckstein who, sixty years earlier, had launched the catering business apart from the tobacco enterprise, the board agreed to create a new company, called LEO Computers Ltd. Representing the family would be Tony Salmon, Neil's older brother, who had a good head for mathematics. Based in a disused workshop in Shepherd's Bush, not far from Cadby Hall, the new company set about building a computer that could be sold to an outside business. Gradually orders came in. Two computers were sold to the Ford Motor Company, another two were purchased by Imperial Tobacco, a third went to the Ministry of Pensions and another to the steelmaker Stewarts & Lloyds. It looked as if Lyons had confounded the doubters and was, once again, forging an entirely new market.

Then, hot on the heels of the debate about computing, the board found itself faced with yet another commercial opportunity. This too it wasn't quite sure how to handle.

One warm day during the spring of 1954, a short American named Edward Vale Gold arrived at Cadby Hall for a meeting with Brian Salmon. At thirty-seven, Brian was considered by Sam and his

Sam Salmon (centre) with LEO computer

contemporaries to be part of the 'younger generation', along with his brothers Neil and Tony and his cousin Geoffrey. As manager of the Corner Houses, Brian dealt with proposals from entrepreneurs looking to base their restaurants at one of Lyons' outlets.

Sitting in Brian's office on the fourth floor, Gold explained that he had opened his first hamburger grill in Bloomington, Indiana two decades earlier. His formula was simply to sell a limited menu – pure-beef hamburgers, fries and ice-cream-based milkshakes – quickly and at an affordable price. Now, he said, he owned seventeen hamburger grills in the USA and was making a proposal: invest in my restaurant business and we will split the profits.

Having worked in the food industry for more than two decades, Brian was well aware of trends both in Europe and North America. He read the trade magazines and attended the international catering conferences that perennially took place in London and other major cities. He spoke with suppliers, distributors and food sellers. His managers often prepared reports on the state of the industry, which Brian read and were then filed neatly away in the company archive by a clerk. He therefore knew all about the new trend for so-called 'fast food': food that was highly standardised, speedily prepared, based on self-service (without waiters) and available across a chain of restaurants.

Although Gold was clearly a pioneer in providing fast food for the masses, there were others not far behind. Since the end of the Second World War more women were working and fewer were cooking at home. Families were looking to purchase their breakfasts, lunches and dinners for a small amount of money and in a short amount of time. Foremost amongst this new wave of catering enterprises were the McDonald brothers, who had opened their first restaurant in San Bernardino, California. Just months before Gold's arrival in London, they had franchised their first store, and by the end of the year there would be four McDonalds in the USA, though still thirteen fewer than Gold had.

Now that beef rationing had been rescinded in the UK, Gold's vision was that Lyons could use its catering expertise to roll out a fast-food hamburger chain in Britain. When Brian asked for the name of the hamburger grill, Gold said it was called 'Wimpy'. This came from the character J. Wellington Wimpy in the *Popeye* comic strip. While Popeye liked to fight and to guzzle spinach, Gold said, Wimpy was his lackadaisical friend with a passion for hamburgers. Bringing the meeting to an end, Brian politely thanked Gold for his time and assured him that he would soon be in touch.

At the next meeting of the board, Brian shared Gold's proposal. He was in favour of exploring it further, but the older board members were resistant. They rejected the idea, partly because the family had no experience in providing fast food, but more importantly because they didn't want the firm associated with snack-bar culture, which they viewed as déclassé. The board instructed Brian to send Gold on his way.

Undeterred, and having been unable to induce any of Lyons' competitors to invest, Eddie Gold returned to Lyons several months later. This time he made a presentation in front of the full board. After quizzing him about the logistics of the operation, and carefully reviewing the financial reports he had brought from America, the board thanked Gold for his time and retired to make a decision. Once again it was the younger members who advocated experimentation, whilst the elders cautioned restraint. Another compromise was agreed: they would trial the Wimpy concept and see how customers responded.

This they did at the 1954 'Ideal Home Exhibition'. To Brian's, Sam's and the rest of the family's great surprise, in just the first week they sold more than 10,000 hamburgers. Later that year they tested the Wimpy hamburger at the Wimbledon Lawn Tennis Championship and then at the Chelsea Flower Show. Each outing was more successful than the last.

Impressed by their customers' euphoric response, Brian typed up a report summarising his findings and proposed that the company invest significant funds in Gold's product. To support his case, Brian pointed out that they possessed the resources to roll out the franchise at scale. Lyons' bakery could produce the buns; its meat subsidiary could supply the hamburgers; and its ice-cream division the milk-shakes. At the next board meeting Sam and the other directors approved Brian's plan, and in September 1954 a small Wimpy snack bar was opened at the Corner House on Oxford Street. Following its success, a larger Wimpy restaurant was opened at the Corner House on Coventry Street in May 1955, which was soon selling 35,000 burgers each week, making it the largest-selling hamburger retail outlet in the world.

J. Lyons was once again fortunate in its timing. By the mid-1950s the British public were increasingly excited by American culture. This was especially true of young people. On the radio they listened to American songs from Doris Day, Johnnie Ray and Frank Sinatra, while at the cinemas they watched Marlon Brando in *On the Waterfront*, Marilyn Monroe in *How to Marry a Millionaire* and James Dean in *Rebel Without a Cause*. At the same time British television was filled with programmes made in the USA, a trend that accelerated in 1955 with the launch of the country's first commercial television station, ITV. These songs, films and TV programmes portrayed America as a land of affluence, innovation and social mobility.

At the same time, following a wave of government deregulation and private investment, Britain and the rest of the Western world were experiencing an economic boom. Instead of being considered the domain of the very wealthy, consumer goods such as televisions, cars, refrigerators and music systems were increasingly considered to be essential items by the general public. During the 1950s car ownership rose by 250 per cent in Britain, while 13 per cent of households had a refrigerator by the decade's end, up from 2 per cent at its start. The arrival of Wimpy came at just the right time to ride this wave of American-style consumerism.

After a year's negotiations, it was agreed that in return for Gold receiving $450,000, a new international Wimpy company would be established, with Lyons owning 51 per cent and Gold 49 per cent. Gold would control his seventeen existing grills in the USA, and Lyons would own any UK restaurants. For their investment, Sam and the rest of the family would be buying Gold's expertise, the menu and the Wimpy name.

With the business arrangements complete, Lyons set about rolling out a chain of Wimpy bars. Unlike the fast-food restaurants then developing in the USA, these would not be counter-service establishments. Instead, waiters would deliver the food on a plate with cutlery. If a customer wished to eat the meal at home, it was available to be taken away. A new Wimpy was started at the Strand Corner House, another at the Maison Lyons at Marble Arch, and a standalone forty-seat store was opened in Hammersmith. Woolworths then paid for the right to include Wimpy bars in their shops, as did a number of greyhound tracks. By 1959, just three years after Lyons' deal with Gold, sixty Wimpy bars were in operation; by 1962, this figure had risen to 227; and by 1965 to 363. By the late 1960s, more than forty million Wimpy hamburgers were being sold each year. This was years before McDonald's opened its first store in Great Britain.

Despite their extraordinary success, market-moulding innovations and sheer buying power, Lyons was still very much at the mercy of world events. The price of flour used in their bread was influenced by the success of the North American cereal harvest. The cost of transporting tea from Nyasaland was affected by the price of oil powering the shipping tankers. Similarly, international currency fluctuations impacted on the cost of linen used for restaurant tablecloths and hotel sheets, along with the price of cacao from West Africa and coffee from South America. It was with great disquiet, therefore, that the family heard that global shipping routes had been disrupted by an incident in the Middle East.

On 26 July 1956, eighty-one years after Disraeli had purchased a 44 per cent stake in the Suez Canal for the British nation, Egypt's President, Gamal Nasser, nationalised the waterway. He believed that, as the canal was located in Egypt, it should by right be his country's asset. He also believed that standing up to the colonial powers would garner domestic support. Losing control of the canal sent shockwaves through the British establishment. The country still relied on it to transport oil from Iraq and the Gulf states, along with raw materials from parts of Asia and Africa.

Three months after Nasser had seized Suez, on 29 October, Israel invaded Egypt's Sinai Desert, in an effort to curtail what they considered to be an overly aggressive neighbour. Within hours, Nasser mobilised his forces and engaged with the Israelis, resulting in the deaths of thirty-eight Israeli and 260 Egyptian soldiers.

The British prime minister Anthony Eden – who had replaced Winston Churchill the year before – now argued that the Suez Canal was Britain's 'great imperial lifeline' and that Nasser was a tyrant who needed to be challenged. When Israel and Egypt refused to agree to a ceasefire, Britain and France dropped paratroopers into Egypt on 5 November, taking up positions along the Suez Canal.

It wasn't long, however, before news leaked out that the Anglo-French incursion into Suez had been pre-arranged with Israel, provoking outrage in the Middle East. In the days that followed, Eden came under tremendous pressure from American president Dwight D. Eisenhower, who considered the Anglo-French interference illegal and was worried that it would antagonise Arab leaders, pushing them closer to the Soviet Union. In a surprise move, the American government also announced that it would rescind the large loans it had made to the Bank of England, unless Britain withdrew its troops. This very public threat was humiliating to Britain and its citizens, yet Eden capitulated and pulled out his forces, effectively handing over control of the canal to the Egyptians. On 9 January 1957, following a wave of public protest and newspaper criticism, Eden resigned.

In the months following the Suez Crisis, the pound became a target of market speculators. To shore up the currency, the new Conservative prime minister, Harold Macmillan, asked the International Monetary Fund (IMF) to underwrite the British economy. The weakened pound made it more difficult for Lyons to borrow money on the international markets and more expensive to purchase overseas products such as tea, coffee and cocoa.

At the annual general meeting held at the Trocadero on 7 June 1957, the Lyons board – comprising Sam and nine of his relatives – reported that the 'year has not been without its difficulties', particularly from the 'fluctuations in world market prices'. The yearly profit, however, was £109,506 greater than the previous year, which allowed for an increased dividend to be distributed to shareholders. Most of this profit came from the new Wimpy restaurants.

Just like Britain, J. Lyons was balanced between the old and the new: the management of a chain of increasingly tired-looking teashops on the one hand, and a network of freshly painted orange-coloured Wimpy bars on the other; the payment of wages according to the old ideas of men deserving more than women, whilst the payroll itself was processed by the very newest of technologies; a management team that was skewed towards the elderly, whilst a cadre of young men agitated for change.

The older generation's tendency towards tradition was an expression of the inherited desire to fit in, to assimilate. Despite all they had accomplished, deep down the family still believed that their position was precarious. And that they were still outsiders. What was happening in the UK at this time did little to assuage their fears.

Chapter 38

1958

Cyril Salmon by Gluck

On a bright autumn day in September 1958, Sam walked through the front doors of the Trocadero and up to Room 14, where the Fund members were gathering for their weekly lunch. Inside, he saw his family clustered around his cousin, Cyril Salmon, a prominent judge at the Old Bailey. All that week the family and the nation had been transfixed by a case of shocking violence and racial hatred, which had fallen to Cyril to adjudicate.

Some weeks before, on the night of 24 August, a gang of nine men aged between seventeen and twenty had gathered in Notting Hill, west London. They were armed with iron bars, a car starting-handle, table leg, various pieces of wood and a knife. Over the next several hours they drove around Shepherd's Bush and Ladbroke Grove, looking for people of colour whom they could beat up. By morning they had conducted sickening attacks on five men, targeted for no other reason than the colour of their skin. Two were lucky enough to escape before being seriously harmed. The other three were left bleeding and unconscious on the pavement. Later in custody, one of the assailants admitted to the police that they had been 'Nigger-hunting'.

The assault took place at the end of a long summer in which west London had been beset by anti-immigrant disturbances. The National Labour Party (unrelated to the Labour Party) was actively promoting racial unrest, with posters demanding: 'Ban coloured immigration'. Another anti-immigrant group was the Britons Publishing Society, which appealed to its followers to 'Keep Britain White'. Oswald Mosley's Union Movement had also, to a lesser extent, been fanning the flames of hatred, handing out flyers about the 'Coloured invasion'. Night after night, thousands of anti-immigrant rioters took to the streets. The windows of homes belonging to recently arrived immigrants were smashed; petrol bombs were thrown in the streets; 108 people had been charged with offences ranging from grievous bodily harm to affray. The 'Nigger-hunting' in Notting Hill, however, was the worst violence seen to date.

The trial, when it began in mid-September, was widely covered in the British press, and Sam had been following it closely. Not least because it was his cousin, Cyril – a man renowned in Fund meetings for his implacable silences – who was tasked with dispensing justice. Looking down from the bench, Cyril had told the defendants, 'As far as the law is concerned you are entitled to think what you like, however vile your thoughts; to feel what you like, however brutal and debased your emotions; to say what you like, providing you do not infringe the rights of others and imperil the Queen's peace. But once you translate your dark thoughts and brutal feelings into savage acts such as these, the law will be swift to punish you, and to protect the victims.' He then added, 'Everyone, irrespective of the colour of their skins, is entitled to walk through our streets in peace, with their heads erect, and free from fear. That is a right which these courts will always unfailingly uphold.'

The punishment was swift and severe. As he was handing down the sentence, Cyril explained that he had decided to make an example of the accused. Crimes of this nature, especially when committed by young men with unblemished records, typically resulted in a stern ticking-off. However, Cyril ordered each of the young men to serve four years in prison. 'There were gasps in court as the sentence was announced,' reported one journalist, 'mothers of some of the youths burst into tears. One woman became hysterical and had to be led out of the court.' But the unusually harsh punishment was widely welcomed in the press. In its article, the *Daily Mirror* said that Mr Justice Salmon 'is a cultured gifted Jew who does everything, slowly, thoughtfully, justly … one of the Salmons of the Salmon and Glucksteins who run the tea-shop Empire J. Lyons and Company'. Moreover, he was a 'likeable Englishman', who, in handing out harsh sentences to the youths, 'has done more to stifle racial hatred than all the theorists. He has become the most talked of man in Britain.'

A week later, the *Daily Mirror* received a letter purporting to be signed by a group of ex-commandos, who stated that 'reprisals would be taken against Mr Justice Salmon and that he would be shot'. The letter was sent to Scotland Yard, to collect fingerprints, and the judge was encouraged to increase his security.

In Room 14, Sam excitedly joined his family in congratulating his cousin for his bravery and his just sentencing. He asked Cyril if he was afraid for his safety; Sam himself was worried. After all, it was not only Cyril – but the company and the family – who had been named in many reports of the trial. Cyril himself shrugged modestly, and said that nothing would stop him from continuing his work.

The trial was not the only moment in the spotlight for the family that year. It was around this time that Sam found himself in the back of the family's shiny black Jaguar, next to his wife and daughter Belinda, who was on her way to be presented to the Queen.

Dressed in a new dress, hat and gloves, Belinda waited in an anteroom at Buckingham Palace alongside forty other young debutantes. Over the previous week she had cut her hair, trimmed her nails and rehearsed her walk again and again. Yet she was still nervous.

At the smallest of gestures from the Lord Chamberlain – dressed in black trousers and a red jacket, whose front was draped in gold tassels – the women were called in one by one. Belinda anxiously watched as the tall ivory-painted door opened and closed. Then it was her turn. As she stepped into a large ballroom, her name was announced. She now saw Queen Elizabeth II. The monarch was enthroned under a crimson canopy directly in front of her. To her right Belinda glimpsed her parents, watching proudly.

She was surprised by how intimidating the situation was. All she had to do was walk a few paces, curtsy, then withdraw. It took all her willpower to retain control. She paused, as she had been instructed, then took three steps forward, gave a graceful dip, her left knee locked behind the right, with her head erect and her hands by her side, waited for two seconds and then rose. After the briefest of pauses she stepped back. And then it was over. It had only taken thirty seconds, but it felt like an hour. She joined the line of other debutantes and waited for the end of the ceremony.

This would be the final year that debutantes were formerly introduced to the monarch – a ritual that had been in place for centuries. A few months earlier, the Lord Chamberlain had announced that there would be no further presentations. Not only did the Queen think the ritual antiquated and exclusive, but her husband thought it 'bloody daft', and her sister, Margaret, famously declared, 'We had to put a stop to it. Every tart in London was getting in.' Already, since the announcement, more than a thousand young women had lined up before the Queen. To many, the termination of this custom was a welcome sign that modernity had finally arrived at the palace. To others, it spoke of grand traditions dying out. Perhaps Britain no longer deserved its prefix: Great.

Now that she had received the royal blessing, Belinda participated in the 'season', a series of breakfast parties, tea dances, horse-racing events and balls in which she would 'come out'. Starting in early spring and continuing until the summer's end, she was introduced to the 'right people' – and, hopefully, her future husband.

In November 1957, Sam and Wendy hosted their daughter's coming-out ball. They chose to hold the event at the London County Council, where Sam had recently been appointed deputy chairman. The evening had been prepared meticulously by the head of Lyons' outdoor-catering team, with every detail of the entertainments, beverages and seating – including the chauffeurs – carefully considered. One by one, the black Daimlers, Rolls-Royces and Bentleys pulled up outside County Hall overlooking the River Thames, and from these executive vehicles climbed out more than 250 young women in ball dresses, pearl necklaces and tiaras, and 250 men in black-tie suits and velvet capes. The young debutantes and their beaux were then ushered into a high-ceilinged reception hall and through to the gilded ballroom. With a live band playing the latest rock-and-roll hits late into the night, and unlimited supplies of alcohol and delicious canapés served by attentive waiters and waitresses, the party was a great triumph.

The following year, 1958, Belinda met Frank, a society boy whose parents had fled Nazi persecution in Germany. The couple started dating and, two years later on the Thames, they were engaged. Belinda and Frank's wedding took place on 30 August 1960. As was the custom, the bride's parents hosted the events. It was as much a matter of logistics as it was of romance. At 2 p.m. exactly, as decreed by the carefully constructed running order, the groom's family were collected from their house in Golders Green. The groom and his brother, the best man – both in morning suits, silk top hats and white gloves – were driven in a Humber Pullman, whilst their parents rode in a Rolls-Royce Silver Wraith. Then, at exactly 2.35 p.m., Sam and his daughter Belinda were picked up in a Rolls-Royce Silver Cloud from the flat in Hyde Park. She looked stunning, dressed in an ivory wedding gown with long sleeves and a silk muslin veil draped over her face. Like his son-in-law, Sam wore a morning suit, top hat and white gloves. Sam's chauffeur, Collins, was given the honour of sitting next to the car's driver.

At 3 p.m. precisely, Belinda and Sam arrived at Hampstead Synagogue on Dennington Park Road. Holding her father's arm, and with her gown's train held by three bridesmaids, Belinda carefully walked up the two stone steps and into the main hall. Inside they were greeted by 500 standing guests. Amongst them were more than 100 members of the wider Salmon and Gluckstein families, a sprawling array of uncles, aunts and first, second and third cousins. Neil and Brian Salmon were there, as were Mimi and Louis Gluckstein and his family. Gluck had been invited, but chose to stay at home in Sussex. The men were all dressed like the groom and the bride's father, with the women in colourful dresses, many with wide-brimmed hats. The most senior relative present was Sam's sixty-five-year-old cousin Barney Salmon, who had recently ascended to the chairmanship of J. Lyons. Barney's grandson Paul was the pageboy.

Like her ancestors before her – Sam and Wendy, Isidore and Kitty, Lena and Barnett, Samuel and Ann, Lehmann and Helena – Belinda was married under a *chuppah,* the embroidered canopy standing in front of the Ark. And just as Isidore would have wanted, it was an orthodox service conducted by an orthodox rabbi in an orthodox synagogue. For although Sam, Wendy and Belinda had joined the Liberal Jewish Synagogue, and the groom and his family belonged to a progressive congregation from the German tradition, the decision had been made to hedge their religious bets. At the time the orthodox rabbinate in Britain would not marry people if their parents had been wed in a liberal or reform synagogue. By marrying in an orthodox synagogue, Belinda and Frank hoped that they would keep their children's options open. Such tactical thinking was a long way from Lehmann's love of the Jewish faith or from Isidore's deep commitment to the traditions of the Bayswater Synagogue.

Later, a reception was held for more than 700 guests at Leighton House in west London, during which 161 bottles of Moët & Chandon 1953 champagne were drunk, along with seven bottles of Haig's Gold Label whisky and three bottles of Gordon's gin. At the end of the evening, the bride and groom changed into their travel clothes and set off for their honeymoon. 'I felt like a doll,' Belinda said later about the day. 'My mother had made all the choices, with the exception of the wedding dress.'

When they returned, there would be one more formality to discuss: the marriage settlement. Like all of her aunts and female cousins, Belinda had always been excluded from the Fund, its weekly family meetings, its decisions its assets. To make up for any perceived inequities, and according to the rules of the Fund, Belinda would, however, receive a 'marriage settlement'. The value of this varied over the years, but at the time of her wedding it was worth £20,000 – equivalent to £400,000 today. This money was put into a trust, to be administered by her father and brother. In addition she was given £1,000 to be spent on her trousseau, including bed linens, cookware and other items deemed necessary for her new domestic life. Belinda was fortunate that her brother and father took a relaxed

Lyons chief's daughter weds

Frank and Belinda's Wedding 1960

attitude towards the trust. When she put in a request to withdraw £10,000 to purchase a house in Hampstead, it was approved. Other women in the family had a much harder time.

When one cousin tried to withdraw capital from her trust to help purchase a house, she was told that the money would instead be invested in government bonds. 'I was shafted,' she later said, 'and have been very angry ever since.' Another cousin, who remarried after her husband died, was forbidden to take money from her trust, and instead had to rely on an annual annuity, which quickly lost its value. This cousin was so infuriated by the way the men in the family controlled her financial affairs that she refused to attend any future family events. A third woman had her marriage settlement taken by her father, to be used to finance his gambling addiction. Later the lost amount was made up by the Fund, a decision again taken by the men.

Yet for all the coming-out balls, society weddings and meetings of the Fund, the family were not immune to world events and the relentless churn towards change. Returning to work after his daughter's wedding, Sam found a crisis waiting for him. Nyasaland appeared to be on the brink of revolution. If this happened, the company's Lujeri tea plantation would be in great peril.

Since the end of the Second World War there had been growing calls for change across the British Empire. The first colony to break off was Jordan in May 1946. Then India gained its independence in July 1947, followed a few weeks later by Pakistan. The next year, in January 1948, Burma declared its independence, as did Sri Lanka the following month and then, two months later, Israel. Then Ireland, which had been self-governed since 1922, announced in April 1949 that it was leaving the British Commonwealth. The 1950s saw other departures: Malaya, Sudan, the Gold Coast and Cyprus had all recently declared their independence. Then, on 3 February 1960, just six months before Belinda's wedding, the prime minister Harold Macmillan had given a speech in South Africa in which he said that 'The wind of change is blowing through this continent. Whether we like it or not, this growth of national consciousness is a political fact.' Many commentators believed that Nyasaland would be the next country to break away.

Over the following months, pro-independence marches and demonstrations erupted across Nyasaland. One of the protestors' main objectives was the nationalisation of European plantations, such as those owned by Lyons. After hearing intelligence that the Nyasaland National Congress was about to launch a 'murder plot' against the white population, the British Parliament had declared a state of emergency. More than 1,000 British and South Rhodesian soldiers had been rushed in to quell the rumoured uprising. In the crackdown that followed, fifty protestors were killed. In the subsequent government investigation, Judge Patrick Devlin reported that the alleged 'murder plot' had never been real and accused Britain of running a 'police state'. This was the only example of a judge-led inquiry criticising imperial Britain or its policies. All of this took place in the weeks before Belinda's wedding.

Now, in the autumn of 1960, following the suspension of the state of emergency, the leaders of the independence movement had been released from prison and the British governor of Nyasaland had been withdrawn to London by the Colonial Office. Without a governor to protect their interests, the future looked uncertain. How would the supplies of tea be affected? Sam wondered. If Nyasaland became independent, would anti-colonial protests spread to other countries? And if so, how would other key crops, such as coffee, sugar and cocoa, be impacted?

After further negotiations with the British government, elections in Nyasaland were held in August 1961, which were won by the renamed Malawi National Congress. With the British press and public increasingly asking difficult questions about human-rights abuses on plantations in former colonies, and recognising that the political future of Malawi was uncertain, Sam and the rest of the board decided it was time to dispose of the Lujeri estate. The property was sold to their chief competitor, Brooke Bond.

From that point forward, Lyons purchased 100 per cent of its raw tea from the auction house in London. In so doing, they would be more reliant on world prices, more dependent on currency fluctuations and, most importantly, less in control of their own fate.

Chapter 39

1965

Sam was sitting in his favourite green-velvet wing-backed chair in his study at home on 30 May 1965 when he received a phone call. He was told that his cousin Barney Salmon had died suddenly of a heart attack. Sam had liked Barney. He was a sweet, kind man who never had a bad word for anyone. He was also the chairman of J. Lyons. Sam suddenly realised that, as the next-oldest board member, it was his turn to lead the company.

Some were surprised at how long Barney had lasted, given his heart condition. Most believed him entirely unfit for the office of chairman. He had been born in the nineteenth century and was brought up with Victorian values. He knew nothing of modern management skills, and his health made him ill-suited to chairing a major multinational corporation.

The same could be said for Sam who, although born in 1900, was increasingly feeling like his age. His responsibilities at the LCC had grown over the years, distracting him from the business of J. Lyons. Recently he had been forced to wear a hearing aid and then, when his heart developed an irregular pattern, he had been equipped with a pacemaker. The times when he had gone out for a ride on his horse were long gone. His was now a sedentary existence, either behind a desk or playing cards on the small bridge table set up in his office.

The issue of age and the succession came to a head at the next meeting of the Fund. Neil argued once again that the company was not modernising quickly enough and that it was time for outside managers with expertise to be brought in. By now a general manager, in charge of the ice-cream division, the Corner Houses, as well as personnel and research & development, Neil found that his arguments were gathering support amongst his relatives. He even raised the question of the succession. Surely, he said, the election to chairman of the company should not be based on who was the oldest; it should be made according to merit. He realised, however, that there was no point in asking for a show of hands. According to the Fund's constitution, all it would take was two members to resist the change and his proposal would be scuppered. He didn't have the votes, yet.

Six weeks after Barney's death, on 6 July, Sam took the stage as chairman at the next annual general meeting of J. Lyons & Company. The gathering took place in the ballroom of the Strand Palace Hotel. With more than 200 shareholders sitting in front of him, along with members of his family and a host of financial journalists and their photographers, this was a big moment for the Prince of Ice-Cream. Taking a deep breath, and having adjusted his hearing aid to full volume, Sam Salmon began reading the report that had been prepared by one of the managers.

Profits were up on the previous year, rising to a little over £3 million, staff morale was high and customers were satisfied. The bakery division had been rebranded as 'Lyons Bakery', which was becoming familiar to the public and had led to an increased market share, whilst the bread and tea divisions were holding steady. Meanwhile they had secured the exclusive catering contracts for all three terminals at Heathrow Airport. New products had also been successfully introduced, including a line of frozen foods, 'Mister Softee' ice-cream sold from mobile vans and a range of instant-coffee labels. Yet, he continued, the past few years had seen 'significant changes in eating habits'. Given the increased traffic in city centres, the public now preferred to eat close to home, preferring quick service and low prices. As a result, and to his profound sadness, he had to announce – he took a deep breath – that the Trocadero would be closing.

At this, a murmur of discontent swept through the hall. The Trocadero had been Lyons' flagship location for more than seventy years. It had been built against the odds, thanks mostly to the perseverance of Monte Gluckstein. Yet what a success it had been, hosting three generations of wondrous entertainments, fine dining and the best cocktails in London. Sam held up his hands to quieten the grumbling. He understood the concerns, but as society changed, so must they. The problem was that the Troc was losing money – a lot of money. They would sell it and use the proceeds to develop new outlets in residential areas and country towns, including a chain of steak houses and a fleet of family-focused restaurants, which they were calling 'The Golden Egg'.

He now moved on to other troubling news. Since the launch of LEO in 1954, three models had been produced, each more powerful than the last. In the past year, the LEO company had sold two LEO III computers and five 326s to the General Post Office – the largest computing contract in Europe. The problem, Sam now explained, was that despite these successes, Lyons could no longer afford to subsidise the experiment. The losses were again too great. 'We are proud,' he said, 'to have been pioneers in applying computers to business operations.' It was time to leave such efforts to firms that were underwritten by the government and the military. He told the shareholders that they had sold their remaining shares in the LEO company, recovering virtually the whole cost of developing the computers. The unspoken truth was that J. Lyons did not have the resources to compete in this rapidly growing field. Other businesses had entered the market, most notably IBM, which had just launched its new System 360, along with a mouth-watering $5 billion investment. It was simply impossible for J. Lyons to get anywhere close to such figures.

The closure of the Trocadero was a sign that Lyons needed to move away from its past. But the selling off of LEO was a measure of an uncertain future. It was unclear where the company should look for its next period of growth.

In the autumn of 1965, Neil was appointed to the main board of Lyons, where he joined his brothers Tony and Brian. He now felt in an even stronger position to influence the course of debate. Once more he made his core arguments: Lyons' management structure was failing to keep pace with changes in industrial organisation; the traditions that had served them so well in the past were becoming a significant obstacle; and if radical changes were not made soon, the company would be unable to adapt to contemporary conditions.

Beyond the warnings of Neil and his brothers, other tensions bubbled beneath the surface of the Fund. One member who did not work for Lyons asked why they should continue contributing their salaries to the Fund, if they could earn more by taking their income directly from their employer. Another member, who also did not work at Lyons, alleged that some people benefited more than he did, because they charged personal expenses to the family business. Someone else argued that those who had married wealthy women were able to enjoy a higher quality of life than those who didn't – something not in keeping with the bundle-of-sticks philosophy. Often the arguments turned petty: one person had their medical bills paid for, while another did not; someone's child's education was paid for, while another's was not.

Behind these discussions was a more existential fear that the Fund itself was at risk. Given that the Fund defied normal classification – it wasn't a partnership or a limited company or a cooperative – and yet had historically benefited from various tax advantages (such as avoiding death duties and inheritance tax), might it be liable for a massive tax bill? After reviewing their case, the lawyer responded that there were no certain answers. The Fund was a unique organisational structure and didn't fit neatly into any category. Best to keep a low profile, he recommended, and hope the tax authorities did not look too closely at their affairs.

With the uncertainty about the Fund's tax status unresolved, and in an effort to heal the growing wounds between the generations, the family hired Harold Bridger, a fifty-nine-year-old psychoanalyst from the Tavistock Institute. His brief was to help them air some of their issues and chart a way forward into the next decade. The Tavistock was a not-for-profit organisation known for introducing psychological concepts to the corporate sector. Bridger was particularly keen on encouraging his clients to identify beneath-the-surface emotions and processes. Surprisingly perhaps, given their conservative and secretive nature, the members of the Fund were open to his methods.

Starting in late 1965, Bridger led a series of group sessions, which all members of the Fund were encouraged to attend. The participants' ages ranged from the early twenties to the late eighties and, as such, their values and experiences varied widely, from the stuffy conservativeness of the Edwardian era to the impatient counter-culture of the 1960s. More than anything else, the group sessions were an opportunity to articulate old grievances. And so the meetings turned fractious, particularly when one member of the younger generation accused an older relative of living off the efforts of others.

1965

When it came to the management of the family business, almost everyone agreed that Lyons needed to be professionalised, and external expertise should be brought in, rather than relying solely on the family. According to the contemporaneous minutes, the phrase that was repeated most often was that the company had to become 'more commercial'. What this meant was an end to the ascension of chairmen on the basis of seniority and the start of senior management position appointments based on competence. In practice, this would mean that Sam would need to retire, becoming the first chairman in the history of the company to relinquish his position for reasons other than death.

This was a tough nut for Sam to swallow. He had worked for J. Lyons for forty-six years. He had grown up seeing his father and uncles run the company with extraordinary success, knowing that one day, if he bided his time, it would be his turn. But if nothing else, Sam was a gentleman. At sixty-eight years old, he felt it was his duty to make way for the younger generation. After yet another lengthy and painful meeting of the Fund, he agreed to step down. The official date of his retirement was set at 31 March 1968. He would be replaced by his cousin, Geoffrey Salmon. As part of the succession plan, the board asked Sam to continue as Lyons' president, which he accepted. Though the position was honorary, it enabled him to retain an office and a secretary, which would allow him, if he wanted, to stay in touch.

Though no longer chairman of Lyons, Sam was not quite ready to disappear from public life. Soon after retiring from the board, he was appointed Mayor of Hammersmith. This was not altogether surprising, given that Cadby Hall was based in Hammersmith, where J. Lyons had played such an active role, and Sam now had time on his hands. The obligations were minimal: occasional luncheons with other mayors, ribbon-cutting and meeting various dignitaries. Best of all, the mayorship would allow him to keep in his hand at politics and feel connected to national events.

As it happened, the spring of 1968 was a febrile moment in British politics. The Labour leader, Harold Wilson, was then prime minster, dedicated to increasing both jobs and government investment in housing and education. But simmering beneath the surface of bread-and-butter issues was mounting concern amongst some parts of the population about the influx of newly arrived immigrants.

In the aftermath of the Second World War, more than 150,000 Polish, Russian, Hungarian and other Eastern Europeans had arrived in the UK. Then, following the British Nationality Act of 1948, which gave all Commonwealth citizens free entry into Britain, a steady stream of migrants had arrived from the West Indies, India, Pakistan and Bangladesh, symbolically starting with the arrival from Kingston, Jamaica of the *Empire Windrush* in June 1948. Between January 1955 and June 1962, net intake to the UK was about 472,000 people. For the rest of the 1960s about 75,000 immigrants arrived annually, doubling the percentage of foreign-born people living in the UK since the end of the Second World War.

One of Sam's political friends was particularly interested in the immigration issue. He was the Shadow Defence Secretary and his name was Enoch Powell. On 20 April 1968, Powell gave a speech to a meeting of the West Midlands Area Conservative Party. The subject was immigration. 'We must be mad, literally mad,' Powell proclaimed, 'as a nation to be permitting the annual inflow of some 50,000 dependants, who are for the most part the material of the future growth of the immigrant descended population. It is like watching a nation busily engaged in heaping up its own funeral pyre.' Most of these immigrants, he went on, came from countries that had formerly been part of the Empire, such as the West Indies and Pakistan. 'As I look ahead,' he thundered, 'I am filled with foreboding; like the Roman, I seem to see the River Tiber foaming with much blood.'

While this so-called 'Rivers of Blood' speech was warmly received at the meeting, it elicited vociferous reactions elsewhere. One Member of Parliament said that Enoch Powell should be prosecuted for incitement, while many in the press called him a racist. For its part, *The Times* called it 'An evil speech', declaring, 'This is the first time that a serious British politician has appealed to racial hatred in this direct way in our post-war history.'

The leader of the Conservative Party, Edward Heath, took swift action, sacking Powell from the Shadow Cabinet. On 22 April, when Heath appeared on the BBC programme *Panorama*, he explained that: 'I dismissed Mr Powell because I believed his speech was inflammatory and liable to damage race relations. I am determined to do everything I can to prevent racial problems developing into civil strife [...] I don't believe the great majority of the British people share Mr Powell's way of putting his views in his speech.'

For his part, Sam was unperturbed. He refused to connect the racial hatred and violence sweeping the UK – typified by the horrific case judged by his cousin Cyril – with Powell's desire to restrict immigration. Above all, they were friends: stalwart Conservatives who attended the same London functions, from receptions with the Mayor of London to events at the London Municipal Society, where both of their wives worked. Unlike some of his family, Sam never considered how Powell would have viewed Lehmann and Samuel when they had arrived in east London a century earlier.

Following Powell's sacking, Sam contacted his friend and asked if there was anything he could do to help. A few weeks later, Sam attended another of Powell's talks at the Junior Carlton Club in London. Midway through, when Powell said that 'some of my best friends are Jews', Sam stood up – as president of Lyons and as a supporter – to demonstrate his backing.

By the spring of the following year, Sam's tenure as Mayor of Hammersmith was over and he was eager to spend more time out of London. Most of all he wanted to be at his thatched cottage in Wiltshire, so that he could grab his fishing rod and box of flies and head out to the banks of the River Kennet.

There he would stay for hours astride a triangular collapsible stool, on a grassy bank overlooking the meandering chalk stream. Though barely able to tie a fly because of his poor eyesight, and therefore rarely hooking a fish, he was happy. No longer responsible for the family business or his children's future, and with nobody to bother him or try to seek his attention, he had at last found peace.

Chapter 40

1969

A new generation was now in charge of J. Lyons & Company. They were led by the forty-seven-year-old Neil Salmon, who was group managing director. In a radical reorganisation, division heads no longer reported to the board, but directly to Neil, who had overall day-to-day authority. He was supported by his brother Brian, who was a senior manager, along with his cousin Geoffrey, the new chairman of the company.

Sam was not the only family member to be pushed out. Before Neil took charge, there had been sixteen Salmons and Glucksteins in senior positions at Cadby Hall, now there were just five. Amongst those forced out were Barney's son, Michael Salmon, who had been in charge of the Regent Palace Hotel and the Ariel Hotel at Heathrow Airport. 'That's the end of the road,' he was told, 'you can't stay.' Sam's brother Julian was also ushered out of the door, as was his cousin Leonard Gluckstein. Such strong-arm tactics caused long-lasting resentment, which festered within the family. According to some of his relatives, Neil was 'intelligent' and a 'mega brain', who sometimes used his mental skills to browbeat those who got in his way. Other family members recalled Neil as 'vicious', a 'bully' and 'an extraordinarily difficult man'. Whatever the truth, such was his force of will that nobody stood up to him.

At the time Neil took over, Lyons' annual group turnover was £100 million, its profit a little over £5.5 million before tax and its property portfolio worth more than £62 million. Lyons' individual product lines were performing well. They were the leader in producing packaged cakes, controlling 26 per cent of the market. Lyons ice-cream controlled 37 per cent of its market, second only to Wall's. They were brand leaders in the ground-coffee market; their tea division was once again seeing growth; as was their instant-cereal product known as Ready Brek. Many of these items were supported by national marketing campaigns, such as the *Thunderbirds*-themed television advertisements for their 'FAB' and 'Zoom' brands. Lyons had also just opened the 600-room Alpha hotel in Amsterdam, the 250-room Albany hotel in Glasgow and another Albany in Northamptonshire. In addition there were more than 1,400 Wimpy stores in operation around the globe. To shareholders and the financial press, Lyons appeared to be doing well, providing quality and innovative products to its consumers – a company that was managed with both diligence and prudence.

Yet despite such a positive outlook, Neil considered Lyons' performance to be unsatisfactory. He believed that the business lacked 'buoyancy', especially in the catering division. Most importantly, he was convinced that if Lyons did not expand rapidly, especially in the face of growing competition from giant corporations in the USA, it would not only lose market share, but would lose its essential business premise. Costs would go up and quality would decline, resulting in devastating damage to the reputation of the teashops, the hotels and Lyons' assorted brands. The only way for the firm to survive, he firmly believed, was exponential growth. And for this he had a plan.

At this time, American corporations were gripped by conglomerate fever. Essential to the logic of conglomeration was that by amassing colossal scale, across sectors, a company could command preferential treatment from banks, government and suppliers. Companies such as Teledyne Technologies, which purchased 100 companies in the 1960s, and ITT, which acquired more than 300 companies during the same period, demonstrated that it was possible to expand rapidly by acquiring businesses through equity swaps and loans, rather than by using the company's cash. Inspired by this model, Neil decided to go on a buying spree.

His initial purchases were based in Britain, targeted to support Lyons' core trades and sufficiently modest to preclude the need for external financing. Within two years, Neil had picked up the flour supplier J.W. French (including eleven flour mills and twenty-four bakeries); the soup and jelly company W. Symington & Co.; the bakery interests held by Scribbans-Kemp; along with Chalmer Holdings Ltd, which made Margetts products (such as apple sauce and toffee syrup); and Tonibells, which owned a fleet of ice-cream vans. He also purchased the Kingsley-Windsor hotel group, White Hall Hotels (London) Limited, and Park Court Hotel Limited. And the family applied for and received permission to build an 830-room hotel next to the Tower of London, which would be called the Tower Hotel, bringing their total number of beds to more than 8,000.

Neil's plan to consolidate control of Lyons took its next logical step when, in January 1972, his sixty-four-year-old cousin Geoffrey Salmon stepped down as chairman. In his place, Neil persuaded the board to appoint his fifty-four-year-old brother Brian. For the first time in its history, J. Lyons was being run by men in their forties and fifties. With the old guard now finally flushed from the board, the younger generation was very much in control. Brian would later say of his elder relatives, 'There was a distinct feeling that the flag was being pulled down over the empire.'

Meanwhile, as Neil prepared for the next big leap forward, the external economy was starting to change.

On 17 February 1972, the Conservative prime minister Edward Heath rose in the House of Commons to give a speech supporting the European Communities Bill. If passed, the bill would trigger the UK joining the European Economic Community (EEC), a trading block comprising France, West Germany, Belgium, Italy, Netherlands and Luxembourg. 'Our prosperity and our influence in the world would benefit from membership,' Heath declared. 'I believed until recently that we could carry on fairly well outside, but I believe now that with developments in world affairs, and the speed at which they are moving, it will become more and more difficult for Britain alone.'

The EEC would make it easier for companies such as Lyons to trade across Western Europe. Heath's proposal was therefore supported by Neil, Sam and the rest of the family. A significant portion of Heath's party, however, as well as the Labour opposition were less than convinced by this argument. Believing that joining the EEC would lead to a reduction in British sovereignty, and still smarting from the loss of British colonies during the 1950s and 1960s, many spoke passionately against the bill. When the vote was taken, 301 voted against, 309 in favour. The bill was narrowly passed.

On 27 July 1972, six months after the Commons vote, Brian Salmon stood up to give the chairman's speech at J. Lyons' annual general meeting in the ballroom at the Cumberland Hotel. He now announced, with much excitement, that Lyons' annual profits had increased to £11.1 million – double what they had been in 1968 – while turnover was up to £189 million, an increase of almost 90 per cent in the same period. Brian concluded by saying that the company's 'drive for continued growth' would remain, and that Lyons would be 'developing increasingly as a European business'.

Following the advice of the leading London bank Rothschild, Neil now approached a number of European banks to raise the necessary finance to pay for his acquisition plan. Based on J. Lyons' good name and its impressive property portfolio, the banks were only too happy to oblige. Most of these loans were taken out in foreign currencies as short-term bridging loans. 'We judged it preferable to raise such funds in the Euro-dollar,' Neil told his shareholders, 'and whilst the terms prevailing were not attractive, we were advised that they would become so in due course.' Thirty years later, the Blackfriar column in the *Daily Express* would describe this as 'the worst advice Rothschild ever gave a client'.

With the money in place, Neil instructed his cousin, John Gluckstein, to purchase an array of European businesses. The search criterion, Neil said, was to find companies with a high turnover, which would boost Lyons' profile as a major multinational company, rather than those that would generate a profit. Despite his lack of experience, John did as he had been told and proceeded to compile a list of possible candidates. First, Lyons purchased the Dutch company Homburg N.V., one of the largest pig-meat processors in Western Europe; followed by Beckers N.V., also in the Netherlands, the country's leading manufacturer of meatballs and other speciality meat products. Next they bought a controlling interest in the Rebyier Group and then in Le Rosemont, two of France's top producers of branded meat and charcuterie. These purchases cost £21million in total.

Not content with these acquisitions, Neil moved on to his next target. On 31 October 1972 – Halloween – Lyons announced that they would be buying the Tetley Tea Company for £23 million ($55 million). At this time Tetley dominated the teabag market – an innovation that, for almost two decades, Lyons had failed to pursue. With their purchase of Tetley, Lyons would once again be the second-biggest provider of tea in the UK; in first place was Brooke Bond. It would also make Lyons the number-two supplier of tea on the eastern seaboard of America, after Lipton. In his report to the shareholders, Neil said that this acquisition would create 'a powerful market force for our UK grocery business'. His investors, however, remained unconvinced and, with their concern about both profligacy and indebtedness, the Lyons share price fell by 1 per cent. Neil ploughed on regardless.

The next significant procurement, while not as big as Tetley's, was more audacious. On 12 January 1974, Neil took out a half-page advert in *The Economist*, in which he announced that Lyons had completed a transaction with the American firm United Brands to acquire 83 per cent of the shares in the Baskin-Robbins Ice Cream Company. Started in 1946 by Irvine Robbins and Burton Baskin, the company had made a name for itself by inviting customers to sample their ice-cream and by having thirty-one flavours: one for every day of the month. At the time of the Lyons purchase, Baskin-Robbins was the largest ice-cream business in the world, supplying 17 million gallons (77 million litres) of ice-cream per year to 1,300 stores in the USA, and many more beyond. The cost of the deal was £15 million ($37 million).

In the course of just a few years, Lyons had increased its non-British activities by an extraordinary amount. Between 1972 and 1974 overseas turnover had grown from representing 8 per cent to 43 per cent of J. Lyons' total business. The final price tag for these and other acquisitions was well over £250 million, which in today's money is more than £2.2 billion.

But while Neil was acquiring businesses at an astonishing rate, the world economy was undergoing a major downturn. The problems had started in October 1973, when a coalition of Arab countries launched a surprise attack against Israel during Yom Kippur, the Jewish Day of Atonement. To support the assault, various countries in the Middle East declared an oil embargo against the UK, the USA and other Israeli allies. The embargo led to a sudden surge in oil prices around the world (rising from $3 to $12 per barrel), triggering a shock to the economic system and, in turn, a two-year recession.

As the recession set in, banks and investors in both North America and Europe took a more careful look at the conglomerates that had formed over the previous decade. They realised that many suffered from lack of focus and reduced levels of productivity. By the spring of 1974, banks were becoming reluctant to support further acquisitions. At the same time interest rates were creeping up, putting pressure on those with existing loans, such as J. Lyons.

To finance his growing debts, Neil told his brothers and cousins that they had no choice but to sell off their prized assets, the hotels. They were not part of their core food and catering business, he said and, more importantly, the banks were unwilling to lend them any more money. The members of the Fund were shocked by this. They had been aware Neil had been purchasing businesses at an amazing rate, but they did not realise that he could not pay for it. But what choice did they have? To their great distress, they agreed to sell off their property portfolio.

The largest tranche went to their competitor, Trust House Forte. This included thirty-five hotels, amongst them the family's most-cherished assets – imagined, built and managed by Salmons and Glucksteins for three generations: the Regent Palace Hotel, the Strand Palace Hotel, the Ariel Hotel at Heathrow Airport and, most painfully, the Cumberland Hotel. The sales price was a meagre £27 million. *The Economist* would later say that Lyons sold its hotels for 'knockdown prices' and 'a song'. It was, they said, the best deal (for Forte) that the stock market would see for the rest of the decade.

Although selling the hotels had been painful, the family felt positive. They had cut their losses and were now prepared for what they had experienced so often before: a pick-up in the business and a pivot to better circumstances.

Chapter 41

1976

Whereas Monte, Isidore, Maurice and Harry had always been fortunate when it came to timing, sadly Neil was not so lucky. At exactly the moment when the family business was at its weakest, the country's economy collapsed.

At the start of 1976, Harold Wilson was once again prime minister, supported by Denis Healey as Chancellor of the Exchequer. Committed to the objective of wealth distribution, their Labour government set the top tax rate at 83 per cent, plus a top tax rate on investment income of 98 per cent – the highest level since the Second World War. During their tenure, inflation reached a height of 26.9 per cent. Believing the British economy to be weak, and weakening, and convinced that Wilson's government was maintaining the pound at an over-inflated value, speculators now attacked the currency with vigour.

By 4 March 1976, the pound stood at 2.01 per US dollar, having depreciated by around 20 per cent since March 1975. The next day, it fell by another 1.48 per cent and went below the 2 per-US-dollar mark for the first time since the end of the Second World War. By 8 March another it had depreciated 3.6 per cent. Eight days later, on 16 March, citing ill health, Harold Wilson announced his resignation, destabilising the economy further. Commenting on his departure, *The Times* wrote, 'The past twelve years have been a period of palpable decline for the United Kingdom: absolute decline in terms of external power and relative decline in respect of living standards. During nine of those years Mr Wilson has been prime minister.'

Watching these events unfold on national television, Sam and the rest of the members of the Fund were in shock. The volatile foreign-currency markets had a dramatic impact on Lyons' balance sheet for, despite selling off the hotels, there remained insufficient assets to pay for Neil's programme of international acquisitions. Now, following the pound's collapse, Lyons found itself paying higher and higher interest rates and was soon heading towards insolvency. The more sterling lost value, the more money Lyons owed to the international banks, and the more impossible their repayments became. It was hard to know what to do. To Sam and the other family members, the events felt completely outside their control.

Since the professionalisation of Lyons, the family's office had been moved out of Cadby Hall and was now based at 199 Piccadilly, just a short walk from Piccadilly Circus. This is where the members of the Fund now met. Gathered around a long oak table, with pictures of various relatives on the wall, twenty-five men sat in silence as Neil explained their predicament. They urgently need to raise £10.5 million in new capital, he said; this would be used to cover the company's debts arising from the devaluation of the pound. Clearly nobody in the room had that kind of money, so they would need to go to outside investors. But considering the state of the company's finances, and the economy in general, Neil knew that the deal would have to be sweetened. He now proposed that they offer an incentive: up till now, as the family well knew, the vast majority of Lyons' shareholders held non-voting shares, allowing the family to retain control of the company. The plan, he said, was to enfranchise these shareholders, giving them the right to vote over the affairs of the company. This would have the effect of reducing the family's voting stock from 67 per cent to 7 per cent. For the first time since they had founded the company in 1894, the Salmons and Glucksteins would lose control of Lyons.

It was a huge price to pay, Neil told his uncles and cousins, but they had no choice; and 7 per cent of something was worth more than 67 per cent of nothing. If they were able to raise the cash, it would provide a lifeline and, for now at least, they would be solvent. Contrary to the usual meetings, the debate was short and even-tempered. What was there to say? Neil's relatives granted him permission to proceed with the proposal.

On 25 March 1976, nine days after Wilson had resigned, Neil sent a circular to the shareholders of J. Lyons summarising the proposal discussed at the Fund meeting, along with the announcement of the £10.5 million rights issue. The shareholders saw a great opportunity to acquire J. Lyons shares with voting rights, and the funds were quickly raised and the rights issue fully subscribed. The story of the family's loss of control was quickly picked up by the newspapers. The headline-writers of the *Daily Mirror* went with 'WHY THEY'RE LOSING THE LION'S SHARE' and interviewed the managing director of J. Lyons. 'At the time these foreign currency loans looked like very cheap money,' Neil told the reporter. 'But they turned out to be bloody expensive.'

Late in the evening of 12 April 1976, Sam received a call from his cousin Brian Salmon. He had some bad news. His twenty-six-year-old son, Simon, had been arrested in Glasgow, he said, for setting up and running a drugs factory. Simon was potentially facing a decade or more in jail.

Sam immediately realised that with Brian being chairman of Lyons the press would have a field day with the story. Simon's arrest could not have happened at a worse time, given the company's financial difficulties and Neil's desperate efforts to project a sense of fiscal and ethical responsibility.

Sam soon learned what had happened. Earlier that year, and partly to prove that he could make it without help from his family, Simon had become involved with a drugs business. He had invested £8,000 into a pop group called Long Vehicle, and had rented a house on Stewart Street in Glasgow. Together with a friend and two members of the band management, Simon was accused of producing amphetamine sulphate, or speed.

To order the raw materials, they set up a fake perfume company called Matthew Jenkins Incorporated, with a false address and telephone number. Their suppliers at a Buckinghamshire chemical laboratory thought one of the orders was rather big, however, and tipped off the police. A team of detectives then followed a hired van to Euston station in London, where the chemicals were loaded onto a Glasgow-bound train. Simon was on board, although he later claimed that he didn't know the chemicals were, too. Upon arrival, the policemen tracked Simon to the house on Stewart Street. The knock on the door came at 8 a.m. the following morning.

After being released on bail, Simon visited many members of the Fund to give them a frank account of what had happened. So it was that he drove from his house in central London to the small village of Mildenhall, outside Marlborough. There he met Sam and Wendy, along with their daughter Belinda. Over lunch, Simon explained his role in the enterprise. To his surprise, Sam was not only compassionate, but showed understanding and support. After lunch, drinking coffee outside on a brick terrace overlooking a water meadow filled with grazing cows, Sam told Simon, 'I hope you find your way through all this.'

A few months later, Simon and his three co-conspirators appeared in a Glasgow court, charged with producing drugs with intent to supply to others. The judge appointed to hear the case was Manuel Abraham Kissen, Scotland's first Jewish High Court justice. Sitting on a wooden bench at the front of the room were Simon's parents, Brian and Annette, who would attend every day of the proceedings. Over the course of the trial the jury heard evidence from the police, along with a number of experts, one of whom reported that the accused had 1.105 kilos of speed in their possession and had ordered enough supplies to make between £1.25 and £4 million worth of drugs.

It took the jury only four hours to make their decision. When the judge asked for the verdict, the foreman said, 'Guilty on all charges'. Before issuing his sentence, Judge Kissen declared, 'I am making no distinction in sentencing because on the evidence the four of you were engaged in criminal activities which must be stamped out.' He sentenced them each to eight years in prison. Simon was devastated. His father and mother held hands as he walked past.

Inevitably, Simon's troubles were widely reported by the media. The *Daily Mirror*'s headline ran 'SON OF JOE LYONS TYCOON HELD IN JAIL'. The *Daily Mail* ran a half-page under the banner 'JAIL FOR MILLIONAIRE'S SON WHO DREAMED OF FAME', while the *Daily Express* headline-writers were more creative: 'WIMPY BAR KID JAILED ON DRUG CHARGE'.

Simon's case was repeatedly discussed at the weekly meeting of the Fund. Many of the members were furious, believing that his actions flew in the face of two of their most important values: honesty and respectability. One cousin put it bluntly: Simon should be thrown out, because he had 'failed to respect the views of the Fund and had committed a serious criminal offence'. Another agreed, saying that 'the Fund would be better off without Simon'.

Other members were anxious that the Fund itself might be at risk. What if the prosecution demanded to go through their accounts?

What if the Crown seized *their* assets, as sometimes happened with drugs cases? These concerns were alleviated, however, when one of the members said they had consulted a lawyer, who reported that the family's assets were unlikely to be seized, given that Simon and his friends had never sold any of the drugs.

After a while it was the turn of some of the quieter members to speak. One of these was Sam, who said that the family's commitment to loyalty was sacrosanct – Simon must be supported, come what may. Others agreed, and soon a consensus formed: as long as the case did not jeopardise the Fund, Simon should remain. This was in line with its principles of 'compassion and mutual support'.

The summer of 1976 arrived with fierce intensity. For sixteen days in a row, the thermostats in London topped thirty degrees. The unprecedented heatwave rendered parts of Britain hotter than Honolulu or Rio de Janeiro. Residents were banned from watering the garden or taking baths. Rivers and ponds dried up. A plague of twenty-three billion seven-spotted ladybirds swarmed south-eastern England. It was so hot at the Wimbledon Lawn Tennis Championship that umpires were allowed to remove their jackets. Nobody remembered seeing anything like this before.

On Thursday, 27 July 1976, in the midst of the scorching weather, Neil and Brian presided over the Lyons annual general meeting. Unlike those of the past, in which the directors had exuded self-congratulation and bonhomie, and the shareholders had responded with applause and speeches full of thanks, this was a tepid, dour, downbeat affair. The fact that the event was held at the Cumberland Hotel, which was no longer owned by J. Lyons, was a reminder of the company's misfortunes and only worsened the mood.

'This has been another difficult year in Europe,' Brian started euphemistically, with his brother Neil sitting next to him. 'The changed situation has meant that the order of priorities in business objectives has altered and it has been necessary to adapt and reorganise for this.' On a more positive note, he continued, and following acquisitions over the proceeding years, the group's turnover had risen sharply to £651 million, generating profits of more than £27 million. The problem, of course, was the company's colossal debts, and of these Brian made little mention. He then wrapped up his statement with as much enthusiasm as he could muster. 'We currently face trading difficulties and are taking energetic steps to meet them,' he said. 'We believe that the end of the year should see your company back to the path of profit growth which remains our foremost objective.'

And that was it. They would soldier on, hoping that the economy would improve quickly enough for them to dig their way out of their financial hole. If not, they would have to find a buyer for the company or, God forbid, go bankrupt. Neither of these were acceptable options for Neil or his relatives.

Unfortunately, the overall economy was going from bad to worse. James Callaghan, who had become prime minister after Harold Wilson's resignation, attempted to cut government spending and shore up confidence in the markets, but his efforts were not sufficient to halt the depreciation of the pound. By the middle of September, the pound fell to an unprecedented 1.7 per US dollar. To prop up the country's economy, Callaghan now approached the International Monetary Fund for a loan of £3.9 billion, the largest loan ever given. In return, the government promised to cut spending by at least 20 per cent.

The request was a humiliating setback for the country. Even Callaghan seemed to have little faith. 'Our place in the world is shrinking,' he said. 'If I were a young man, I should emigrate.' The press portrayed the crisis as the final proof, if proof was needed, that the British Empire was over. The *Wall Street Journal* captured the moment with its headline: 'Goodbye, Great Britain. It was nice knowing you.'

Chapter 42

1977

With the economy in tatters, Simon in jail and Lyons' bottom line still not improving, Neil decided to make some radical decisions. The losses flowing from the collapse of the pound were compounded by the fact that many of the businesses they had purchased at the start of the 1970s were haemorrhaging money. Either the company books that they had been given were in error or they – Neil, John and the other members of the board – had not investigated them properly. Or both. Either way, the cashflow problems were one burden too many for the struggling company.

Neil's first big decision was to close the teashops and the Corner Houses, initially outside London, then in the capital itself. For some time they had been losing money, and with the company doling out cash to the banks, Lyons simply could not afford to keep them going, even for history's sake. As the teashops shut their doors one by one, the general public became aware that the era of Lyons might be coming to an end. The nostalgia and loss were felt by three generations of customers who had sat at the gleaming tables and given their orders to a fleet of efficient waitresses.

Amongst those mourning was Susan Goodman, a journalist for *The New York Times*. 'To visitors here between the wars, a Lyons Corner House was almost as much of an institution as Buckingham Palace,' she wrote. With the news that the last Corner House was to be closed, she continued, customers had written letters pleading for the eateries to be reopened. These letters 'recalled a sentimental courtship and sanctuary during a raid in the Blitz'. One man remembered the name of his favourite Nippy back in 1928 – Violet. Another wrote from Wales, recalling a childhood visit with her parents to one of the Corner Houses. 'I had a Knickerbocker Glory sundae,' she remembered, 'and no ice cream has ever tasted so good to me since.'

The British press were equally forlorn. 'There can be few Londoners who have not slipped into a Joe Lyons for a quick breakfast or snack,' wrote John Stanley, a journalist at the *Evening News*, 'or perhaps as a child enjoyed the treat of tea in town with thick-buttered bread, creamy eclairs and meringues. They were the meeting place of young London. How many proposals or sad partings were made under the benevolent auspices of J. Lyons?' Stanley then added that he had visited one of the teashops just before its close, hoping for one last sentimental cup of tea. Instead he had been jostled by tourists, was served undercooked chips and was never brought his cup of tea. 'So dies a legend,' he concluded. 'In the good old days one could have eaten like a king for eight bob. Life with Lyons, as we knew it, has gone for ever.'

Lyons' sorry state of affairs was noted by a writer in *The Economist*, the newspaper that had been launched the very week Samuel Glückstein had arrived in England. 'Would any large and cash-happy American or European company like to buy a distressed British company with a world turnover of $1 billion,' the article began. 'Hoary and somewhat sleepy, it was rejuvenated by the impatient younger scions of the founding family, whose ambitions outran their prudence.' Is Lyons for sale? asked the *Economist*. If it was, 'Would anyone want to buy a load of debt?'

This was Neil's second big decision. He could not see any other choice. It was time to look for a buyer to purchase Lyons. Given the sorry state of the company's books, and the family's inevitable reluctance, this would not be an easy task. But time was short. If an interested party was not found soon, the company would become insolvent, which Neil believed to be the worst outcome – not only for the company's staff and creditors, but also for the Salmons and Glucksteins. Bankruptcy would leave an indelible stain on the family's legacy. Discreetly and quietly, Neil began to reach out to possible purchasers.

In the midst of the financial crisis the family lost one of its greatest personalities. On 10 January 1978, Gluck died alone, at home, following a series of heart attacks and a stroke. She was eighty-two years old. She had remained in Sussex since the war's end. Most of her time had been spent campaigning for improved art supplies, particularly encouraging the use of oil paints over acrylics. In recent years she had returned to her studio to produce some works, and she had been delighted when, in 1973, the Fine Arts Society had held a retrospective, exhibiting fifty-two pieces of her work.

The Times reported on Gluck's death. This was the first instance in which an obituary for a female member of the family was printed in the national paper of record. Noting her wearing of men's clothes and her short-cropped hair, the newspaper said that Gluck 'felt it necessary to rebel against a family which expected daughters to do no more than marry acceptably'. As for her art, *The Times* said that her blend of 'authority, determination and will are all evident in her work'. Most flattering of all, her portraits told 'a truth about their sitters'.

Twenty people gathered for a non-denominational service at a chapel in Worthing, a half-hour's drive from Gluck's home in East Sussex. In attendance were her brother Louis and his wife Doreen, who had returned from Switzerland. Irritated either by the interruption of his holiday or by decades of arguing with his sister over money, or both, Louis refused to speak and sat in the front row, glowering. The eulogy was instead given by his son, Roy. Nesta did not attend the ceremony. Afterwards an awkwardly silent tea was held at Gluck's house. A few days later, her ashes were scattered in the garden.

In a letter to a friend two years earlier, Gluck had written about the significance of her work. 'By what content would one recognise a picture was mine?' she asked. 'I, of course, am the last person to be able to answer such a question. So?? It will be too late for me when posterity decides.'

Another of the family's grandes dames was also thinking about posterity. Neil's mother, Mimi, had long been considered the matriarch of the family. She lived by herself in a flat on Great Cumberland Place, supported by a cook, a maid and a chauffeur. She was often visited by her nephews, nieces and grandchildren, whom she entertained at her club near the Hilton Hotel or at the L'Epée D'Or restaurant at the Cumberland Hotel. There she enjoyed recalling the early years of J. Lyons, paying particular attention to the ideas of family unity and loyalty.

Now eighty-four years old, she decided to set down her memories in writing. Often she caveated a story with phrases such as 'The following is absolutely true and accurate even though it happened oh so long ago' or 'That which I am about to write will be accurate'. She recalled that the 'boys', as she called her father and his brothers, relied on their wives and daughters for advice. And she wrote that 'The unity in the 1st World War was stronger than ever and only equalled at the time of the 2nd World War. I noticed this and remember it with pride and maybe conceit. What an anchor!'

There were certain stories that she worried over. The time, for instance, when one of the fathers prevented his son from marrying a 'Goy' (a non-Jew) – 'Good kind Families can at times be very cruel,' she wrote. Or the controversial departure of one of the early members of the Fund. If others approved, she suggested, such stories should be 'added to what I have written'.

About her grandson Simon and his drugs conviction, Mimi wrote that he had 'behaved stupidly' and 'is now paying the price of his folly'. The family's response had pleased her, however, and she described their compassion towards Simon as a 'miracle'. She also noted that she herself had been in touch with Simon, and that he was relieved 'the family motto holds good'. As for Gluck, all Mimi said was that she 'became a very respected artist'.

Most of all, she spoke about her father, Monte. When, as a young girl, she had displayed signs of ingratitude, her father decided she needed to learn to appreciate what she had. So he drove Mimi down to Whitechapel to show her where he lived as a boy. Two lads were playing marbles on the pavement. 'It's better than Kensington, where you can't play anything in the street,' she had said. In response, he drove her through a neighbourhood of slums, before returning home. She got the message, appreciating the gifts and opportunities provided by her family. 'Looking back,' she wrote, 'he was always in the centre of all that took place, pleasures, troubles, quarrels etc., and that's how I remember him.' She then added, 'I suppose he was the greatest peacemaker and peace keeper I ever met.'

It was perhaps no coincidence that Mimi was writing about her father, his talents and skills at the very point when his company, J. Lyons, was facing its stiffest test – the company that was being led by her son, Neil Salmon.

★

Throughout the spring of 1978, Neil worked tirelessly to find someone to buy Lyons, a difficult task, given the weak economic environment. Several offers were made, but all were felt by the board to be well below the company's true value. Neil continued his search for the right buyer.

The stress was getting to him. He smoked more and his diet worsened: a three-course meal for lunch and dinner, heavy with red meat, butter, cream and sugar, and washed down with lashings of red wine. He rarely left his desk and never exercised. He was significantly overweight, which was unusual at this time. The doctor said his blood pressure was dangerously high and he needed to change his lifestyle. But Neil didn't.

Lyons' economic woes mirrored those of the country. When James Callaghan became prime minister, 600,000 people were unemployed, but now the figure was more than 1.5 million. Meanwhile job vacancies were falling, and the price of household goods such as milk, bread and petrol was rising. In an attempt to control government debt, Callaghan announced in July 1978 that public pay rises would be capped at 5 per cent per year, far lower than the rate of inflation. The unions angrily rejected this proposal, promising to launch a series of coordinated strikes that would grow throughout the year. Any hope of a swift resolution to the financial crisis was over.

Callaghan's chief political opponent was Margaret Thatcher, the former Lyons employee, who had recently been elected as the Conservative Party leader. Thatcher was supported by Keith Joseph, whom she would describe as her 'closest political friend'; and by Nigel Lawson, who would later become her Chancellor of the Exchequer. Both happened to be members of the Salmon and Gluckstein families (Keith Joseph was Samuel and Ann Gluckstein's great-grandson, Nigel Lawson married Alfred Salmon's granddaughter Vanessa). As part of her efforts to overthrow Callaghan, Thatcher referred back to a time when Britain was an industrial powerhouse, when it oversaw a massive empire. In an interview with Granada Television's *World in Action* programme, she made clear her views on immigration. 'By the end of the century there would be four million people of the new Commonwealth or Pakistan here,' she said. 'Now, that is an awful lot and I think it means that people are really rather afraid that this country might be rather swamped by people with a different culture', and she added that the British people would 'be rather hostile to those coming in'.

Meanwhile, Britain was gripped by the horror of a serial murderer who was active around Yorkshire in northern England. One woman was brutally killed in Leeds, a second in Manchester and a third in Huddersfield. The *Daily Mirror* received a letter from a man who claimed to have murdered a woman in Preston and signed his name as 'Jack the Ripper'. Women in the North of England felt it was unsafe to go out at night. Politicians and journalists criticised the police for their inaction and lack of progress with the case.

It was against this background of economic and social turmoil that Neil was forced to return to the negotiations. The company's cash position had grown truly alarming, and if they didn't identify a buyer by the summer's end, there was a real risk of liquidation. Finally, in August 1978, after protracted talks, Neil announced to the board that he had a firm deal. Allied Breweries, Britain's second-largest brewing group, was offering to purchase Lyons for £63.6 million. The companies were of approximately the same size, both selling close to £800 million in goods – equivalent to £4.8 billion today – but where Allied Breweries had declared a healthy profit the previous year, Lyons had registered a significant loss. Yet according to Sir Keith Showering, chairman of Allied Breweries, the 'two companies were sufficiently concordant to enable us to achieve new growth'.

At the next meeting of the Fund, Neil recommended that the family accept the offer. There were more than twenty members present that day, including Sam, Brian and Geoffrey. For many in the room, it was hard to imagine how things had turned calamitous so quickly. It was well known that many family businesses struggled to maintain their success decade after decade – as summed up in the adage 'clogs to clogs in three generations' – but few, if any, of the cousins had anticipated such a precipitous collapse. They were distressed, yet the decision was not theirs to make. Now that the family had lost control of the voting stock, they could not actually block the sale of the company.

As for their feelings towards Neil, many felt sick with anger. Not only were they letting themselves down, but also their parents and grandparents, who had worked so hard to build the company and had felt such great pride in handing it over to the next generation. But what use was anger? All the way along they had made decisions by consensus. And while it was true that Neil had been opinionated and forceful – often far too forceful, some said – he had asked them about every major decision along the way and they had voted with him. If mistakes had been made, they had been complicit. After a surprisingly short discussion, a vote was called. Each of the men raised their hands in approval. Neil's proposal was agreed.

By the end of the summer of 1978 the proposed merger was signed off by the boards and shareholders of both companies. After it was reviewed by the government minister Roy Hattersley (who decided not to refer the deal to the Monopolies Commission), it was finally approved in September 1978.

Over the winter of 1978, the trade unions accelerated their coordinated strike action. It started with more 6,500 production workers at the Ford Company in Merseyside and Southampton, and grew to more than 50,000 of their colleagues demanding to be paid above the 5 per cent wage cap. The industrial action then spread to the Bakers, Food and Allied Workers' Union, civil servants, lorry drivers, ambulance men, railway workers, waste-collectors and Health Service employees. The protest even extended to the cemeteries, when eighty gravediggers went on strike in Liverpool. As the industrial action stretched into January 1979, and then into February, its effects were exacerbated by the abnormally cold weather, which arrived in the form of snow blizzards and freezing winds.

On 29 March, after months of economic instability and industrial unrest, the House of Commons voted to dissolve Parliament and discussed the date for the next general election. 'The Government have failed the nation,' Margaret Thatcher declared, 'they have lost credibility, and it is time for them to go.' This vote was the first step in the next political cycle, which would lead, inexorably, to the ascension of Thatcher as Britain's first female prime minister, ushering in an era of national pride, economic vigour and profound (many would say traumatic) social change.

That very same day – 29 March 1979 – the industrialist and financier Sir Alex Alexander was appointed chairman of J. Lyons. He was the first non-family member to run the company. After more than 130 years, the family no longer had its own business. Although clearly the individual members were in vastly better shape than they had been when they left Belgium's shores in the 1840s, they were, in some ways, adrift once again.

Chapter 43

1980

Sam's 80th birthday with Wendy (rear) and grandchildren
Thomas Harding (left) and Amanda Harding (right)

On 18 October 1980, eighteen months after Alex Alexander was named chairman of Lyons, Sam Salmon turned eighty. To celebrate, Wendy hosted a lunch party for him at their apartment in Carlos Place in Mayfair. The only people invited were their immediate family: their two children, their two in-laws and their nine grand-children. They had decided on a small affair, as Sam's health was fading. The meal was served at the large round dining table. Afterwards a family picture was taken in the drawing room, with Sam at the centre, smiling from behind his thick glasses at the camera.

Two weeks later, Sam complained of acute abdominal pain. He woke up nauseous and found it hard to eat. After a visit from a doctor, he was diagnosed with advanced pancreatic cancer. Considered too frail to survive surgery, they discussed chemotherapy, but it was hard to imagine that Sam could withstand the treatment, given that he felt too weak even to leave his bed. When his children, Belinda and Jonathan, came to visit, Sam recognised them and was able to speak clearly, but he soon ran out of energy and had to rest. Then on 10 November 1980, less than two weeks after being diagnosed, Sam died.

Unlike his relatives, Sam did not want to be buried. Instead his body was cremated and his ashes were scattered at the foot of his parents' grave in the Willesden orthodox cemetery. Several days later, a memorial service was held for Sam at the Liberal Jewish Synagogue in St John's Wood – the same synagogue that Isidore had forbidden him to be *bar mitzvahed* in sixty years earlier.

At the front of the hall sat Sam's sixty-three-year-old wife Wendy, along with her two children and their families. The wider clan was of course present, including all of Mimi's sons – Neil, Brian, Tony and Christopher – and Sir Keith Joseph. Also attending were the Lord Mayors of Westminster and Hammersmith and many other notables, such as Enoch Powell. The eulogy was given by Sam's cousin, the High Court judge Cyril Salmon.

Sam's death marked the end of an era – a relay race of sorts, in which the baton of the business had passed across the generations, from Lehmann to Samuel, from Monte to Isidore, and then to Sam. Beyond a small notice in *The Times*, there was little public acknowledgement of his passing. According to those who ran the Fund, Sam was 'kind' and 'sweet', but 'not very intelligent'.

In his four-volume internal history of Lyons, David John Richardson mentioned Sam's name only four times. And the author of a book about Lyons' foray into computing said that its family board members, including Sam, never attended university – though they did. No memorial attests to Sam's contribution to the development of ice-cream, the Elstow bomb factory or the early days of British computing. No history books account for his lifetime of work. Beyond his immediate family, Sam would barely be remembered.

As for the business, which had survived from 1873 until 1979, the family's connection with J. Lyons was finally over. Over the next few years its brands were sold to other companies, its departments split up, its assets stripped and packaged off. During the early 1980s there was an attempt to relaunch the Corner Houses, but this soon failed, for lack of public interest. In 1983, Cadby Hall was demolished to make way for a new development. By the middle of the decade there was scant physical trace left of the great catering empire.

The Fund, however, whose assets included various properties in central London – and which was Monte's primary bequest – continued.

Chapter 44

1986

It took most of the 1980s for the family to accommodate to the disbelief and hurt of Lyons' collapse. The recovery was not helped by the fact that many of the company's products remained on sale. Every time they saw an advert for Tetley tea on television or drove past an ice-cream van selling Lyons Maid, it triggered a sense of loss.

Meanwhile the family had become embroiled in debates about the Fund. Should they keep it, or should they distribute its £60 million-plus in assets? For while its members no longer worked for the family business, they continued to pool their incomes. If the bundle-of-sticks philosophy was to be respected, argued the older generation, then the Fund should continue, to take care of the needy, the disabled and the retired, to keep the family close and to honour their ancestors' heroic efforts. One of the fundamental and most-cherished values of the Fund was that the strong took care of the weak. It was abhorrent to these men even to raise the prospect of dissolution.

An alternative argument was aired by the younger generation with increasing force: while the Fund had served its purpose admirably, it was now out of date. They resented the fact that they had little autonomy, requiring approval from the group for even the most basic expenditure, such as medical bills, motoring expenses and house renovations. This made them feel like supplicants. Equally, it was not fair for everyone to be paid the same, they said, if some worked hard whilst others did not. Moreover, why should they share their income, others asked, if it was possible to earn more by working for another firm than they would receive from the Fund? Perhaps most upsettingly – at least for the traditionalists – these younger members did not believe that spending time together was sufficient reason in itself to keep the Fund going.

To resolve the growing tensions, the family turned once again to the Tavistock Institute. Harold Bridger, who had helped them in the 1960s, said that he would like to help but, at seventy-seven, he felt too old. Instead he recommended Penny Jones, a forty-three-year-old psychologist who also worked at the Tavistock. In early March 1986, Jones arrived for her first encounter with the Salmons and Glucksteins. The weekly meetings were now held at 51 Great Cumberland Place, around the corner from Marble Arch. The building's ground-floor flat had been converted into a meeting space, and it was here that she was introduced to the twenty-five men, ranging from their eighties to their twenties, sitting in an assortment of armchairs, sofas and other easy chairs set around the walls of the room. It was an extraordinary situation: a woman in her forties being asked to lead this all-male group. Yet, with Harold Bridger's endorsement, the atmosphere was not unwelcoming. Jones felt deeply honoured, but also a little intimidated.

Before long, the men were opening up to her, sometimes in the group sessions, but more often when she had a chance to speak to them one-to-one, over tea and sandwiches (prepared by one of the member's wives), outside in the street or later, by phone. She was struck by the respect the members showed to each other, by their strong culture of caring and their deep commitment to continue the Fund. She also felt their discomfort and pain. There was profound sadness: about the loss of J. Lyons; about the challenges facing the Fund; about the prospect of loosening family ties. But there was also a hurt that went much deeper, which had been handed down the generations. She picked up that there was an intense need to protect each other. Such feelings were expressed financially – in conserving the capital in the Fund, in the provision of money to the widows, and in the distribution of cash to those unable to look after themselves – but she could tell it was about much more than that. Jones had never seen anything like the Fund. They were more than a family: they felt like a clan. The discussions often gave her goosebumps.

After reviewing Bridger's notes and having met members of the Fund a few more times, Penny Jones wrote a psychoanalytic history of the family. She reported that the Fund's problems had started back in the 1870s, when the dispute between the family members was in the law courts and Monte Gluckstein's father sent him to listen. This had led to Monte's 'subsequent horror' and the 'lifelong efforts that he made on behalf of family unity'. Everyone knows the 'effects on children of rowing parents, or families,' she went on, and while some children run away and others become violent or delin-quent, Monte's response was to 'promote harmony and produce reconciliation in the face of conflict'. The issue, she continued, was that Monte's solution itself contained a new set of problems, for in addition to providing a benevolent and caring context for the family to live in, 'it exerted immense control and obligation in order to prevent members behaving abominably [...] and took away from individuals their right and obligation to parent their children in some very marked ways – connected primarily in concretised form in money and property.'

[The Fund] thus catered for Monte's inevitable anger and fury and wish to control the conflict in the family, as well as for the clear vision and wish to provide security, safety and comfort. The problem was that whilst consciously providing for the latter the shadow of the former was bound to remain a latent force with great potential just under the surface between the people.

In looking after the family members' homes and finances, the Fund had taken on the role of 'unconscious parent', Jones concluded. In untangling people's emotions, and in resolving some of the conflicts between the generations, she suggested that the members should split into smaller groups and embark on a series of facilitated frank discussions, in which everyone was encouraged to share their feelings.

On 5 May 1988, a memo was circulated by seven of the younger members, who would become known as the Group of Seven. The signatories included Neil's son Roger and Sam's son Jonathan. They wrote that they wanted to keep their earnings (rather than deposit them in the Fund) so that they could take care of their own families. They said they 'took a very gloomy view' of the Fund's future and that if no action was taken, then 'disaster will strike'. By this, they meant that they would leave the Fund. Most hurtfully, they asked: 'how can we trust people we hardly know to manage the Fund on our behalf?' Many of the members were enormously offended by this memo.

Amongst those most vehement in their opposition to change were Neil, Geoffrey and Brian Salmon. These elder members came straight to the point, accusing their sons and nephews of a 'lack of loyalty and goodwill' and even of 'greed'. As far as they were concerned, the Fund was central to their lives, an essential part of their life's work. They said that the views of the Group of Seven came as a shock, and that they had 'failed' the younger generation.

In response, the Group of Seven said they felt manipulated and oppressed by their elders, and that instead of promoting unity, the bundle-of-sticks philosophy felt claustrophobic, as if the bond that had held them together for more than a century was now the cause of their problems. In response, the elder men withdrew, refusing to engage and claiming a presumption of wisdom and authority. This further antagonised the Group of Seven. More meetings were convened, but little was resolved. It was all a far cry from the early idealism of Monte Gluckstein.

After all, much had changed over the previous century. Horse and carriages had been replaced by motorised buses, cars and aeroplanes. Women had gone from being disenfranchised to winning elections; from being banned from eating out in public to owning their own restaurant chains; and from being unable to secure bank loans to managing banks. There also had been a technological and communications revolution, with the arrival of radio and television, and later computers and mobile phones.

Within this massively changed context, it was hard to justify, the younger generation argued, a financial arrangement that had been established more than a century earlier. In addition, few – if any – of the younger generation could see how they could benefit from the Fund, when their sisters and mothers did not. Indeed, many of the women were speaking out about the inequity and bristled at the idea that, if and when they married, their brothers or fathers would manage a trust in their name.

Meanwhile, in the middle of these family rows, a new cohort of young men was preparing to join the Fund, including Alastair Salmon, Sam's grandson. At sixteen, Alastair had been given a signet ring engraved with an ear of wheat, and he had a vague idea about the bundle of sticks. That, however, was the limit of his education. Nobody had told him about Lehmann's flight from Germany, Samuel's bruising fight in the courts or the creation of Lyons. Yet he was keen to join the Fund and learn how it all worked.

Another member-in-waiting was Felix Salmon, Neil's grandson, who was born in 1972. Now eighteen, he had attended a few meetings and was similarly eager to find out more. 'I was weirdly aware that I was the only person at school whose family income was completely unrelated to the amount his parents made,' he later recalled. 'There was a strange secrecy about it.' His parents had told him not to talk about the family business, and never to discuss the Fund.

On 25 July 1988, Neil circulated a memo to the members of the Fund entitled 'The Nature of the Fund'. By now he was sixty-seven and in deteriorating health, but he was driven to secure the cohesion and financial well-being of future generations. In the sixth draft of the paper, he wrote that the Fund was not a means for common ownership, nor did its wealth belong to its members. Instead the money 'is held in trust for all its beneficiaries and the members are in this sense trustees'. Any proposal to close the Fund and distribute its assets to the members without taking care of windows or children would be 'outrageous'.

With such a stark red line having been drawn by Neil, and supported by many other members of the Fund, it was impossible to move the debate forward. In this way the 1980s edged towards the 1990s, and still no decision was made on the Fund's future, for few wanted to offend the older men. The Group of Seven waited for those holding out to change their mind, or die.

It was therefore only after Neil and Geoffrey Salmon had passed away, in 1989 and 1990 respectively, and the rest of those holding out either changed their mind or gave in to younger voices, that it was agreed the Fund should be dissolved. The only question now was how to distribute the assets fairly. This proved to be a complicated actuarial process. As part of the plan, each person was to receive the title to their own house. To make the distribution equitable, each house was evaluated by an independent appraiser, and any differences in value were made up in cash and shares. Senior members would be paid their current incomes for the rest of their and their widows' lives, it was quickly agreed. The family would also have to take care of any widows and other dependants, as well as set aside sufficient funds for pensions and taxes.

There were further issues. Should stepchildren, for instance, receive the same sum as biological children? Should boys of nineteen and twenty, who were close to the age of joining the Fund and might have planned their lives accordingly, receive the same as full members? The process was supervised by Brian's son Simon and Neil's son Roger. It could easily have descended into acrimony and petty squabbles, but curiously it didn't. In the end, the terms of the allocation were laid out in a convoluted spreadsheet. Most received close to £2 million in property, shares or cash. Those who were on the cusp of joining the fund received close to half a million pounds. Finally, on 4 April 1991, and after years of discussion, the Fund was broken up and its assets distributed. Remarkably, everyone was still talking to each other at the end of the process.

And so while it was the end of an era, Monte's original objective – providing security to his family members – had been achieved. Nobody would be forced to live in a neighbourhood beset by poverty and crime. The elderly and sick would be comfortably taken care of, well into the future. Most importantly, as far as Monte would have been concerned, and despite all the various pressures and conflicts, the family had not torn itself apart. On the contrary, they had managed to sell the business and close down the Fund with care and honour, and with friendly relationships intact.

Surprisingly, then, this was a happy ending. The Fund was no more, and yet, after all the debts had been paid and the pot divided, there was plenty to go round. There was no rancour at what had happened, little anger towards Neil, no festering grudges. Somehow, through the turbulent years of the 1970s and 1980s, family members had reached the balance that Monte had espoused, striving for improvement when need be, but, when they had enough, walking away and smelling the roses. Or, in Sam's case, fishing.

Less clear was what would happen next. Without the business or the Fund, would family members seek each other's company? Would the next generation of parents tell their children about the legends? Would anyone take the trouble to update Lehmann and Joseph's family tree? Above all, for the current generation's children and their children's children, what would be the story of Lyons and the Fund? What – if anything – would be the family's legacy?

EPILOGUE

—————————

I stood outside the open wrought-iron gates, coffee in hand, waiting for my friend Hester Abrams. This was Hackney, east London, just a few minutes' walk from Victoria Park, and beyond, Whitechapel. A red bus rolled past. Two women sat at a café, rocking buggies and catching up on the latest news. Besides the 'Beware! Security!' sign on one of the columns next to me, there was no indication that this was a cemetery, let alone a Jewish one.

Earlier that week I had discovered that this was where Helena and Lehmann Glückstein were buried, and I had asked Hester to join me, as she was not only an expert in reading Hebrew-lettered headstones – not an easy task – but also knew about the customs surrounding Jewish burial rites during the Victorian period. A few minutes later she arrived, also holding a coffee and, having greeted each other, we walked in.

From the gates to the crumbling brick wall at the rear of the lot it was about 100 metres; from side to side, about 50 metres. The red-brick mortuary hall that used to stand just beyond the entrance had long fallen down, leaving a gravelly shadow. In all, there were probably no more than 200 burial sites: a variety of chest tombs surrounded by low iron rails, headstones made either of sandstone or granite, and vaults topped by stumpy marble obelisks. There were also a number of horizontal stone markers, which were half-covered by moss. Around these long-forgotten graves, a beefy man in a red T-shirt and shorts was driving a mower through the grass.

Hester told me that the custodian who used to manage the cemetery had died more than two decades before and the place had been closed ever since. It was only open today because the grass was being cut. While she spoke to the gardener, I went in search of my ancestors' graves. I knew that Helena and Lehmann were buried in the 1850s, but was unable to find any headstones from that period. Confused, I asked the gardener for help. 'Try the two at the front,' he said patiently.

Hester and I walked back towards the iron gates and there, right next to the entrance, were two graves. On one was the name of Helena Glückstein, on the other Lehmann Glückstein. I was surprised by my reaction. I had never known these people, and they had died more than 150 years ago, yet I felt something. A connection.

It was almost impossible to read the writing on Helena's stone, as the elements had worn away the letters and it looked as if the top edge had fallen off. Lehmann's was even worse. The back was cracked and crumbling; algae was eating away the surface. Without help, these stones would not last much longer. 'You know the synagogue that is responsible for this cemetery is about to start some major repairs,' said Hester over my shoulder. 'Now would be a good time to fix up the graves. Given how close they are to the entrance, it might also be a nice idea to add an interpretative sign.'

An interpretative sign. A good idea, I agreed.

During my research, I had spoken to a dozen or so members of the Salmon and Gluckstein families, mostly of the older generation, who could remember all the way back to the Second World War. To carry out the grave-renovation project properly – it was now a project in my mind – I would have to secure their support. I first obtained an estimate from a grave-restorer and then wrote an email to my relatives. I was surprised by the swiftness of their response. 'I'm in,' said one elderly cousin. 'Sure, no problem,' said another. 'Good idea,' said a third. Okay, that was the money problem taken care of. But what to say on the interpretative sign?

Surely any summary had to mention the pogroms in Germany and then the epic flight to England. The traumatic trial in the 1870s that had almost torn the family apart would come next, then the bundle of sticks and Monte's inspirational idea for the Fund. Then the 'Venice in London' exhibition – it would be impossible not to include that – and, of course, the tobacco company. After this, the teashops, the Trocadero, the Corner Houses and the hotels. I also wanted to mention Jack the Ripper, but really it would take too long to explain. The same was probably true of the royal visits. How could I not speak about the Nippies, though, or the 'British Empire Exhibition'? And there's no way I could leave out the bomb factory. What about after the Second World War? Wimpy and Lyons Maid, and Baskin-Robbins? And there was a whole universe of computer historians who would never forgive me if I failed to include LEO.

My first attempt ran to 350 words – not bad, I thought. Perhaps a little long. I tried again, and then again. I cut out all the extraneous words and adjectives. I was down to 228 words. Nobody could complain about that. So I sent the text to the man in charge of cemetery renovations, who forwarded it to a stonemason.

The next day, an email arrived with a graphic of how the stone would look. The word 'handsome' came to mind: curly edges, rectangular, marble. Then I saw the dimensions, '48 inches by 36 inches'. That was the size of a child's bed! Not only would it cost a small fortune, but it would look ridiculous amongst the austere graves in east London. Clearly that would not work. To shrink the sign, I was going to have to reduce the text severely. And if I was going to do that, I couldn't just make a list of dates and accomplishments. To get to the heart of the legacy – its essence – I had to reach out to many more of my relatives and ask them what Lyons meant to them today. The problem was that, beyond my uncle's children, I didn't know any cousins of my generation. Even worse, even if I spoke to them, I would be faced with the frightening question: why are *you* writing the legacy of the family?

I called Susan, great-granddaughter of Izzy Gluckstein, who over the past year had helped me with my research. With trepidation, I explained Hester's idea for a sign by our ancestors' graves and that I needed help with the words. Susan immediately said that she liked the idea and offered to put me in touch with other family members. This was a huge relief. I was no longer doing this by myself.

I started making phone calls. One relative put me in touch with two others. 'Have you spoken with … ?' I was asked, and the connection was made. I dialled the number, introduced myself and said where I fitted in the family tree – 'I'm the son of Belinda, the grandson of Sam and Wendy, the great-grandson of Isidore and Kitty' – and then, assuming an intimacy that was not there, asked about their lives, what the family meant to them, how it had made an impact. I pressed them about the Fund; about the inequality between men and women; about religion, anti-Semitism, immigration and assimilation. Some of the conversations were over in five minutes; others went on for more than an hour. I spoke to one cousin in Wellington, New Zealand; another in Rio de Janeiro, Brazil; a third in Paris. I travelled to people's homes. I met them in cafés. I almost made one cousin miss a plane in Portland, Maine. 'My wife's good at this stuff,' he yelled down the line as he hurried to the boarding gate, 'we'll send our comments by email.' I kept a note of our conversations, compared people's responses and, before long, realised there was a pattern.

Many of the descendants are still actively involved in family-related enterprises. First, there are the foodies. Alastair Salmon, for instance, is head chef for the Lord Mayor of London, while Nigella Lawson has made a career hosting cookery shows and writing about food. Then there are the storytellers. Felix Salmon writes for Reuters and Axios, Nick Salmon is one of London's most successful theatre producers, while Sebastian Meyer is an award-winning photographer for *The New York Times* and *Time* magazine, Dominic Lawson is a columnist for *The Sunday Times*, and George Monbiot writes for *The Guardian*.

There is also a strong line of entrepreneurs, such as Vicki Salmon, who is a partner at a law firm specialising in intellectual properly, and Andrew Salmon, who is CEO of one of the UK's most successful merchant banks. And there is a whole raft of lawyers, such as Baroness Shackleton of Belgravia LVO, who represents members of the British royal family and celebrities such as Sir Paul McCartney. Finally, there are the public servants, such as Dr Harriet Walford, who keeps a general practice in Hampshire, and Kirsten Hagon, who works for the International Federation of the Red Cross and Red Crescent Societies (IFRC).

It was an impressive, powerful, intimidating bunch. Not everyone had a Wikipedia page, but they all came across as confident, secure and possessing a profound sense of belonging. It was hard to imagine that the foundation of Lyons, and all that came with it, did not have some influence on their lives.

Speaking to my new-found kinfolk, I learned that the legacy of the Salmons and Glucksteins was a mixed bag. To most, it evoked awe and profound nostalgia; memories of luxury and the crème de la crème. To some, particularly the women, it triggered anger, reminding them of how they were cut out, and how their lives had once been controlled by others. Most agreed that the family was remarkable, although there was little consensus on why. Some shared childhood anecdotes (eating at the Carvery, free lunches at the Troc), while others spoke of common family traits (such as sending badly cooked food back at restaurants, 'out of respect for the chef').

Several were keen to forget, to sweep it all under the carpet and move on. Quite a few believed that Lyons and all it stood for was yesterday's news, with little of interest today. With these last views, I disagreed.

It is indisputable that the Salmons and Glucksteins had a profound impact not only on their family members, but on the tens of thousands of staff and suppliers they worked with; on the tens of millions of customers around the world who enjoyed their products; and on the society upon whose social fabric they impacted. Objectively, the family business revolutionised gender employment and business computing, tobacco trading and high-street food retailing, the training of catering staff, food distribution (particularly fast-food), product advertising … and the list goes on. They were pioneers, democratising luxury and globalising taste. Avid proponents of free trade, whilst understanding that capitalism must be tempered by compassion and government intervention. They proved that history is not only forged by politicians, celebrities, kings and queens, but also by those working quietly but assiduously in the background, the grafters.

More than this, the family's story spoke of something bigger. Of a country built on the extraordinary efforts – cultural, scientific and economic – of immigrants. And it struck me that whilst other countries like the USA honour those arriving at their shores, through myths like the American Dream and Melting Pot, we in Britain do not. We have rags-to riches stories, such as Arthur who draws a sword from a stone and Dick Whittington who comes to London barefoot and later becomes Lord Mayor, but no legend that celebrates the British Dream. Surely this omission is problematic.

I spent the weekend drafting and redrafting the legacy text. I worried that I wouldn't get it right. Distilling 200 years into fewer than fifty words: that was one word for every four years. It sounded not only difficult, but perhaps a fool's errand. And I wasn't even sure it was my task to complete. I had never worked for Lyons. I was too young to remember the family in its heyday. I had grown up with little knowledge of the family.

Early on Monday morning, and feeling not a little insecure, I pinged a copy of the shortened legacy text to Susan. To my relief, she said she liked it. She then forwarded it to her cousin Joanna, who lived in New York and was very ill with cancer. For years Joanna and Susan had worked together, exploring their Salmon and Gluckstein history. Susan explained our plan to erect a sign next to Lehmann's headstone in Hackney Cemetery. That evening Susan told me that Joanna really liked my words, particularly the last line: 'Pass it on'.

On Wednesday, Susan sent me another message. Joanna was now at home in her apartment in New York, with her hospital bed set up next to the window facing Riverside Park. Not wishing to endure more pain, Joanna had requested that she be put into an induced coma. Her two adult daughters and adult son had travelled to her bedside to be with her. They shared memories and said how much they loved each other. All of this they recorded on a tape recorder. And then Joanna was given a morphine injection.

On the Friday, I received an email from Joanna's son:

Dear All, it's with a very heavy heart that I'm writing to let you know that Joanna died this afternoon. For the past three days Mom has been in a peaceful sleep-like state. Before I turned my recorder off, mom asked Amelia to read the legacy of the family patriarch Lehmann Gluckstein who's buried in Hackney Cemetery. Joanna was the very personification of this family creed. Her death is heartbreaking, but she lived a life full of excitement, adventures and discoveries. What a thing to pass on.

The legacy text would do.

With the words agreed, the next question was: what material should the sign be made of? Susan and I agreed that stone was a little boring. Too similar to what was already in the cemetery. Better a medium that had some meaning, told a story and was part of the narrative.

Two weeks later, we were being led around the Trocadero in central London by Guy, the chief engineer. Each of us wore high-visibility jackets and hard hats. The building was finally being redeveloped, after languishing for a decade. Guy told us they were building a 740-room hotel, over eleven storeys. In addition there would be a ground-floor restaurant complex (including a 500-seat Chinese restaurant), a roof terrace with a 360-degrees view over London and a 1,400-square-metre interfaith centre. More than 300 men were working on the site, and we saw safety notices in four languages pasted on the walls.

When Susan explained the purpose of our visit, and a brief story of our family, Guy said that he too was interested in history. 'What excites me about this project,' he said, 'is that in a hundred years, people will still be using this building.' He then added with a smile, 'You could say that we are building the history of tomorrow.' Back in the office, Guy handed us a piece of rusty steel. It was 20 centimetres wide, 16 centimetres tall, and heavy, weighing perhaps five kilos. He said they had cut it out of the fourth floor. It wasn't serving any structural purpose, he reassured us. At the back of the beam we could see the heads of six rivets. Guy told us that in the old days the steel's quality was inconsistent and had to be reinforced. 'It must be one of the original beams,' he said, 'from 1896.'

Two months later, Susan and I were back in the old Jewish cemetery in Hackney. With us was my friend Hester and my wife and daughter, along with fifty members of the Salmon and Gluckstein families. In front of us stood the two graves of Helena and Lehmann Glückstein, both beautifully restored, cleaned of their algae, with their chipped edges smoothed and the Hebrew and English letters now clearly legible. In the soil before them were two steel poles holding the metal beam from the Trocadero, which was covered with a cloth.

Susan thanked everyone for coming, saying a few words of explanation: the story of how we came to be there today. Hester then shared her plans for renovating the cemetery, saying that the old mortuary hall next to the entrance would be rebuilt as a synagogue, and that the family graves would be the first ones that visitors would see. Then it was the turn of Susan's teenage grandsons, Ben and James. As the youngest family members present, it seemed fitting that they would be the ones to do the honours.

With a flourish, they pulled off the cloth, revealing the text that I'd sent to Joanna:

Here lie Helena and Lehmann Glückstein.
Matriarch and patriarch of the family,
who founded the catering firm J. Lyons
and the tobacco retailer Salmon & Gluckstein.

Whose legacy was:

Find a safe place. Love your family and friends.
Give back to society. Savour the good things.
Tell your story.
Pass it on.

We clapped. Some stepped forward to read the text, and we talked for a while. Then it was over. Later, a few of us had coffee at the café next to the cemetery's entrance. After an hour or so we said goodbye, promising to stay in touch.

As we walked home, my daughter said that she was glad she now knew more about the Salmons and Glucksteins. 'What do you think was the family's legacy?' I asked her. 'Togetherness and unity,' she

Lehman and Helena's grave with new sign, Hackney

said. Then, after another step or two, she added, 'We might not be meeting at the Trocadero or the Lyons teashops any more, but it doesn't really matter where we get our drinks – the important thing is that we're still meeting.'

I'll toast to that.

For more information on the Salmons and Glucksteins, and on J. Lyons, please visit:

www.salmonandgluckstein.com

THE RULES OF THE FUND

The Fund was created in 1873 by Monte and five of his brothers and brothers-in-law. Twenty years later, on 11 December 1893, the Fund was formed into a 'formal partnership' and the first Deed was signed. The Deed was updated and executed in a new form in 1928. The rules of the Fund were passed down orally from one generation. This document is a summary of some of the basic principles.

- The Fund keeps the family together.
- Only male family members aged twenty-three or older are eligible to join.
- A job in the family company will be found for all members, if requested.
- Meetings are held every week; attendance is expected where reasonably practicable.
- Once a member, you must contribute all of your earnings to the Fund (even if you do not work for a family business).
- All members are treated equally. Each receive a similar wage, drawn from the Fund (appropriate to age and family size).
- All members receive a company car and driver.

- The Fund will purchase homes for members within guidelines agreed. The home is owned by the Fund. Members receive an initial allowance for renovation and furniture and then periodic payments for renovations.
- The fund pays for private medical care and education for all members and their families.
- Spouses are allowed to retain their own assets, providing they do not lead to members enjoying a materially different standard of living from other members.
- Upon the death of a member, a member's widow will continue to receive his income in perpetuity.
- Decisions are made by consensus. If we cannot reach a consensus, no decision is made. (The Deed provides that if two or more members reject a proposal, the proposal is not approved. In practice we never get to this point.)
- If and when a daughter of a member marries, she will receive a one-time payment from the Fund. This will be paid into a trust fund for her.
- The Fund is for life. Members have a right to leave at any time, but if they do, the entitlement under the Deed will be a modest amount compared to expectations as a member.
- The Fund is not a Trust or a company. It is a 'community of interests'.
- Members cannot tell anyone about the Fund.

NOTES

Prologue

xix, **'A newspaper described this railway convoy'**: From the *Leeds Mercury* (27 September 1906). *The Illustrated London News* (29 September) called the banquet 'gargantuan' and *The Bystander* magazine (26 September) said it was 'colossal'. The *Daily Mirror* (27 September), *The Times* (28 September), *The Sphere* (29 September) and the *Aberdeen Daily Journal* (26, 27 and 28 September) also covered the event.

Chapter 1

3, **'Now that he was eighteen years old'**: Lehmann's date of birth is unclear. According to Lehmann's *Lexicon*, he was born on 17 July 1794. His grave-stone in Hackney states that he was sixty-nine years old when he died in 1859, suggesting that he was born in 1789 or 1790. His marriage certificate records him as being thirty-two years old in August 1819, giving a birth year of 1787. The birth certificate of Lehmann's son Harry (Arnhem, 11 May 1832) states that Lehmann was forty-five years old, so again born around 1787. Finally, the 1851 census states Lehmann's age as sixty, giving him a date of birth of 1790 or 1791. Taken together, it appears that Lehmann was born between 1787 and 1794. I have opted for the former date.

5, **'In Hooksiel, a fishing village on the North Sea'**: The sources for this section come from Niedersächsisches Landesarchiv. The critical comments from Hooksiel [signature NLA OL, Bestand 76-18 422] and the kosher slaughterman [signature: NLA OL Best. 70 Nr. 3009-1].

6, **'In his spare moments, Lehmann wrote *Eduth Aschereth*'**: The book was published by Carl Schünemann, based in Bremen. Although it received little attention at the time of its publication, it would be quoted by the Catholic priest Anton Joseph Binterim in his book *Über den Gebrauch des Christenblutes bei den Juden*, published in Düsseldorf in 1834. In this study, Binterim used Lehmann's book to demonstrate that the blood-libel rumours were, in his words, *'Albernheiten'* or follies.

7, **'A brotherly forbearance has united us for ages'**: Heinrich Heine witnessed the Hep-Hep riots at first hand, which prompted him to write this poem, entitled 'Edon', to his friend Moses Moser on 25 October 1824.

9, **'anti-Jewish pogroms that had erupted three days earlier'**: According to *The Times*, 9 September 1819, this took place in the towns of Sommerach and Rimpon on 18 August 1819.

9, **'"Hep! Hep!" – meaning the destruction of Jerusalem'**: This definition was given by the Dormagen village chronicler, Joan Peter Delhoven, around the time of the pogroms. According to *The Times*, 9 September 1819, page 2, 'Hep! Hep!' was a rallying cry that had become 'terrible for the Jews of Germany'.

10, **'on 12 October 1819, at the end of the summer festival'**: This was the annual *Kirmes* carnival.

10, **'were recorded by Joan Peter Delhoven, in the *Rheinische Dorfchronik*'**: The references to Dormagen come from Stefan Rohrbacher's essay, *Die Hep-Hep-Krawalle und der Ritualmord des Jahres 1819 zu Dormagen*, in: R.Erb/M.Schmidt (Hrg.), Antisemitismus und deutsche Geschichte, Berlin 1987, S. 135–147.

11, **'The French-language paper *La Renommée*'**: The article was reprinted in *The Times* on 29 September 1819, under the headline 'On the late persecution directed against the Jews in Germany'.

12, **'Helena gave birth to a boy, Samuel'**: According to Lehmann Glückstein's handwritten notes, Samuel's Hebrew name was Isaac.

Chapter 2

14, **'Lehmann Meyer Glückstein, who had faked his death'**: The evidence supporting the theory that Lehmann faked his death has two parts. First, that Lehmann was buried at Rheinberg stadtarchiv; and second, his motivation. According to the Rheinberg archive, there are many headstones missing at the cemetery, due to vandalism during the Nazi period. In 1984, a historian named Klaus Schulte pieced together a list of 'families' interred in Rheinberg cemetery who were missing headstones. This list included '*Lehmann Glückstein, Lehrer 1824,* * *Jever, 1787*'. In his 1993 book *Land Zwischen Rhein und Maas*, researcher Dieter Peters also cited a list of nine 'families' buried in the cemetery who were missing headstones, including '*Lehmann Glückstein 1787–1824, aus Jever, Lehrer*'. The names on both lists are identical. It is worth noting that the Rheinberg stadtarchiv has death certificates for eight of the nine individuals on these lists, but no certificate for Lehmann. There is, however, a death certificate for Lehmann's infant daughter Adelheid, who died in 1820. It is possible that the missing headstone was Adelheid's; however, infants were rarely given headstones at that time, and the date listed for Lehmann Glückstein's death is 1824 (not 1820), the year Lehmann and his family travelled to Arnhem. The lack of a death certificate for Lehmann is not particularly surprising for the period, either. As for his motivation: in 1824 the Prussian state passed legislation requiring Hebrew teachers to be certified. As Lehmann was not certified, this meant unemployment. In addition, the general economy was bad for Jews in Rheinberg, and some Jews (including the family of Lehmann's wife) were burdened with old protection-fee debts. Furthermore, debt collectors from Jever may also have been chasing Lehmann for his father's old debts. Finally, faking one's death may have provided not only legal benefits, but also social ones. Given the small community in Rheinberg, a death may have provided a cleaner break for those left behind. Since Lehmann was actually buried in Hackney, London, in 1859 (according to the headstone, death certificate, travel and census records), the existence of a grave for 'Lehmann Glückstein' in Rheinberg, in 1824, suggests that he took the only option that would have resulted in him avoiding the debt, and passing it on to family members: a faked death.

16, **'a lexicon of ancient Hebrew and Chaldean words'**: The title of the book was *Lexicon Hebraicum et Chaldaicum complectens*. It was written by Johannes Buxtorf (1564–1629), and the first edition was published in 1615 by Conrad Waldkirch in Basel.

21, **'their son Gershom died, at the age of four years and ten months'**: In his 1954 edition of *Family Trees*, Louis Gluckstein noted that 'For some undiscoverable reason this entry was obliterated by Lehmann Meyer Gluckstein[sic]. There is no trace of this son having died.' Sadly, the latter was not the case, and confirmation of Gershom's death comes from the Rotterdam archives.

21, **'Holland's economy had weakened significantly'**: Figures taken from 'The European subsistence crisis of 1845–1850: a comparative perspective' by Eric Vanhaute, Richard Paping and Cormac Ó Gráda.

Chapter 3

23, **'moving from one sleepy Dutch or Belgian city to the next'**: Belgium won its independence in 1830.

25, **'In 1843, the death rate in Whitechapel was 21 per cent higher'**: According to the Medical Officer of Health for Whitechapel report in 1877 [Wellcome Library].

25, **'By mid-century, 25–30 per cent of Jews in London were receiving poor relief'**: From *The Jews of Britain, 1656 to 2000* by Todd Endelman.

25, **'Whitechapel was known as a haven for pickpockets and prostitution'**: Charles Dickens, whose godfather lived in the area, wrote frequently about the squalor and sordidness of Whitechapel. In *The Pickwick Papers* the character Sam Weller surveys 'the crowded and filthy street through which they were passing' and calls it 'not a wery nice neighbourhood'.

26, **'described Germany's press that year as existing "under the thraldom"'**: *The Times*, 20 January 1843.

28, **'2,083 residents had died from fever'**: From the Medical Officer of Health for Whitechapel report, 1877 [Wellcome Library]. The numbers for London in 1843 were: scarlet fever (1,867), diarrhoea (834), whooping cough (1,908), smallpox (438), measles (1,442), and fever (2,083).

28, **'Her father had been found guilty of stealing lottery tickets'**: In April 1830, Ann's father (Conraad Joseph, aka Conraad Sammes) was charged by Amsterdam police with stealing a red leather satchel, an IOU worth 12 guilders, eighty lottery tickets and a pawn-shop receipt. In his defence, he said he had received the tickets from an 'unknown German' and that he was a victim of anti-Jewish persecution. The prosecutor called him a liar and sentenced him to eighteen months in jail. Ann's father appealed the decision. On 23 September 1830, the High Court recorded that Ann's father 'has already left for England'. On 29 September, the High Court rejected the appeal because Ann's father was 'guilty of either stealing satchel or being an accomplice'. He never returned to the Netherlands [National Archive in The Hague 2.09.17, inv. no. 321, and City of Amsterdam Archive, no. 5225 / pdf no. KLAB036820000148].

29, **'he walked with Ann to the local town hall in Whitechapel'**: On his marriage certificate in 1845 Samuel stated that he was a 'Dentist'. By 1851 he stated on his eldest son's birth certificate that he was a 'Cigar dealer', and then in July of the same year he took out an insurance policy as a 'Dealer in cigars', registered at his home on Freeman Street [General Registry Office / National Archives].

30, **'They called her Lena, after Samuel's mother'**: The name on Lena's birth certificate was 'Leah', but from an early age the family called her 'Lena' (after her grandmother, Helena). She was recorded as 'Lena

Gluckstein' on her marriage certificate with Barnett Salmon on 24 June 1863. The confusion between Leah and Lena was such that on 23 May 1866, Lena's brother-in-law, Abraham Abrahams, signed a statement confirming that her real name was 'Leah', though she was also known as 'Lena'.

30, **'a second girl was born – a twin, whom they named Julia'**: Although the birth certificates are hard to read, it appears that Lena (Leah) was born at 'half past five in the afternoon' and Julia at 'thirty one minutes past five in the afternoon'. Lena's birth-certificate number is 178, one before that of Julia, which is 179.

30, **'half of their neighbours were born in England'**: According to the 1851 census.

Chapter 4

33, **'sourced almost entirely from Virginia'**: According to *Tobacco: Its History, Varieties, Culture, Manufacture and Commerce* by E.R. Billings, Virginia's high tobacco yield relied on a system of 'cultivating immense plantations with gangs of slaves, bossed by overseers, who forced the work without let or hindrance'. Of the twelve million slaves stolen from Africa, at least 40 per cent were transported on British ships. A shocking 15 per cent died during the Middle Passage crossing.

33, **'Samuel Glückstein was well aware that the tobacco he purchased'**: Many of the London papers had covered the slave rebellion headed by Nate Turner, which had violently raged through the tobacco plantations of southern Virginia in 1831. A few justified the division of labour on biological grounds. 'White men,' *The Times* recommended to its readers on 2 September 1839, 'cannot in that climate perform the necessary labour for the cultivation of tobacco.' Even members of the British and Foreign Anti-Slavery Society could not agree on whether they should purchase goods produced by slaves. At a meeting on 3 June 1844, some argued that there was no point in boycotting tobacco made by slaves, if a similar action was not taken against sugar, coffee and cotton. Others said that the responsibility lay with the slave owners, not the consumers of slave products. Still more declared that any boycott would be contrary to the principles of free trade and would harm British workers.

35, **'Importers of Cuban cigars'**: According to William Morgan's paper, 'Cuban Tobacco Slavery: Life, Labor and Freedom in Pinar del Rio, 1817–1886', by 1842 the number of slaves in Cuba had risen to 436,495 – the equivalent of 43 per cent of Cuba's population.

36, **'Samuel was now able to pay for a thirty-year-old servant from Ireland'**: According to the 1851 census.

37, **'and transported it by horse and cart to the cemetery in Hackney'**: The cemetery was opened in 1788. At various times it has been called the 'Jews' Burial Ground', 'Grove Street Cemetery', 'Hackney Cemetery' and 'Lauriston Road'. It was closed to burials in 1886.

38, **'the men stood guard, wooden staffs in hand, to ensure that nobody stole the body'**: On 12 December 1848, *The Times* reported a case of a body-snatcher visiting a surgery in Dudley who offered a doctor bodies 'dead or alive'. When the physician said that bodies were no use to him alive, the resurrectionist said he would 'settle' the victim. When the doctor asked how, the man said, 'I'll give him something to drink.'

39, **'For these things I weep, mine eye, mine eye runneth'**: From the Book of Lamentations, Chapter 1, Verse 16.

Chapter 5

45, **'They adored their mother and feared their father'**. This quote, and Mini's others, come from a series of letters to her nephew, Geoffrey Salmon, and her grandson, Roger Salmon, written between 1973 and 1977. On 8 November 1974, Geoffrey wrote a note on the back of a brown envelope that contained these letters: 'I told Mimi that I would rather leave these notes as they are and not try to weave them into a narrative. They would then be part of the material for a future historian. She said that she had no objection to this at all and that I could do with them as I liked. I asked if she wanted to have another look at them and she said that she didn't.'

50, **'his father Aaron suffered from severe mental illness'**: According to Barnett Salmon's wedding certificate, his father was a 'dealer' and his last name was Solomon. The 1841 census recorded his father as a 'clothes dealer'.

51, **'The wedding took place at the Great Synagogue'**: The Great Synagogue was first built on Dukes Place in 1690, after the return of the Jews following their expulsion from England in 1290. It was destroyed in a German air raid on 11 May 1942.

52, **'in the squalid slums of Whitechapel'**: Jack London wrote about his time in east London in his book *The People of the Abyss* (1902), as did George Orwell in his book *Down and Out in London and Paris* (1933) and Clement Atlee in his poem 'Limehouse' (1909).

52, **'After losing his ten-year-old daughter to tuberculosis, Charles Darwin'**: In their paper 'It's Ok, We're Not Cousins by Blood: The Cousin Marriage Controversy in Historical Perspective' (*PLOS Biology*, December 2008), Diane Paul and Hamish Spencer reported that Darwin later worried that his marriage to his first cousin was 'a factor' in Annie's death.

Chapter 6

54, **'To his right sat his two uncles and their lawyer'**: The information about this case can be found in National Archive file C 15/545.

56, **'hatred of loan sharks and moneylenders was never forgotten'**: Mimi recalled that Monte not only encouraged his synagogue to ban moneylenders from the congregation, but would not allow them to enter his house. Once, on a cruise ship, he had seen a young man in evident distress. Approaching him, Monte offered to help, and when the man explained that he was in debt for £200 to a moneylender, Monte offered to pay the sum. The man thanked him and said, 'a bunch of Jews broke me. One good one saved me. God bless you.' Years later, Monte's bank manager called to say that a sum of £200 had been deposited in his account. The young man who had left the money didn't leave a note [Mimi's letter to her nephew, Geoffrey Salmon, 23 October 1977].

57, **'Samuel was buried in West Ham'**: His wife, Ann, was buried next to him in West Ham on 10 March 1885.

58, **'The will, he said, provided that Samuel's "dear wife"'**: Interestingly, on her marriage certificate, dated 4 June 1856, Bertha gave her father's profession as 'Teacher' and his name as 'Seymour Gluckstein'. The name 'Seymour' was sometimes given to immigrants from France and the Low Countries.

Chapter 7

64, **'a "community of family interests" – or, more simply, as "the Fund"'**: On 25 April 1974, Geoffrey Salmon started an unpublished history of 'The Fund'. He said that its first iteration was created in 1873 by Monte and his five brothers and brother-in-laws. Twenty years later, on 11 December 1893, the Fund was formed into a 'formal partnership' known as 'Barnett Salmon & Co.' or, more simply, 'B. S. & Co.' This was signed by Barnett Salmon, Izzy Gluckstein, Samuel Joseph, Monte Gluckstein, Joseph Gluckstein (in that order, as senior partners) and then, as junior partners, by Alfred Salmon and Julius Kopenhagen (who had married Monte's sister Bertha in 1883). Later, Isidore Salmon would sign as a junior partner. In 1903, the next iteration of the Fund was formed, for the next generation, and was known as 'Gluckstein, Joseph and Salmon', or 'G. J. & S.' A few years after that, in 1928, the two legal entities were amalgamated. According to Geoffrey Salmon, 'The Fund is unique as far as we know, it falls within no category. It is not a company, it is not a partnership, it is not a trust. The nearest that we have to a legal definition is that it represents a contractual relationship between its members, and even that definition has only emerged during the last few years.' According to Roger Salmon [email to author], the 1928 deed for the Fund 'was distinctly different' from the original agreement. 'There were scales for drawings, so older members drew more than younger up to age 45 when they reached a maximum. Single members normally drew less. Members were able to save from their drawings and (not in the deed) were allowed to spend their wives' income so long as this was in "hundreds not thousands"'.

65, '"**Don't tell the women**"': In his note written to members of the Fund on 13 June 1979, Geoffrey Salmon added that 'even the Members' wives were not told about what was going on, or at least that was the avowed principle, although I always had doubts as to how far it was carried out in practice'.

Chapter 8

76, '"**Smoke More, Pay Less**"': It appears that Karl Marx was one of those who smoked Salmon & Gluckstein cigars. According to Wilhelm Liebknecht's book *Karl Marx: Biographical Memoirs*, Marx purchased cheap cigars from a shop in Holborn: 'I believe for one shilling and sixpence per pound and box. That brought forth his political-economic talent for saving: with every box he smoked he "saved" one shilling and sixpence. Consequently, the more he smoked the more he "saved." If he managed to consume a box per day, then he could live at a pinch on his "savings".'

76, '**the smoking of tobacco was not widely believed to be bad for your health**': It would not be until the 1890s that medical researchers began widely to assert that smoking led to lung cancer and vascular disease.

Chapter 9

82, **'The wedding would be in February the following year'**: When Monte and Tilly honeymooned in Paris, they attended the spring Masquerade Ball. Monte insisted that Tilly wore the same long pink dress she had worn the day they became engaged. She obliged.

82, **'It was she who had encouraged him to marry Tilly'**: According to Mimi, 'Aunt Lena, full of wisdom and heart encouraged Father to marry "little Tilly". According to Father his sister Lena never gave bad advice. Aunt Lena was big-hearted as well as clear headed' [Mimi's letter to Roger Salmon, 1977].

Chapter 10

86, **'"The tobacco business was successful"'**: From Monte's article in the *Daily Mail*, 5 October 1921. This article is also the source of Monte's thoughts on the 'Newcastle Exhibition' and of the subsequent quote: 'Any man moving about the country ...'

88, **'Joseph Nathaniel Lyons was born on 29 December 1847'**: Over the years the relationship between Joe Lyons and the family would be obscured – probably intentionally. In the popular imagination, Joe came to be known as a member of the Salmon and Gluckstein family. His name has never been included, however, in the extensive Family Trees that was published and republished by the family. He was never invited to become a member of the family Fund. And when it came to reserving a place in the cemetery where family members were buried, he was not allocated a space in the Salmon and Gluckstein plot. In a letter to her nephew Geoffrey, 23 and 24 October 1977, Mimi described the relationship as follows: 'Aunt Rose Gluckstein introduced Joe Lyons to father. He was a distant relation of hers and had done her father a good turn when he was in trouble.' She added that Rose (Izzy Gluckstein's wife) had met Joe Lyons 'in Australia'. In the same letter, Mimi described Joe Lyons as 'on his uppers at this time'.

Perhaps a more accurate portrayal of Joe's relationship with the family was later given by the Lyons Catering Division. In their internal memo they would describe Joe Lyons merely as a 'friend', and not a family member.

91, **'According to the fair's programme, the *Jubilee Chronicle*'**: As quoted in the *Newcastle Daily Chronicle*, 8–12 May 1887.

91, **'They needn't have worried'**: According to the *Newcastle Daily Chronicle*, 31 October 1887, the total number of visitors to the exhibition was 2,092,273, excluding season-ticket holders.

93, **'successfully delivered catering contracts in Glasgow, London and Paris'**: According to a frothy interview with Joseph Lyons in *Variety*, published on 3 March 1910, the impresario wished to take the waitresses he had employed for the Glasgow exhibition to Paris. They were, apparently, 'crazy to go'. The French were less sure, believing that Joe's 'establishment fell within the category that usually was attended by the *Police de Moeurs* [vice squad] and would have to be licensed'.

Chapter 11

99, **'it was his belief "that the murderer was a Jew"'**: Chief Inspector Donald Swanson was referring to the testimony of Israel Schwartz, who recalled seeing one of the Whitechapel murder victims being attacked by a man and an accomplice. According to Schwartz, the assailant had shouted, 'Lipski'. At this time 'Lipski' was used as a pejorative term for a Jew, following the previous year's trial of Israel Lipski, who had killed a woman.

100, **'five more women were murdered in and around the district'**: Those who study the Whitechapel murders disagree as to whether these additional killings were committed by the same person as the earlier crimes. Many believe that Jack the Ripper killed no more than five women, known as the 'canonical five'.

100, **'including Alice McKenzie a prostitute'**: Alice was also known as 'Clay-pipe Alice', on account of her smoking habit. The police found a pipe under her body.

100, **'found on the pavement of Castle Alley'**: On 20 July 1889, the *East London Observer* described Castle Alley as 'probably one of the lowest quarters in the whole of East London, and a spot more suitable for the terrible crime could hardly be found on account of the evil reputation borne by this particular place, and the absence of any inhabitants in the immediate vicinity'.

100, **'Aaron Kosminski, a Jewish–Polish immigrant'**: In his 2104 book *Naming Jack the Ripper*, Russell Edwards says that he is 'definitely, categorically and absolutely' convinced that Kosminski was Jack the Ripper.

Chapter 12

102, **'outside Olympia exhibition hall'**: Olympia had opened in 1886 with the Hippodrome Circus, featuring 400 performers, 300 horses and six 'funny' elephants, followed soon afterwards by 'An Exhibition of Sporting Dogs' organised by Mr Charles Cruft.

103, **'Many were calling this economic contraction the "Great Depression"'**: This name was changed to the 'Long Depression' after the economic turmoil of the 1930s.

106, **'They would call it "Venice in London"'**: Joe Lyons told *Titbit* magazine (2 February 1895) that 'A horse is a curiosity in Venice. It occurred to me that a gondola would be equally novel in London. Besides, the London public were pining for something new, and my idea was not merely to depict beautiful scenes from beautiful lands upon the stage, but to place that stage in the centre of a replica of the locality.' Joe went on to say that he had travelled to Venice himself, procured more than fifty gondolas at £40 each and, 'if I remember rightly', taken more than 400 photographs of some of the city's most picturesque streets, and persuaded scores of gondoliers to come to London. In truth, Monte had done most of the work.

108, **'she brought her four young nieces to live at her house'**: This was part of Mimi's recollections to Geoffrey Salmon.

108, 'On 25 December 1891 ... to celebrate *Chanukah*': Approximately every quarter-century *Chanukah* happens to fall on Christmas Day. The two holidays rarely line up, because the Jewish calendar is based on the lunar cycle, which takes approximately thirteen months, whilst the Christian cycle is linked to the sun, which takes twelve months.

108, 'in his dishevelled state, Kitty barely recognised him [Abraham]': In her letters to Geoffrey Salmon, 1974–1977, Mimi wrote '[Abraham] enjoyed his whiskey but had to go out for his morning drink.' She also described Kitty as his 'not so loving daughter'.

110, 'One tour operator was running occasional trips from London to Constantinople': The operator was known as the International Sleeping Car Company, and a return trip cost £40. For a useful report on the Constantinople exhibition, see *The Times*, 27 December 1893, and *The Illustrated London News* of the same time.

110, 'With the help of more than 1,000 workmen': The spectacle was produced by Bolossy Kiralfy, the brother of Imre Kiralfy.

111, 'In early 1893, while preparations for the "Constantinople" exhibition were in full swing': The next exhibition was called 'The Orient', featuring a host of Nubians, Arabs and 'other beauties', along with a reproduction of the Taj Mahal and the Red Fort, supported by circus-style performers who worked with twelve dromedaries, sixty horses, four elephants and a pack of Bengal tigers. 'The Orient', which opened in December 1894 and closed the following July, was not as successful as the previous spectacles. According to an article of 31 July 1895 in the *Standard*, this could be partly explained by appalling weather that winter and an outbreak of influenza.

111, '"this aroused the Ambassador's ire"': *The New York Times*, 3 November 1893.

112, 'everyone was calling her Mimi': According to Roger Salmon, when Emma started to talk she struggled to say her name, calling herself 'Mimi'. The name stuck.

Chapter 13

121, **'Isidore, who had recently completed an apprenticeship at the Bristol Hotel'**: Geoffrey Salmon had fond memories of his uncle Isidore Salmon. 'He enjoyed life to the full, worked very long hours and he had a great variety of interest but he could always find time to do something more. I remember the occasions when I was at school at Malvern and mother and father were away on a long business trip, he found time to come and visit me, which meant that he had to spend the night in Malvern. I was not ill, nor in any form of trouble, but he just thought that in father's absence he would come and see for himself that I was all right' [Geoffrey Salmon, unpublished family history, 1974].

121, **'By now Alfred and Isidore'**: The source for this description of Alfred comes from a letter written in 1974 by his son Ivor to Geoffrey Salmon.

123, **'As the public face of the company, Joe Lyons took the position of chair'**: For the first eighty years of the company's existence, the role of chairman was unlike that of many other companies. For the chairman not only reported to the corporate board, but was instructed by a management board made up only of family members who worked at the company (and who were also, of course, members of the Fund). According to Roger Salmon, viewing the Chairman as 'Head of the Company' is misleading. 'Joe Lyons was clearly never this, and I understand the position was simply given to the oldest serving family member and did not, I think, carry any authority.' The general public, however, were afforded a different view, with the chairman often portrayed in a position of considerable power by the popular press. Joe Lyons is also likely to have had more than an honorary role in the company. According to Mimi, Monte Gluckstein viewed Joe Lyons as 'invaluable' and a 'great showman' [letter to Geoffrey Salmon, 1977]. In truth, power was probably split between the chairman and the management board and the nature of the role probably depended on the person who was chairman (for example, it is probable that Monte Gluckstein had more authority than Isidore Salmon). For the sake of clarity, therefore, I have considered the role of chairman as significant though not all-powerful in this story.

125, **'This was partly because women had, until recently, been excluded from the trade-union movement'**: It wasn't until 1875 that the first female delegates were elected to the Trade Union Congress.

126, **'A resolution was adopted which read'**: The meeting also discussed the possibility of joining the Women's Trade Union League – the country's first female union, which had only recently been set up – but after some discussion this proposal was voted down.

126, **'the strike was widely and positively reported in the national and regional newspapers'**: The *St James's Gazette* coverage was breathless. 'A preliminary tour of some of the West End shops yields nothing at the moment,' wrote the journalist, adding that 'Everything seems to be going on as usual during the luncheon hours' with the exception of the Piccadilly shop which 'appeared short-handed'. The journalist called Lyons' payment arrangements 'novel' and concluded that there was a considerable range in payments, with the highest going to 'the quickest and most skilful and possibly the most attractive'. When asked for comment, a company spokesman responded with rather a tin ear: 'Lyons has no difficulty hiring staff on the 2.5 per cent basis' and 'if there is further difficulty they will put men in the place of women'. [*St James's Gazette* and other newspaper coverage 24 & 25 October 1895].

127, **'Isidore now visited all the teashops personally'**: According to *The New York Times*, 13 December 1920, J. Lyons was the first firm of restaurateurs in England to outlaw the payment of tips to waiters.

Chapter 14

130, **'In the end, it was the Fund that provided the necessary loan'**: According to certain family records held in the London Metropolitan Archive, of the £75,000 required, Monte and Joe Lyons were on the hook for £25,000 each, whilst two of Monte's brothers underwrote the rest. This is surely incorrect, as Monte and his relatives did not own capital, which was instead held by the Fund.

132, **'Finally, on 1 October 1896, the big day arrived:'** The menus for the early years of the Trocadero were bound in a book. Its use came to an end when someone, perhaps a disgruntled staff member, entered names such as 'Shithole', 'I fart' and other blue words, under the alphabetised guest list.

138, **'Following Barnett's death, the Fund now included five of the original partners'**: 'It is difficult after 50 years to recapture the atmosphere of a family meeting in those days,' Geoffrey Salmon later wrote. 'The meetings were, to say the least, unstructured. Everyone talked at once and interrupted constantly. Sometimes there were important decisions to be made, but one of the main purposes of the meetings was that Members should meet together.'

140, **'George Orwell went further'**: From his essay 'Such, Such Were The Joys' first published in *Partisan Review*, September–October 1952.

142, **'the orthodox Bayswater Synagogue in west London'**: Formed in 1863, the synagogue continued until 1965, when the site was acquired by the Greater London Council and demolished to make way for a motorway development. It was one of the five original synagogues that formed the United Synagogue in 1870, of which it remained a constituent member until its closure.

142, **'No thought was given to the fact that she was his first cousin'**: Isidore and Kitty were the children of twin sisters Julia and Lena.

143, **'Consanguinity was not unusual in the late nineteenth century'**: In their paper 'It's Ok, We're Not Cousins by Blood', Diane Paul and Hamish Spencer wrote that public opinion in late-Victorian Britain was 'strongly against cousin marriage'. According to the historian David Sabean, researchers 'concur in the description of a high point in consanguineal marriages reached between 1880 and 1920', followed by a decline through to the 1950s. No laws, however, were passed in Europe banning cousin marriage. In contrast, the first ban in the USA on consanguinity was enacted by Kansas in 1858, followed by seven other states in the 1860s.

Chapter 15

148, **'At the next meeting of the Fund, Monte stood'**: In a letter to Geoffrey Salmon in 1974, Mimi said that the scales of justice in the Olympia trial had not been fair: 'Bribery of sorts gave his opponents the victory.' She did not shed any light on who was doing the bribing, or for what reason.

Chapter 16

155, **'Monte now sat down with his brother Izzy at their cigarette factory in east London'**: According to Geoffrey Salmon, Izzy 'was a very good and a very kind man. Although he had not the vision or brilliance of his brother [Monte], he had plenty of ability and great industry. He was one of the principal architects of the Fund and it was the bond between himself, his brother [Monte] and also his sister [Lena] which provided the strength and the leadership for the whole family.'

155, **'the *Financial Times*, reported that "Salmon & Gluckstein threaten to scoop"'**: Article published 3 September 1896.

156, **'After all, who wouldn't want to purchase their cigarettes at a cheaper price?'**: As the *Cigar and Tobacco World* trade magazine pointed out, 'What then is the net result so far? Simply a splendid advertisement for S&G and the arousing of the public to a scene that their interests are in danger and that free trade is being obstructed to their detriment.' Quoted by D.J. Richardson in his unpublished biography of J. Lyons.

158, **'The new concern had been registered on 10 December 1901'**: Imperial Tobacco launched a large-scale marketing campaign, informing the public of the existential threat facing the nation's tobacco. They said that the Americans aimed to seize control of the British trade, a move that would increase prices and reduce the number of products available to the consumer. If the public wished to keep control, and if they wished to support British jobs, they should protest against the arrival of American Tobacco.

159, **'The family was now wealthy'**: The Fund still owned 13,535 shares after this original sale, which was gradually reduced to 2,000 shares by 1927. While each of the directors of S&G (including Monte) had their service contracts with the tobacco company renewed for the next fourteen years, their workload remains unclear. In 1904, for example, Monte attended twenty-four S&G board meetings. In 1905, the secretary wrote to Monte complaining about the 'lengthened absence of Mr Joseph Gluckstein [Monte's brother] from his duties concerning Salmon & Gluckstein Ltd'. According to the family's official biographer, D.J. Richardson, 'it is probable that Salmon & Gluckstein duties became less time-consuming as time passed, and even in the first years the new position allowed the directors to spend more time on their catering interests in J. Lyons'.

159, **'Those who were members of the Fund migrated en masse into far larger houses'**: Monte and Tilly lived on Addison Gardens, as did Monte's brother Isidore M. Gluckstein, Sam and Hannah Gluckstein, Harry and Emma Gluckstein, Alfred and Frances Salmon, Isidore and Kitty Salmon and Harry and Lena Salmon, and Sydney Gluckstein. His cousins Isidore Gluckstein, Montague and Hannah Gluckstein, Monte and Marion Salmon, Joe and Julius Salmon, Maurice and Kate Joseph lived on Lyndhurst Road or Lindfield Gardens in West Hampstead.

159, **'Next to them awaited a coachman wearing a black silk top hat'**: This description comes from Yvonne Mitchell's *The Family*.

160, **'Monte's relationship with his seven-year-old daughter Mimi was special'**: At school a boy had approached Mimi and said, 'Joe Lyons only makes bread, my father makes cakes too', so she hit his ear. After a severe reprimand from her mother, Monte took her aside and said, 'Always stand up for the family, J. Lyons can look after itself' [Mimi's letter to Geoffrey Salmon, 1973].

Chapter 17

164, **'infant mortality was 50 per cent higher here than in the rest of the capital'**: In the neighbouring district of Spitalfields it was even higher, with 62.5 per cent of all deaths being children under five years of age.

166, **'In particular, a dim view was taken of any perceived slowness of cognitive skills'**: In her book *The Family*, published in 1967, Yvonne Mitchell (great-granddaughter of Samuel Glückstein) wrote about the Gregorys and Dances, a thinly veiled imitation of the Salmons and Glucksteins. She depicted her relatives' propensity for intermarriage, concluding that 'the children of such a union could be mentally weak'. She then described the family's obsession with acuity: 'No Gregory or Dance [Salmon or Gluckstein] ever thought so highly of any Dance or Gregory's mental powers. "Bit of a fool" and "not very bright" were said among themselves.' One character, Maude the cook, goes on to say, 'Well what can you expect, intermarriage weakens the blood.' This fixation on intelligence, or lack of it, probably stemmed from the family's high rate of cousin-marriage and their worry about possible genetic defects. That anxiety would linger for decades, finding its expression in the continued value the family placed on cognitive speed.

171, **'Lord Carrington was a few sentences into his address when a female voice shouted'**: According to the reporter from the *Gloucestershire Echo* (4 November 1908), 'Lord Carrington and the gentlemen around him took the interruption composedly. But the feminine part of the audience expressed audible disapproval.' The protest was also covered in the *Evening Standard* on 4 November 1908, which reported that twelve women were ejected during the speech. *Votes for Women* published their article on 5 November 1908.

172, **'his mother Lena had played a crucial role'**: Towards the end of 1907, Isidore's mother Lena became increasingly lethargic and confused. She was now sixty-one years old and living with her sister, Rose, at 32 Frognal Lane in north-west London. The doctor had diagnosed a kidney failure but, after giving birth to fifteen children, of whom six had died, her relatives believed it to be exhaustion more than anything else. A strong, determined woman, Lena fought till the end. In early December, after experiencing a number of exhausting seizures, she fell into a coma. Finally, on 4 December, with her sons Isidore, Alfred and Harry in the room, she let go. According to her death certificate, Lena's profession was 'widow of Barnett Salmon, a cigar manufacturer'. But she was much more than that. Having been one of the first to work at the family's cigar workshop, co-manager of Salmon & Gluckstein's first retail shop, co-founder of J. Lyons, co-creator of the Fund, real-estate manager for J. Lyons properties, and mother and grandmother to the people who would take J. Lyons forward over the next seventy years, Lena was in many ways the first matriarch of the family, although at the time – at least publicly – her death was entirely overlooked.

Chapter 18

174, **'At the same time, according to an inquiry by the Board of Trade'**: As published in *The Times*, 25 January 1908.

182, **'Buoyed by the success of the Strand Palace'**: The Royal Palace Hotel took up a city block, comprising the island of land between Brewer Street, Air Street and Glasshouse Street. The hotel included 1,280 rooms, making it the largest at that time in Europe. Each room had a bathroom with running hot and cold water. Its telephone number was Regent 7000 and its telegram name was 'Untippable London'. The hotel's launch was supported by a massive advertising campaign, including an advert in the *Daily Mail* taking up the entire front page, a full-page advert in *The Times*, along with adverts in ten other national newspapers.

Chapter 19

187, **'In late 1913, Monte was invited to join the new synagogue's founding council'**: According to the council minutes held at the Liberal

Jewish Synagogue archive, Monte was nominated to join the council by O.S. Lazarus in January 1914, and his first meeting as a council member took place in February 1914.

188, **'and their two children Louis and Gluck'**: For consistency's sake, I have used 'Louis' and 'Gluck' throughout the text. In fact Louis was called 'Luigi' by the family, whilst Gluck's birth name was 'Hannah Gluckstein'. In addition, she was also called 'Hig' by the family, 'Tim' by Nesta and on at least one occasion she called herself 'Peter'.

189, **'Sam attended Colet Court school'**: At the age of four years and six months, Sam had started at the Froebel kindergarten near the family's home. 'He plays quietly with the other children,' the school told his parents, 'and shows an affectionate and unselfish disposition.' In another report, the head teacher wrote that Sam was a good and dutiful boy and had done 'very good work', adding the qualifier 'considering the drawbacks of eyesight'.

189, **'he had to perform his *bar mitzvah*'**: The most recent *bar mitzvah* in the family had been that of Sam's cousin, Louis Gluckstein, in 1911. To keep track of his presents, Louis had made careful notes in a navy-blue notebook, observing the name of each contributor, their address, the item received, along with 'how disposed of'. While there is no trace of what Louis received from his parents or his elder sister Gluck, Monte and Tilly are reported to have given a ten-volume set of William Shakespeare, to be placed in the family library. Sam's parents contributed an eight-volume set of Edward Gibbon's *The History of the Decline and Fall of the Roman Empire* (also in the library). Uncle Maurice's gift was more thrilling, a gold-mounted pocket book, while Mimi's was best of all: a crisp £5 note. The last two were placed securely in the safe. The entries in the notebook were given different colours, with red ink reserved solely for 'members of the family who attended without invites'. It is worth noting that Joe Lyons was not listed in red ink – in other words, he was not considered to be within the inner family circle. Some of Louis' presents were later re-gifted; for instance *Life of Napoleon*, which was given by the Fishers, was re-gifted to Cyril Salmon on 5 June 1917 on the occasion of his *bar mitzvah*. Louis was given £3 in compensation, by his parents.

191, **'instead he could take part in a "confirmation"'**: Harry Salmon's son, Alfred, was the first in the family to choose confirmation over *bar mitzvah* in 1920. He was followed by Geoffrey Salmon, Anthony Salmon, Douglas Gluckstein, Kenneth Gluckstein, Roy Gluckstein, Michael Salmon, Jonathan Salmon and Belinda Salmon. The LJS has a 'confirmation book' in its archive listing all of those confirmed.

Chapter 20

193, **'By 1914, 60 per cent of all Indian imports came from Britain'**: Quote from *The Rise & Fall of the British Empire* by Lawrence James.

193, **'the British standard of living had risen sharply'**: These figures come from the paper 'The Condition of the Working-Class in England, 1209–2004' by Gregory Clark, University of California, Davis, 2005. According to the National Literacy Trust, as many as 15 per cent of adults in the UK today are functionally illiterate.

194, **'Whereas Britain's GDP had been 40 per cent larger than Germany's in 1870'**: Figures quoted from *Empire: How Britain Made the Modern World* by Niall Ferguson.

195, **'50 million Africans and 250 million Indians'**: From A.J.P. Taylor's *English History 1914–1945*: 'The white population of the Empire rallied eagerly to the mother country. Some 50 million Africans and 250 million Indians were involved, without consultation, in a war of which they understood nothing, against an enemy who was also unknown to them.'

196, **'Belgian refugees began arriving in London'**: According to Mimi's letter to Geoffrey Salmon, 23 & 24 October 1977, the family ran a home for Belgian refugees during the First World War. Her husband Julius arranged the food, she said, and Mimi and the other 'family dames organised everything else'. Amongst the refugees were a Mrs Monbiot and 'her two handsome children'. Her son Maurice went on to marry Ruth Salmon, Lena and Harry's only daughter. He then became head waiter at the Trocadero. Their grandson, George Monbiot, is a journalist for *The Guardian*.

196, **'J.S. Smith, the head of Lipton's tea department'**: Smith was fifty years old and had worked for Lipton's for more than twenty years. He worked in the office next to Thomas Lipton After he heard that Lyons might sue for libel, Smith wrote to his agents asking them to remove any evidence that he, Smith, had encouraged them not to purchase from Lyons [London Metropolitan Archives ACC/3527].

Chapter 21

201, **'a scandal that was widely covered by the papers'**: For instance the *West London Observer* 19 February 1915, *Evening Dispatch* 13 February 1915, *Whitstable Times and Tankerton Press* 13 March 1915, and *Pall Mall Gazette* 12 February 1915.

203, **'anti-German riots had erupted across Britain'**: *The Times* and *Daily Sketch* covered this story on 10–13 May 1915. The latter also carried pictures of police officers protecting a German bakery from an angry crowd in Kentish Town, north London.

204, **'all German men of fighting age would be interned'**: The size of the German population in the UK dropped from 57,000 in 1914 to 22,254 in 1918. Figures from *Germans in Britain since 1500* by Panikos Panayi.

206, **'In the spring of 1915, Sam received a wedding invitation at school'**: According to her letter to Geoffrey Salmon, 6 November 1977, 'When Mother was sending out my wedding invitations […] Father collected them and unbeknown to her destroyed the ML's [money-lender's] invitations'.

207, **'Ten days after Mimi and Julius' wedding'**: Mimi was not always impressed by her husband's behaviour. 'On one occasion I mentioned to Julius that a male cousin of ours was paying me a lot of attention

– would he please ask him to desist. His prompt reply was "put up with him else he might fall for one of the firm's staff." I didn't' [Mimi's letter to Roger Salmon, 1977].

Chapter 22

212, **'To counter the German blockade, the Royal Navy deployed a flotilla of destroyers'**: Meanwhile, the USA, the UK and other Allied powers ran a counter-blockade against Germany. These dual efforts had a dramatic impact on world trade. According to a September 1916 report published in *The Economist*, annual exports from the USA to Germany had fallen from more than $300 million to less than $300,000 over the previous four years. During this same period, exports to Britain from the USA trebled in size.

216, **'Later that evening Joe Lyons died at his flat in the Hyde Park Hotel'**: Mimi wrote to her nephew Geoffrey Salmon about Joe Lyons' wife Psyche, 'a wonderfully good horsewoman having worked in a circus from childhood. She also had a soft beautiful speaking voice.' She then added, 'When Joe Lyons was dying Psyche would not allow any member of the Family to visit him not even when he was first ill. My Father felt this terribly and showed his distress. Their house was but a few yards from where we lived at 14 West Kensington Gdns (long since demolished) and the land taken over by the Olympia. One morning on my way to school (the Froebel) I made my way into their house via the back door. I knew she was out riding – I saw Joe, he hugged me and said come again. I was late for school, I explained to Mrs Yelland the Head Mistress what I had done. Her reply was "do it every day". I did and was never found out. I gave up when he no longer knew me.'

219, **'In one letter, Louis' mother described her belief'**: Not all the letters that Louis received from his parents were serious. 'I did intend to write you a long letter this morning, but I have done a very silly thing,' wrote Joseph in one letter. 'I left home in a hurry and left in my coat pocket all my memoranda and your last two letters,' adding, 'I also left behind the little sugar box you gave me, so you see I have left behind all the sweet things.' These letters are quoted in the family's unpublished biography of Louis Gluckstein.

Chapter 23

224, **'Of these, 239 had died in combat and hundreds had been injured'**: On 7 October 1922, an obelisk was erected on the Lyons playing fields in Sudbury, west London, containing the 239 names, along with the following words: 'Erected by J. Lyons and company Limited, in memory of the staff who fell in the Great War 1914–1918'. From this point forward, the company directors and staff gathered each year to lay wreaths and remember the valour of those who had made the ultimate sacrifice.

229, **'in which Meinertzhagen prophesied that'**: In this same letter, dated 19 March 1939, Meinertzhagen betrayed his prejudice, comparing the Jews and the Arabs: 'The Jew, virile, brave, determined and intelligent', and in contrast 'The Arab, decadent, stupid, dishonest and producing little [...] the Arab is a poor fighter, though adept at looting, sabotage and murder.'

232, **'After three years of study, and quite a bit of cavorting'**: Geoffrey Salmon later recalled, 'As young men we were very indulged, but we were expected to conform to certain standards of conduct. We did so because of the respect we had for our elders, not because we necessarily believed in them ourselves [...] Appearances mattered, how you dressed, who you were seen with, who were your friends. Regard was paid to "what was done" and what "wasn't done"' [Geoffrey Salmon, unpublished family history, 1974].

Chapter 24

239, **'According to the *Financial Times*, the *Pall Mall Gazette*'**: Two decades earlier, during the Olympia scandal, *The Times* had reported how Lord Macnaghten (who had presided over the Olympia case) had accused Monte of fraud and dishonesty. Later, on 13 February 1913, *The Times* had written that Macnaghten had perhaps treated Monte with 'undue severity'. Now, on 9 October 1922, *The Times* declared that Monte 'had been the actual head of the family firm since its inception', adding that he 'was a man of remarkable business capacity'. It appeared that, at the end of his life, at least some people were willing to look past Monte's errors and appreciate his impressive achievements.

Chapter 25

250, **'Of course like the merry go rounds they have to be attended to by minders'**: from Thomas Crosland's essay in *The Times*, 28 June 1923, as well as the comment: 'largest and most up-to-date cream-ice factory not only in the United Kingdom but in Europe'.

255, **'killing as many as 1,000 people and wounding up to 1,500 others'**: Historians disagree on the precise number of casualties at what was known as both the Amritsar Massacre and Jallianwala Bagh. The official British report concluded that 379 people were killed and 1,100 were injured. The Indian National Congress said that 1,000 died and 1,500 were injured.

257, **'Later Isidore took Kitty around the exhibits'**: One of the most popular attractions at the 'British Empire Exhibition' had been the rodeo hosted by Charles Cochran. 'Outlaw horses with wicked records,' proclaimed advertisements pasted around the event, 'not merely untamed but untamable'. Some were upset by Cochran's apparent ill-treatment of animals. A suit was filed by the RSPCA and, despite Cochran winning the case, his reputation appeared ruined. Fortunately he had become acquainted with the Salmon and Gluckstein family at the exhibition (he later thanked them in his autobiography for giving him a 'restart') and was hired to produce a nightly entertainment at the Trocadero.

260, **'Eventually a vote was taken'**: Decisions were made by consensus in the Fund, if two or more members objected a proposal was rejected.

263, **'It would take a few years for this decision to be enacted as legislation'**: This legislation was known as the 'Natives on Private Estates Ordinance, 1928'.

Chapter 26

265, **'but from the formal tone of the letter'**: In this letter Isidore addressed his colleague as 'Dear Mr Chamberlain', whereas when the recipient was ill in 1940, he wrote to him more warmly as 'Dear Chamberlain' [Neville Chamberlain archives at Birmingham University].

268, **'which was about to be vacated by a man called Oswald Mosley'**: For the back-story, see Robert Skidelsky's biography, *Oswald Mosley*.

269, **'He was also helped by the local branch of the Imperial Federation League'**: The IFL's proposal was to federate the Empire, in which a large territory, or territories, could be locally managed while maintaining a central representative authority.

270, **'Election day fell on Wednesday, 29 October'**: Harrow general-election results in 1929: Major Isidore Salmon (Conservative), 23,466; Captain H. Beaumont (Labour), 15,684; C. Taylor (Liberal) 12,054. The results in 1931: Major Isidore Salmon (Conservative), 48,068; G. Sandilands (Labour), 14,241; H. Banting (Liberal) 5,444.

Chapter 27

272, **'on 20 October 1925, a small parcel arrived'**: Seven months earlier, on 4 March 1925, Isidore had stood up for his maiden speech in the House of Commons during a debate on the Royal Commission on Food Prices [Hansard: HC Deb, 04 March 1925, vol. 181, cc549–97].

273, **'"it tells us where we came from"'**: So said Barnett Samuel Gluckstein, or BSG as he was known, who was the Fund's treasurer. Apparently when someone in his office said that 'mistakes will happen', BSG had replied: 'not here they won't' [Geoffrey Salmon, unpublished family history, 1974].

276 'the Corner House on the Strand had become the unofficial centre
for London's male gay community...' In his book *Queer London*, Matt
Houlbrook wrote that the Lyons Corner House on the Strand was the
'absolute Mecca of the gay scene in London' and 'one of queer London's
landmarks.' In his book *It's Not Unusual*, Alkarim Jivani reported that
'Almost every gay man who had contact with other gay men went at
one point or another to the Lyons Corner House [on the Strand]. It
became the unofficial headquarters for London's male gay population.'
Jivana added that there were limits to the tolerance. Men who 'sported
lipstick' and called each by names such as 'Greta' and 'Marlene' were
escorted outside.

282, 'By 1924 the word "Nippy" held such value that Lyons registered
it as a trademark': In a speech to the shareholders [reported in *The
Times*, 23 June 1927] Alfred acknowledged that the family did not coin
the term 'Nippy', but this would not stop them pursuing those who
tried to use it.

283, 'Lyons now hosted an annual Miss Lyons beauty pageant': On 11
June 1949, the *News of the World, Evening News* and *Star* reported that
the winner of the Lyons 'Loveliest Girl' contest was the nineteen-year-
old Miss Joan Rice of Clapham, London. Within days she had been
picked up by a talent agent. Rice went on to train at the Rank
Organisation's Charm School and then acted in a variety of films,
including as Dalabo in *His Majesty O'Keefe* (1954).

285, 'it was time that a woman be made a board member': This was
at the 1917 Lyons annual general meeting, as reported in *The Economist*
of 17 June. Of the sixty-one directors of Lyons, not one was a woman
[see Appendix 9 in *The First Food Empire* by Peter Bird].

Chapter 28

286, 'suffragettes had thrown stones at one of the Salmon & Gluckstein
tobacconist shops': The protest took place on 1 March 1912. Although

the family had sold most of its shares in S&G, it still held a stake in the company.

288, **'One way, which I do not advocate, would be, of course, to murder the women innocents'**: Quoted in Hansard: HC Deb, 29 March 1928, vol. 215, cc1359–481. Astonishingly, not one newspaper reported Cockerill's suggestion that female infanticide was the solution to women's suffrage.

292, **'Back in London, Sam returned to his parents' house'**: The following morning he fell ill with a bad case of flu. After a few days in bed, Sam resolved to go out. Having dressed, he descended the stairs and headed for the front door, where he was intercepted by Kitty. 'Am I your mother or am I not?' she cried out. 'I told you to go to bed, so go to bed!' Sam nodded and returned to bed. A world traveller perhaps, but he was still under the wing of his mother [Sam Salmon's 1915 diary].

Chapter 29

296, **'The socialite Nesta Obermer made an appearance'**: Five years later, in 1937, Gluck painted a picture of Nesta and herself, which she called *Medallion (YouWe)*. This painting was later used as the cover of Radclyffe Hall's 1928 novel *The Well of Loneliness*.

301, **'The Board of Deputies was inundated with calls to support the boycott'**: The Montreal *Jewish Daily Eagle* requested a comment. The British Non-Sectarian Anti-Nazi Council invited the Board to talk at a demonstration in Hyde Park. It was also invited to speak at public rallies, with speakers such as Sylvia Pankhurst and Eleanor Rathbone [London Metropolitan Archives: Board of Deputies files ACC/3121].

304, **'she engaged in a lengthy correspondence with her twelve-year-old son, Neil'**: Correspondence held by Neil's son, Roger Salmon.

306, **'Addressing him variously as "Dear Salmon" and "Sir Isidore"'**: For letters, articles and minutes of the Palestine, Aliens and Foreign

Affairs committees, see London Metropolitan Archives: Board of Deputies files ACC/3121.

Chapter 30

311, **'In another front-page article, a writer "blushes to admit"'**: the *Blackshirt* published this article in May 1939, under the headline 'Spot the Gentile'.

312, **'In attendance were a number of press barons'**: One was Lord Camrose, who owned the *Dispatch*, *Manchester Evening Chronicle* and a host of other papers.

318, **'Leaving the building by the Blythe Road entrance'**: This story was reported in the *Taunton Courier and Western Advertiser* on 13 June 1934, and was provided by a witness named J.H. Bentley of Brondesbury Road, London, to the *News Chronicle*.

318, **'It was the worst violence seen on the London streets in a generation'**: In his book *Oswald Mosley*, Robert Skidelsky called Olympia the 'epic battle of the 1930s'.

319, **'Isidore decided it was time to take action. He tracked down Viscount Rothermere'**: In his article for the *Spectator* on 27 December 1963 Randolph Churchill wrote: 'I have seen the *Daily Mail* abandon the support of Sir Oswald Mosley in the thirties under the pressure of Jewish advertisers.' In his book on Mosley, Robert Skidelsky said, 'Since Randolph Churchill worked for Lord Rothermere at the time this statement is not without weight.' In his book *Blackshirt*, Stephen Dorril notes that Rothermere's split with Mosley was reported by the German attaché in London to his bosses back in Berlin. Of two names given, one was that of 'Lyons'. On 2 June 1940, Mosley gave evidence to a government committee. The transcript of this meeting was not released until 13 December 1983, when the *Sunday Times* printed it. When asked if it was true that Rothermere was 'giving you large sums of money', Mosley said, 'yes, certainly'.

Then he spoke about the cause of Rothermere's withdrawal of support. 'I subsequently found to be true that his advertisers threatened to boycott him,' said Mosley, 'and that was why the *Daily Mail* stopped backing us. The Jewish advertisers, Lyons and those sorts of people.'

319, **'According to Mosley's colleague William Joyce, Rothermere later'**: From Joyce's book *Twilight Over England* (1940). Also the quote 'Thus a multi-millionaire and a man of very strong character [...] Oriental confectioner.'

320, **'Shortly after Rothermere's decision to withdraw his support'**: Mosley was attending the January Club, a social group consisting of people who were friendly towards the BUF.

322, **'The result of this debate was the Government of India Act, introduced in late 1934'**: Isidore Salmon voted in favour of this act on 5 June 1934, as did his friend Neville Chamberlain. Churchill voted against.

323, **'*The Times* published a twenty-eight-page special supplement'**: Published on 3 May 1935.

325, **'This idea of a Minister of Pleasure was happily picked up by the press'**: On 13 June 1935, the *Yorkshire Post* gave four times as much space to Isidore's proposal as they gave to the demand by Hitler's ambassador-at-large, Joachim von Ribbentrop, that Britain's naval rearmament be matched, battleship by battleship, to that of Germany.

326, **'Now, thirteen years later, Chamberlain was Chancellor of the Exchequer'**: As both Chancellor and Prime Minister, Chamberlain greatly expanded the RAF's budget, from £16.78 million in 1933 to £105.702 million in 1939, surpassing the Army's budget in 1937 and the Royal Navy's in 1938.

326, **'called for a dramatic increase in military spending'**: In the early 1930s, Isidore chaired the Private Members of the House of Commons Economy Committee. In June 1932, the committee issued a report summarising Britain's military capacity and calling for an increase in military spending. This was later used by Chamberlain as part of his argument for urgent rearmament. Quoted by Paul Smith in *Government and Armed Forces in Britain 1856–1990* which gives a source of: Treasury Papers General Files 1888–1948 [National Archive T 163/7/5/8].

Chapter 31

329, **'like the rest of the employees, addressed him as "Mr Sam"'**: When his mother Kitty visited, she was greeted as 'Mrs Isidore'.

331, **'Sam described himself as a "stage-door Johnny"'**: Thinking back on her father's romances at this time, Belinda said that 'He believed that he was always in total control.'

336, **'Wendy's mother was pleased by Sam's interest in her daughter'**: Shortly after the couple had started dating, Sam gave Wendy's brother Peter a silver cigarette case engraved with his name. 'It is from one of my previous girlfriends,' Sam confided to Peter, 'so perhaps it's best that you have it now.' When it came to walking his sister down the aisle, Peter recalled that 'I was too frightened to be nervous.'

336, **'Upon discreet enquiries, Isidore learned that Wendy's mother'**: The first husband was called Edward Barnett, and they married on 18 January 1910; the second was Alec Benjamin, who died in 1933.

337, **'Finally, over the New Year, Sam asked Wendy to marry him'**: On 9 January 1937, Sam paid for a notice in *The Times* announcing that he and Wendy were engaged.

Chapter 32

341, **'Now, in a booming, gravelly voice, Churchill declared'**: *The Times* covered this speech in an article the following day under the headline 'Rape of Austria'.

342, **'the British government now asked Isidore Salmon to review the army's catering procedures'**: National Archive: WO 339/100965 and WO 32/13378. See also the Army Catering Corps Association archives in Aldershot. Since 2002, the British Army has given the annual Sir Isidore Salmon Award to the "best" warrant officer class in the food service. The winner is selected by army chefs themselves. The silver plate is housed in a display cabinet outside the Sir Isidore Salmon dining room at the Food Services Wing, Worthy Down, Hampshire.

342, **'Indeed, Isidore described the cookhouse as the "Cinderella of the Army"'**: As quoted in the *Daily Express* the day after Isidore's appointment.

344, **'That night's gala was featured in the next issue of *Life* magazine'**: America's best-selling magazine described Mrs Chamberlain as having 'a reputation for coldness despite her feeding birds in public parks' [*Life*, 9 May 1938].

345, **'Over the next three weeks, politicians debated the upcoming budget'**: The Chancellor gave his budget statement on 26 April 1938. *The Times* headline the following day was 'REARMAMENT BUDGET'. The budget included an increase in tea. Despite this, Isidore voted in favour [Hansard: HC Deb, 26 April 1938, vol. 335, cc66–7].

347, **'Like most of his colleagues in the House, he had cheered'**: Like Isidore, Louis Gluckstein was in the House of Commons when Chamberlain gave his statement about Munich. 'My subconscious was saying to me "This is completely out of order, it's improper for everyone getting up and shouting like this." Whilst my real self was saying, "this is quite splendid, perhaps we shan't have war after all." It is interesting that the people who were subsequently most vitriolic, unpleasant and critical about the Munich talks, were the people who were foremost in surging across the floor of the house to wring Chamberlain's hand and wish him well, and there were many who were in tears.' According to his biographer, Louis always thought Chamberlain was 'unfairly judged and did all that was humanly possible to secure a peaceful solution to the threats hovering over Europe'. Unpublished biography Louis Gluckstein.

348, **'Hearing these words, Isidore and his colleagues'**: At the end of the debate, Isidore voted in favour, as did the vast majority of his colleagues. [Hansard: 21 November 1938, Vol. 341].

351, **'Who is the head of the army? A Jew, Hore-Belisha'**: In the 'Letter from London' column, published in the *Nottingham Journal*, 7 June 1939.

Chapter 33

355, **'Gluck appeared more interested in matters of the heart than in matters of war'**: Or, as Diana Souhami would later write in *Gluck: Her Biography*, 'Gluck's preoccupations were with Art and Love and her own feelings. Her battles were within and her war was to come a little later.'

357, **'To compile the list, Schellenberg and his team'**: There were two members of the Salmon and Gluckstein family on the list. In addition to Isidore, the other was 'Louis Glückstein' [*sic*], who was included for his work as a Conservative Party politician. [Black Book viewable at the Hoover Institution digital collection 55425].

358, **'Sun Works, Lyons' tea factory on the island'**: According to Peter Bird in *The First Food Empire*, J. Lyons' stock was seized by the Nazis, but the factory was never requisitioned, although it was 'threatened on a number of occasions'.

362, **'With the Blitz terrorising the capital, Isidore and Kitty's son'**: During the thirty-seven-week Blitz, the capital was targeted seventy-one times. For a map of where the bombs fell, see: www.bombsight.org.

366, **'Isidore sent a letter to the Ministry of Food'**: As reported by the *Portsmouth Evening News* on Monday 18 August.

366, **'That afternoon, Isidore underwent an operation'**: According to reports in the *Yorkshire Post and Leeds Intelligencer*, published on 20 August 1941.

366, **'More than 500 letters of condolence arrived for Kitty'**: One came from a friend called Damson Weina who wrote, 'I remember you saying that if he could not get well enough to be able to take part in life you could not wish him to live on. After the last complication, he could never have been himself again. I can only hope that in your sorrow you will find solace with the thought of a life which has travelled its course with courage, confidence, and gaiety, and has achieved in many fields auspicious lasting benefits for his country' [Family collection]. Two years after death Isidore's, the Labour minister Ernest Bevin would remark, 'In the Services we have had amazing success. In the army alone we have over 100,000 men and women trained in catering. We are indebted to the late Member for Harrow (Sir Isidore Salmon) for laying the foundations. I think he did magnificent work' [Hansard, 9 February 1943, Volume 386].

367, '**Obituaries recounting Isidore's life and achievements**': Including the *Manchester Guardian*, *The Times*, the *Express*, the *Scotsman* and the *Daily Telegraph*, along with overseas papers, such as Melbourne's the *Age*, the *Auckland Star*, *Natal Daily News*, *Hindu Madras*, *New York Herald Tribune* and *The New York Times*. Most focused on Isidore's creation of the Army Catering Corps. One oft-repeated point was that in the two years since the outbreak of war, 60,000 cooks and 5,500 messing officers in the British army had received instruction in the arts of catering. Some obituaries reflected racial prejudice, such as the *Guardian*'s of 17 September 1941: 'His influence was felt behind the scenes, in committees and consultations. And like so many of his race, he was a tremendous worker.' Many of the papers – for instance, *The Daily Telegraph* of 17 September, *Jewish Chronicle* of 19 September and *Manchester Guardian* of 17 September – spoke of Isidore's founding of the Union Jack Club (which supports returning veterans). Yet the Union Jack Club's website states that it was founded by Mrs Ethel McCaul and it makes no mention of Isidore Salmon. When I contacted the Union Jack Club, its chief executive, Simon Atkins, replied that 'sadly we do not have any archives with the details of the founding of the Union Jack Club'. This is an example of the precariousness of establishing someone's legacy.

367, **'When it was time, Rabbi Ephraim Levine walked across the red carpet'**: Ephraim Levine also said, 'The mere recital of the many and varied interests that engaged his busy life would be impressive. But this would be something in the nature of a catalogue. And catalogues can be dead records unless we breathe into them the spirit of humanity. The man is greater than his work.'

372, **'Edna Gluckstein, the wife of one of Izzy's grandsons, was working in Bletchley Park'**: The record of Edna's service is as follows: 'FO Civilian, TA [Temporary Assistant]. For service in support of the work of Bletchley Park during World War Two' [Bletchley Park Roll of Honour]. According to her granddaughter, Karen Prochazka, 'She also told me that she lived in the Amiens area of France under the name "Louise" while undercover for the SOE as the wife of a Frenchman. The similarities to the story of Nancy Wake are ridiculous. It has made it very difficult to find any information as all searches come back to her. As you know SOE records were largely destroyed in a fire after the war.'

Chapter 34

375, **'Just a few months earlier, two Germans'**: For more on this, see *The Times* article published on 7 August 1941.

375, **'In early February 1942, the first buildings were complete'**: For more on the Elstow factory [National Archive: TS 62/31 1941–5], see also *The Tinkers of Elstow* by H.E. Bates.

376, **'Remarkably, only one worker died during the course of the war'**: When her family later sued for damages, the courts found the factory managers and the Lyons board innocent of any wrongdoing [*The Times*, 19 October 1946].

378, **'In private, the Chief Rabbi of Britain, Joseph Hertz'**: In June 1942, Hertz and the Archbishop of Canterbury, William Temple, created the Council of Christians and Jews. Amongst other actions, they wrote letters to the newspapers and communicated with Anthony Eden and other government officials. For example, see *The Times* of 5 December 1942, when Temple wrote of his 'burning indignation at this atrocity to which the records of barbarous ages scarcely supply a parallel'. Also *The Times* of 9 December 1943, in which Hertz stated that two million Jews 'had been slaughtered'.

379, **'the *Scharnhorst* and *Gneisenau*, became known as "Salmon and Gluckstein"'**: According to *Tatler* magazine (6 August 1941): 'it was Air Marshall Peck who called [the *Scharnhorst* and *Gneisenau*] "Salmon and Gluckstein".'

Chapter 35

382, **'one-seventh of all the high explosive dropped by Bomber Command on Germany'**: This figure from *The Tinkers of Elstow* by H.E. Bates. In addition: 96,488 tonnes of bombs were made at the factory between February 1942 and May 1945.

383, **'On 8 May 1945, after almost six years of combat'**: On 20 April 1945, Jacques Tratsart shot his father, stepmother and brother at the Lyons Corner House on Oxford Street, London. Most of the press placed the story on the next day's front page: 'Café Tragedy' (*Scotsman* and *Liverpool Echo*) and 'Belgian accused of Double Murder' (*People, Birmingham Mail* and *Coventry Evening Telegraph*). One of the few exceptions was the *Morning Advertiser*, which went with 'Corner House Shooting'. Luckily, for J. Lyons given the great events then shaking the world, the story would not attract too much attention. The main story on the front page of the *Coventry Evening News*, for instance, was 'Russians search Chancellery for Hitler's Body'.

383, **'in which at least fifty million people had lost their lives'**: Some historians give the figure of eighty million. This is based on deaths relating to war-related illnesses and starvation.

385, **'Bruce Gluckstein ... was killed [... on] the beach-head at Anzio'**: Bruce died on 4 March 1944. According to Mimi, 'Bruce's death [was] actually due to medical neglect and not because of his minor wound. He was left unattended for a long while and eventually when moved to a hospital, it was too late.' Two weeks earlier, Second Lieutenant Eric Waters was killed during the battle for the beach-head at Anzio. Waters' son Roger later wrote the song 'When the Tigers Broke Free' for Pink Floyd, in memory of his father and describing his death.

385, **'Mimi's son Neil was still with the Intelligence Corps.'** The source for Neil's time with the Intelligence is Alan Judge from the Intelligence Corps Museum archivist in Chicksands. In an email he wrote: 'Sergeant Neil Lawson Salmon died in August 1989 aged 68. He joined the TA in February 1941 and subsequently served in 31 FSS and 37 FSS in UK and later in 108 Wireless Intercept Section in North Africa and N W Europe from 1942–1945. His last posting was to the Staff of the Depot in 1945–1946.' However, Roger Salmon questions some of this history. 'I never heard of him travelling to Italy or North Africa, still less of guarding a DP camp. Or of anything called FSS or Field Security (though wireless intercept sounds right). His main role in the I Corps was in understanding the uncoded interchanges between German operators at the beginning and end of coded messages, in order to derive information about movements of units etc. He had this role in part because he spoke German.'

386, **'Sam was now put in charge of the ice-cream division'**: One of the problems, as Sam explained in a speech to the Wholesale Ice Cream Federation, was that Lyons' pre-war advantage of maintaining ice-filled storage chests within shops had become a handicap. The war had left the company 'with a legacy of thousands of refrigerator cabinets all over the British Isles,' he said, 'which for seven years had neither proper maintenance nor much needed parts' [quoted in D.J. Richardson's biography of Lyons].

388, **'Lyons was now once again the second-largest ice-cream maker in the UK, after Wall's'**: Lyons' success was helped in part by a health scare. On 15 August 1946, *The Times* reported that a thirteen-year-old girl named Pearl Barrow had contracted typhoid from eating ice-cream during a school trip. Over the next few days more than 100 people were infected, some as far afield as Dublin and Glasgow. In the wake of this typhoid outbreak, the government passed emergency legislation mandating that all ice-cream had to be pasteurised through a process of heat treatment. Anybody failing to comply would be fined £20 for a first offence, and would face up to three months' imprisonment if found guilty a second time. The cost of installing the pasteurising equipment was beyond the means of most ice-cream manufacturers, and Lyons purchased a number of smaller ice-cream makers, including Walker Dairies in Liverpool, Massarella in Doncaster and Glacier Foods on the south coast.

391, **'Their initial correspondence blossoming into something more serious'**: Sam's son Jonathan said that he believed his father probably knew about his mother's romance with Pierre. And there would be others, such as a man named McCaddy, whom Wendy met while visiting Australia. Sam, however, chose not to say anything. 'It was because of her beauty,' Jonathan recalled, 'that mother got away with murder.'

Chapter 36

399, **'Sam was now a Freemason'**: Over the previous 200 years, Masonic lodges were headed by society's most powerful men, who were at the centre of Britain's great imperial project – men such as Lord Hastings (secretary of the Committee of Imperial Defence); Lord Kitchener (Secretary of State for War); Lord Wolseley (who famously rescued General Charles George Gordon from the siege in Khartoum); the Duke of Connaught (Governor-General of Canada); as well as the Prince of Wales. Commenting on this interconnectedness, the Secretary of State for the Colonies (himself a senior Mason), Lord Carnarvon, said, 'Following closely in the wake of colonisation, wherever the hut of the settler has been built, or the flag of conquest waved, there Masonry soon has equal dominion [...] it has reflected [...] and then consolidated the British Empire.' By the decade's end, Sam was appointed Worshipful Master, becoming responsible for the initiation of a new generation of Freemasons.

399, **'Izzy Gluckstein's son, Major Monte Gluckstein'**: Major Monte played a key role in the development of J. Lyons, particularly its marketing and public relations. For instance, according to the company in-house magazine *Lyons Mail* (December 1958), Major Monte was responsible for the term 'Nippy' and the popular 'Where's George – Gone to Lyonch' advertising campaign, in addition to the Cochran shows at the Trocadero. He also took over Isidore Salmon's role as honorary adviser to the Ministry of Food during World War Two. According to his granddaughter Susan Burton, members of the family still talk of his kindness when dealing with those who got into trouble and that 'he followed in his uncle Monte's footsteps as the main peacekeeper in the family.'

400, **'Simmons announced that LEO was ready'**: According to *Guinness World Records*: 'The earliest business computer was LEO I (Lyons Electronic Office). It began operations in November 1951 at the Lyons headquarters, London, UK. The first of its many business applications was the valuation of the weekly output of bread and cakes from Lyons.' On 14 October 2016, Eric Schmidt, executive head of Alphabet, parent company of Google, gave a lecture at the London School of Economics, whose theme was entitled 'From LEO to Deep Mind'.

Chapter 37

405, **'some worried that automation might lead to the loss of clerical jobs'**: On 17 February 1954, the *Shields Daily News* compared it to the automation that had emerged during the Industrial Revolution: 'What was the result of extra power? Simply that output increased, more workers and technicians were required, wages increased and conditions improved, working hours diminished and time and money for leisure were given to those who never previously dreamed of it.' They added, 'The prospect for LEO is full of promise.'

410, **'This was years before McDonald's opened its first store in Great Britain'**: McDonald's opened its first British shop on Powis Street, east London, on 3 November 1974.

412, **'a management team that was skewed towards the elderly'**: By the early 1960s, Lyons employed more than 30,000 people, the vast majority of whom were women. Yet there were still no female members in the senior executive, nor was there a female board member. Similarly, as with most other companies in Britain at this time, female employees were not paid the same as their male counterparts. They would have to wait another ten years for the Equal Pay Act, which came into law in 1970.

Chapter 38

417, **'Sam and Wendy hosted their daughter's coming-out ball'**: Belinda's coming-out party was organised by a relative named Sir Norman Joseph, whose other responsibilities included Wimbledon and royal garden parties.

Chapter 39

424, **'in his study at home on 30 May 1965 when he received a phone call'**: The story was reported in the *Daily Mirror* under the headline 'Lyons man dies'. On 3 June, *The Times* announced that the new Lyons chairman was to be Sam Salmon, under the headline 'New chief at Cadby Hall'. Michael Salmon said of his father, Barnett Salmon, 'he had a serious heart condition in the 1950s. It was a miracle he survived as long as he did. He longed to be chairman of Lyons, but he really was not fit. And he really was not suited to the job. He was not brought up with modern management skills.' Barnett Salmon was known as both 'Barney' and 'Uncle Bill' by his family.

Chapter 40

434, 'the *Thunderbirds*-themed television advertisements': In the summer of 1966, Lyons ran a series of advertisements featuring characters from the *Thunderbirds* television show. One spot began with the *Thunderbirds* theme tune over the image of a spaceship, which then cut to two puppets standing in front of a console. 'Emergency, we are under attack,' shouts John Tracy to Virgil. 'Fire new Zoom!' replies Jeff Tracy. A multicoloured ice-cream then shoots out of the spaceship as the narrator says, 'Zoom, the big ice lolly with three fruit-flavoured stages.' The Zoom then blows up another spaceship – presumably the enemy's. Also available that summer was FAB. This too was promoted via a *Thunderbirds* advert. Miss Penelope is in the back seat of her pink limousine being driven by a peak-capped Parker, who takes them across a swing bridge. 'Oh, the heat,' she says in a sultry voice. 'Pass me a FAB, Parker.' He hands her the pink-and-white ice-cream, and we see a rope snapping. The car just makes it across as the bridge collapses into the ravine, although the passenger does not seem to notice. 'FAB, Parker,' she continues, 'just think, all those hundreds of thousands on an iced lolly to keep a girl cool. FAB, especially for girls, from Lyons Maid.'

435, 'Geoffrey Salmon stepped down as chairman': Geoffrey produced the third version of *Family Trees* in December 1973. He also included a four-page history of the Fund, along with a chart of its fifty-nine male members across five generations. Strikingly, although it was laid out like a family tree, it was devoid of women, except for Samuel's wife and three daughters.

436, 'trigger the UK joining the European Economic Community': Ireland and Denmark would join the EEC at the same time as the UK, on 1 January 1973.

437, '"the worst advice Rothschilds ever gave a client"': *Daily Express*, 22 June 2001. The article went on, 'Rothschilds had advised them to borrow at low rates in Switzerland. But the pound collapsed and Lyons' borrowings ballooned. Eventually Lyons had to merge with Allied Breweries.'

437, **'purchasing the Tetley Tea Company for £23 million'**: Lyons purchased Tetley from the American business Beech-Nut Nutrition Corporation.

439, **'The largest tranche went to their competitor, Trust House Forte'**: Later, Lyons sold the Tower Hotel next to Tower Bridge to EMI, and the Wimpy chain to United Biscuits.

Chapter 41

443, **'rented a house on Stewart Street in Glasgow'**: Later *The Daily Telegraph* (20 November 1976) would describe this house as 'Britain's most sophisticated drugs factory'.

444, **'It took the jury only four hours to make their decision'**: Simon's trial took place on 1–20 November 1976.

Chapter 42

450, **'Another of the family's grandes dames was also thinking about posterity'**: Around the same time, Geoffrey Salmon asked his male relatives for their memories. Cyril Salmon wrote that his father thought the 'Fund should be run more formally' (for example, the figures ought to be audited, and cheques above a certain amount should bear two signatures). He had no illusions about what a rumpus this might have caused in his day – 'I daresay it might cause an equal rumpus now! Perhaps however we should look to the future, and the dangers that could arise in the years ahead.' Another cousin said that Maurice Salmon enjoyed provoking people into an argument. 'I recall, for example, him leading Sam Salmon and myself into a debate,' wrote John Dick, 'and when I was carefully preparing a hole for Sam to fall into, M.S. was as delighted as a schoolboy, seeing the trap coming and, being quite unable to contain himself, jumping about in his chair shouting "Don't answer him, Sam! Don't answer him, Sam!"' Not all of the submissions were amusing. One of Geoffrey's cousins alleged that after Howard Gluckstein (one of Monte's nephews) had died in a riding accident, his father had refused to honour the customary agreement that the Fund would make a financial settlement to the widow. This was because the father 'was convinced that Howard had been trapped into the marriage'.

452, **'Thatcher was supported by Keith Joseph'**: In *The Path to Power* Margaret Thatcher wrote, 'I could not have become the leader of the opposition, or achieved what I did as prime minister, without Keith [Joseph].' It is worth noting that Thatcher appointed many Jews to her government. In addition to Joseph and Lawson, there was Malcom Rifkind, Leon Brittan and David Young. She also appointed Immanuel Jakobovits to the House of Lords, the first rabbi to sit in that chamber. She also represented Finchley, north London, which has a sizeable Jewish population. For more on this see *'Margaret Thatcher – the Honorary Jew'* by Robert Philpot.

453, **'Allied Breweries ... was offering to purchase Lyons for £63.6 million'**: According to an *Economist* article published on 14 September 1985, the tea, cake and ice-cream divisions of Lyons' business was valued seven years later at £600 million.

454, **'After [the merger] was reviewed by the government minister Roy Hattersley'**: His decision was taken after the chairman of Allied Breweries offered assurances that the reorganisation of Lyons would not result in large-scale redundancies.

455, **'they were, in some ways, adrift once again'**: The mood of the family was not subsequently helped by the death of Mimi on 1 June 1979.

Chapter 43

458, **'Beyond a small notice in *The Times*'**: This short obituary mentioned Sam's role in the family business and his time in public office, at the London County Council and as Mayor of Hammersmith. Taking up equal space were obituaries for the Soviet Deputy Defence Minister and the Dowager Empress of Annam, then part of Vietnam.

Chapter 44

462, **'Many of the members were enormously offended by this memo'**: This and other documents on the Fund are collected in the unpublished volume 'G.J. & S., Pre-finite life, entry and leaving 1985–1989'.

Epilogue

470, **'Many of the descendants are still actively involved in family-related enterprises'**: Their relations to the older generation are as follows:

Alastair Salmon = Isidore Salmon's great-grandson
Baroness Shackleton of Belgravia LVO = Alfred Salmon's great-granddaughter
Dominic Lawson = Alfred Salmon's great-grandson
Felix Salmon = Mimi's great-grandson
Nick Salmon = Mimi's grandson
Sebastian Meyer = Samuel and Ann's great-great-great-grandson
George Monbiot = Harry Salmon's great-grandson
Vicki Salmon = Harry Salmon's great-granddaughter
Andrew Salmon = Alfred Salmon's great-grandson
Fiona Shackleton = Alfred Salmon's great-granddaughter
Dr Harriet Walford = Izzy Gluckstein's great-great-granddaughter
Kirsten Hagon = Mimi's granddaughter

LIST OF ILLUSTRATIONS

LIST OF ILLUSTRATIONS

BIBLIOGRAPHY

Salmon and Gluckstein family and Lyons history

Bates, H.E., *The Tinkers of Elstow* (Bemrose, 1946). The best book on the Lyons munitions factory in Bedfordshire.

Bird, Peter, *The First Food Empire* (Phillimore, 2000). A fact-heavy book about the history of Lyons.

—— *LEO, First Business Computer* (Hasler Publishing, 1994). The story of the Lyons computer.

Bridges, T.C. and Tiltman, H.H., *Kings of Commerce* (Harrap, 1928).

Cook, Matt, *A Gay History of Britain: Love and Sex Between Men Since the Middle Ages* (Greenwood World Publishing, 2007)

De la Haye, Amy and Pel, Martin, *Gluck: Art and Identity* (Yale University Press, 2017). An academic book on the artist.

Denham, Andrew and Garnett, Mark, Keith Joseph (Acumen Publishing, 2001). Biography of Margaret Thatcher's all including his roots to Salmon and Gluckstein family.

Ferry, Georgina, *A Computer Called Leo: Lyons Tea Shops and the World's First Office Computer* (Fourth Estate, 2003). About the people who invented the Lyons computer.

Gluckstein, Joseph, *Family Trees* (first edition, 1925). Unpublished history of the Salmon and Gluckstein families, including an introduction, notes and extensive family trees. In the copy on my shelf there is a letter: 'Dear Joe and Babs. I am sending herewith a complete set of the family Trees made up to 1st June 1925 ... In the hope that they will prove as interesting to you as the compilation has been to me. Your affectionate Uncle. J Gluckstein.'

Gluckstein, Louis Halle, *Family Trees* (second edition, 1954). Unpublished history of the Salmon and Gluckstein family, including an introduction, notes and extensive family trees.

Houlbrook, Matt, *Queer London: Perils and Pleasures in the Sexual Metropolis, 1918-1957* (University of Chicago Press, 2005)

Jivani, Alkarim, *It's Not Unusual: A History of Lesbian and Gay Britain in the Twentieth Century* (M. O'Mara Books, 1997)

Lyte, Charles, *Sir Louis Halle Gluckstein: A Biography*. Unpublished authorised biography by a leading journalist.

Mitchell, Yvonne, *The Family* (Heinemann, 1967). Semi-fictional account of the Salmons and Glucksteins. It is fun trying to work out who is who.

Richardson. D.J., *History of J. Lyons & Co. Ltd* (1976). In 1970, Richardson completed a two-volume PhD thesis on Lyons in the Economic History department at the University of Kent. The full title was 'The History of the Catering Industry with special reference to the History of J. Lyons and Co. Ltd to 1939.' Lyons then commissioned Richardson to build on this work, and he produced an authorised but unpublished four-volume study of the company from its origin up to the mid-1970s. In October 2018, I spoke to librarian Andrew Cook at Kent University and was told there was a note attached to Richardson's work: 'Thesis cannot be consulted'. The reason for this was unknown.

Salmon, Geoffrey, *Family Trees* (third edition, 1973). Unpublished history of the Salmon and Gluckstein families, including an introduction, notes and extensive family trees and chart of the Fund.

Souhami, Diana, *Gluck: Her Biography* (Pandora Press, 1989). The life of Monte Gluckstein's niece, the painter, Gluck.

Sturgeon, Leo Michael, *Salmon & Sturgeon: A Faithful Memoir.* Unpublished book, written by Sam and Wendy Salmon's driver.

Wykes, Alan, *Pride of Lyons.* Unpublished, unauthorised history of Lyons.

Jewish history

Aris, Stephen, *The Jews in Business* (Jonathan Cape, 1970)

Berger, Doreen, *The Jewish Victorian: Genealogical Information from the Jewish Newspapers 1871–80* (Robert Boyd Publications, 1999)

Birmingham, Stephen, *Our Crowd: The Great Jewish Families of New York* (Harper & Row, 1967)

Cowen, Anne and Roger, *Victorian Jews through British Eyes* (Littman Library, 1998)

Elon, Amos, *The Pity of It All: A Portrait of Jews in Germany 1743–1933* (Metropolitan Books, 2002)

Endelman, Todd, *Broadening Jewish History* (Littman Library, 2001)

—— *The Jews of Britain, 1656 to 2000* (University of California Press, 2002)

—— *Radical Assimilation in English Jewish History 1656–1945* (John Wiley, 1990)

Ferguson, Niall, *The House of Rothschild, Volumes I and II* (Weidenfeld & Nicolson, 1998)

Keshen, Ann and Romain, Jonathan, *Tradition and Change: A History of Reform Judaism in Britain* (Vallentine Mitchell, 1995)

Kosofsky, Scott-Martin, *The Book of Customs: A Complete Handbook for the Jewish Year* (HarperOne, 2004)

Lebzelter, Gisela, *Political Anti-Semitism in England 1918–1939* (Holmes & Meier, 1978)

Lipman, V.D., *A History of Jews in Britain since 1858* (Leicester University Press, 1990)

—— *Three Centuries of Anglo-Jewish History* (W. Heffer & Sons, 1961)

Miller, Rory, *Divided Against Zion* (Routledge, 2000). Provides insight into arguments over Zionism within British Jewry, including the role of Louis Gluckstein.

Williams, Bill, *The Making of Manchester Jewry, 1740–1875* (Manchester University Press, 1976)

British history

Blake, Robert, *Disraeli* (Trafalgar Square Publishing, 1966). Definitive and very well written.

Brendon, Piers, *The Decline and Fall of the British Empire 1781–1997* (Jonathan Cape, 2007)

Cochran, Charles B., *I Had Almost Forgotten* (Hutchinson, 1932)

—— *The Secrets of a Showman* (Heinemann, 1925)

Dorril, Stephen, *Blackshirt: Sir Oswald Mosley and British Fascism* (Viking, 2006)

Edwards, Ruth Dudley, *The Pursuit of Reason: The Economist 1843–1993* (Hamish Hamilton, 1993). Brilliant book on the history of *The Economist*.

Evans, Stewart and Skinner, Keither, *The Ultimate Jack the Ripper Sourcebook* (Robinson, 2000). Terrific compendium of source material.

Falk, Bernard, *He Laughed in Fleet Street* (Hutchinson, 1933). A brief but interesting section on Joe Lyons.

Ferguson, Niall, *Empire: How Britain Made the Modern World* (Allen Lane, 2003)

Fontane, Theodor, *A Prussian in Victorian London* (Austin Macauley, 2014). About Fontane's time in England.

Holmes, Colin, *Searching for Lord Haw-Haw* (Routledge, 2016)

James, Lawrence, *The Rise and Fall of the British Empire* (Little, Brown, 1994)

Morris, James, *Pax Brittanica Trilogy* (Faber, 1968–78)

Mosley, Oswald, *My Life* (Nelson, 1968). In his own words – take with pinch of salt.

Panayi, Panikos, *Germans in Britain since 1500* (Hambledon, 1996)

Skidelsky, Robert, *Oswald Mosley* (Macmillan, 1975). The definitive biography.

Taylor, A.J.P., *English History: 1914–1945* (Oxford University Press, 1965)

Food and tobacco history

Billings, E.R., *Tobacco: Its History, Varieties, Culture, Manufacture and Commerce* (1875). A superb contemporary view of tobacco, including hand drawings and amusing songs.

Corina, Maurice Trust in Tobacco (Michael Joseph, 1975). Useful description of early Anglo-American fight for market share in nineteenth-century including purchase of S&G.

Dickinson, Sue, *The First Sixty Years* (1965). The history of Imperial Tobacco.

Griffiths, John, *Tea: A History of the Drink that Changed the World* (André Deutsch, 2007)

Kroc, Ray, *Grinding it Out: The Making of McDonald's* (McGraw-Hill, 1977. The king of McDonald's franchises tells its history from the inside.

Love, John F., *McDonald's: Behind the Arches* (Bantam, 1986)

Renders, Pim, *Licks, Sticks and Bricks: A World History of Ice Cream* (Unilever, 1999)

Robbins, John, *Diet for a New America* (1987). By the son of one of the co-founders of Baskin-Robbins – a critical read.

Schlosser, Eric, *Fast Food Nation* (Houghton Mifflin, 2001)

ACKNOWLEDGEMENTS

Special thanks to Peter Bird, who did such groundbreaking research on the J. Lyons story. Sadly, Peter died while I was writing this book. His publication *The Fast Food Empire* served for a long time as the principal guide to the history of J. Lyons. I met Peter twice, corresponded with him often and was extremely thankful that he generously donated his archive to the London Metropolitan Archives, which is available for the public to explore.

Thank you to my researchers: John Owen (Germany), Daniel Bussenius (Germany), Gerard van Vuuren (Holland), Rob Boeman (Holland), Sam Harding (Steep) and Sipan Marceau (London).

I was helped by a large number of experts, archivists and supporters, including: Nancy Anderson, Christopher Andrews, Jonathan Clarke, Anna Crutchley (Jesus College, Cambridge), Todd Endelman, David Frei (United Synagogue), Rachel Garside (Union Jack Club), Colin Gray, Claire Harrop (Westminster Kingsway College), Jamie Hutch, Nathanja Hüttenmeister (Steinheim Institute in Essen), Penny Jones, Anne Kershen, Tony Kushner, Cinde Lee (LJS), Chris Partsch, Dieter Peters, Panikos Panayi, Mordechai Pinchas, Harmen Snel (Amsterdam archive), Hamish Spencer, Sabine Sweetsir (Rheinberg archive), Rose

Wild (*The Times*), Roxana Willis and Alexandra Wright (LJS). *About Joe Lyons the man*: Neville Lyons, Tim Lyons, Wendy Salter. *About the LEO computer*: Peter Byford, Mary Coombs, Frank Land, Anthony Morgan, Bob Stevenson and Hilary Caminer. *About the history of food*: Lucy Newton, Mark Casson, Peter Scott and Neil Rollings. *About Bedales*: Ruth Whiting and Jane Kirby. *About the Army Catering Corps*: Dougie Dau (Army Catering Corps Association) and Fiona Jenkins (National Army Museum).

For those interested in the archives, I relied on the following – thank you to each and every one of them: London Metropolitan Archives, which holds the J. Lyons & Co. papers and photographs, as well as documents relating to the Board of Deputies of British Jews. The Royal Logistics Museum, which contains the Army Catering Corps archives. The National Archive, which holds the 1937 'Salmon Report' regarding the Army Catering Corps, 1940–45; Elstow Factory confidential documents; the 1870 Gluckstein court case; and the Jacques Tratsart murder (in April 2015, I successfully obtained a Freedom of Information Act to open this file). Churchill College, Cambridge archive, which holds the Enoch Powell archive. Birmingham University, which holds the Neville Chamberlain archive. Bedales library and archives (including *Bedales Chronicles* and *Bedales Reports*). Jesus College, Cambridge archive, which holds information on Sam Salmon's time at Cambridge. The National Portrait Gallery, which has photographs and other images of key family members. *The Times* newspapers archive, which has extensive coverage of Lyons, Monte Gluckstein, Joseph Salmon, Isidore Salmon, Sam Salmon and other family members; British Library *Daily Mail* archive, which includes Monte Gluckstein's article 'Survey of Lyons History', published in October 1921; the British Newspaper Archive (including *The Blackshirt*), which contains an enormous number of articles about the family and the companies they ran, including articles on Isidore Salmon and other family members, 1900–90.

ACKNOWLEDGEMENTS

A huge thanks to my family members for their time, their private archives and, most importantly, their trust. First, to Roger Salmon, Jeremy Salmon, David Salmon and Felix Salmon, who encouraged me at the project's start. To Joanna Anderson (Meyer), for her blessing of the legacy wording, and her children – Jessica, Sebastian and Amelia – for allowing me to celebrate this moment. To Susan Burton, my hard-hat-and-neon-jacket companion-in-arms. To Joanna Davison, for her super-clear digital family trees, to which I referred a gazillion times. And more generally to: Peter Benjamin, Phillippa Cook, John Gluckstein, Nigel Gluckstein, Penny Gluckstein, Roy Gluckstein, Kirsten Hagon, Amanda Harding, Belinda Harding, David Harding, Frank Harding, Kate Harding, Charles Joseph, Polly Joseph, Caroline Knapp, Dominic Lawson, William Makower, Karen Prochazka, Alastair Salmon, Andrew Salmon, Chloe Salmon, Harry Salmon, Jess Salmon, Jonathan Salmon, Michael Salmon, Nick Salmon, Patrick Salmon, Paul Salmon, Rhian Salmon, Robert and Vera Salmon, Roger Salmon, Shirley Day Salmon, Fiona Shackleton, Jane Stockel, Michelle Vaughan, Harriet Walford and Julian Walford. The names of some family members have been changed to protect their identity.

Thanks to Asif Aziz, for so generously giving access to the Trocadero; and to Guy Finkelstein, for retrieving the old steel beam from its ruins. To Hester Abrams, Mark Williams, Melvyn Hartog, and Gang Colling for making it possible to erect the sign at Hackney Cemetery (United Synagogue). To Martin Poole and his team at PMP Laser Technology in Hampshire, for their brilliant work in cleaning, engraving, polishing and mounting the steel block and Joshua Reed for the design.

Once again, a big thank-you to my regular readers: Amelia Wooldridge, Lucy Baring, Niall Barton, Moritz Groening. Amanda Harding, Debora Harding, James Harding, Dr Kate Harding, Sam Harding, Rupert Levy, Cait Morrison, Zam Baring, Jane Hill and Nick Viner.

Yet again I must thank my brilliant editor, Tom Avery, at William Heinemann, Anna Argenio and Arenike Adebajo for their editorial help and for photo research, Glenn O'Neill for cover design, Darren Bennett for maps, Janet Smith for Family Trees, and all the team at Penguin Random House. Also my superb agents, Sarah Chalfant and James Pullen at The Wylie Agency.

And, finally, Deb and Sam, for your support, tolerance and love.

INDEX

Page numbers in *italics* indicate illustrations.

INDEX